DAILY LIFE IN

THE MONGOL

EMPIRE

Blue wolf, creation myth creature. Courtesy of Xinjiang Qinshan Culture Publishing

DAILY LIFE IN

THE MONGOL

EMPIRE

GEORGE LANE

The Greenwood Press "Daily Life Through History" Series

GREENWOOD PRESS
Westport, Connecticut • London

Library of Congress Cataloging-in-Publication Data

Lane, George, 1952–
    Daily life in the Mongol empire / by George Lane.
    p. cm. — (Greenwood Press "Daily life through history" series, ISSN 1080–
4749)
    Includes bibliographical references and index.
    ISBN 0–313–33226–6 (alk. paper)
    1. Mongols—Social life and customs. I. Title. II. Series.
DS19.L345   2006
950'.2—dc22   2005026896

British Library Cataloguing in Publication Data is available.

Library of Congress Catalog Card Number: 2005026896
ISBN: 0–313–33226–6
ISSN: 1080–4749

First published in 2006

Greenwood Press, 88 Post Road West, Westport, CT 06881
An imprint of Greenwood Publishing Group, Inc.
www.greenwood.com

Printed in the United States of America

(∞)™

The paper used in this book complies with the
Permanent Paper Standard issued by the National
Information Standards Organization (Z39.48–1984).

10 9 8 7 6 5 4 3 2 1

CONTENTS

EPIGRAPH

IBN AL-ATHIR "ON THE TATARS, 1220–1221 CE":[1]

For some years I continued averse from mentioning this event, deeming it so horrible that I shrank from recording it and ever withdrawing one foot as I advanced the other. To whom, indeed, can it be easy to write the announcement of the deathblow of Islam and the Muslims, or who is he on whom the remembrance thereof can weigh lightly? O would that my mother had not born me or that I had died and become a forgotten thing ere this befell! Yet, withal a number of my friends urged me to set it down in writing, and I hesitated long, but at last came to the conclusion that to omit this matter could serve no useful purpose.

I say, therefore, that this thing involves the description of the greatest catastrophe and the most dire calamity (of the like of which days and nights are innocent) which befell all men generally, and the Muslims in particular; so that, should one say that the world, since God Almighty created Adam until now, has not been afflicted with the like thereof, he would but speak the truth. For indeed history does not contain anything which approaches or comes near unto it. For of the most grievous calamities recorded was what Nebuchadnezzar inflicted on the children of Israel by his slaughter of them and his destruction of Jerusalem; and what was Jerusalem in comparison to the countries which these accursed miscreants destroyed, each city of which was double the size of Jerusalem? Or what were the children of Israel compared to those whom these slew? For verily those whom they massacred in a single city exceeded all the children of Israel. Nay, it is unlikely that mankind will see the like of this calamity, until the world comes to an end and perishes, except the final outbreak of Gog and Magog.

For even Antichrist will spare such as follow him, though he destroy those who oppose him, but these Tatars spared none, slaying women and men and children, ripping open pregnant women and killing unborn babes. Verily to God do we belong, and unto Him do we return, and there is no strength and no power save in God, the High, the Almighty, in face of this catastrophe, whereof the sparks flew far and wide, and the hurt was universal; and which passed over the lands like clouds driven by the wind. For these were a people who emerged from the confines of China, and attacked the cities of Turkistan, like Kashghar and Balasaghun, and thence advanced on the cities of Transoxiana, such as Samarqand, Bukhara and the like, taking possession of them, and treating their inhabitants in such wise as we shall mention; and of them one division then passed on into Khurasan, until they had made an end of taking possession, and destroying, and slaying, and plundering, and thence passing on to Ray, Hamadan and the Highlands, and the cities contained therein, even to the limits of Iraq, whence they marched on the towns of Azerbaijan and Arran, destroying them and slaying most of their inhabitants, of whom none escaped save a small remnant; and all this in less than a year; this is a thing whereof the like has not been heard. And when they had finished with Adharbayjan and Arraniyya, they passed on to Darband-i-Shirwan, and occupied its cities, none of which escaped save the fortress wherein was their King; wherefore they passed by it to the countries of the Lan and the Lakiz and the various nationalities which dwell in that region, and plundered, slew, and destroyed them to the full. And thence they made their way to the lands of Qipchaq, who are the most numerous of the Turks, and slew all such as withstood them, while the survivors fled to the fords and mountain-tops, and abandoned their country, which these Tatars overran. All this they did in the briefest space of time, remaining only for so long as their march required and no more.

Another division, distinct from that mentioned above, marched on Ghazna and its dependencies, and those parts of India, Sistan and Kirman which border thereon, and wrought therein deeds like unto the other, nay, yet more grievous. Now this is a thing the like of which ear has not heard; for Alexander, concerning whom historians agree that he conquered the world, did not do so with such swiftness, but only in the space of about ten years; neither did he slay, but was satisfied that men should be subject to him. But these Tatars conquered most of the habitable globe, and the best, the most flourishing and most populous part thereof, and that whereof the inhabitants were the most advanced in character and conduct, in about a year; nor did any country escape their devastations which did not fearfully expect them and dread their arrival.

Moreover they need no commissariat, nor the conveyance of supplies, for they have with them sheep, cows, horses, and the like quadrupeds, the flesh of which they eat, naught else. As for their beasts which they ride, these dig into the earth with their hoofs and eat the roots of plants, knowing naught of barley. And so, when they alight anywhere, they have need of nothing from without. As for their religion, they worship the sun when it rises, and regard nothing as unlawful, for they eat all beasts, even dogs, pigs, and the like; nor do they recognise the marriage-tie, for several men are in marital relations with one woman, and if a child is born, it knows not who is its father.

Therefore Islam and the Muslims have been afflicted during this period with calamities wherewith no people hath been visited. These Tatars (may God confound them!) came from the East, and wrought deeds which horrify all who hear of them, and which you shall, please God, see set forth in full detail in their proper connection. And of these was the invasion of Syria by the Franks (may God curse them!) out of the West, and their attack on Egypt, and occupation of the port of Damietta therein, so that Egypt and Syria were like to be conquered by them, but for the grace of God and the help which He vouchsafed us against them, as we have mentioned under the year 614 (A.D. 1217–18). Of these, moreover, was that the sword was drawn between those who escaped from these two foes, and strife was rampant, as we have also mentioned: and verily unto God do we belong and unto Him do we return! We ask God to vouchsafe victory to Islam and the Muslims, for there is none other to aid, help, or defend the True Faith. But if God intends evil to any people, naught can avert it, nor have they any ruler save Him. As for these Tatars, their achievements were only rendered possible by the absence of any effective obstacle; and the cause of this absence was that Muhammad Khwarazmshah had overrun the lands, slaying and destroying their Kings, so that he remained alone ruling over all these countries; wherefore, when he was defeated by the Tatars, none was left in the lands to check those or protect these, that so God might accomplish a thing which was to be done.

It is now time for us to describe how they first burst forth into the lands. Stories have been related to me, which the hearer can scarcely credit, as to the terror of the Tatars, which God Almighty cast into men's hearts; so that it is said that a single one of them would enter a village or a quarter wherein were many people, and would continue to slay them one after another, none daring to stretch forth his hand against this horseman. And I have heard that one of them took a man captive, but had not with him any weapon wherewith to kill him; and he said to his prisoner, "Lay your head on the ground and do not move," and he did so, and the Tatar went and fetched his sword and slew him therewith. Another man related to me as follows: "I was going," said he, "with seventeen others along a road, and there met us a Tatar horseman, and bade us bind one another's arms. My companions began to do as he bade them, but I said to them, 'He is but one man; wherefore, then, should we not kill him and flee?' They replied, 'We are afraid.' I said, 'This man intends to kill you immediately; let us therefore rather kill him, that perhaps God may deliver us.' But I swear by God that not one of them dared to do this, so I took a knife and slew him, and we fled and escaped." And such occurrences were many.

NOTE

1. From Edward G. Browne, *A Literary History of Persia,* vol. 2 (London: T. Fisher Unwin, 1915), 427–31. Scanned by Jerome S. Arkenberg, California State Fullerton. The text has been modernized by Professor Arkenberg. This text is part of the Internet Medieval Source Book, "Internet History Sourcebooks Project," ed. Paul Halsall, http://www.fordham.edu/halsall/source/1220al-Athir-mongols.html. The sourcebook is a collection of public domain and copy-permitted texts related to medieval and Byzantine history.

PREFACE

Because no standardized system of transliteration exists to render foreign scripts into English text, Arabic, Persian, and especially Chinese names, titles, and expressions can appear in a bewildering array of forms, fashions and spellings. Often these renderings are decorated with a profusion of confusing and varied diacritical marks. For example, the Persian Sufi poet of the thirteenth century, Mawlana Jalaladdin Rumi, is referred to in scholarly works as Rūmī, Jalāl al-Dīn Rūmī, Jalálu'ddín Rúmí, or even Jalálu'l-Din Rúmi. In Turkey he is known as Mavlana, in popular works he is known simply as Rumi or Jalaluddin Rumi, and in Iran as Maulānā. The Persian historian ᶜAṭā Malik ᶜAlā al-Dīn Juwaynī appears often as Juvaini, or Juvainī, or Ata-Malik Juvaini, or combinations of these. Chinese names are even more varied and confusing, and when consulting other books and maps these variations should be borne in mind. Chinggis Khan (Genghis Khan, Chingiz Khan) attacked the Xi-Xia early in his career. These early targets are also called the Xixia, the Hsi-hsia, or the Hsi-Hsia. Before it became the Mongol capital, Da-du, or Ta-tu, was referred to as Zhong-du, Chung-du, Chang-tu, or Chong-du. Until an internationally accepted system of transliteration is established this confusion will continue. However, an awareness of the problem and a flexible attitude to spelling and transliteration will greatly alleviate the difficulties in the meantime.

I would like to express my gratitude for the generosity of the *Committee for Central and Inner Asia* (CCIA), Faculty of Oriental Studies, Cambridge University whose funding contributed towards the costs of travel incurred during the research for this book. My thanks also to Florence Hodous for her time and hard work in the final stages of getting the book into print. And a final word of thanks in recognition of the patience and endurance shown by Assumpta, Oscar and Ella over the long months that I have been engrossed by this project.

Chronology

1125	Liao dynasty (Khitans) driven out of north China by Jurchens, who become the Chin dynasty. The seminomadic Khitans flee westward and eventually found the Qara Khitai empire in Central Asia.
1141	The Saljuq sultan Sanjar defeated by Qara Khitai at Qatwan steppe near Samarqand. It is the advance of the Qara Khitai (Black Cathays) that gives rise to the legend of Prester John.
1167	Temüjin (Chinggis Khan) is born. The years between 1155 and 1167 are also claimed as his date of birth.
1174	Temüjin engaged to Börte, daughter of Dei-sechen of the Onggirat. Yesügei (father) poisoned by Tatars.
1180	Temüjin murders half-brother Bekhter. Later held in Tayichi'ut captivity.
1183–84	Börte abducted by Merkits. Toghril and Jamuka assist in rescue. First-born child, Jochi, is born shortly after Börte's release.
1187	Temüjin is defeated at the battle of Dalan Balzhut. Gap in Temüjin's life history; possibly in exile in China.
1200	'Alā' al-Dīn Moḥammed II, Khwārazmshāh, accedes.
1206	Chinggis Khan proclaimed supreme ruler of the tribes, at a *quriltai* in Mongolia. Reign of the Delhi sultans in northern India/Pakistan until 1555.

1209	Mongols invade Hsi-Hsia (Xixia, Xi-Xia).
1211	Mongols invade Chin (Jurchen) empire of north China.
1215	Chin capital, Chong-du (Zhongdu, Chung-tu), falls to Mongols. Zhongdu later rebuilt and renamed Da-du, Ta-tu, Khan Baliq.
1218	Mongol troops under Jebe occupy Qara Khitai empire.
1219	Chinggis Khan invades empire of the Khwārazmshāh.
1221–23	Ch'ang Ch'un journeys from China to Hindu Kush.
1223	Chinggis Khan returns to Mongolia.
1227	Chinggis Khan dies. Final conquest of Hsi-Hsia.
1229	Ögödei elected as Great Khan.
1234	Chin resistance to Mongols ends.
1235	Ögödei builds walls of Qaraqorum, Mongol imperial capital.
1237–42	Mongol campaigns, conducted under Batu in Russia and Eastern Europe.
1241	Ögödei dies; battles of Liegnitz and River Sajo. Regency of Töregene until 1246.
1245–47	John of Plano Carpini (Giovanni Diplano Carpini) journeys to Mongolia.
1246	Güyük elected as Great Khan.
1248	Güyük dies. Regency of Oghul Ghaymish lasts until 1251.
1250	Mamluks seize effective power in Egypt, 'Izz al-Dīn Aybak Ayyubid Sultan al-Malik al-Ashraf al-Mūsā nominally on throne.
1251	Möngke elected as Great Khan.
1252–79	Mongols conquer Sung empire of south China.
1253–55	William of Rubruck journeys to Mongolia.
1253	Hülegü's forces set off for Persia.
1254	'Izz al-Dīn Aybak assumes full powers in Egypt. The Bahrī line of Mamluks of Egypt and Syria, 1250–1390 (Ethnic Qipchaq Turks originating from Russian steppes).
1255	Batu, first khan of Golden Horde dies. Sartak briefly khan of Golden Horde, succeeded by his brother, Ulaghchi.
1256	Hülegü takes Assassin castles in north Persia.
1257	Berke accedes as khan of Golden Horde. His accession follows mysterious death of both Sartak and Ulaghchi.

1258	Baghdad falls to Hülegü. Last 'Abbasid caliph dies.
1259	Möngke dies. Hülegü travels east.
1259	The Mamluk Qutuz assumes power in Egypt.
1260	Ket-Buqa invades Syria with a small force, then withdraws. Battle of 'Ain Jālūt takes place. Rival *quriltais* elect Qubilai and Ariq-Buqa as Great Khan; civil war ensues. Ket-Buqa, a Christian Mongol, is captured and killed.
1260	al-Malik al-Zāhir Baybars I al-Bunduqdārī assumes Mamluk throne (Baybars 1260–77).
1261–62	Warfare breaks out between Hülegü and Berke.
1264	Qubilai is victorious over Ariq Buqa.
1265	Hülegü, first Il-Khan, dies. Abaqa succeeds.
1266	Building begins at new Mongol capital of China, Ta-tu (Da-du, Beijing).
1267	Berke, khan of Golden Horde, dies.
1271	Marco Polo, with his father and uncle, sets off for China (arrives 1275).
1272	Qubilai adopts Chinese dynastic title, Yuan.
1273	Jalāl al-Dīn Rūmī dies.
1274	First Mongol expedition against Japan takes place.
1276	Hangzhou, capital of Sung empire, falls to Mongols.
1279	Sung resistance to Mongols ends.
1281	Second Mongol expedition launched against Japan.
1282	Abaqa Khan dies through alcohol abuse and succeeded by Ahmad Tegüdar. Ottomans begin to form a statelet and reign until 1924.
1284	Ahmad Tegüdar dies and Arghun succeeds.
1287	Rabban Sauma sent to Europe by Il-Khan Arghun.
1292	Persian poet from Shiraz, Sa'dī, dies.
1294	Qubilai dies. John of Monte Corvino arrives in China. Ch'ao is introduced disastrously into Iran.
1295	Ghazan accedes as Il-Khan. Mongols in Persia become Muslim.
1299–1300	Major Mongol invasion of Syria takes place. Syria is briefly occupied by Il-Khanid forces.
1304	Il-Khan Ghazan dies. Öljeitü succeeds.

1313	Özbek, under whose rule the Golden Horde becomes Muslim, accedes. Öljeitü Khan builds his capital, Sultaniya.
1316	Öljeitü dies.
1318	Rashīd al-Dīn, a vizier of tremendous talents, is executed, and his son remains in power.
1335	Abū Saʿīd, last Il-Khan of line of Hülegü, dies. Jalayrids (Baghdad), Karts (Herat), Sarbadārs (Sabzevar), and Muzaffarids (Shiraz) form successor states.
1346	Black Death breaks out among Mongol force besieging Kaffa in the Crimea and from there spreads to Europe.
1353–54	Major outbreak of disease takes place in China. The Moroccan traveler-writer Ibn Battuta dictates his journals.
1368	Mongols driven from China by Ming forces.
1370	Toghon Temür, last Yuan emperor, dies in Qaraqorum. The renowned North African historian Ibn Khaldun writes *Muqaddima* in 1375.

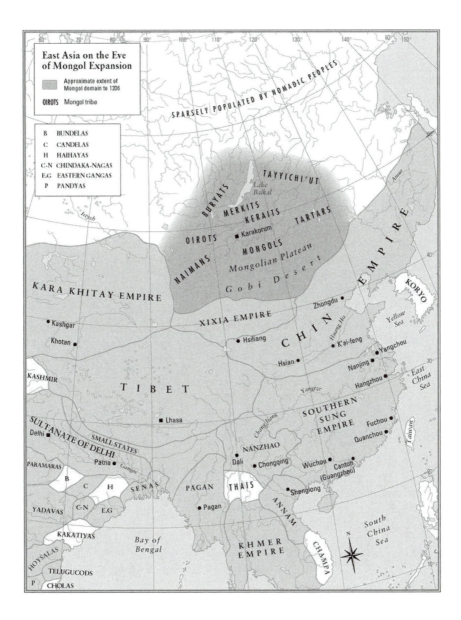

East Asia on the Eve of Mongol Expansion

Approximate extent of Mongol domain to 1206

OIROTS   Mongol tribe

B   BUNDELAS
C   CANDELAS
H   HAIHAYAS
C-N   CHINDAKA-NAGAS
E.G   EASTERN GANGAS
P   PANDYAS

SPARSELY POPULATED BY NOMADIC PEOPLES

BURYATS
TAYYICHI'UT
Lake Baikal
MERKITS
KERAITS
OIROTS
Karakorum
TARTARS
NAIMANS
MONGOLS
Mongolian Plateau
Gobi Desert

Irtysh

KARA KHITAY EMPIRE

XIXIA EMPIRE
Kashgar
Khotan

Zhongdu
Hsiliang
CHIN EMPIRE
Huang Ho
K'ai-feng
Yangchou
Hsian
Nanjing
Hangzhou

KORYO

Yellow Sea

East China Sea

KASHMIR

TIBET

Lhasa

Yangtze

SOUTHERN SUNG EMPIRE

Fuchou
Quanchou

Taiwan

SULTANATE OF DELHI
Delhi
SMALL STATES

PARAMARAS
Patna   Ganges
B
C
H
SENAS
YADAVAS
C-N
E.G

KAKATIYAS

HOYSALAS
TELUGUCODS
P
CHOLAS

Changjiang

NANZHAO
Dali   Chongqing
PAGAN   THAIS
Pagan
Wuchou
Canton (Guangzhou)
Shenglong
ANNAM

Bay of Bengal

KHMER EMPIRE

CHAMPA

South China Sea

xvii

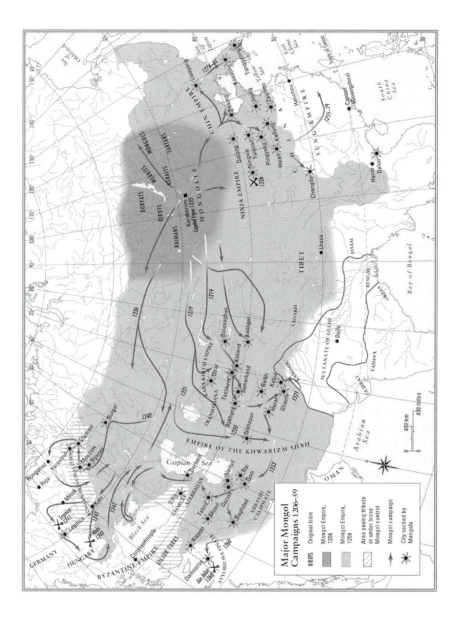

Major Mongol Campaigns 1206–59

OIROTS	Original tribe
	Mongol Empire, 1206
	Mongol Empire, 1259
	Area paying tribute or under loose Mongol control
→	Mongol campaign
✳	City sacked by Mongols

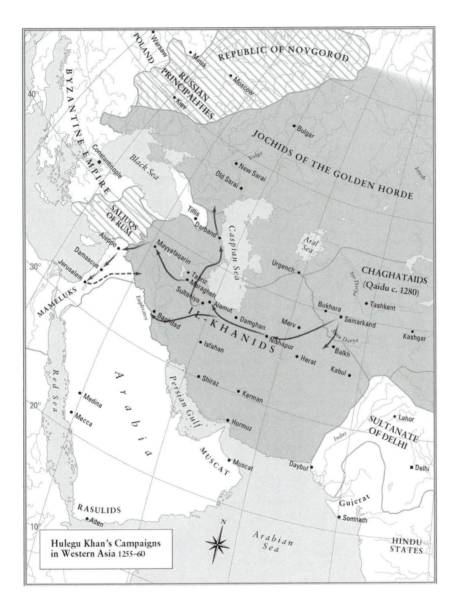

POLAND

• Warsaw

• Minsk

REPUBLIC OF NOVGOROD

RUSSIAN

PRINCIPALITIES

• Moscow

40°

• Kiev

BYZANTINE EMPIRE

• Bulgar

JOCHIDS OF THE GOLDEN HORDE

Irtysh

Constantinople

Black Sea

Volga

• New Sarai

• Old Sarai

SALJUQS OF RUM

Aral Sea

Tiflis

• Darband

Caspian Sea

• Urgench

CHAGHATAIDS
(Qaidu c. 1280)

Aleppo

Mayyafaqarin

Syr Darya

• Bukhara

• Tashkent

Damascus

30°

Jerusalem

• Tabriz

• Maragheh

Sultaniya

• Alamut

• Damghan

Euphrates

Baghdad

I L - K H A N I D S

• Merv

• Samarkand

Amu Darya

• Balkh

• Kashgar

MAMELUKS

• Isfahan

• Nishapur

• Herat

• Kabul

Red Sea

Arabia

Persian Gulf

• Shiraz

• Kerman

SULTANATE
OF DELHI

• Lahor

Indus

20°

• Medina

• Mecca

• Hormuz

MUSCAT

• Muscat

• Daybul

• Delhi

Gujerat

RASULIDS

10°

• Aden

N

Arabian
Sea

• Somnath

HINDU
STATES

Hulegu Khan's Campaigns
in Western Asia 1255–60

xix

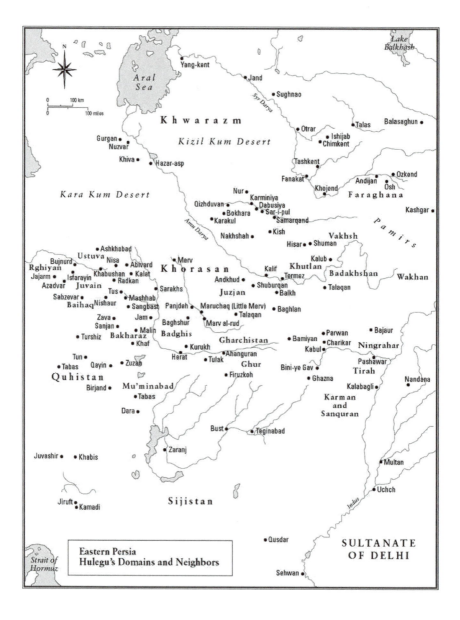

Eastern Persia
Hulegu's Domains and Neighbors

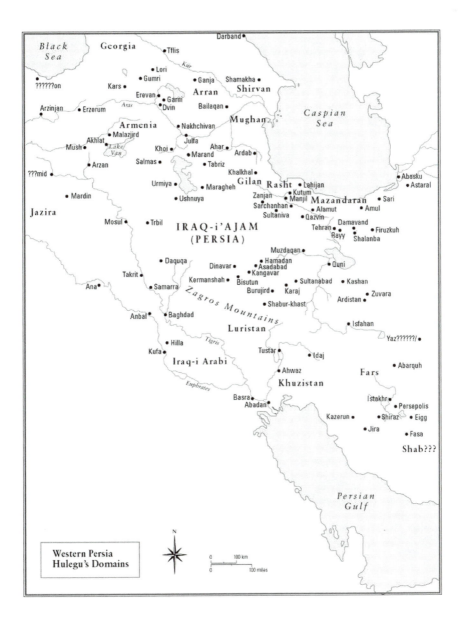

Black Sea

Georgia

Tflis

Darband

Lori
Gumri

Kür

Kars

Ganja

Shamakha

??????on

Erevan
Garni
Dvin

Arran

Shirvan

Arzinjan

Erzerum

Aras

Bailaqan

Nakhchivan

Mughan

Caspian Sea

Armenia

Malazjird

Akhlat

Julfa

Ahar

Mush

Khoi

Marand

Ardab

Arzan

Salmas

Tabriz

Khalkhal

Abasku

???mid

Mardin

Urmiya

Maragheh

Gilan

Rasht

Lahijan

Astaral

Ushnuya

Zanjan

Kutum

Manjil

Mazandaran

Sari

Jazira

Mosul

Trbil

IRAQ-i'AJAM
(PERSIA)

Sarchanhan

Sultaniva

Qazvin

Alamut

Damavand

Amul

Tehran

Firuzkuh

Rayy

Shalanba

Muzdaqan

Daquqa

Dinavar

Hamadan

Asadabad

Quni

Takrit

Kangavar

Kermanshah

Bisutun

Sultanabad

Kashan

Ana

Samarra

Burujird

Karaj

Zuvara

Zagros Mountains

Shabur-khast

Ardistan

Anbal

Baghdad

Isfahan

Luristan

Yaz??????/

Tigris

Kufa

Hilla

Iraq-i Arabi

Tustar

Idaj

Fars

Abarquh

Euphrates

Ahwaz

Khuzistan

Basra

Abadan

Istakhr

Persepolis

Kazerun

Shiraz

Eigg

Jira

Fasa

Shab???

Persian Gulf

N

0   100 km
0   100 miles

Western Persia
Hulegu's Domains

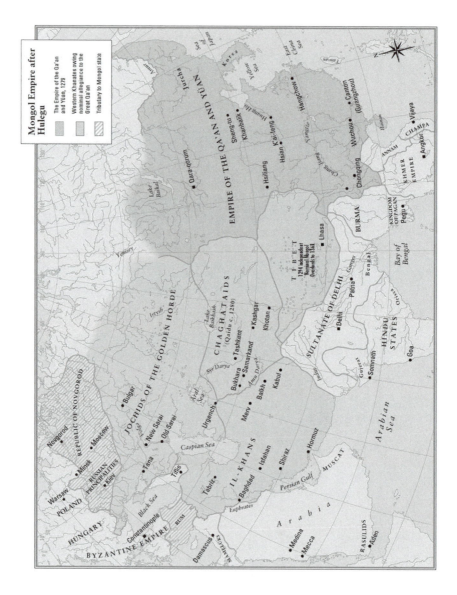

Mongol Empire after Hulegu

The Empire of the Qa'an and Yüan, 1279

Western Khanates owing nominal allegiance to the Great Qa'an

Tributary to Mongol state

EMPIRE OF THE QA'AN AND YÜAN

Qara-qorum

Sheng-tu

Khanbalïk

Kai-feng

Hsian

Hsiliang

Chongqing

Wuchou

Canton (Guangzhou)

Hangchow

Hamy Hills

Yellow Sea

Sea of Japan

Korea

Jurcha

Lake Baikal

Yenisey

East China Sea

NIPPON

VIJAYA

CHAMPA

ANNAM

KHMER EMPIRE

Angkor

KINGDOM OF PAGAN

Pegu

BURMA

Lhasa

T I B E T

1294 independent normal Mongol overlords to 1354

Bay of Bengal

SULTANATE OF DELHI

Delhi

Patna

Gangas

Bengal

HINDU STATES

Goa

Somnath

Gujarat

Kashgar

Khotan

CHAGRATAIDS

(Qaidu c. 1280)

Samarkand

Tashkent

Bukhara

Lake Balkhash

Syr Darya

Amu Darya

Aral Sea

Balkh

Merv

Kabul

Arabian Sea

MUSCAT

Hormuz

Shiraz

Isfahan

IL-KHANS

Baghdad

Tabriz

Euphrates

Persian Gulf

Arabia

Medina

Mecca

RASULIDS

Aden

Arab Sea

Urgench

Caspian Sea

Tana

Old Sarai

New Sarai

Bulgar

Volga

JOCHIDS OF THE GOLDEN HORDE

Irtysh

REPUBLIC OF NOVGOROD

Novgorod

Moscow

Minsk

Kiev

Warsaw

POLAND

HUNGARY

RUSSIAN PRINCIPALITIES

Tiflis

Black Sea

Constantinople

BYZANTINE EMPIRE

RUM

Damascus

MAMLUKS

N

xxii

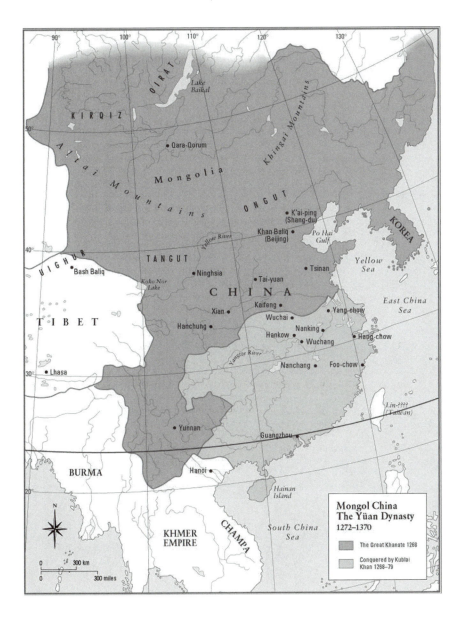

90° 100° 110° 120° 130°

O I R A T

Lake
Baikal

K I R Q I Z

50°

Qara-Qorum

Altai Mountains

Mongolia

Khingai Mountains

O N G U T

K'ai-ping
(Shang-du)

Khan Baliq
(Beijing)

Po Hai
Gulf

KOREA

UIGHUR

40°

TANGUT

Yellow River

Ninghsia

Koko Nor
Lake

Bash Baliq

Tai-yuan

Yellow
Sea

Tsinan

C H I N A

East China
Sea

T I B E T

Xian

Kaifeng

Hanchung

Wuchai

Yang-chow

Hankow

Nanking

Wuchang

Hang-chow

30°

Lhasa

Yangtze River

Nanchang

Foo-chow

Lin-????
(Taiwan)

Yunnan

Guangzhou

BURMA

Hanoi

20°

Hainan
Island

N

KHMER
EMPIRE

CHAMPA

South China
Sea

Mongol China
The Yüan Dynasty
1272–1370

The Great Khanate 1268

Conquered by Kublai
Khan 1268–79

0   300 km

0   300 miles

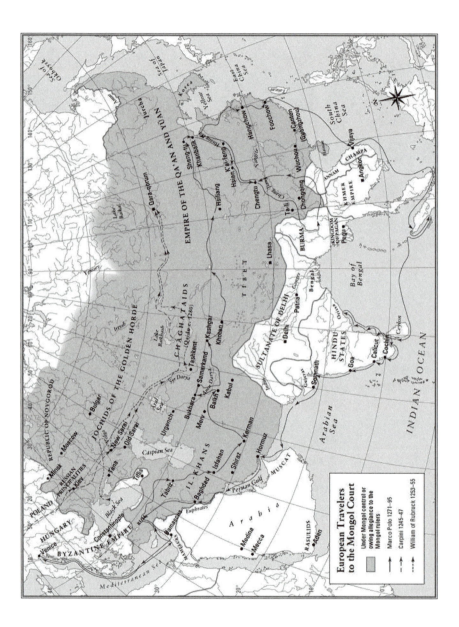

European Travelers to the Mongol Court

Under Mongol control or owing allegiance to the Mongol rulers

→ Marco Polo 1271–95

-→ Carpini 1245–47

··→ William of Rubruck 1253–55

1

HISTORICAL OVERVIEW: GENGHIS KHAN AND MONGOL RULE

The present century and much of the last century are commonly viewed as a time of unprecedented change and of events with global rather than local ramifications. It is widely believed that the world had never undergone such a shared traumatic transformation on such a scale anytime before. The sweeping changes that overtook much of Asia and Eastern Europe in the thirteenth century had as profound an effect on that century's political, cultural, economic, mercantile, and spiritual environment as the forces of globalization are having on the world today. Whereas the causes and reasons for the pervasiveness of globalization today are complex, the spread of the globalization that swept the medieval world can be traced to one man. That man was Genghis Khan (Chinggis Khan),[1] born Temüjin, son of Yisugei, and it was he who united the Turco-Mongol tribes of Eurasia behind him and swept out of the steppe with devastating and radical effect. Initially Chinggis Khan had sought wealth through plunder in order for him to consolidate his power base and keep the tribes happy. Eventually, this zeal for booty transformed into a taste for power and grew into a conviction of spiritual righteousness, and suddenly the Mongol armies were carrying with them the banner of Tengri, the god of the sky, and their continued success was proof of their god's omnipotence and support.

Temüjin's harsh rise to power was the catalyst that resulted in the formation of the largest contiguous land empire. He emerged first as the young son who desperately fought for his fatherless family, then as tribal leader surrounded by a core of staunchly loyal supporters, and thereafter as supratribal leader unifying the peoples of the Asian steppes with promises of untold wealth and prestige, and finally as Chinggis Khan, world conqueror whose issue initiated actions, concluded agreements, and accomplished feats the impact of which resounds to this day. The treaty between Tibet and China was first drafted by a Mongol ruler and remains the basis for their union today; the Sufi songs of Rūmī that resound around the world from California to Tokyo were nurtured and first heard under Mongol rule; Beijing was built by the Mongols as their capital of a united China, a status it enjoys to this day; the cultural and spiritual links between western Asia and the East were cemented under Mongol auspices. From Temüjin, whose name once evoked derision, to Genghis Khan, who cowed and roused the princes of Russia and Eastern Europe and who would awe emissaries from a fearful outside world, this Mongol emperor is more deserving of fame than of infamy. He was not only a world conqueror but also a world unifier.

Chinggis Khan, Hohhut Museum. Courtesy of Xinjiang Qinshan Culture Publishing

THE LEGACY

The legacy of Genghis Khan and the Mongol hordes has been shrouded and obscured by the myth makers of history and indeed by the propaganda of the Mongols themselves. Those who suffered humiliation and defeat needed to justify and explain their shame through hyperbole, whereas the Mongols, eager to deter any who would challenge their rise, were content that the terror inspired by these tales provoked inaction rather than reaction. The result is that today for many the name of Genghis Khan is synonymous with evil and the Mongols with barbarian rule and destruction. Their defenders are few and, until recently, their apologists rare. In Europe the echo of their horses' hooves resonated with dread on the pages of the chronicles of Matthew Paris, whereas in Japan it was believed that only the divine intervention of the kamikaze winds prevented the collapse of that island empire into a sea of barbarism. In Russia the *Chronicle of Novgorod* still inspires horror at the memory of the events of the thirteenth and fourteenth centuries, and the Islamic world continues to quote less than objective sources such as the doom-laden words of Ibn al-Athir rather than those historians who wrote from firsthand knowledge.

Such sentiments are not universal, however, and among not only Mongolian people but also among the Turkish people both in Turkey and

Early copy of the Secret History in Hohhut Museum. Courtesy of Xinjiang Qinshan Culture Publishing

Turkish Central Asia, the appellations Genghis, Hülegü, Möngke, Arghun, and other such names from the Mongol golden age can still be found and are worn with honor. In the Turkish-speaking world and within the countries straddling the Eurasian steppes, Genghis Khan and his Mongol hordes are becoming a source of pride, and the tales told of his deeds and progeny are a source of inspiration.

Recent academic thinking has also begun to look again at the legacy of the Mongols and at the period of Mongol rule itself. Beneath the rhetoric and propaganda, behind the battles and massacres, hidden by the often self-generated myths and legends, the reality of the two centuries of Mongol ascendancy was often one of regeneration, creativity, and growth. Two recent exhibitions, one in the United States and the other in London have celebrated the glorious legacy of the peoples from the Eurasian steppe. In New York and Los Angeles in 2002 an exhibition entitled *The Legacy of Genghis Khan* paid tribute to the cultural achievements of the Mongols who ruled in Iran and quieted the myth that the period of Il-Khanid rule in Iran (1256–1335) was barbaric. Likewise in London in 2005, a major exhibition celebrated the Turks' more than 1,000 years of glorious history, covering their rule and influence in a swath of countries from China to Europe. The aim of this book is to explore this more objective portrait of Genghis Khan and the period of Mongol rule following his death in 1227 C.E. and seek a more dispassionate view of life under Mongol rule.

CHINGGIS KHAN AND MONGOL RULE

The next chapter will examine the lands into which Temüjin was born. It will give an overview of the Eurasian steppes and the society that thrived there in the twelfth and thirteenth centuries. Genghis Khan, or Chinggis Khan as his name is more correctly written, drastically reshaped the relationship between the pastoral, nomadic societies of the northern Eurasian steppes and their southern urban, agriculturist, and sedentary neighbors. This first chapter will consider why this occurred and the political and social pressures that built up to cause this major upheaval.

The Mongol Empire comprising the Eurasian steppes officially came into being in spring 1206, the year of the Tiger, with the symbolic rising of the white standard of the protective spirit of the nation and the enthronement of Temüjin as emperor of the nation of archers, supreme leader of the "people of the felt-walled tents." The white standard had nine points, each representing one of the Turco-Mongol tribes. Temüjin was awarded the title Chinggis, which is thought, not conclusively, to mean "Oceanic Ruler," a term with Uyghur roots, though it has been pointed out that *ching* in Mongolian means "firm, strong." Temüjin's greatest achievement had been to unite the tribes and subdue forcibly and very ruthlessly all dissent. The tribes united behind Chinggis for one reason only, however, and if this reason were not to remain a reality, neither would the tribal unity.

The tribes believed that unity under Chinggis would bring them power and wealth. As long as Chinggis delivered, the tribes would remain loyal. As long as loyalty was in their interest, the tribes would remain loyal, and it was Chinggis Khan's dilemma to ensure that he could continue to deliver booty, power, and prestige, without which his empire would unravel and his position would be challenged. Chinggis Khan succeeded where so many before had failed, and he was able to lead a steppe empire out of the steppe and transform it into a world empire ruling both steppe and sown.

Once unleashed, the Mongol led forces spread quickly in all directions. Numbering two million, the Mongols represented a confusion of tribes rather than a single ethnic race. War was a way of life. In 1207 they struck out from the steppe and defeated the Tangut kingdom of Xixia (northwest China), and then turning eastward and braving the burning sands of the Gobi they hit hard at the seminomadic Chin of northern China. The prize they sought was the fabulous wealth of the Chin capital of Chong-du. Though unbeatable in open battle on the plain or in the mountains, the Mongols had no experience of siege warfare, but they were quick learners. From their experiences with the fortresses in Xixia and their smashing of the Great Wall, using captured Chinese engineers in 1215 they finally broke down the walls of the imperial Chin capital and laid the city to total ruin and a "glorious slaughter." The carnage cemented their awesome and horrifying reputation. It was to be another 17 years before the rest of Chin northern China was subdued, but Chinggis Khan was not to enter the country ever again. He now turned his attention westward.

After the Qara khitai had fallen to the forces of the Mongol general Jebe in 1217, the Mongols found themselves neighbors to the lands of Islam. Chinggis Khan held the Khwārazmshāh, Sultan Moḥammad, the emperor of central Asia, Afghanistan, and Iran in awe. He is quoted as having declared, "I am the sovereign of the Sun-rise, and thou the sovereign of the Sun-set."[2] Rather than risk confrontation, Chinggis Khan sought alliance. But when the arrogant Sultan Moḥammad allowed a trade delegation and envoys from the Mongols to be ignominiously slaughtered, the fate of the Khwārazmian empire was sealed. In 1219 an army of 200,000 men, including 10,000 siege engineers, moved westward under the command of Chinggis Khan. The cities of the Khwārazmshāh crumbled before the mighty advance, and the Khwārazmshāh fled for his life. In Bokhara, Chinggis Khan admonished the terrified citizens, "I am the punishment of God. If you had not sinned he would not have sent me."

Within a few years, Iran, the Caucasus, Ukraine, the Crimea, Russia, Siberia, Central Asia, Afghanistan, Pakistan, and Kashmir had all fallen to the Mongol forces. Meanwhile, news reached the Great Khan that back east the Tangut had arisen in revolt in Xixia. Not only had they refused his call to arms and had failed to send soldiers for his campaign against the

Silk merchant in Kashgar bazaar. Courtesy of Xinjiang
Qinshan Culture Publishing

Khwārazmshāh, but now they were in open defiance. The Mongol emperor
personally led his armies eastward to punish the wayward king, but in
1227, after a series of victories as he sat waiting to receive the homage of the
humbled Tangut monarch, Chinggis Khan developed a fever and died. In
only 20 years Chinggis Khan had not only led the nomadic tribes out from
the Eurasian steppes to conquer the mighty Chin empire of northern China
but had also overrun the Islamic kingdom of the Khwārazmshāh who had
ruled the west.

   Already changes had begun to transform the nature of the Mongol expansion. The Mongols were becoming a minority in the multiethnic makeup
of the army. Foreign bureaucrats, Uyghurs in particular, were filling the
burgeoning administration. The leaders were assuming the trappings of
power and prestige, and their *ordus* had been transformed by the luxury

Mongol dagoba or stupa, the White Tower in Hohhut.
Courtesy of Lan Tien Lang Publications

and sumptuousness they now were able to affect. Perhaps most significant was the growing belief in Tenggerism, the belief that their success and continuing triumph was divinely ordained and that they were following the will of their God, Tengri. Their subjects accepted that the Mongols were divine visitations, though their view was that they had come from hell, and there was a growing conviction among the Mongols themselves that destiny had cast them in the role of world conquerors and that all must therefore submit unquestioning to their divinely inspired rule. Their ultimatums to those they would conquer were given in the name of God.

POST-CHINGGIS

Two years after the Great Khan's death, his son Ögödei had been confirmed in office and the conquests were resumed. The hold on the Chin lands was consolidated and Korea was taken; military rule was tightened in Persia, Armenia, Mesopotamia, and Azerbaijan; and the Sung empire of southern China was given notice that they would be next in line for conquest. In Iran various military governors meant that the country remained unstable and chaotic and the Ismāʿīlīs, Jalāl al-Dīn Khwārazmshāh, and other local warlords disrupted life and security for the mass of the people. The poet Saʿdī left his beloved Shiraz to escape the chaos, returning only when he heard of the advent of Hülegü Khan and a central government in the 1250s. In the 1230s, Batu Khan and his Golden Horde were extending their territory deep into Eastern Europe, and terrifying tales of the Mongols began to enter the nightmares of Europeans. In 1240 Kiev was captured and destroyed. In 1241 the Polish army was defeated at Liegnitz, and the victorious Mongols then continued to devastate Moravia and Silesia before capturing Hungary itself.

In December 1241 all campaigning was abruptly stopped, however. The Qaʾan, the Great Khan Ögödei, had died, and all Mongol leaders, princes, and nobles of the Golden family, as the Chinggisids were known, were summoned to the capital at Qaraqorum for a *quriltai* to elect a new leader. It was from this point that the cracks that had been faintly discernable from the beginning of Ögödei's reign began to become more pronounced. After a long regency when Ögödei's widow presided over the vast empire, his son Güyük ruled for a short and tense time until his death in 1248. Batu and his Golden Horde had been opposed to Güyük's election, and after his death, Batu was determined not to allow the crown to fall to the house of Ögödei.

Batu himself and, by extension, his progeny were barred from the top position because of rarely expressed but pervasive doubts about his paternity. His mother Börte had been kidnapped by the Merkit tribe early in her marriage to Temüjin. Approximately nine months after her rescue she gave birth to Jochi, Batu's father. Chinggis had insisted that Jochi should be awarded all the respect due to an eldest son and would allow no allusions to the circumstances of his birth. Rarely spoken doubts persisted, however, and it seemed an unwritten law that Batu remain kingmaker rather than king and that he be treated with the same deference and respect as that given the actual Qaʾan.

RISE OF THE TOLUIDS

With Batu's backing, Möngke, son of Tolui Khan, the youngest son of Chinggis Khan, successfully seized the throne in 1251 after a bitter and very bloody civil war in which his cousin's support was crucial. His rise to power cost the houses of Ögödei and Chaghedai dearly, and his supporters decimated their ranks ruthlessly. Möngke Khan was to be the last Great Khan to rule over a united Mongol Empire, though the unity was tenuous by this stage.

Möngke Khan moved to consolidate his and his family's, the Toluids', grip on power. He dispatched one brother, Qubilai, eastward to subdue the Sung of southern China, and another brother, Hülegü, to consolidate Toluid control of Persia, Anatolia, and the lands of Islam. Hülegü destroyed the mountain strongholds of the so-called fanatical, suicidal terrorists of the day, the Assassins (or more correctly, the Ismāʿīlīs), and then marched on Baghdad to oust the caliph from his position of power. He accomplished this in 1258 with the help of local Kurdish warlords and the disgruntled Shiites of the region. Möngke left his youngest brother, Ariq Buqa, to guard the Mongol homelands as he went southward to help Qubilai in the conquest of the Sung. Möngke died of dysentery while on campaign in China, and once again the worldwide campaigns of the Mongols came to a sudden halt and a *quriltai* was called to which the increasingly disunited Golden family were summoned.

DIVISION

The death of Möngke in 1259 marked the end of the Mongol Empire as a united whole. Civil war flared between the brothers Qubilai and Ariq Buqa over the succession; the disputed accession of Berke Khan, a Muslim, in place of Batu Khan marked the beginning of open hostilities between the Persian Il-Khanate and the Golden Horde, and in 1260 the Mamluks of Egypt defeated a Mongol army at 'Ain Jālūt, proving Mongol fallibility.

Qubilai Khan elected himself Qa'an (Great Khan) not at a *quriltai* in Qaraqorum, the Mongol capital, but in his summer capital, Shang-du (Xanadu), while Ariq Buqa proclaimed himself true ruler of the Mongols. This dispute between the brothers has been downplayed in the Persian sources, which remain the main source of information on Mongol history. They portray Ariq Buqa as a usurper and front man for the estranged and alienated tribes who had suffered in the purges following Möngke's assumption of power. Because these chroniclers were supporters of the house of Tolui, however, they were not unbiased observers, and their words must be treated carefully. In fact, Ariq Buqa represented a sizable part of the Mongol Empire, especially those who disapproved of the direction toward which their leadership was moving. The supporters of Ariq Buqa represented the more traditional-minded Mongols who remained attached to the steppe and the nomadic way of life. They saw the Toluids as having become too close to the people over whom they ruled, namely the Chinese and Persians. The civil war of the early 1260s was a battle for the soul of the Mongols, but the outcome was not decisive. When Ariq Buqa was proclaimed Qa'an, Qubilai was able to move against him with the power and wealth of China behind him. His younger brother could not match such a challenge. The year 1264 saw Qubilai Khan victorious, but he was recognized only by his brother, Hülegü, in Iran. The Golden Horde and the Chaghedaids did not recognize his sovereignty.

THE GOLDEN AGE

The years following 1260 saw the empire irrevocably split but also signaled the emergence of the two greatest achievements of the house of Chinggis, namely the Yüan dynasty of greater China and the Il-Khanid dynasty of greater Iran. In Iran the Mongol rulers eventually converted to Islam when Ghazan Khan acceded to the throne in 1295. Many have seen the reign of Ghazan Khan and his prime minister, the vizier Rashīd al-Dīn, as the Il-Khans' golden age. This, however, has had more to do with the fact that the later historians were Muslim who preferred to award merit and praise to a fellow Muslim, especially a convert, than to "infidels." In fact, both Hülegü and his son Abaqa presided over a culturally and economically prosperous period of Iranian history that was also relatively peaceful. Abū Saʿīd, the last Il-Khan, died in 1235 without heir, and thereafter the line of Hülegü effectively disappeared. Short-lived Mongol dynasties such as the Jalayrids in western Iran with their capital in Baghdad, the peasants' regime of the Sarbadārs in the north of the country, the Persian Karts in Khorasan, and the Muzaffarids of Shiraz all appeared and prospered briefly, but by 1400 they had all fallen to a new storm from the East. This storm was led by Timurlane (1335–1405), another leader of a Turco-Mongol tribe.

In China, Qubilai Khan's successors never matched his achievements, though the dynasty continued for another 74 years. No more territorial expansion occurred, but the seeds that Qubilai Khan had planted prospered. After two disastrous attempted invasions of Japan, expansion in the east stopped. Just as the Mongol defeat by the Egyptian Mamluks at 'Ain Jālūt in 1260 ended the myth of Mongol invincibility in the West, so the defeats by the Kamikaze winds and the Japanese in 1274 and 1281 marked the demise of their reputation in the East. But if the military superiority had come to an end, the legacy of Mongol rule lived on. The highly efficient communications network and the new roads emanating from the new capital Ta-tu (Beijing) ensured that China continued to thrive on international trade. When eventually the regime collapsed and the Ming, an ethnically Chinese dynasty, assumed control of the country, there was no attempt to deny the legitimacy of the Yüan for decades. Though it had been Mongol, the Yüan was accepted as an authentic Chinese dynasty. Zhu Yuanzhang proclaimed himself the new emperor in 1368, and the Ming dynasty he founded ruled until 1644.

It was the two empires founded by the Toluid brothers, Hülegü and Qubilai, that ensured the Mongols the lasting prestige and glory to match their martial reputation for indestructibility and ruthlessness. Both the Il-Khanate and the Yüan dynasty left an indelible mark on the culture and history of both Iran and China. In both states, which remained close for many decades, there was considerable assimilation between the rulers and the ruled. Although Mongol traditions continued to be respected in both the Yüan and the Il-Khanate, the cultural influences of the cities were

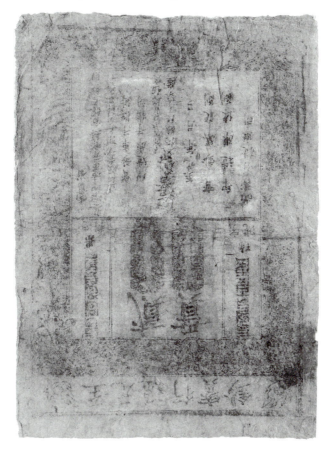

Legal tender in use during the Yuan period. Courtesy of
Lan Tien Lang Publications

unmistakable and contrasted with life in the north. Ghazan Khan, ruler
of Iran from 1295 to 1304, converted to Islam in 1295, but he maintained
his extremely close links with the Great Khans of China and recognized
the supremacy of Mongol law, the *yasa* of Chinggis Khan. In China, too,
Chinese laws and administrative practices were adopted, but Mongol law
and custom remained an important element in all institutions.

The quality and style of daily life in the Mongol Empire depended very
much on where that life was spent. In the north, life in many ways went on
as it had for centuries. The nomadic tribes continued to roam from winter
to summer pastures, though now their world had opened its borders to
wealth, trade, and influences that would have been unimaginable a generation earlier. In the northwest the Golden Horde had assimilated the Qipchaq
Turks, and there had been little attempt to infiltrate the world of the princes
of Rus. The steppe kept its distance from the sown. The sedentary world

of the Rus and the people of Eastern Europe paid their Mongol masters tribute, and the tribes kept themselves to the rolling steppes away from the cities and farmlands of their neighbors. Daily life in the grasslands of the Golden Horde had not changed much since the papal envoys of Carpini in the 1240s and then William of Rubruck in the 1250s passed through. Even in these regions where Mongol tradition remained strong, however, the court life had been transformed since the early days, and the luxuries that were the norm farther south in the courts of Persia and China would also have been enjoyed here.

For everyone, life after the *quriltai* of 1206 was transformed. The empire passed through three main periods, and these periods were reflected in lifestyle changes for many who lived under Mongol rule. The initial period of expansion was dominated by military confrontations and triumphs. After the death of Guyuk in 1248, a period of internal strife and consolidation followed as the power bases became more entrenched. The last period, beginning around 1260, saw the formation of the Yüan and the Il-Khanate and the complete transformation of the Mongol court. In Beijing and Tabriz the monarch enthroned in those glorious courts was no longer a rude warlord from the steppe but an emperor, receiving obsequious envoys from around the world. The empire had created a new political reality over nearly half the land area of the planet. With the new political reality there were new military alliances, confrontations, and networks. In addition, the empire had also given birth to a new cultural awakening. Just as the empire had combined and mixed political institutions, practices, people, and networks from all over the Mongol-dominated world, so too had the emerging culture, be it gastronomical, artistic, astrological, literary, or scientific. In the realm of politics, it was the Mongols who held the reins of power for more than a century, just as they dominated the military institutions. In the world of culture, they were present as well, as brokers, financiers, and movers. The world they created was a long way from the steppe, but it was from the steppe that the inspirational wind blew.

NOTES

1. Though commonly known as Genghis Khan, the spelling Chinggis Khan more correctly reflects the pronunciation of his name.

2. Maulana Juzjani, Minhaj-ud-Din Abu 'Umar-i-Usman, *Tabakat-i-Nasiri. A General History of the Muhammadan Dynasties of Asia; from 810–1260 A.D. And The Irruption of the Infidel Mughals into Islam*, trans. H. G. Raverty (1881; reprint, Calcutta: The Asiatic Society, 1995), 966.

2

STEPPE LIFE

The Mongols were the last of the great nomadic invaders of the sedentary world.[1] Over the centuries there had been successive intrusive migration of nomadic hordes from their Eurasian heartlands westward into Europe, southward into Persia and Sind, and in the east, southward into China. The peoples of the Eurasian steppe had a long tradition of mounting raids and irruptions into the sown, that is, periodic invasions of the agriculturally domesticated lands, from the vast expanses of uncultivated grasslands and savanna that compose most of the Eurasian steppe lands. Europe, China, and the lands south of the Oxus River all had a long history of repelling and accommodating their horse-mounted neighbors with varying degrees of success. In Iran the legends and myths surrounding and based on these successive raids and wars between the peoples of the steppe and the peoples of the sown were enshrined in the stories of the Persian national epic, the *Shahnameh* (Book of Kings), and in particular the *Shāhnāmeh* of the eleventh-century poet Firdowsī (920–1025). North of the mighty Oxus River (Amu Darya, Amuyieh) lay the nomadic peoples of Turan, who cast envious aspirations on the lands south of the Oxus, which were ruled by the people of Iran. The Iranians had kept the Turanians at bay until the thirteenth century, when the Khwārazmshāh openly defied, insulted, and challenged Chinggis Khan. The Mongol invasion was so devastating because it was a prolonged and sustained attack, and in many ways a retreat of the nomads back from the sown to the open steppe never occurred.

This chapter will examine the nature and structure of steppe society and the transformation that Eurasian tribal society underwent during the

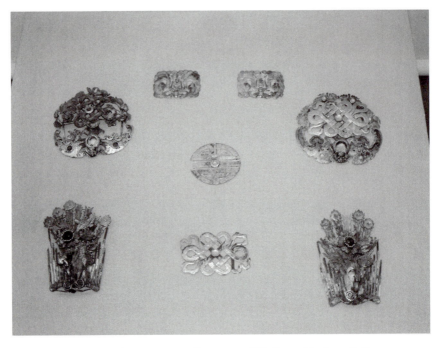

Mongol jewelry, Hohhut Museum. Courtesy of Xinjiang Qinshan Culture
Publishing

rule of the Mongols and Chinggis Khan. It will provide an overview of the
nature of the nomadic tribal society that Chinggis Khan was born into and
its relationship with its sedentary neighbors to the south.

TRIBES

The nomadic tribes of the Eurasian steppe are often known collectively
as Mongols. This is solely because of the dominance of Chinggis Khan's
tribe over all other Turco-Mongol tribes. They have also commonly been
called Tatars, and before the rise of Chinggis Khan, *Tatars* was the standard
appellation for all Eurasian nomads. This was because the Tatars were the
most powerful and dominant group within the Turco-Mongol world. Even
though with the rise of Chinggis Khan the use of the term *Mongols* spread,
the label Tatar continued to be attached to the invaders. In Asia this was simply habit, but in Europe the word Tatar corresponded to the medieval Latin
Tartarus, meaning "hell," and this tied in well with the prevalent belief in
Europe at that time that the Mongols were denizens of the underworld, sent
by the biblical demons Gog and Magog to punish the sinners of the world.
Until recently, central Asia was known as either Turkistan or Tartary.

Though the major tribal confederations at this time are often divided
into Mongols, Tatars, Naimans, Onggirats, Merkits, and Keraits, with

Pipes, Hohhut Museum, Inner Mongolia. Courtesy of Xinjiang Qinshan
Culture Publishing

numerous subdivisions, these groups were in no way either linguistically
or ethnologically distinct. Mongols could be found in Naiman tribes, for
example, and Turkish or a form of Turkish would be used as a first language in any number of these groupings. In the *Secret History* there is a
reference to the peoples of the Eurasian steppes as "the peoples of the Nine
Tongues," which points to their recognized linguistic diversity.[2] Mongols
were found in all the other tribal confederations, and Turks were of course
a major component of the Mongol confederation. This ethnic and linguistic
blurring became far more pronounced with Chinggis Khan's rise to power.
Chinggis made a point of breaking up the traditional tribal divisions and
instilling a new loyalty based on his reformatted decimal tribal structures.
Religion was not a divisive factor among the tribes, and a variety of religious beliefs coexisted without rivalry and usually adapted themselves
to each other. Shamanism[3] was the most prevalent belief, but Nestorian
Christianity,[4] for example, was common among the Naiman, Ongut, and
Merkits, and Buddhism was often professed, among the Uighur in particular. Religious tolerance was a defining trait among the tribes and among
the Mongols under Chinggis Khan in particular. Loyalty and identity
was often associated with individuals and tribal leaders or ancestors. The
tribe was the basic unit of society, and, especially when linguistically or

ethnically mixed, it was the tribe that promoted unity and the idea of a common identity. The practice of exogamy (marriage outside the tribe) and polygyny (multiple wives) can help to explain the linguistic and ethnic diversity of the tribes, but despite such diversity all members of the tribe still considered themselves descendants of a common ancestry, however tenuous and mythical that ancestry might be.

GEOGRAPHY

The Turco-Mongol nomadic tribes pastured their flocks over a vast area that is commonly referred to as the Eurasian steppes. The Eurasian steppes cover a wide zone stretching from Eastern Europe to Manchuria and passing through the south Russian steppe, Kazakhstan, Zungharia, Tsinghai province and Mongolia. The immense central Asian plateau, lying at between 900 and 1,500 meters above sea level and bounded by the Altai and Tian Shan mountain ranges in the west and by the Great Khinghan heights in the east, was the home of the Mongol tribes. South of this region the steppe transforms into desert, a vast arid zone punctuated with islands of urban and sedentary settlements. In contrast, the prairies, grasslands, and gentle mountain slopes of the steppes were devoid of farming settlements or towns. Those who would dwell on the steppe were

The vast Lake Sayram high in the Tian Shan mountains, the Chaghataid heartlands. Courtesy of Xinjiang Qinshan Culture Publishing

pastoral nomads and hunters, and life necessitated their seasonal migration in constant search of water and grass. Though the nomads generally renounced fixed settlements and fixed dwellings, their migration routes were often rigid. As a result, cultivation on a limited scale was practiced by these steppe migrants who would sow suitable crops that they would then be able to harvest later, on their return migration. Constantly on the move, constantly alert to the environmental, climatic, and human changes around them, and constantly prepared for danger and threats, the pastoral nomads were a natural martial force, and war was everyone's business. Every herdsman doubled as a fighter and raider, and the culture of the steppe resounded with tales and songs of their warrior heroes. These nomads were pastoral armies.

COHESION

Fiercely independent, there was little social cohesion above the level of the tribe, and tribal leaders generally resisted the formation of supratribal authority unless the forfeiting of their autonomy promised very great rewards. Wealth was generally measured by the possession of livestock, the protection and amassing of which were the overriding concerns of the tribe. When alliances, confederations, and supratribal arrangements were entered into, the motivation behind such moves was the protection or amassing of wealth. Chinggis Khan was remarkable from the outset in that he was able to form so cohesive and unified a supratribal polity out of such a fiercely independent collection of warrior tribes.

The tribes of Turco-Mongols in the twelfth century can very generally be divided into the pure pastoralists (cattle and sheep grazers) and the forest-hunters/fishers. The less numerous forest-hunters could be found around Lake Baikal, the source of the Yenisey River, and the upper reaches of the Irtysh River, whereas the pastoralists occupied the lands south of this region, from the foothills of the Altai Mountains to Lake Buyr and Hulun. However, just as some hunters tended cattle, so did the pastoral nomads hunt. In fact, the hunt, referred to as the *nerge,* played an extremely important role in the life of all the Mongol tribes. The targets of the organized hunts were wild donkeys, antelope, boar, game, and even lions as well as rival tribes and enemies. Lassoes, bows and arrows, and spears were all employed. The *nerge* served the function of recreation, military training, and food gathering, and it was an event in which the whole tribe partook. Horses, cows, sheep, goats, and camels were all reared to provide the tribe's basic needs.

The other basic need, women, were also "hunted" because the tribes were strictly exogamous (marrying outside the clan or tribe), and this would frequently lead to intertribal conflict. However, under other circumstances, brides would also be used to cement intertribal alliances. Polygyny was common among those who could afford it, even though women enjoyed a

Copper seal, Hohhut Museum. Courtesy of Xinjiang Qinshan Culture Publishing

very high status among the Turco-Mongols. They played a role in all aspects of the tribe's life, including the fighting. Women often exercised considerable real power, as is demonstrated by the regency of Töregene Khātūn (widow of the Great Khan Ögödei; regency 1241–46) and Oghul Ghaymish (widow of the Great Khan Güyük; regency 1248–51). The principal wife and her children were invariably awarded special status. Only the sons borne by Chinggis Khan's principal wife, Börte Füjin, were considered eligible for succession. Upon the father's death, his wives, considered part of his estate, were inherited by his youngest son, following the practice of ultimogeniture. The natural mother was not included in this inheritance package.

POWER

Primary political power lay with the khan or tribal chief. The tribal chief generally rose from among the aristocratic elite, though not necessarily. The choice of chief was arrived at through a process governed by the principles of tanistry, which demands that succession fall to the best-qualified and competent candidate, rather than by the dictates of primogeniture, ultimogeniture,[5] or any other system of seniority. Usually the chief would be chosen from among the members of the chiefly house, but Chinggis Khan is an obvious example in which such a rule was not followed. Such a system often led to succession struggles. In the case of larger tribes or confederations, such struggles could lead to the formation of new break-away tribes or adjusted tribal realignments. Nobles *(noyan)* within the tribe often had their own personal following of friends and allies *(nöker)*, who in turn would be served by their own household and retainers, the commoners *(haran)*. These *haran* would rarely break from their particular noble and would follow him if he split from the tribe or realigned himself within another confederation.

SHAMANS

Another source of political power, independent of the tribal nobility, was the shaman *(böge)*. The shaman was the tribe's link with the spiritual world. His ability to foretell the future and interpret order from the per-ceived chaos of the world around the tribesmen gave the shaman enor-mous prestige and authority. It was generally believed that in addition to the gift of prophecy, the shaman possessed supernatural resources and magical powers. He was the tribe's intermediary with the spirit world. The tribe's leading shaman could fulfill the role of the chief's principal *nöker*, or his close advisor. He could also be a source of alternative, even rival, political authority. In some cases, the shaman himself could assume the role of chief.

The shaman's services were called upon for choosing auspicious days for celebrations, important events, commencing battle; for advice on elect-ing new chiefs or leaders; for the treatment of the sick and disabled; for the curing of childlessness; and for warding off evil spirits; exorcism; and the casting of spells. His major role remained his ability to foretell the future. His insights were gained by the careful reading and interpretation of the cracks that opened up across the shoulder blades of sheep after ritual burning. Shamanism is believed to have originated from ancestor worship, and most Mongol tents contained images of the family's ancestors *(ongghot)*. Heaven (Tengri) was worshipped, and the mother Earth (Itügen) was vener-ated. Between *köke* (blue) or *möngke* (eternal) Tengri and Itügen lived a mul-titude of spirits, and it was in this realm that the shamans were most active and influential. The shaman's voice was disregarded at the chief's peril because the whole tribe believed in the power of the holy man's magic and the authority of his words. This peril was made all the more real because the shaman was usually associated with a shaman's "guild," which linked and supported shamans among various tribes and clans.

THE KHAN

As head of the tribe, the ruling khan's main duties concerned the allot-ment of pastures, the plotting of migration times and routes, and deci-sive leadership. The shaman and the other nobles, effectively a tribal council, both confirmed and counterbalanced the chief's authority. The tribe operated on a minimum of two administrative levels. At the highest level was the tribal chief, who exercised direct control over the tribal nobles. At a lower level, individual nobles controlled their own retinue of commoners, who were solely answerable to them.

Sometimes it was considered in the tribes' interest to form alliances or join confederations or even seek the protection of a stronger tribe. However, this invariably involved some loss of independence, something that any tribe was loath to suffer. The reality of the steppes dictated that the smaller or weaker tribes had to sometimes sacrifice their independence in order to merely ensure their continued existence. Where the supratribal arrangement existed, it took on the form of an enlarged reflection of the tribe, incorporating common myths, beliefs, practices, traditions, and institutions. Often a royal lineage, a golden lineage in the case of the Mongols, became a unifying theme with which to command an extra sense of unity and identity.

Mongol *paiza* granting free passage to the bearer. Courtesy of Xinjiang Qinshan Culture Publishing

After Chinggis Khan assumed the leadership of the "people of the felt-walled tents,"[6] his clan, the Borjigid, dominated the other clans and tribes, who then declared their allegiance or submission *(il)*[7] and also took on the collective name of Mongols. The supratribe could be joined by outsiders by one of three methods. First, a whole tribe could pledge loyalty and be incorporated in its entirety into the larger polity (political unit). Second, after suffering defeat a tribe could be broken into individuals, tents, or family units and distributed as booty among all the component parts of the supratribe. Third, and especially with nontribal military elements, outsider units could be assigned to individual military commanders to act under his personal command. These supratribal polities were extremely fluid, and their composition frequently changed, expanding or shrinking over time, though the idea of a vague "people" or "nation" or *ulus* persisted and provided a continuing sense of identity. When Chinggis Khan reached the pinnacle of his power in the third decade of the thirteenth century, he allotted new *ulus*[8] named after his sons, and these *ulus* were to form the basis of political and even geographical entities for centuries after his death. Individual tribes, to conclude, would submit and relinquish some of their independence to a supratribal polity when material gain, usually in the form of war-generated booty, was offered or when the tribe's security or very existence was threatened.

MAINTAINING POWER

Chinggis Khan built his power base and his tribal empire through battle, and with each victory he added more men to his army and more tents to his following, but it should be realized that those independent-minded tribal chiefs remained with him not out of fear but out of choice. The tribes flocked to the Mongol banner not in defeat but in the belief that united they would cause others' defeat. Chinggis Khan offered his followers rewards and plunder aplenty. The tribes harkened to his call and submitted their independence to him because they believed that they would gain and prosper in his service. If he could not deliver, his support would have soon dissolved, and the supratribe would have dwindled once again into scattered tribes. His authority and the tribes' continued support both depended on his victories and political and military success.

Certain elements were necessary to maintain the unity and preservation of the steppe empire. The charisma of the leader was crucial. A supratribal power would often dissolve on the death or defeat of its leader. If the tribal leaders' expectations of wealth and prosperity did not continue to be met, the union would quickly dissolve. Sometimes a confederation of tribes might be formed and unified in order to achieve a single goal. Such was the case when the steppe tribes wished to confront China in order to win concessions. The tribal sovereign would be a nominal figure and act as a spokesman for the collective tribes. The principles of tanistry[9] would rule his succession, and the supratribal union would persist because the need for a united front would still be present.

As Chinggis Khan grew in stature, so also did the expectations of his followers. The union behind him existed because Chinggis Khan met those expectations. Without him there would be no expectations and no unity. The steppe leader had no need of pomp and ceremony. He was not clothed in the regality of a Persian *Shahanshah* (King of Kings) or a Chinese emperor. A great Khan was not bathed in the mystery of majesty so crucial for the preservation of the "civilized" world. He was awarded respect, authority, and even adulation because he delivered wealth and prosperity to his followers. He was admired for his generosity and for his martial skills. He was expected to lead his army, which in effect was his people and tribes, into battle and win for them riches. These were very real expectations and concrete rewards. The object of his martial adventures could, of course, be other tribes, but ideally and increasingly as the supratribe became larger, that object was the sedentary communities of the sown and their rich urban centers, cities, and caravans.

EMPIRE

Steppe empires rather than steppe confederations were built by immensely charismatic, ambitious, and powerful men. A Great Khan (Qa'an) ruled a steppe empire, whereas a khan reigned over a steppe confederation. Chinggis Khan was the greatest of the steppe khans. As the expectations of his followers rose, so too did his own ambition, and neither were disappointed.

The Great Khan might well have achieved his position as undisputed leader of the tribes after a long and bloody civil, intertribal war and possibly also an intratribal succession conflict. A reckoning would invariably follow with payoffs and paybacks all being called for. A *quriltai* (a Mongol princely assembly) would be summoned, and all the leading players, tribal chiefs, military commanders, and factional elements would be called upon to participate and decide the fate of the rebels. Part of the fate of the rebels or losing side would be their becoming the source of booty from which the allies of the winner could be rewarded.

Eventually the losing side would be incorporated into the winning supratribal entity, and the enlarged force would then seek richer pastures. In order to retain the loyalty of the increasing number of equally ambitious subordinate khans and chiefdoms, the leader of the steppe empire would have to find increasingly challenging and rich adventures and sources of wealth to occupy his expanding army of warriors and tents. As the last of the Eurasian steppe tribes fell to his forces, Chinggis Khan found himself in this position in the early thirteenth century. For the Great Khan, therefore, there seemed only one natural and obvious choice he should make.

He should turn his attentions to that inexhaustible source of booty and plunder: the urban centers of Manchuria and China.

Relations with the settled peoples were not always antagonistic. The nomads were nonautarkic in the economic, political, and cultural spheres.[10] Trading was mutually advantageous, and protection was a commodity that the tribes were always willing to barter. Metals for their tools and weapons, grain for bread, textiles for their tents and clothing and for their lords and ladies, precious metals and gems, and especially *nasij,* or brocades and fine fabrics, embroidered in gold and silks, were among the items that they sought to procure in exchange for meat, wool, horses, and hides.[11]

Though Chinggis Khan is credited toward the end of his days with the desire to return to the simple life away from fineries and pomp, among the elite and the steppe aristocracy an appetite for epicurean indulgence in more sophisticated food and drink was growing. Koumiss, the alcoholic

Mongol seal, Hohhut Museum. Courtesy of Xinjiang Qinshan Culture Publishing

fermented mare's milk of the steppe, could not compete with the fine wines available in the towns and cities. Though these nomad lords continued to view the settled realms with arrogant disdain, they were appreciative of the luxuries and comforts this rival world had to offer.

NEW WORLD ORDER

With the attention of his forces now directed outward, two strategies remained to bind these armies into a cohesive force. One was through a thorough structural overhaul of the army, and the other was the use of religion and the shamans to forge a common identity and purpose. However, with the number of rebel tribes rapidly dwindling, the only realistic option for sustaining a large booty-hungry army was a major and prolonged incursion into the sown.

The classical army formation employed by steppe leaders as far back as the confederation of nomadic central Asian tribes known as the Hsiung-nu, or Huns, at the end of the third century B.C.E. and perfected by Chinggis Khan was decimalization, the division of the army into deci-mal units of tens, hundreds, thousands, and so on. Ideally, a decimal sys-tem would have replaced the tribes, but even Chinggis Khan was unable to achieve this. To varying degrees, however, decimalization, that is the division of the fighting forces into units of ten *(harban)*, one hundred *(jagun)*, one thousand *(minghan)*, and ten thousand *(tümen)*, each headed by an answerable commander, was able to circumvent and sometimes overrule the tribal command structure and tribal loyalties. It also greatly facilitated the incorporation of outside or defeated forces into the main body of the army. In reality these formations rarely contained the exact number of assigned men, especially in the higher divisions of thousands, and it was not uncommon for a tribal chief to be assigned command of a *minghan* or a *tümen*.

With the downplaying of tribal loyalty, the cohesion of the supratribe stemmed from a common spirituality that transcended individual tribal religious affiliations and by a belief in Tenggeri, the universal sky god whose favor bestowed victory. This idea of a single supreme god around which the Mongols' spirituality was based was seized upon in later years by their Muslim subjects to justify their own submission to the Mongols' infidel rule. Tengri bestowed his favor by granting victory to his chosen agent, and therefore the mark of Tengri's approval was victory in battle, and the sign of divine disfavor was defeat. As long as the ruler was granted victory, his faithful followers believed him blessed with Tengri's favor and would therefore remain loyal. The royal mandate survived only so long as victories could be achieved. In addition to victory, it was also necessary for the would-be steppe ruler to obtain the endorsement and support of the tribe's shaman. The shaman would often act as an intermediary with Tengri, who would demonstrate his bestowal of a mandate on the aspiring steppe king through the offices of the shaman. In such circumstances the shaman had a very powerful and influential role.

With his tribes suitably organized into decimal rather than tribal units and the endorsement of Tengri vouched for by a well-respected, independent shaman, the steppe warrior/king would then be in a position to assail the rich agricultural lands and prosperous urban centers to the south.

STEPPE VERSUS SOWN

Pastoral steppe nomads repeatedly invaded China over many centuries for various reasons. Their greed and a predatory nature that their lifestyle encouraged predisposed them to raiding. Second, climatic change affected the pattern of their lives and their prosperity. A third reason was population increase and the demands that entailed. Related to these reasons were the resulting economic pressures that change invariably brought. A further reason was a growing trade imbalance caused by the Chinese that brought resentment in the steppe. This was strengthened by a desire to periodically assert steppe dominance over the inferior culture of the sown. Finally, there was the reality of developing a supratribal polity that entailed military adventure.[12] To a greater or lesser extent all of these reasons played a part in the motivation of the nomadic invasions, but it is the final point that was crucial for a prolonged and sustained invasion. Without an invasion of the sown, the supratribal polity could not be sustained. Chinggis Khan united a warrior culture that was perpetually on the move, which by tradition had lived with their agrarian neighbors through controlled and limited extortion and whose lifestyle barely sustained a very fragile economy. It was a society that chose its leaders because of their ability to wage successful war and to increase the tribe's prosperity at the expense of their neighbors. It is hardly surprising that such a society, upon uniting and reaching its peak of power, invaded its ill-prepared and weak, agrarian neighbors. Any other outcome would have been unthinkable. The explanation of why the pattern of periodic raids from the steppe to the sown transformed into full-scale occupation under Chinggis Khan must simply be that having attained such a degree of unity, it was only the wealth of the lands and cities of the sown that could provide the booty to satisfy the fully united tribes of the steppes, who no longer had themselves to fight. Whereas before, the settled communities of China could pay off invaders or employ selected stronger tribes to act as their border guards, under Chinggis Khan the combined might of the steppe had become too great to be bought.

Unlike previous steppe rulers the Mongols continued to grow and rule. In the past the pattern of nomadic incursions into the sown had been one of attack, plunder, rapine, destruction, and retreat. Another facet of the relationship between steppe and sown, often overlooked or marginalized, should be emphasized. The Eurasian nomads enabled lines of commercial activity and cultural exchange to operate between east and west and especially between Iran and China. Under the Chinggisids the Mongols became cultural and economic brokers, and these links between Iran and China in particular became cemented.[13] Merchants had long traversed the steppes, and they did so only with the acquiescence of the steppe lords. These same merchants would have facilitated the exchange of goods between steppe and sown, and their safe passage would have been mutually beneficial to all concerned. The establishment of this commercial relationship in addition to the political ties between the dominant tribe and the Chinese rulers had long regulated and constrained the more predatory inclinations of the tribes, and the nomads would have long learned that the prosperity of the sedentary regions could provide them with real benefits beyond booty. When Chinggis Khan found that he controlled considerable regions of agricultural and urban settlement, he was able to utilize his contacts among the merchant, often Muslim, community to harness for mutual benefit these new resources. Taxation and trade replaced booty as the new sustenance for his emerging empire.

THE END?

It has often been asked why the Mongols suddenly disappeared. They did not disappear as such but simply became assimilated as nomadic culture became marginalized, hastened by the use of gunpowder. In Iran the Mongol Il-Khan, Ghazan, converted to Islam around 1295, and thereafter the Mongol elite became increasingly Persianized, increasingly adopting Persian habits, dress, manner, and speech. The Golden Horde in the Russian steppes became increasingly Turkish-dominated, and a breakaway faction possibly gave birth to the Ottoman state.[14] In China the Yüan dynasty, often disparaged by traditionally minded Mongols for its adoption of Chinese ways, was replaced by the Ming dynasty (1371–1644), but their heritage and even their treaties have persisted to the present. In India the Moguls, who traced their descent from the Chinggisids, went with the advent of the rule of the British Raj (ruled 1760–1947).

Chinggis Khan differed from previous steppe leaders. The Mongol leader possessed many qualities that have distinguished him from other military strategists, nomadic chieftains, and conquering emperors, and some of these characteristics will be examined in later chapters. However, an overriding difference relevant to this introductory chapter should be emphasized. This was his recognition of the nature, worth, and strength of the sedentary world and his willingness and ability to utilize those qualities in order to advance his own cause. Chinggis Khan achieved celebrity and greatness as a steppe ruler, but he went down in history as a world conqueror and empire builder, and two of his grandsons, Qubilai and Hülegü, ruled over two of the world's greatest and most sophisticated civilizations: China and Persia.

KINGSHIP AND THE MONGOLS

Family relations, inheritance, and authority were a complex matter with the Turco-Mongol tribes of the Eurasian steppes. With the advent of Chinggis Khan and their rise to power, the matter became far more complex. It was a polygynous society, and men were permitted a number of wives. Economics was the determining factor in the number of wives a man might have, so there was often a resulting rivalry among the siblings of the various wives, especially when a major wife had not been clearly appointed. Add to this the widespread acceptance of the principles of tanistry (election of the strongest or worthiest of the ruling family) among the steppe people, and it can be seen why empires and dynasties based on or arising from the steppe lands of Eurasia have not been noted for their longevity or stability.

MARRIAGE MORES

Though it was a polygynous society, most families were limited to one wife, and fidelity was prized and adultery frowned upon. In fact, earlier chroniclers such as Carpini and Rubruck claim that adultery was punishable with death. Intercourse with a virgin was also considered a capital offence. Wives had to be bought, and the marriage was considered eternal, the couple being reunited in the afterlife. This belief gave rise to the practice of sons marrying all his father's wives, other than his natural mother, on the father's death. The son, often the youngest, had the option to merely look after the well-being of these wives or to take them as full wives. If these wives returned to the father in their afterlife, it was not considered such a loss because they were still kept within the family circle. In the case of Hülegü Khan, Mongol ruler, or Il-Khan, of Iran (ruled 1256–65), his inherited wife, Dokuz Khatun, became his principal wife, and their sons and descendants sat on the Il-Khanid throne until 1335. She was the last and youngest of his father's, Tolui's, wives, and it was claimed the marriage had not been consummated. According to Rubruck the Mongols observed the prohibitions on first and second degree of sanguinity that forbade marriage with first cousins or with aunts or uncles. However, there were no restrictions on affinity, that is on marrying two sisters, for example, in succession or at the same time. Chinggis Khan had innumerable wives, and modern estimates claim that 16 million of his descendants are walking the planet today, spreading his genes to places Mongol hooves never trod.

When a marriage contract was drawn up, it was the father who organized the banquet. Meanwhile, the daughter was obliged to flee and hide from her future husband at the home of her relatives. The father would then announce the disappearance of his daughter and would tell her fiancé that if he could find her he could keep her. At this the man would ride out with his friends to hunt for his betrothed. Upon finding her, he was supposed to feign violence and forcibly seize her, taking her away with him bound and struggling. As their daughter was being abducted, her family would be at home mourning their loss while the husband's family would be preparing a welcoming feast to greet his newly won wife.

FLEXIBILITY

Rules and principles did exist to regulate social life and to determine inheritance rights, but they were extremely flexible. As the Mongols spread from their roots in the high steppes, their social norms and institutions developed and adapted. This development and change can be seen in tribal institutions, inheritance practices, and in the assumption of leadership. The emergence of the empire was mirrored in the change from a nomadic way of life to varying degrees of sedentarization. Where once the various camps and clusters of tents belonging to a particular tribe or clan could be found in the same general neighborhood of valleys and hills, now a tribe's *ordus* might be separated by many thousands of miles, and messages could takes weeks or months to pass from one brother to another. Close contacts were maintained, however, and the periodic calling of *quriltais*, especially when a new Great Khan had to be decided by election, demanded that all key members of the family be present. During campaigns all members of the family would be represented in the army on the move, and all the princes would receive their allotment of occupied lands and of captured artisans. The last campaign composed of *tamma* contingents, as the troops donated by the various princes were called, was Hülegü's march on Iran in the 1250s, after which the splits rendering the empire asunder became too great to allow such a united force to assemble again.

TRIBAL UNITY

People were divided into clans and tribes, though it should be noted that these were rather loosely organized institutions and not restricted to blood relationships at all. The fact that they were theoretically based on blood connections has led to many spurious genealogical claims and other misunderstandings. Most tribal groupings claim common heritage and ancestry, but this is generally agreed to be a political device to engender common cause and unity with little basis in reality. The loose tribal structure enabled Chinggis Khan to radically reorganize the tribal structure of nomadic Eurasian society and so enforce his own discipline and chain of command over his extraordinarily disparate, unruly tribal people. With his regrouping in tribally mixed units, loyalty was encouraged to the military commanders and certainly to the Golden family, though ultimately loyalty was engendered to Chinggis himself.

As units before and certainly after this radical reconfiguration of the clans, these Turco-Mongol tribes were not linguistically, racially, or

Mongol *paiza* from Hohhut Museum. Courtesy of Xinjiang Qinshan Culture
Publishing

religiously united polities. So great was Chinggis Khan's prestige and so
great were his conquests and the resulting wealth and prosperity that his
successes generated that his name and authority were enough to embolden
and inspire the reconstituted Turco-Mongol tribes. Within these tribes the
clans formed a subdivision, but even at this level blood ties did not necessarily take precedence, and the institution of *andas* (sworn brotherhood)
was commonplace. An exchange of blood accompanied the swearing of
allegiance, loyalty, and trust when two friends declared themselves *anda*.
One notable example of this kind of close tie was the case of the young
Chinggis Khan, Temüjin, and his boyhood friend Jamuqa, detailed in the
Secret History of the Mongols. Anda-ship was recognized as an equal, though
voluntary, relationship to a blood tie and could be utilized as such as when
Temüjin called on his late father's *anda*, Toghril, the powerful leader of the
Kereit tribe, to honor this relationship and come to his *anda*'s son's aid.
Another voluntary relationship that involved renouncing other blood ties
was the position of the *nöker*, which can be loosely translated as "com-
rade" or "associate," though with a suggestion of "follower" attached to
the term. The subordinate status of the *nöker* became more pronounced
later until eventually the term was used to denote a servant or lackey.
Many of Chinggis Khan's greatest generals began their careers as his
nökers. The openness of the clan was further ensured by the strict practice

of exogamy, or marriage outside the clan or tribe. One of the results of the constant warfare that characterized pre-Chinggisid steppe society was the incorporation of various tribes by their conquerors and the parceling out of the men and women as slaves or concubines. These people and their offspring could eventually be assimilated into the tribe, adding to its ethnic, religious, and linguistic mix.

INHERITANCE

Inheritance conventions among the Mongol tribes were also flexible. The father's *ordu* (camp) and possessions, including wives and slaves, were inherited by the youngest son of the chief wife, though it should be added, not the son's actual mother. By convention the eldest son would retain seniority but would inherit the *ulus* (subject people, effectively lands) farthest from the family homelands. Other *ulus* would be granted to other sons until, as mentioned, the youngest would inherit the homelands or homestead itself. With Chinggis Khan this pattern was followed with Jochi, his firstborn, receiving lands to the west "as far as Mongol hoof had trod" and Tolui receiving the lands of the Mongol steppes. However, when Jochi died, just before his father, it was his younger son, Batu, who inherited his father's lands and position. Traditions did exist, but flexibility and adaptability ruled. It should be noted that Chinggis Khan's chief wife, Börte, retained her high status even though she had been kidnapped early in their marriage. Virginity was not a particularly prized attribute for women even though both parties to adultery were severely punished. Questions regarding the parentage of Börte's firstborn, Jochi, were not allowed to affect his standing in the royal family, and Chinggis Khan always gave him the respect due his status as firstborn son of the emperor.

The laws governing inheritance of kingship were also flexible to a degree and were influenced by the tribal custom of tanistry. During the debate over Chinggis Khan's succession Ögödei Qa'an (ruled 1229–41) expressed reservations, first, because "in accordance with Mongol custom, it is the youngest son from the eldest house that is the heir of his father,"[15] and second, because he had elder brothers and uncles whose familial seniority gave them priority. In this case the ruling and choice of Chinggis Khan himself was followed, but in later cases the precepts of tanistry, nemesis of would-be steppe dynasties in which kingship fell to the strongest aspirant, were followed. The principle of tanistry awarded the leadership of the tribe to the best-qualified member of the ruling family by a meeting of tribal elders. Disputes frequently led to civil war and the breakup of the tribe. With two succession traditions very much alive, patrilineal, which followed father to son, and lateral, which followed familial seniority through uncles and brothers and so forth, disputes were inevitable, and it was such disputes that eventually split the Mongol empire. The Mongol

Il-Khanid dynasty of Iran (1256–1335) followed an often bloody mixture of these traditions, the kingship passing from father to son to brother to uncle through rarely smooth successions.

Kinship was a valued and important factor in Mongol society. However, it was a far more flexible institution than its adherents possibly realized, and though blood links were considered important, tribal and clan and even close family relationships could be manipulated, changed, manufactured, and created without undue controversy. Chinggis Khan's rise to power was due in part to his ability to mold the ties of kinship within Turco-Mongol society to his own ends.

NOTES

1. For a detailed study of many of the issues raised in this chapter, see Joseph Fletcher, "The Mongols: Ecological and Social Perspectives," *Harvard Journal of Asiatic Studies* 46 (1986): 11–50.

2. Urgunge Onon, trans., *The History and Life of Chinggis Khan (The Secret History of the Mongols)* (Leiden, Netherlands: Brill, 1990), 129.

3. Shamanism is a religion characterized by the belief in the existence of good and bad spirits that can be controlled by priests or shamans.

4. Nestorian Christianity is the doctrine that Christ was two distinct persons, divine and human, implying a denial that the Virgin Mary was the mother of God. It is attributed to Nestorius and survives today in the Iraqi church.

5. Primogeniture refers to the rights of the first born; ultimogeniture refers to the rights of the youngest or last born.

6. Onon, The History and Life, 102.

7. Note the Il-Khans of Iran (1256–1335), who recognized the sovereignty of the Great Khan (Qa'an) in Qaraqorum. The opposite of *il* is *bulgha* (unsubmitted).

8. *Ulus* refers to the tribes or people over whom a prince was appointed. Strictly speaking, people constituted the *ulus*, in reality it came to mean land.

9. Tanistry is the succession practice whereby the leadership of the tribe would fall to the strongest of the princes, often determined through battle.

10. Meaning they were not totally independent but were dependant for many things on their settled neighbors, to use Anatoly M. Khazanov's phrase (*Nomads and the Outside World* [Madison: University of Wisconsin Press, 1994], 69–84.

11. On the Mongols' love of and trade in fine brocade, see Thomas Allsen, *Commodity and Exchange in the Mongol Empire: A Cultural History of Islamic Textiles* (Cambridge: Cambridge University Press, 1997).

12. From Ch'i-ch'ing Hsiao, cited in Fletcher, "The Mongols," 32.

13. See Thomas Allsen's superb study of this subject in *Culture and Conquest in Mongol Eurasia* (Cambridge: Cambridge University Press, 1991).

14. This is a highly controversial view convincingly argued by the Ottoman scholar Colin Heywood, "Filling the Black Hole?: the Emergence of the Bithynian Atamanates 1298–1304," (Yeni Turkiye Dergisi, 1999), 1–10.

15. Ala-ad-Din 'Ata-Malik Juvaini, *The History of the World Conqueror*, trans. John Andrew Boyle, intro. David Morgan, (Manchester, U.K.: Manchester University Press, 1997), 186.

3

APPEARANCE

EARLY REPORTS

Many of the early reports of the Mongols that came to the west, both to Europe and the Middle East, in the thirteenth century carried horrific descriptions of the barbarian hordes, the Tatars, or denizens of Hell. These descriptions appeared very much to confirm the earlier reports of the carnage, savagery, and monstrous invincibility of this satanic storm from the east. Many of the earlier reports from the east were wholly fanciful and bore little resemblance to reality. Fabulous tales of strange beings and wondrous lands predominated, but as news of the Tatar invasions began to infiltrate, the stories of horror began. Even though descriptions and pictures that began to be available later in the thirteenth century bear closer resemblance to reality, these early accounts of the appearance of the Mongols remain of great interest because they convey the emotional impact the devastating appearance of the Mongols made on the medieval societies of Europe and the Islamic world.

The Armenian historian Kirakos of Ganjak (1201–1272), a cleric and onetime captive of the Mongols, described them as "hideous and frightful to look upon." He remarked upon their lack of facial hair and "narrow and quick-glancing" eyes, "shrill and piercing" voices and notes that they were "long-lived and hardy." A contemporary of Kirakos, another Christian Armenian cleric, Grigor of Akanc, is more colorful in his depiction of the invaders from the Nation of Archers, as he called the Mongols.

Mongol horseman, Xi'an Museum. Courtesy of Lan Tien Lang
Publications

They were terrible to look at and indescribable, with large heads like a buffalo's,
narrow eyes like a fledging's [young bird], a snub nose like a cat, projecting snouts
like a dog's, narrow loins like an ant's, short legs like a hog's, and by nature no
beards at all. With a lion's strength they have voices more shrill than an eagle's.[1]

The Persian poet Amir Khosrow (1253–1324) describes several hundred
Mongol prisoners taken by the Muslim armies from Sind whose Delhi
Sultanate (1206–1555) provided a haven from the Mongols for many of
those seeking asylum and safety:

Their eyes were so narrow and piercing that they might have bored a hole in a
brazen vessel, and their stench was more horrible than their colour. Their heads
were set on their bodies as if they had no necks, and their cheeks resembled
leather bottles full of wrinkles and knots. Their noses extended from cheekbone

Graven images, Baku early thirteenth century. Courtesy of Lan Tien Lang
Publications

to cheekbone. Their nostrils resembled rotting graves, and from them the hair
descended as far as the lips. Their moustaches were of extravagant length, but
the beards about their chins were very scanty. Their chests, in colour half-black,
half-white, were covered with lice which looked like sesame growing on a bad
soil. Their bodies, indeed, were covered with these insects, and their skins were as
rough-grained as shagreen leather, fit only to be converted into shoes.[2]

A more measured account is given by a Franciscan monk and papal
emissary who accompanied Friar Giovanni DiPlano Carpini's intelligence
gathering party traveling (1245–47) to Qaraqorum, capital of the Mongol
Empire. He reports that the Tatars are usually:

of low stature and rather thin, owing to their diet of mare's milk, which makes
a man slim, and their strenuous life. They are broad of face with prominent
cheekbones, and have a tonsure [shaven circle] on their head like our clerics
from which they shave a strip three fingers wide from ear to ear. On the forehead, however, they wear their hair in a crescent-shaped fringe reaching to the
eyebrows, but gather up the remaining hair, and arrange and braid it like the
Saracens [Muslims].[3]

The Franciscan Friar William of Rubruck traveled to the court of the
Great Khan Möngke between 1253 and 1255, and on his return he sent a
full account of his journey to King Louis IX of France. He mentions their
shaved heads but describes the bald patch as square rather than round,
and he says that the forehead and temples are also shaved of hair, leaving a

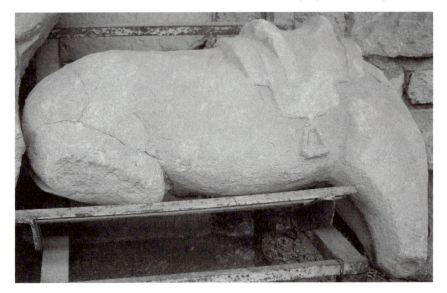

Horse from Baku, early thirteenth century. Courtesy of Lan Tien Lang
Publications

long tuft of hair hanging from the crown to the eyebrows. Rubruck further
describes the men as having long hair behind, which they braid in two
plaits right up to the ears. He notes that girls, on the day following their
marriage, shave their heads from the middle toward the forehead. Interestingly, he adds a detail about hygiene, explaining that in order to wash their
hair, the Mongols first take water into their mouths. They then allow this
water to trickle from their mouths into their cupped hands, which they use
to wet their hair and wash their heads.

Though less emotional in his description than others, William of
Rubruck is quite pointed in his account of the women.

The women are astonishingly fat. The less nose one has, the more beautiful she
is considered; and they disfigure themselves horribly, moreover, by painting
their faces.[4]

Later, he describes the wife of a local Mongol commander, Scacatai,
whose appearance he finds particularly repellent. In order to enhance her
nasal features, the snub nose being a prized sign of beauty, this lady had,
it seemed to Rubruck, amputated the bridge of her nose. The horrible
result was the almost complete lack of any discernable nose, and worse
still she had apparently applied some black ointment to that disfigured
spot as well as to her eyebrows. She "looked thoroughly dreadful" concludes the Friar.

Baku, early thirteenth century. Courtesy of Lan
Tien Lang Publications

TRANSFORMATION

Though the earlier reports of their appearance are rarely very compli-
mentary, the Mongols were ambitious not only for land, conquests, and
power but also for the luxuries of the outside world and the fineries of that
world with which to adorn themselves. Chinggis Khan is credited by the
Persian statesman and historian Rashīd al-Dīn with expressing the following ambition for his wives and daughters.

My wives, daughters-in-law, and daughters are as colourful and radiant as red
fire. My only aspiration and wish is to delight their mouths with the sweetness
of the sugar of benevolence, to adorn them front and back, top and bottom, with
garments woven with gold, to seat them upon sure-footed steeds, to serve them
sweet, clear water, to provide their animals lush, verdant meadows, and to clear

Figures from Rashid al-Din's *Jami' al-Tavarikh*. Courtesy of Lan Tien Lang
Publications

thorns and brambles and all that might be injurious from the roads and highroads,
and to prevent thorns and weeds from growing in their pastures.[5]

For his people Chinggis Khan also wanted a world distant from the
frugality and coarseness of the steppe in which he grew up. He foresaw a
change in the Mongols' appearance and in the image they projected.

After us, our off-spring will wear garments of sewn gold, eat fatty and sweet delicacies, ride well-formed horses, and enjoy beautiful ladies.[6]

To enhance their image and reflect their new status, and no doubt embar-
rassed by their reputation as primitive, dirty barbarians, the Mongols who
ruled in the later thirteenth century adorned not only themselves but also

Uyghur seamstress with traditional silk cloth, Kashgar. Courtesy of Xinjiang Qinshan Culture Publishing

their living quarters with sumptuous, delicate embroideries and brocades, woven with gold and precious stones. The opulence of their palace-tents became legendary, and along with the sophistication of their courts, it stood in stark contrast to the appearance they projected when first they emerged from the steppe.

This transformation of the appearance of the Mongols, from their depiction in the annals of the English chronicler Matthew Parris as cannibalistic savages to the later images of imperial splendor that emerged from their appearance in the Yüan (Chinese) courts, is aptly illustrated through the words of another European cleric, Friar Odoric of Pordenone (died 1331) whose extensive travels took him to the Yüan court (Mongol dynasty in China, 1260–1370). Here he describes how the Great Khan rode between his winter and summer palaces.

The king travelleth in a two-wheeled carriage ... all [made] of lignaloes [perfumed wood] and gold, and covered with great and fine skins, and set with many precious stones. And the carriage is drawn by four elephants ... and also by four splendid horses, richly caparisoned.... Moreover, he carrieth with him in his chariot twelve gerfalcons; so that even as he sits therein upon his chair of state or some other seat, if he sees any birds pass he lets fly his hawks at them.[7]

MONGOLS AND CLOTHING

William of Rubruck was a close observer of the Mongols and in his report to King Louis IX of France he described not only their habits but their dress as well. The Mongol court had changed drastically since the days of Chinggis Khan's youth. The Mongols were rich and powerful and they were able to adorn themselves with fabrics from every corner of their expanding empire. William betrays his awe and admiration in this extract from his long report covering his epic journey from 1253 to 1255:

> Of their clothing and customs you must know, that from Cataia, and other regions of the east, and also from Persia and other regions of the south, are brought to them silken and golden stuffs and cloth of cotton, which they wear in summer. From Ruscia, Moxel, and from greater Bulgaria and Pascatir, which is greater Hungary, and Kerkis, all of which are countries to the north and full of forests, and which obey them, are brought to them costly furs of many kinds, which I never saw in our parts, and which they wear in winter. And they always make in winter at least two fur gowns, one with the fur against the body, the other with the fur outside exposed to the wind and snow; these latter are usually of the skins of wolves or

Mongol image from Baku Fortress c. 1222. Courtesy of Lan Tien Lang Publications foxes or papions; and while they sit in the dwelling they have another lighter one. The poor make their outside (gowns) of dog and kid (skins).

When they want to chase wild animals, they gather together in a great multitude and surround the district in which they know the game to be, and gradually they come closer to each other till they have shut up the game in among them as in an enclosure, and then they shoot them with their arrows. They make also breeches with furs. The rich furthermore wad their clothing with silk stuffing, which is extraordinarily soft, light and warm. The poor line their clothes with cotton cloth, or with the fine wool which they are able to pick out of the coarser. With this coarser they make felt to cover their houses and coffers, and also for bedding. With wool and a third of horse hair mixed with it they make their ropes. They also make with felt covers, saddle-cloths and rain cloaks; so they use a great deal of wool. You have seen the costume of the men.

The men shave a square on the tops of their heads, and from the front corners (of this square) they continue the shaving to the temples, passing along both sides of the head. They shave also the temples and the back of the neck to the top of the cervical cavity, and the forehead as far as the crown of the head, on which they leave a tuft of hair which falls down to the eyebrows. They leave the hair on the sides of the head, and with it they make tresses which they plait together to the ear.

And the dress of the girls differs not from the costume of the men, except that it is somewhat longer. But on the day following her marriage, (a woman) shaves the front half of her head, and puts on a tunic as wide as a nun's gown, but everyway larger and longer, open before, and tied on the right side. For in this the Tartars differ from the Turks; the Turks tie their gowns on the left, the Tartars always on the right. Furthermore they have a head-dress, which they call *bocca*, made of bark, or such other light material as they can find, and it is big and as much as two hands can span around, and is a cubit and more high, and square like the capital of a column. This *bocca* they cover with costly silk stuff, and it is hollow inside, and on top of the capital, or the square on it, they put a tuft of quills or light canes also a cubit or more in length. And this tuft they ornament at the top with peacock feathers, and round the edge (of the top) with feathers from the mallard's tail, and also with precious stones. The wealthy ladies wear such an ornament on their heads, and fasten it down tightly with an amess, for which there is an opening in the top for that purpose, and inside they stuff their hair, gathering it together on the back of the tops of their heads in a kind of knot, and putting it in the *bocca*, which they afterwards tie down tightly under the chin. So it is that when several ladies are riding together, and one sees them from afar, they look like soldiers, helmets on head and lances erect. For this *bocca* looks like a helmet, and the tuft above it is like a lance. And all the women sit their horses astraddle like men. And they tie their gowns with a piece of blue silk stuff at the waist and they wrap another band at the breasts, and tie a piece of white stuff below the eyes which hangs down to the breast. And the women there are wonderfully fat, and she who has the least nose is held the most beautiful. They disfigure themselves horribly by painting their faces. They never lie down in bed when having their children.[8]

Cloth and clothing held great symbolic significance for the medieval Mongols even before the days of empire. The great number of Muslim weavers transported to China under the Yüan dynasty attest to the importance textiles and dress continued to occupy in Mongol society. Both the wearing and presenting of clothes and items of clothing carried messages and meaning for the peoples of the steppe and for the Mongols in particular.

Thirteenth-century Mongol figurine, Xi'an Museum.
Courtesy of Lan Tien Lang Publications

Fur, leather, wool, camel's hair, and felt constituted the basic dress fabric, and cotton and silk were also available from their sedentary neighbors. Standard wear was an ankle-length robe cut from a single piece of material. Loose trousers would be worn under this, and round the waist a belt made of soft material would be fastened. As protection from the weather, they wore felt capes, fur hoods, and leather boots or buskins made of felt. Friar William of Rubruck, who traveled through Russia to Mongolia between 1253 and 1255, describes their summer wear as being made of silk, gold, and cotton, whereas in winter they wore garments made from a wide variety of furs. He explains that the fur clothes were double-layered so that the fur was inside as well as out. These pelts were often obtained from the wolf, fox, or lynx, though the poor used the skins

Traditional Mongol dress, Hohhut Museum. Courtesy of Xinjiang Qinshan Culture Publishing

Bactrian Camel on the shores of Lake Sayram. Courtesy of Xinjiang Qinshan
Culture Publishing

of dogs or goats. Their breeches were also made from pelts, with silk lining for the rich and cotton for the poor.

Friar Carpini, an emissary for Pope Innocent IV, though some say spy,
traveled east from 1245 to 1247, earlier than Rubruck. His detailed descriptions of the Mongols report that men and women would often be dressed
identically and that he had problems telling the sexes apart. They wore
tunics of buckram, fine linen, or silk, split open on one side and fastened
by cords with the material folded back double over the chest. Married
women wore full-length tunics opened at the front.

THE *BOGHTA*

All reports, including Carpini's, mention *boghta*, the very distinctive
headdresses worn by married women. Li Chih-Chang, who accompanied
the Taoist monk Ch'ang Ch'ung to central Asia to visit Chinggis Khan,
elaborates. The headdress was made "of birch-bark, some two feet high.
This they generally cover with a black woollen stuff; but some of the richer
women use red silk. The end [of this headdress] is like a duck." Later
reports describe the *boghta* as a three-foot iron wire frame adorned with

Thirteenth-century Mongol figurine, Xi'an Museum.
Courtesy of Lan Tien Lang Publications

red and blue brocade or pearls and later still as frames wrapped with red silk or gold brocade. By the time Rubruck was writing in the 1250s, the *boghta* had become more elaborate and garishly decorated. Peacock and mallard tail feathers along with precious stones now festooned this status symbol of the rich, the whole contraption attached to the lady's head with a fur hood in which was gathered her hair. In addition, the *boghta* was secured around the throat by straps.

The *boghta* could convey more than social status. Chinggis Khan's mother, Hö'elün, signaled her intention to commence an arduous venture by girding her belt and securing her *boghta*. The Mongol ruler of Iran, Arghun Khan (ruled 1284–91), signaled his acceptance of Tudai Khātūn (Lady Tudai) as his wife by placing a *boghta* on her head.

CLOTHES AS PRESENTATIONS

The giving and presenting of clothes often held great symbolic significance for the Mongols. When Temüjin (the young Chinggis Khan) presented his powerful uncle, Ong Khan, ruler of the mighty Kereyid tribe,
with a black sable coat, it was generally understood that Ong Khan's
acceptance of the gift signified that the protection of his tribe had henceforth been extended to Temüjin. Between friends, the exchange of belts
reinforced that friendship and tied them closer, as was the case with the
young Temüjin and his neighbor, Jamuqa, who had already declared
themselves *anda* (blood brothers). Gold and silver satins of many colors
were always presented to officials on the occasion of royal births. Likewise, to express condolences and loyalty to Mongol custom and tradition,
robes and a *boghta* would be presented to a widowed wife, even while plots
and intrigues were in the making. Such was the case when the third Great
Khan, Güyük (1249), died and his wife, Oghul Qaimish, the acting regent,
accepted such gifts from her cousins' family, even as they were plotting the
annihilation of her whole family line, the Ögödei Chinggisids. When peace
and reconciliation were sought, the presentation of clothes was always
expected. Gold, gems, gilded tunics, and gilded hats heavily decorated in
jewels and precious stones would be exchanged or offered. Conversely, the
taking away of clothes also carried symbolic meaning. Before praying to
the Sky God, Tenggeri, Chinggis Khan removed his hat and belt to signify
his powerlessness and his need for help. When Chinggis Khan removed his

Thirteenth-century Mongol figurines, Xi'an Museum. Courtesy of Lan Tien Lang
Publications

brother's, Jochi Qasar's, hat and belt, he was expressing the ending of his trust in his sibling. During the accession ceremonies of the Great Khans, all those present were expected to remove their hats and drape their belts over their shoulders. Their replacement symbolized the subjects' acceptance of the new order.

THE ROBE OF HONOR: THE *KHIL^{C}AT*

Another essential item of clothing for the Mongols, increasingly so as their courts took on an imperial air, was the Robe of Honor or *khil^{c}at*. This was awarded to nobles, princes, sultans, and other rulers who had proved their loyalty to their masters, the Mongols. These Robes of Honor became more elaborate and splendid as the empire expanded, and they

Thirteenth-century Mongol figurines, Xi'an Museum.
Courtesy of Lan Tien Lang Publications

are reflective of the value put on fine fabrics and clothing by the Mongol nobility. Ceremonial dress in general was composed mainly of gold-weaved brocade.

Recent studies have shown that the need for gold and precious stones, used in the manufacture of the Mongols' ceremonial dress, was one of the driving forces behind the expansion of the Mongol empire into the settled lines. Sources for the raw materials and artisans to fashion these metals, stones, and fabrics into clothing were a major preoccupation with all the Mongol rulers. The importance of dress in Mongol society has not been fully appreciated until recently.

Marco Polo was well aware of the importance that the Mongols attached to clothes and fineries, and in the following extracts from his *Travels* he records the awarding of the traditional *khilᶜat,* a custom also found commonly at courts in the mediaeval Islamic world. The whole subject of gold fabrics, brocade, *nasīj,* and *khilᶜats* has been explored by the American scholar Thomas Allsen. He has found that these costly fabrics formed the basis of much of the commerce and trade in the empire, and it was the search for raw materials and craftsmen that fueled much of the drive for expansion and the acquisition of new territory. Marco Polo discerns this obsession with extravagant raiment in the following two selections.

Thirteenth-century Mongol figurines, Xi'an Museum. Courtesy of Lan Tien Lang Publications

CHAPTER XVI

CONCERNING THE TWELVE THOUSAND BARONS WHO RECEIVE ROBES OF CLOTH OF GOLD FROM THE EMPEROR ON THE GREAT FESTIVALS, THIRTEEN CHANGES A-PIECE

Now you must know that the Great Kaan hath set apart 12,000 of his men who are distinguished by the name of Keshican, as I have told you before; and on each of these 12,000 Barons he bestows thirteen changes of raiment, which are all different from one another: I mean that in one set the 12,000 are all of one colour; the next 12,000 of another colour, and so on; so that they are of thirteen different colours. These robes are garnished with gems and pearls and other precious things in a very rich and costly manner. And along with each of these changes of raiment, i.e., 13 times in the year, he bestows on each of those 12,000 Barons a fine golden girdle of great richness and value, and likewise a pair of boots of Camut, that is to say of Borgal, curiously wrought with silver thread; insomuch that when they are clothed in these dresses every man of them looks like a king! And there is an established order as to which dress is to be worn at each of those thirteen feasts. The Emperor himself also has his thirteen suits corresponding to those of his Barons; in colour, I mean (though his are grander, richer, and costlier), so that he is always arrayed in the same colour as his Barons, who are, as it were, his comrades. And you may see that all this costs an amount which it is scarcely possible to calculate.

Now I have told you of the thirteen changes of raiment received from the Prince by those 12,000 Barons, amounting in all to 156,000 suits of so great cost and value, to say nothing of the girdles and the boots which are also worth a great sum of money. All this the Great Lord hath ordered, that he may attach the more of grandeur and dignity to his festivals.

And now I must mention another thing that I had forgotten, but which you will be astonished to learn from this Book. You must know that on the Feast Day a great Lion is led to the Emperor's presence, and as soon as it sees him it lies down before him with every sign of the greatest veneration, as if it acknowledged him for its lord; and it remains there lying before him, and entirely unchained. Truly this must seem a strange story to those who have not seen the thing![9]

CHAPTER XIV

CONCERNING THE GREAT FEAST HELD BY THE GRAND KAAN EVERY YEAR ON HIS BIRTHDAY

You must know that the Tartars keep high festival yearly on their birthdays. And the Great Kaan was born on the 28th day of the September moon, so on that day is held the greatest feast of the year at the Kaan's Court, always excepting that which he holds on New Year's Day, of which I shall tell you afterwards.

Now, on his birthday, the Great Kaan dresses in the best of his robes, all wrought with beaten gold; and full 12,000 Barons and Knights on that day come forth dressed in robes of the same colour, and precisely like those of the Great Kaan, except that they are not so costly; but still they are all of the same colour as his, and are also of silk and gold. Every man so clothed has also a girdle of gold; and this as well as the dress is given him by the Sovereign. And I will aver that there are some of these suits decked with so many pearls and precious stones that a single suit shall be worth full 10,000 golden bezants.

And of such raiment there are several sets. For you must know that the Great Kaan, thirteen times in the year, presents to his Barons and Knights such suits of raiment as I am speaking of. And on each occasion they wear the same colour that he does, a different colour being assigned to each festival. Hence you may see what a huge business it is, and that there is no prince in the world but he alone who could keep up such customs as these.[10]

NOTES

1. Grigor of Akanc, *History of the Nation of Archers*, trans. R. Blake and R. Frye (Cambridge: Harvard University Press, 1954), 295.

2. Kulliyat-i-Amīr Khosrow (Tehran, 1996), 532.

3. R. A. Skelton, T. E. Marston, and George D. Painter, *The Vinland Map and the Tartar Relation* (New Haven, Conn.: Yale University Press, 1995), 86.

4. William of Rubruck, *The Mission of William of Rubruck,* trans. and ed. Peter Jackson with David Morgan (London: Hakluyt Society, 1990), 89.

5. Rashīd al-Dīn, *Jāmi' al-Tavārīkh*, eds., Mohammad Roushan and Mustafah Mūsavī (Tehran: Nashr albaraz, 1994), 587–88.

6. Ibid, 585–86.

7. "The Travels of Friar Odoric," in Henry Yule, *Cathay and the Way Thither* (Millwood, N.Y.: Kraus Reprint, 1967), 228–29.

8. William of Rubruck, *The Journey of William of Rubruck to the Eastern Parts of the World, 1253–55, as Narrated by Himself, with Two Accounts of the Earlier Journey of John of Pian de Carpine,* trans. from the Latin and ed., with an introductory notice, by William Woodville Rockhill (London: Hakluyt Society, 1900), ch. 6.

9. Marco Polo, Complete Yule-Cordier Edition of Marco Polo's travels by Marco Polo and Rustichello of Pisa, *The Project Gutenberg EBook of the Travels of Marco Polo,* vols. 1 and 2, available at: http://www.gutenberg.net.

10. Ibid.

4

DWELLINGS

As nomads the Mongols were not renowned for their city-building skills, and it was urban destruction rather than urban construction for which they were justly famed. They did not live within the confines of solid, brick walls and were initially suspicious of those who voluntarily did so. Their home was the open steppe, and their walls were the sky and the looming mountains. The elements were their decorations and furnishing, and the elements formed the constant back-drop to their lives. Just as they had a dramatic impact on the lives of city dwellers, however, cities and the denizens of those cities had a profound and dramatic impact on the Mongol hordes.

EARLY DWELLINGS

Long before the Mongols began to actually build their capital cities on permanent sites with buildings designed to withstand the arduous tests of time, they constructed what have been described as cities on wheels and indeed were mobile homes within a mobile community of mobile institutions. Friar Giovanni DiPlano Carpini, a papal intelligence agent traveling across the Eurasian steppes in 1245, came across Mongol yurts too large and complex to be efficiently taken apart each time the *ordu* (camp) moved on. Carpini, an unlikely medieval James Bond, related how "the smallest [yurts] are put on a cart drawn by one ox, the larger by two or three or more depending upon how large it is and how many are needed to move it."[1] William of Rubruck, traveling nearly 10 years later, reported seeing yurts on

Mongol yurts on the road from Yining to Lake Sayram. Courtesy of Xinjiang
Qinshan Culture Publishing

wagons with axles "as large as a ship's mast" pulled by as many as twenty-
two oxen.[2]

Before the Great *Quriltai* of 1206, which saw Temüjin proclaimed
Chinggis Khan and ruler of all the Turco-Mongolian tribes of the
steppe, the only contact that these nomads had with urban communities was through military conflict or military alliances. The steppe
dwellers and the urban settlers lived in separate, different worlds, and
both viewed the other with a certain degree of disdain and distaste.
Yet within two generations the most sophisticated of urbanites could
be found writing and partaking in learned debate while indulging in
the most sumptuous and refined of gastronomic delight at the heart of
their Mongol masters' camp. Also within two generations the children
of those same nomad warriors who a few years previously had been
terrorizing their sworn enemies—city dwellers—could be found laying the cornerstones of cities that have since developed into the most
powerful and magnificent metropolises in the world.

In 1255 William of Rubruck was still able to write of the Mongols,
"Nowhere have they any 'lasting city,'" and he continued to describe his
hosts as purely nomadic pastoralists. Though no longer quite accurate by
that time, with the establishment in 1272 of the Yüan dynasty in China by

Qubilai with Ta-tu (Khan Baliq, Beijing) as its capital and the founding in 1258 of the Il-Khanid dynasty in Iran by Hülegü with Maragheh as its capital, the Mongols had ceased to be steppe emperors. The transformation had been gradual, and their living conditions would have reflected these changes. More and more their nomad camps were resembling mobile cities composed of increasingly elaborate yurts sumptuously decorated in fineries acquired through an insatiable appetite for gold embroidery and brocade commonly referred to as *nasij* or as the "cloth of Tartary" by European sources.

At the time of the visits by the two Franciscan friars, however, less majestic dwellings were commonly in evidence. William of Rubruck (circa 1210–70) describes their dwellings in some detail.

Nowhere have they fixed dwelling-places, nor do they know where their next will be (J: Nowhere have they any "lasting city"; and of "the one to come" they have no knowledge [cf. Heb. 13:14]). They have divided among themselves Cithia [Scythia], which extendeth from the Danube to the rising of the sun; and every captain, according as he hath more or less men under him, knows the limits of his pasture land and where to graze in winter and summer, spring and autumn. For in winter they go down to warmer regions in the south: in summer they go up to cooler towards the north. The pasture lands without water they graze over in winter when there is snow there, for the snow serveth them as water.

They set up the dwelling in which they sleep on a circular frame of interlaced sticks converging into a little round hoop on the top, from which projects above a collar as a chimney, and this (framework) they cover over with white felt. Frequently they coat the felt with chalk, or white clay, or powdered bone, to make it appear whiter, and sometimes also (they make the felt) black. The felt around this collar on top they decorate with various pretty designs. Before the entry they also suspend felt ornamented with various embroidered designs in color. For they embroider the felt, colored or otherwise, making vines and trees, birds and beast.

And they make these houses so large that they are sometimes thirty feet in width. I myself once measured the width between the wheel-tracks of a cart xx feet, and when the house was on the cart it projected beyond the wheels on either side v feet at least. I have myself counted to one cart xxii oxen drawing one house, eleven abreast across the width of the cart, and the other eleven before them. The axle of the cart was as large as the mast of a ship, and one man stood in the entry of the house on the cart driving the oxe.

Furthermore they weave light twigs into squares of the size of a large chest, and over it from one end to the other they put a turtle-back also of twigs, and in the front end they make a little doorway; and then they cover this coffer or little house with black felt coated with tallow or ewe's milk, so that the rain cannot penetrate it, and they decorate it likewise with embroidery work. And in such coffers they put all their bedding and valuables, and they tie them tightly on high carts drawn by camels, so that they can cross rivers (without getting wet). Such coffers they never take off the car.

When they set down their dwelling-houses, they always turn the door to the south, and after that they place the carts with coffers on either side near the house at a half stone's throw, so that the dwelling stands between two rows of carts as between two walls. The matrons make for themselves most beautiful (luggage) carts, which I would not know how to describe to you unless by a drawing, and I would depict them all to you if I knew how to paint. A single rich Moal or Tartar has quite c or cc such carts with coffers. Baatu has xxvi wives, each of whom has a large dwelling, exclusive of the other little ones which they set up after the big one, and which are like closets, in which the sewing girls live, and to each of these (large) dwellings are attached quite cc carts. And when they set up their houses, the first wife places her dwelling on the extreme west side, and after her the others according to their rank, so that the last wife will be in the extreme east; and there will be the distance of a stone's throw between the iurt of one wife and that of another. The ordu of a rich Moal seems like a large town, though there will be very few men in it. One girl will lead xx or xxx carts, for the country is flat, and they tie the ox or camel carts the one after the other, and a girl will sit on the front one driving the ox, and all the others follow after with the same gait. Should it happen that they come to some bad piece of road, they untie them, and take them across one by one. So they go along slowly, as a sheep or an ox might walk.

When they have fixed their dwelling, the door turned to the south, they set up the couch of the master on the north side. The side for the women is always the east side, that is to say, on the left of the house of the master, he sitting on his couch his face turned to the south. The side for the men is the west side, that is, on the right. Men coming into the house would never hang up their bows on the side of the woman.[3]

Friar Giovanni DiPlano Carpini paints a simpler picture, explaining that the tents were round and cleverly prepared from laths and sticks. A chimney was fashioned in the center, which as well as allowing smoke to escape, allowed light into the interior. The walls and doors were lined in thick felt, though Carpini does not mention the sumptuous nature of some of these wall linings. Yurt or *ger* size, explains the friar, reflects wealth and social status of the owner. The smaller *gers* could be easily dismantled and loaded onto a wagon, whereas the larger size *ger* had to be loaded intact onto their ox-drawn wagons.[4] These mobile tents were called *ger tergen*. Marco Polo, traveling a few decades later, noted these same dwellings used by the common people and noted that the doors were usually set to face south, a characteristic of many central Asian people.

The wagons, which as noted previously come in different sizes and are often richly adorned, are also employed to carry provisions and the women and children. Marco Polo noted that the wagon and wheels are sometimes covered by thick black felt, which he claimed was so effective that "if it rained all day on the cart water would soak nothing that was in the cart under the cover of felt."[5] He added that the wagons served a dual purpose. Not only were they used to carry provisions, the yurts themselves, and women and children, but they were utilized by the women to conduct trade, and the buying and selling would be carried on from atop the wagons themselves.

MOVABLE VERSUS IMMOVABLE

Nomads live in tents, and the Mongols as nomads continued to live in tents even though the sumptuous gilded cloth palaces bore little resemblance to the threadbare yurts of the days prior to the *qurïltai* of 1206. Even in the early days, however, their dwellings also contained permanent structures. These solid structures would be utilized each time the tribe returned to their winter *(qïshlaqs)* or summer *(yaylaqs)* pastures. Remains of permanent structures have been found dating from the time of Chinggis Khan. Rock and brick platforms were used to support wooden and cloth structures. These features were developed over the years to include immovable walls, and divides and foundations became deeper and sturdier. Eventually these features outnumbered the movable elements, and the camps were transformed into cities. Even in the great cities of China the Mongol princes and generals liked to remind themselves of their roots, and spaces were allocated for the pitching of tents and the erection of yurts and the employment of the movable features of their former lives. The chronicler of the Mongols of Persia, Qāshānī, kept a detailed record of the itinerary of the Il-Khan Öljeitü (ruled 1304–16) and itemized in detail the king's travels during his reign. This chronology of Öljeitü's regular migrations throughout his reign illustrates what Charles Melville has termed "the continuum of the interaction between the nomadic and sedentary ethics of government."[6] Though Öljeitü was mobile throughout his period on the Iranian throne, neither the gentle pace of his migration nor the limited area in which he roamed caused him to be absent from his central administration or from the day-to-day affairs of his country. During the rule of the Mongol administrator of western Asia, Arghun Aqa, more than 60 years before, the historian Juwaynī complained that the constant traveling of what has been described as a "mobile secretariat" interfered with the writing of his famous history. In contrast, Öljeitü's administration carried an air of semipermanence, and foreign envoys had little difficulty tracking his whereabouts. The paraphernalia of government, the files, documents, archives, and the clerical staff, were also always at hand or nearby, and the growth in the number of permanent structures ensured that the hardware of the administration was provided for wherever the court settled. The summer and winter camps were well documented; Ala Tagh (Ala Dau) in Turkey, Siyah Kuh northwest of Hamadan, Sughurlukh or Takht-i-Suleiman, Khonkhur Öleng, which became the capital Sultaniya, Ujan southwest of Tabriz, Sayn south of Ardabil, and Hasht-rud east of Maragheh were frequently mentioned *yaylaqs* (summer camps). Often-mentioned *qïshlaqs* (winter camps) included Jaghatu south of Lake Urumia, Baghdad, Hulan Mören, Qarabagh northeast of Nakhchivan, and various unspecified sites in Arran, Mazandaran, and Mughan. From this it can be seen that both the Il-Khan's summer and winter camps were in a relatively restricted area corresponding to the region known today as Azerbaijan. Tabriz became a capital in the full sense of the word under the reign of Ghazan Khan (ruled 1295–1304), as did Sultaniya under Öljeitü, who despite his itinerant habits furnished his capital with government, public, and imperial buildings and constructed six highways spreading out from this center to various points in his kingdom. He was resident in his capital during the summer months.

The increasingly elaborate tents that the princes lived in during their journeys around the country would often remain standing for months at a time, and when they were not in use they would simply be packed up and stored until the court returned the following year. The actual material

Royal *ordu*, Dengsheng. Courtesy of Lan Tien Lang Publications

making up the tent would not be carried from location to location but would remain in storage until needed. Sira-Ordu, mentioned later, was one such semipermanent structure that attracted the attention of its many illustrious visitors. Sira-Ordu, which was predominantly yellow, was used for quriltais along with the usual white tents.

In the Yüan period permanent and semipermanent structures were used together though increasingly the semipermanent structures were primarily for decoration and entertainment only. The summer residence of Shangdu (Xanadu) contained a structure called the *da'ange*, which was used for audiences, but in addition in another part of the city permanent structures were also employed for feasting and receiving foreign dignitaries. Shangdu was home to the fabulous Cane Palace constructed in the city's northern area of Beiyuan, which also housed a zoo and botanical gardens. This enormous semipermanent structure, the Zongdian or Zongmaodian, was made of canes supported by gilt and lacquered columns, each bearing a gilded dragon. Yesun Temür (ruled 1323–28) in 1325 ordered this imposing movable palace revamped and refurbished, and some records of this work have survived and provide an indication of the size and expense of these so-called tents. Two carpets were specially woven and together covered an area of 850 square yards or one-sixth of an acre. They used 3,000 pounds of blue and white wool.

Four kinds of palatial building can be identified as having been used by the Great Khans: temporary buildings such as the Sira-Ordu; structures that combined permanent and temporary features, as have been found at sites used seasonally by Chinggis Khan; buildings on sites used for permanent and semipermanent structures, as seen in Shangdu; and structures built to last, as were the buildings of Qubilai's capital Da-du, today's Beijing.

LAVISH TENTS

The Mongols' taste for tents never disappeared, and it was recognized that in order to impress a prince of the Golden family a sumptuous feast was prerequisite, but in addition the feast had to be served in an exceptionally lavish setting. Hülegü's leisurely invasion of Iran was punctuated by frequent feasting stops where the local administrators would spare no expense to squander luxuries on the Great Khan Möngke's brother. In Samarqand the Mongol governor of central Asia, Mas'ud Beg, erected a tent woven in *nasij* (gold and silk cloth) with a covering of white felt that served the royal party for their 40 days of revelry and merrymaking. Shortly afterward in spring 1256, near the town of Tus, Arghun Aqa, the Mongol governor of Khorasan, laid on another feast for which another fabulous tent was constructed. The tent comprised an antechamber and an audience hall, and a thousand gold nails were used to hold it in place.

In Rabi'II [April–May] they pitched a tent of *nasij* in Jinhal-Fuqara near Tus at the gate of a garden that had been laid out by the Emir Arghun, ... That tent was one which the World-Emperor Mengu Qaan had ordered the Emir Arghun to prepare for his brother. In obedience to the Emperor's command the master craftsmen had been called together and consulted, and in the end it had been decided that the tent should be made of a single sheet of cloth with two surfaces. And in executing the weaving and dyeing of it they had surpassed the art of the craftsmen of San'a [Yeman]: the back and front were uniform and the inside and outside in the exact correspondence of the colours and designs complemented one another like the simple-hearted. The teeth of the scissors had been blunted with the cutting of it. That gilded cupola and heaven-like tent, the disc of the sun, lost its brightness out of jealousy of the truck of this tent, and the resplendent full moon wore a sulky expression because of its roundness.[7]

Just as their cousins in China were doing, the Mongols in Iran combined the permanent and the semipermanent in the construction of their palaces, and the differences between the two continued to blur. Ghazan Khan pitched his golden tent in Ujan, a site he visited each summer that contained, according to Rashīd al-Dīn, "kiosks, towers, baths, and lofty buildings" on a permanent basis. The tent took his engineers a month to erect. The Il-Khans, princes and nobles, Mongols, and their Persian administrators often named their permanent structures after themselves, and as a result there is to this day an area of Tabriz called Rashidiya or Raba'-i-Rashidi. Father and son are responsible for Arghuniya and Ghazaniya, both complexes in the Tabriz region, built for the two Il-Khans. Öljeitü built the magnificent Sultaniya, ruins of which still impress visitors to northwest Iran today.

Activities in these lavish tents and buildings, both permanent and semipermanent, were the same in Iran and China. They served as pleasure palaces and seats of government. Enthronements took place here, as did all major *quriltais*. As early as 1257 Hülegü celebrated the Mongolian New Year, *Keyünükemishi*, at a camp near Qazvin, northern Iran. All the Il-Khans celebrated their official enthronements at their seasonal camps rather than at their nominal capital cities. Before Ghazan ascended the Il-Khanid throne in 1295 the Il-Khans kept their treasuries at their seasonal camps rather than at the capital, though the guards and security were of course permanent and fixed. Hülegü's vast wealth, considerably fattened following the sack of Alamut in 1256 and Baghdad in 1258, was stored on an island in Lake Urumiya. He was buried at this site after his death in 1265 along with treasure, food and wine, and six virgins. The site has never been discovered, and as far as is known the treasure remains buried somewhere on Shahi (now Islamia) Island on the east side of Lake Urumiya.

Much government business was conducted at the seasonal sites, and usually any major works were initiated by feasting and revelry, a practice found throughout the empire. The khan would sit on a platform at the northern end of the hall facing south. His major wife would be seated next to him on his left. Male revelers would sit on his right with the ladies seated opposite. Feasts would last for days rather than hours, and sometimes participants had to dress in a certain style or color, which would then be changed each day. Princes of the Golden family would take turns hosting these prolonged revelries. "Each in turn gave a feast, and they cast the die of desire upon the board of revelry, draining goblets [*jamha*] and donning garments [*jamaha*] of one color, at the same time not neglecting important affairs."[8]

One of the major attractions for the Mongols of their seasonal camps was the opportunity to indulge their appetite for hunting, archery, and falconry. All Mongols learned horse riding from a very early age, and archery was a skill at which they excelled.

Even with the establishment of cities and palaces, the Mongols never completely abandoned their nomadic roots, and the *ger* would often be transported into the heart of the city and reconstructed. In Qubilai Khan's new capital, Ta-tu (Beijing), the emperor ordered the construction of tents in the parks and gardens of his new capital. These were for the use of his sons and their cousins and also, it is interesting to note, for the use of royal ladies in the last weeks of pregnancy. To make these ties between steppe and sown all the stronger, Qubilai ordered the transference of steppe soil and grass to his parks. In addition to this transposed flora, he tried to add authenticity to his urban steppe scene with some imported fauna in the form of model reclining tigers operated mechanically to appear alive.

QARAQORUM

It was Ögödei Qa'an who established the first permanent Mongol city. Unlike his father, he did not believe that a kingdom conquered on horseback must be ruled from horseback, and therefore he determined to build his own capital using traditional nomadic standards to choose the ideal setting. Qaraqorum, which means "black stones" or "black walls," was constructed in the heart of Mongol territory on Orkhon River on territory that had once belonged to Ong Khan's Kereyid tribe. It had also been the site of previous Turkic kingdoms, and the remains of a wall called Ordu-Baligh were in evidence. Qaraqorum was situated on open steppe, allowing for wind that would keep the air clear of mosquitoes. Water supplies were near but far enough away so as not to become polluted by the close proximity of human settlement. Mountains were also close for a seasonal haven for the flocks of animals. It was a perfect site for a nomad's camp, but it was doomed as the chosen site of a fixed capital. No protection was offered in winter against the bitter cold that swept across the steppe. Food supplies had to be brought in from afar because there was no means of production locally. Actual construction was probably begun after Ögödei shot an arrow to determine the placement of the first stone and the length of the building, one bowshot and new wall; another arrow and another wall and a pavilion to connect them. And so Qaraqorum, capital of the empire, was born.

Rashīd al-Dīn claims that the Qa'an (Ögödei), told that Baghdad was the most beautiful city in the world, ordered that his city be built in order to outshine that fading capital. Craftsmen and artisans in plenty had already been imported from throughout the conquered lands to start on the construction. *Yam* stations were established every 15 miles to link Qaraqorum with the cities of Cathay, totaling 37 *yams*.[9] A *hazara*, a military unit of 1,000 soldiers, was assigned to each *yam* to provide security for the cartloads of provisions and material, including foodstuffs and drink, which passed along this road, reportedly 500 wagons daily. The wagons of *bägni* and *sorma* (beer and ale) needed six oxen to pull them.

Initially it was a sumptuous palace for himself that he had ordered constructed, but then he commanded that each of his brothers, sons, and other princes should also have residences built in the vicinity, and it was in this way that the Mongols' first capital grew. The Qa'an saw this as "laying the foundations of world sovereignty and raising the edifices of prosperity."[10] His palace was "exceedingly tall in structure and with lofty pillars, such as was in keeping with the high resolve of such a king,"[11] and it was finished in a variety of colorful paintings and designs fashioned by his Khitan artists. When the other tall pavilions were also finished, the emerging city covered a very wide area. Typically, Ögödei ensured that priority be given to the installation of ornate wine cellars, and he had distinguished goldsmiths and silversmiths fashion utensils from precious metals in the shape of elephants, lions, horses, and the like that spouted wines and kumiss from their mouths into silver or gold basins.

As Chinese architects and artisans continued to work on the new capital, many of the Mongol nobles lived in their private *gers* short distances away from Qaraqorum itself. Some building may have actually begun as early as 1220, but it was not until 1235 that the city was walled. The royal court was often at least a day's ride away depending at which semipermanent site Ögödei was resident. Muslim *uzan* (craftsmen) built a family pavilion, the Sa'uri Palace, for him at Gegen-Chagan, famed for its falconers, where he would hunt waterfowl. Juwaynī waxes lyrical about this "very tall castle filled with all kinds of many-coloured, jewel-studded embroideries and carpets" and describes the Qa'an's 40-day sojourn here in spring where as usual "he would give himself up to the joys of drinking and spread the carpet of bounty, which was never rolled."[12] Other pavilions and palaces were erected in the general area of Qaraqorum, and Ögödei would share his time in each of them.

There was a Chinese pavilion, Sira-Ordu, that was particularly noteworthy, it being mentioned by many sources, including European. It had walls of latticed wood, a ceiling of gold-embroidered brocade *(nasij)*, the whole structure swathed in thick, white felt. These pavilions were very sumptuous and were very large, possibly large enough to accommodate 10,000 people, though Sira-Ordu could accommodate only 1,000. Sira-Ordu was a permanent fixture, with its exterior adorned with gold nails and its interior with thick *nasij*. The Franciscan friar Carpini visited Guyuk here and described a "tent supported by columns covered with gold plates and fastened to other wooden beams with nails of gold, and the roof above and the sides on the interior were of brocade"[13] and also a small palace situated on a hilltop only three or so miles from his capital.

In fact, Qaraqorum resembled more a giant storehouse and a base for the craftsmen, administrators, and merchants who serviced the Golden family and their retainers. Though it produced little, it received prodigiously. Serving as the symbolic heart of the empire it was the destination of the trains and caravans of tribute and envoys from around the known world. The royal princes and their families might not have remained long within its thick and solid walls, but a third of the city was permanently occupied by the bureaucracy needed to run the Mongols' burgeoning empire, including scribes and translators from every nation now under Mongol sovereignty.

Above the town a garden had been built for the Qa'an containing four gates, each gateway assigned its separate task. One was reserved for the Qa'an himself, another for his princesses, a third for his children and relatives, and the last for the use of the general populace. Within the garden Chinese builders constructed a four-gated castle inside of which they situated a royal throne approached by three flights of stairs; one flight for the Qa'an, one for his ladies, and one for his cupbearers and table deckers. Vats of alcoholic beverages, usually too heavy to move, were placed in the cupbearers' quarters along with elephants, camels, and horses along with their attendants, ready for public feasts when these casks had to be lifted. All the Qa'an's utensils were, of course, fashioned in gold and silver and studded with jewels. The emperor enjoyed these luxuries twice a year "whenever the sun entered Aries, and the world was glad, and the face of the earth, because of the weeping of the clouds, smiled and shone forth through the mouths of flowers" as Juwaynī described his stays.[14]

In Qaraqorum itself a thriving religious community began to grow, reflecting the spiritual diversity of the empire. Places of worship for Taoists, Buddhists, Christians, and Muslims found space in the emerging capital, and public debates often were held for the amusement of the great khans. One such debate held before Möngke Khan in which William of Rubruck took part opened with a warning to all participants.

This is Mangu's decree, and let nobody dare claim that the decree of God is otherwise. He orders that no man shall be so bold as to make cause any commotion that might obstruct these proceedings, on pain of death.[15]

At this time there were 12 idol temples of unspecified religions, two mahumneries or mosques, and one church. Mud walls surrounded the city, and each of the four city gates conducted different commercial activity. At the east gate millet and other grain were sold, sheep and goats could be found at the western gate, cattle and wagons were traded at the southern gate, and at the northern gate was found the horse bazaar. William of Rubruck was not overimpressed with the Mongol capital when he visited it in April 1254, dismissively claiming that "it is not as fine as the town of St Denis, and the monastery of St Denis is worth ten of the palace."[16] Other than the royal enclosures, the city was divided into two parts. The quarter of the Saracens, as Europeans called the Muslims of western Asia, contained the bazaars, and it was here that the merchants and traders would congregate close to the campgrounds and, therefore, close to the newly arrived envoys and visitors. The other quarter was that of the Cataians, or Chinese, who William of Rubruck claims were all craftsmen.

The papal envoy found Möngke's palace far more impressive than the city, which only really came alive when the royal court moved into town. He described the palace as resembling a church with "a middle nave and two sides beyond two rows of pillars and three doors to the south side,"[17] though he does not supply the detail given by Juwaynī. The friar instead describes in detail the famous drinking tree made by the silversmith William of Paris, who became a friend and companion of William of Rubruck.

Once the great lands of the Persians and the southern Song had fallen to the Mongol hordes, their capitals moved south, and Qaraqorum lapsed slowly into decay and neglect. Other cities served the Mongol Qa'ans.

BEIJING (KHAN BALIQ, TA-TU, TAIDU, DA-DU, JUNG-DU, ZHONGDU)

Beijing became the Mongol capital when Qubilai claimed the greatest of all possible prizes, the throne of a united China. It was Chinggis Khan himself who, in 1215, first seized the city from the Chin who used what was then Zhongdu as their northern capital. Chinggis later appointed his loyal Muslim administrator, Yalavach, as the city's first governor. Waṣṣāf, the historian administrator for the Mongols in Iran circa 1320, described Khan Baliq (Turkish for Imperial city) in his history of the Il-Khans of Persia. He wrote that Qubilai built the walls of the city at the height of his power and named it Taidu (Daidu, Chinese for "Great City"). The walls were painted white and were crenellated. He peopled it with artists and craftsmen from all over his empire. It quickly became "a place of assembly resplendent and ornamented overall." Rashīd al-Dīn claimed it had 17 towers spaced at one-*parsang* intervals. It had boulevards rather than the maze of small streets typical of Chinese cities, and from one city gate there was an uninterrupted view across the city to the opposite city gate. The boulevards were wide enough for nine horsemen to gallop side by side. Within the walls, gardens were laid, and orchards were formed with trees, shrubs, hedges, and bushes imported from throughout the growing empire. Most of these plants bore fruit. Qubilai chose this site for his capital rather than Shangdu (Xanadu), which had been the location of the *quriltai* that proclaimed him Great Khan, in order to appease his Chinese citizens who saw Shangdu as belonging to nomad territory and associated it with its role as a staging post for raids and incursions.

Providing for the new capital was a major concern. Even in the thirteenth century "the land of Khitai [was] an exceedingly broad and vast country and very thickly populated [and] in the whole of the inhabitable quarter there is no other country with such populousness or multitude of people as here."[18] The site of the capital was 24 *parsang* (72 miles) from the gulf of Bo Hai. Flowing through the city, the Yungting, or Sankan River,

From the Yuan Observatory, Beijing. Courtesy of Lan Tien Lang Publications

From the Yuan Observatory, Beijing. Courtesy of Lan Tien Lang Publications

provided water and a navigable connection to the interior and to the gulf. It came via the Chamchiyal (Nankow) pass and provided a route to the summer residence and hunting lodge at Shangdu (Xanadu). However, it proved inadequate for the city's needs, and Qubilai ordered reconstruction and extension of the Grand Canal, which had long suffered from neglect since its construction in the seventh century. The north needed to import grain and food from the more fertile south, and the canal would prove more efficient than the sea route. Rashīd al-Dīn claimed the canal provided a 40-day link with Zaitun from where ships could sail to and from India and boats could connect with other ports of Māchīn (South China).

The lengthening and strengthening of the Grand Canal was an extremely costly and ambitious undertaking. Qubilai's chief minister, Sangha, later known as a "villainous minister," was charged with the project, which involved the building of 1,090 miles of canal by two and a half million workers. The canal, 40 meters wide in parts, was provided with regular sluices to accommodate large seafaring vessels and was walled with stone. A major highway was constructed at the same time and was also made with stone and lined with willows and other trees to provide shade

The Yuan Observatory, Beijing. Courtesy of Lan Tien Lang
Publications

for the road and its travelers. Villages and roadside shops and eater-
ies were also established along the whole length of the new highway.
This ensured that the famed *yam* postal relay system could now be fully
extended to eastern China, connecting Tabriz with Beijing by riders who
could cover 250 miles per day.

To further its identity as an international city, Qubilai designated
certain sections of the city to particular peoples. Hence, there was a
Muslim area of the city, an Indian section, areas where Europeans were
concentrated, and districts where certain trades and professions were
practiced. Marco Polo mentioned that the Lombards, the Germans,
and the French each had their own designated area. In this aspect it
resembled Qaraqorum but on a vastly bigger scale. A reputed 20,000

The Yuan Observatory, Beijing. Courtesy of Lan Tien Lang Publications

prostitutes lived and worked in the city. These women were regulated, with an officer put in overall control of their activities through a corps of constables, each in charge of between 100 and 1,000 women. Some of these courtesans were expected to entertain the many ambassadors who arrived as the Great Khan's guests. The ambassadors and their retinue would be furnished nightly with different women, and these courtesans were expected to offer their services free as a form of taxation to the state. Most people actually resided in the suburbs, which spread for three or four miles in each direction. There were many fine houses and inns for the merchants who came from all over the world to trade in this booming city. Marco Polo claimed that 1,000 cartloads of silk arrived in the city each day. He said that the reason such vast quantities of silk and gold were woven in Khan baliq was because of a scarcity of flax, cotton, and hemp. He reckoned that the new capital directly served 200 surrounding cities. "To this city everything that is most rare and valuable in all parts of the world finds its way."[19] Qubilai's capital was a true international metropolis.

Qubilai's new capital quickly achieved supremacy and recognition, not least because the Qa'an built his empire's mint in the capital.

CHAPTER XVIII

OF THE KIND OF PAPER MONEY ISSUED BY THE GRAND KHAN, AND MADE TO PASS CURRENT THROUGHOUT HIS DOMINIONS

In this city of Kanbalu is the mint of the grand khan, who may truly be said to possess the secret of the alchemists, as he has the art of producing money by the following process. He causes the bark to be stripped from those mulberry-trees the leaves of which are used for feeding silk-worms, and takes from it that thin inner rind which lies between the coarser bark and the wood of the tree. This being steeped, and afterwards pounded in a mortar, until reduced to a pulp, is made into paper resembling (in substance) that which is manufactured from cotton, but quite black. When ready for use, he has it cut into pieces of money of different sizes, nearly square, but somewhat longer than they are wide. Of these, the smallest pass for a denier tournois; the next size for a Venetian silver groat; others for two, five, and ten groats; others for one, two, three, and as far as ten besants of gold. The coinage of this paper money is authenticated with as much form and ceremony as if it were actually of pure gold or silver; for to each note a number of officers, specially appointed, not only subscribe their names, but affix their signets also; and when this has been regularly done by the whole of them, the principal officer, deputed by his majesty, having dipped into vermilion the royal seal committed to his custody, stamps with it the piece of paper, so that the form of the seal tinged with the vermilion remains impressed upon it by which it receives full authenticity as current money, and the act of counterfeiting it is punished as a capital offence. When thus coined in large quantities, this paper currency is circulated in every part of the grand khan's dominions; nor dares any person, at the peril of his life, refuse to accept it in payment. All his subjects receive it without hesitation, because, wherever their business may call them, they can dispose of it again in the purchase of merchandise they may have occasion for; such as pearls, jewels, gold, or silver. With it, in short, every article may be procured.

Several times in the course of the year, large caravans of merchants arrive with such articles as have just been mentioned, together with gold tissues, which they lay before the grand khan. He thereupon calls together twelve experienced and skilful persons, selected for this purpose, whom he commands to examine the articles with great care, and to fix the value at which they should be purchased. Upon the sum at which they have been thus conscientiously appraised he allows a reasonable profit, and immediately pays for them with this paper; to which the owners can have no objection, because, as has been observed, it answers the purpose of their own disbursements; and even though they should be inhabitants of a country where this kind of money is not current, they invest the amount in other articles of merchandise suited to their own markets. When any persons happen to be possessed of paper money which from long use has become damaged, they carry it to the mint, where, upon the payment of only three per cent, they may receive fresh notes in exchange. Should any be desirous of procuring gold or silver for the purposes of Manufacture, such as of drinking-cups, girdles, or other articles wrought of these metals, they in like manner apply at the mint and for their paper obtain the bullion they require. All his majesty's armies are paid with this currency which is to them of the same value as if it were gold or silver. Upon these grounds, it may certainly be affirmed that the grand khan has more extensive command of treasure than any other sovereign in the universe.[20]

From the Yuan Observatory, Beijing. Courtesy of Lan Tien Lang Publications

The walled city had each of its 12 gates guarded by 1,000 armed guards. The heavy guard was not for fear of rebellion but was there to enhance the prestige and status of the Great Khan. Likewise, Qubilai's personal body-guard, the Keshikten, numbered 12,000 cavalrymen, not for fear of attack but because he had the means and wealth to maintain such a personal guard. The city guards imposed a curfew within the city walls that was draconically enforced. The peals of a great bell would warn the citizens to shutter their homes and get off the streets. Groups of 30 guards would nightly patrol the city streets, arresting any they found breaking the curfew. Interrogation would take place in the morning, and if any offence was found to have been committed, the culprit would be severely beaten. Executions would take place outside the city walls because spilling blood within the city precincts was forbidden. Cremations and burials were also forbidden within the walls.

Qubilai Khan's own palace (*qarshi*) was built of wood and planks and measured 400 paces on each side. Qubilai was usually in residence here during the winter months. Waṣṣāf, in his usual painfully extravagant style, described the interior of this opulent pavilion, this "elysian structure endowed with cupola and windows," in Greek mythological

The Yuan Observatory, Beijing. Guo Shoujing's celestial tables. Courtesy of Lan Tien Lang Publications

imagery, but the message is clear. Qubilai's residence, "putting to shame the pinnacles of the celestial tabernacle" possessed a fabulous palace far removed from the dwelling in which his grandfather would have grown up. Its floors were inlaid with jasper, the grilles on the windows were made of gold and silver, and statues graced the hall and complemented the paintings, which reflected "both art and wit." Rashīd al-Dīn also commented on the marble floors and pillars, remarking on their cleanliness and extreme beauty. He explained that each of the walls had its special function. The outside wall was for the tethering of horses, an inside wall was for emirs to sit for the daily morning assembly. A third wall was reserved for guards and a fourth for courtiers. Friar Oderic of Pordenone, traveling through China in the 1320s, also expressed his awe on visiting the palace.

Tiananmen Square, Beijing. Courtesy of Lan Tien Lang Publications

[Taydu] hath twelve gates, between every two of which there is a space of two long miles; and betwixt the two cities [old and new site] also there is a good amount of population, the compass of the two together being more than forty miles. Here the Great Khan hath his residence, and hath a great palace, the walls of which are some four miles in compass. And within this space be many other fine palaces. (For within the great palace wall is a second enclosure, with a distance between them of perhaps half a bowshot, and in the midst between those two walls are kept his stores and all his slaves; whilst within the inner enclosure dwells the Great Khan with all his family, who are most numerous, so many sons and daughters, sons-in-law, and grandchildren hath he; with such a multitude of wives and councilors and secretaries and servants, that the whole palace of four miles' circuit is inhabited.)

And within the enclosure of the great palace there hath been a hill thrown up on which another palace is built, the most beautiful in the whole world. And this whole hill is planted over with trees, wherefrom it hath the name of the *Green Mount*. And at the side of this hill hath been formed a lake (more than a mile round), and a most beautiful bridge built across it. And on this lake there be such multitudes of wild-geese and ducks and swans, that it is something to wonder at; so that there is no need for that lord to go from home when he wisheth for sport. Also within the walls are thickets full of sundry sorts of wild animals; so that he can follow the chase when he chooses without ever quitting the domain.

But his own palace in which he dwells is of vast size and splendour. The basement thereof is raised about two paces from the ground, and within there be four-and-twenty columns of gold; and all the walls are hung with skins of red leather, said to be the finest in the world. In the midst of the palace is a certain great jar, more than two paces in height, entirely formed of a certain precious stone called *Merdacas* [jade] (and so fine, that I was told its price exceeded the value of four great towns). It is all hooped round with gold and in every corner thereof is a dragon represented as in act to strike most fiercely. And this jar hath also fringes of network of great pearls hanging there-from, and these fringes are a span in breadth. Into this vessel drink is conveyed by certain conduits from the court of the palace; and beside it are many golden goblets from which those drink who list.

In the hall of the palace also are many peacocks of gold. And when any of the Tartars wish to amuse their lord then they go one after the other and clap their hands; upon which the peacocks flap their wings, and make as if they would dance. Now this must be done either by diabolic art, or by some engine underground![21]

Marco Polo was very impressed with the palace and its gardens, and he described the winter residence in some detail. "The walls inside are covered with silver and gold and there are paintings of horsemen, dragons

Tiananmen Square, Beijing. Courtesy of Lan Tien Lang Publications

and every kind of bird and animal."[22] This style of decoration continued over the vaulted ceilings of the reception room, which could seat 6,000 people. There were countless other rooms, and for the Italian no architect anywhere on Earth could have bettered the design of that palace. Separate buildings were situated nearby containing the private property of the monarch including "his treasure in gold and silver bullion, precious stones, and pearls, and also his vessels of gold and silver plate."[23] Here too were the private quarters of his wives and concubines. Descriptions of the palaces at this time all stress the colorful nature of the buildings, the roofs in particular, which were painted in vermilion, green, azure, blue, and yellow and shone in the sun like jewels. The buildings, which it was stressed were built to last, were visible from miles around.

Marco Polo also mentioned the Green Mount, the gardens, and the lake with their abundance of wildlife and exotic animals. Between the inner and outer walls of the palaces, gardens, coppices, and orchards were planted, all stocked with fauna. Stags, roebucks, harts, and fallow deer, populated the green areas, the central feature of which was an artificial mound of earth one hundred paces in height with a circumference of one mile. The earth was transported to the mount by elephants from deep excavations nearby that were dug to create an artificial lake well stocked with teeming fish. The Green Mount was capped with a pavilion and dressed in evergreen trees from all over the empire. It was said that whenever Qubilai heard tales of a new kind of tree he would order that same tree to be dug up and transported for planting on his Green Mount. The lake at its base supplied Qubilai's tables with an abundance of fish and aquatic fowl, including swans.

XANADU (KEMIN-FU, CHEMEINFU, K'AI-P'ING, SHANG-TU, SHANGDU)

> In Xanadu did Kubla Khan
> A stately pleasure dome decree:
> Where Alph, the sacred river, ran,
> Through caverns measureless to man
>   Down to a sunless sea.
>
> Samuel Taylor Coleridge, *Kubla Khan*

This summer capital existed, and it possessed a stately pleasure dome, and such was the impression it created in those who visited the newly built town that it acquired the trappings of legend. It was named K'ai-p'ing by Qubilai, who selected its location, about 125 kilometers north of modern Beijing, on the basis of geomancy using the principles of wind and water and the advice of Chinese sages. By building a major urban center on the edges of the steppe and on the borders of the Chinese agricultural lands (the sown), Qubilai was sending a message to his new subjects. He was not an invader but a ruler, and his domains stretched across the boundaries of what had been steppe and sown. In 1263 he changed the name again, and K'ai-p'ing became Shang-tu, or Upper Capital, and the growing town assumed the function of a summer residence and a hunting preserve. It displayed both Mongol and Chinese influences with its accommodation of the "chase" and the reflection in the buildings and city planning of Chinese urban styles.

The town had three sections surrounded by a square earthen wall between 12 and 18 feet in height. Six gates, two on the east and west walls and one on the north and south walls, allowed access. Protection was enhanced by six watchtowers on each wall. Most of the 200,000 citizens lived within the outer section in mud and board housing. Buddhist temples were also found in this outer section, in keeping with traditional Chinese practice. Other important buildings were situated according to guidelines found in the *I Ching*, the *Book of Changes*, a text still widely consulted today.

The second section of K'ai-p'ing, the Inner City, contained Qubilai's residence and the houses of his retinue, and it also was planned as a square. It was enclosed in a brick wall 10 to 16 feet high with four turrets overlooking them. The imperial palace was constructed on an earthen platform strengthened with rocks and wooden beams because the land was often wet and marshy. Rashīd al-Dīn claims that

since the water was trapped in the bowels of the earth, it seeped out over time in other places in meadows some distance away, where it surfaced as springs and flowed forth. On the plinth a Chinese style palace was built.[24]

The palace raised above the surrounding land, which would have been dotted with springs, must have presented an enchanting scene. Inside, the palace was equally impressive with the walls of the hallways and chambers brightly painted with hunting scenes, birds, animals, flowers, trees, and other delightful images. The palace and the other government buildings located within the inner walls were made of marble, and though no buildings remain standing today, the scattered pieces of tile work, ceramics, marble, and glazed roofing attest to the wealth and luxury of the summer city.

The third section of the city was the hunting preserve, something not many Chinese cities possessed. This hunting park was located west and north of the outer walls and was composed of meadows, woods, coppices, streams, and small lakes. Fountains and streams dotted the artificial landscape where tame animals, mostly varieties of deer, were free to wander.

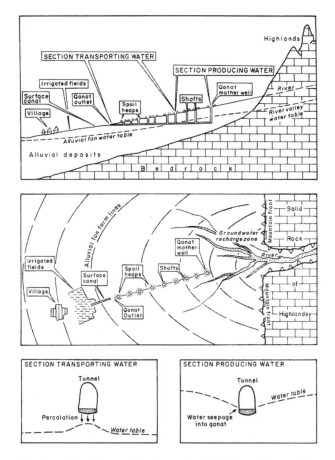

Qanats—irrigation methods used to this day in Iran and Afghanistan. Courtesy of Lan Tien Lang Publications

Falconry, a very popular sport among the Mongol elite, was also practiced here. Reputedly the park was also home to special breeds of white mares, and cows' milk was strictly reserved for the Great Khans. The park was enclosed in an earthen wall and a moat and accessed by four gates. Little of this game park has survived to the present, and once again it is Marco Polo's vivid description which has preserved its memory. Surrounded on all sides by mountains, rich in trees and flora, with abundant wildlife and running water, this little town must have been a welcome retreat in the hot, sticky summer months, though its appearance made many of the traditionally minded Mongol elite uneasy about the way in which their leadership were leading. They perceived the new city as too Chinese and a betrayal of Mongol nomadic values and virtues. It was from this time onward that the divisions in the empire became overtly cultural rather than merely political.

HANGZHOU

The Song capital fell to the Mongols in 1276. This was the city of Kinsai, which so enraptured Marco Polo, especially its idyllic lake, which is still today an escape from the city with its houseboats and floating restaurants. In 1275 the Mongol general Bayan was slowly advancing on the Song dynasty's capital, and Empress Dowager Hsieh (1208–82), with whom real power resided following the death of her son, Tu-tsung, was reluctant to abandon her beloved capital for an uncertain exile. Eventually she compromised, and she consented to the royal family leaving for safety in the south while she remained behind with the four-year-old emperor. The Song-held cities and towns and their military positions fell to Bayan usually without a fight, but the formidable empress dowager was determined to negotiate a deal rather than surrender as a conquered foe. On December 23, 1275, she sent negotiators to bargain with Bayan, offering to pay regular tribute in return for his abandoning of his expedition. But at this late stage, the general was too close to victory to even consider such an audacious compromise. The emissary was dismissed with a curt reminder that a Mongol envoy had already lost his life at Song hands and that Qubilai's Confucian advisor, Hao Ching, had been disgracefully detained. Even a formal offer of a yearly tribute of 250,000 tael of silver and 250,000 bolts of silk could not deflect Bayan's insistence on unconditional surrender. Only in late January when the emperor described himself as a subject of Qubilai would Bayan consent to negotiations. But it still took long, protracted bargaining before the empress agreed to hand over the Song dynasty's seal of office, an unambiguous symbol of surrender. Though Bayan was aware that most of the royal family had fled southward and had eluded his search parties, he chose to ignore what could have been interpreted as duplicity, and the emperor and his grandmother were treated well, and their palaces and the family vaults and tombs were not plundered or abused. In fact the whole city escaped sacking, ordinary Song officials were kept in their jobs, and Hangzhou was helped to restore itself to its former glory. The emperor was granted a title, awarded provisions and a stipend to keep him comfortable, and was then exiled to Tibet where he eventually became a monk.

The following is an extract from Marco Polo's *Travels* and recounts the fall of Hangzhou to the Mongol forces under the renowned general Bayan. Bayan gained great prestige and fame during his lifetime, and this is reflected in the number of pages devoted to his exploits found in the early sources. Not only are his adventures recorded in the Chinese chronicles, such as the Yuan Shih, but Rashīd al-Dīn and the Persian historians also devote considerable space to his successes and character.

Sedan chair from the Song Village in Hangzhou. Courtesy of Lan Tien Lang Publications

He advanced to five cities in succession, but got possession of none of them; for he did not wish to engage in besieging them and they would not give themselves up. But when he came to the sixth city he took that by storm, and so with a second, and a third, and a fourth, until he had taken twelve cities in succession. And when he had taken all these he advanced straight against the capital city of the kingdom, which was called KINSAY [Hangzhou], and which was the residence of the King and Queen.

And when the King beheld Bayan coming with all his host, he was in great dismay, as one unused to see such sights. So he and a great company of his people got on board a thousand ships and fled to the islands of the Ocean Sea, whilst the Queen who remained behind in the city took all measures in her power for its defence, like a valiant lady.

Now it came to pass that the Queen asked what was the name of the captain of the host, and they told her that it was Bayan Hundred-Eyes. So when she wist that he was styled Hundred-Eyes, she called to mind how their astrologers had foretold that a man of an hundred eyes should strip them of the kingdom. Wherefore she gave herself up to Bayan, and surrendered to him the whole kingdom and all the other cities and fortresses, so that no resistance was made. And in sooth this was a goodly conquest, for there was no realm on earth half so wealthy. The amount that the King used to expend was perfectly marvellous; and as an example I will tell you somewhat of his liberal acts.

In those provinces they are wont to expose their newborn babes; I speak of the poor, who have not the means of bringing them up. But the King used to have all those foundlings taken charge of, and had note made of the signs and planets under which each was born, and then put them out to nurse about the country. And when any rich man was childless he would go to the King and obtain from him as many of these children as he desired. Or, when the children grew up, the King would make up marriages among them, and provide for the couples from his own purse. In this manner he used to provide for some 20,000 boys and girls every year.

I will tell you another thing this King used to do. If he was taking a ride through the city and chanced to see a house that was very small and poor standing among other houses that were fine and large, he would ask why it was so, and they would tell him it belonged to a poor man who had not the means to enlarge it. Then the King would himself supply the means. And thus it came to pass that in all the capital of the kingdom of Manzi [China], Kinsay by name, you should not see any but fine houses.

This King used to be waited on by more than a thousand young gentlemen and ladies, all clothed in the richest fashion. And he ruled his realm with such justice that no malefactors were to be found therein. The city in fact was so secure that no man closed his doors at night, not even in houses and shops that were full of all sorts of rich merchandize. No one could do justice in the telling to the great riches of that country, and to the good disposition of the people. Now that I have told you about the kingdom, I will go back to the Queen.

You must know that she was conducted to the Great Kaan, who gave her an honourable reception, and caused her to be served with all state, like a great lady as she was. But as for the King her husband, he never more did quit the isles of the sea to which he had fled, but died there. So leave we him and his wife and all their concerns, and let us return to our story, and go on regularly with our account of the great province of Manzi and of the manners and customs of its people. And, to begin at the beginning, we must go back to the city of Coiganju, from which we digressed to tell you about the conquest of Manzi.[25]

Song Dynasty buoy, West Lake, Hangzhou. Courtesy of Lan Tien Lang Publications

West Lake buoy, thirteenth century. Courtesy of Lan Tien Lang Publications

Hangzhou was a favorite resort among the Mongols and their courtiers, including Marco Polo. It has retained its status as a popular recreational centre to the present day. The central hall of the city's main mosque, the Phoenix Temple, was constructed in the 1270s, and West Lake, filled with boats and floating restaurants today, attracted water-loving visitors seven hundred years ago as well.

DESCRIPTION OF THE GREAT CITY OF KINSAY, WHICH IS THE CAPITAL OF THE WHOLE COUNTRY OF MANZI

When you have left the city of Changan [Xi'an] and have travelled for three days through a splendid country, passing a number of towns and villages, you arrive at the most noble city of Kinsay, a name which is as much as to say in our tongue "The City of Heaven," as I told you before.

And since we have got thither I will enter into particulars about its magnificence; and these are well worth the telling, for the city is beyond dispute the finest and the noblest in the world. In this we shall speak according to the written statement which the Queen of this Realm sent to Bayan the conqueror of the country for transmission to the Great Kaan, in order that he might be aware of the surpassing grandeur of the city and might be moved to save it from destruction or injury. I will tell you all the truth as it was set down in that document. For truth it was, as the said Messer Marco Polo at a later date was able to witness with his own eyes. And now we shall rehearse those particulars.

First and foremost, then, the document stated the city of Kinsay to be so great that it hath an hundred miles of compass. And there are in it twelve thousand bridges of stone, for the most part so lofty that a great fleet could pass beneath them. And let no man marvel that there are so many bridges, for you see the whole city stands as it were in the water and surrounded by water, so that a great many bridges are required to give free passage about it. (And though the bridges be so high the approaches are so well contrived that carts and horses do cross them.)

The document aforesaid also went on to state that there were in this city twelve guilds of the different crafts, and that each guild had 12,000 houses in the occupation of its workmen. Each of these houses contains at least 12 men, whilst some contain 20 and some 40,—not that these are all masters, but inclusive of the journeymen who work under the masters. And yet all these craftsmen had full occupation, for many other cities of the kingdom are supplied from this city with what they require.

The document aforesaid also stated that the number and wealth of the merchants, and the amount of goods that passed through their hands, was so enormous that no man could form a just estimate thereof. And I should have told you with regard to those masters of the different crafts who are at the head of such houses as I have mentioned, that neither they nor their wives ever touch a piece of work with their own hands, but live as nicely and delicately as if they were kings and queens. The wives indeed are most dainty and angelical creatures! Moreover it was an ordinance laid down by the King that every man should follow his father's business and no other, no matter if he possessed 100,000 bezants.

Inside the city there is a Lake which has a compass of some 30 miles: and all round it are erected beautiful palaces and mansions, of the richest and most exquisite structure that you can imagine, belonging to the nobles of the city. There are also on its shores many abbeys and churches of the Idolaters. In the middle of the Lake are two Islands, on each of which stands a rich, beautiful and spacious edifice, furnished in such style as to seem fit for the palace of an Emperor. And when any one of the citizens desired to hold a marriage feast, or to give any other entertainment, it used to be done at one of these palaces. And everything would be found there ready to order, such as silver plate, trenchers, and dishes [napkins and tablecloths], and whatever else was needful. The King made this provision for the gratification of his people, and the place was open to every one who desired to give an entertainment. (Sometimes there would be at these palaces an hundred different parties; some holding a banquet, others celebrating a wedding; and yet all would find good accommodation in the different apartments and pavilions, and that in so well ordered a manner that one party was never in the way of another.)

The houses of the city are provided with lofty towers of stone in which articles of value are stored for fear of fire; for most of the houses themselves are of timber, and fires are very frequent in the city. The people are Idolaters; and since they were conquered by the Great Kaan they use paper-money. Both men and women are fair and comely, and for the most part clothe themselves in silk, so vast is the supply of that material, both from the whole district of Kinsay, and from the imports by traders from other provinces. And you must know they eat every kind of flesh, even that of dogs and other unclean beasts, which nothing would induce a Christian to eat.

Since the Great Kaan occupied the city he has ordained that each of the 12,000 bridges should be provided with a guard of ten men, in case of any disturbance, or of any being so rash as to plot treason or insurrection against him. Each guard is provided with a hollow instrument of wood and with a metal basin, and with a time-keeper to enable them to know the hour of the day or night. And so when one hour of the night is past the sentry strikes one on the wooden instrument and on the basin, so that the whole quarter of the city is made aware that one hour of the night is gone. At the second hour he gives two strokes, and so on, keeping always wide awake and on the look out. In the morning again, from the sunrise, they begin to count anew, and strike one hour as they did in the night, and so on hour after hour.

Part of the watch patrols the quarter, to see if any light or fire is burning after the lawful hours; if they find any they mark the door, and in the morning the owner is summoned before the magistrates, and unless he can plead a good excuse he is punished. Also if they find any one going about the streets at unlawful hours they arrest him, and in the morning they bring him before the magistrates. Likewise if in the daytime they find any poor cripple unable to work for his livelihood, they take him to one of the hospitals, of which there are many, founded by the ancient kings, and endowed with great revenues. Or if he be capable of work they oblige him to take up some trade. If they see that any house has caught fire they immediately beat upon that wooden instrument to give the alarm, and this brings together the watchmen from the other bridges to help to extinguish it, and to save the goods of the merchants or others, either by removing them to the towers above mentioned, or by putting them in boats and transporting them to the islands in the lake. For no citizen dares leave his house at night, or to come near the fire; only those who own the property, and those watchmen who flock to help, of whom there shall come one or two thousand at the least.

Moreover, within the city there is an eminence on which stands a Tower, and at the top of the tower is hung a slab of wood. Whenever fire or any other alarm breaks out in the city a man who stands there with a mallet in his hand beats upon the slab, making a noise that is heard to a great distance. So when the blows upon this slab are heard, everybody is aware that fire has broken out, or that there is some other cause of alarm.

The Kaan watches this city with especial diligence because it forms the head of all Manzi; and because he has immense revenue from the duties levied on the transactions of trade therein, the amount of which is such that no one would credit it on mere hearsay.

All the streets of the city are paved with stone or brick, as indeed are all the highways throughout Manzi, so that you ride and travel in every direction without inconvenience. Were it not for this pavement you could not do so, for the country is very low and flat, and after rain 'tis deep in mire and water. (But as the Great Kaan's couriers could not gallop their horses over the pavement, the side of the road is left unpaved for their convenience.) The pavement of the main street of the city also is laid out in two parallel ways of ten paces in width on either side, leaving a space in the middle laid with fine gravel, under which are vaulted drains which convey the rain water into the canals; and thus the road is kept ever dry.

You must know also that the city of Kinsay has some 3000 baths, the water of which is supplied by springs. They are hot baths, and the people take great delight in them, frequenting them several times a month, for they are very cleanly in their persons. They are the finest and largest baths in the world; large enough for 100 persons to bathe together.

And the Ocean Sea comes within 25 miles of the city at a place called GANFU, where there is a town and an excellent haven, with a vast amount of shipping which is engaged in the traffic to and from India and other foreign parts, exporting and importing many kinds of wares, by which the city benefits. And a great river flows from the city of Kinsay to that sea-haven, by which vessels can come up to the city itself. This river extends also to other places further inland.

Know also that the Great Kaan hath distributed the territory of Manzi into nine parts, which he hath constituted into nine kingdoms. To each of these kingdoms a king is appointed who is subordinate to the Great Kaan, and every year renders the accounts of his kingdom to the fiscal office at the capital. This city of Kinsay is the seat of one of these kings, who rules over 140 great and wealthy cities. For in the whole of this vast country of Manzi there are more than 1200 great and wealthy cities, without counting the towns and villages, which are in great numbers. And you may receive it for certain that in each of those 1200 cities the Great Kaan has a garrison, and that the smallest of such garrisons musters 1000 men; whilst there are some of 10,000, 20,000 and 30,000; so that the total number of troops is something scarcely calculable. The troops forming these garrisons are not all Tartars. Many are from the province of Cathay, and good soldiers too. But you must not suppose they are by any means all of them cavalry; a very large proportion of them are foot-soldiers, according to the special requirements of each city. And all of them belong to the army of the Great Kaan.

I repeat that everything appertaining to this city is on so vast a scale, and the Great Kaan's yearly revenues wherefrom are so immense, that it is not easy even to put it in writing, and it seems past belief to one who merely hears it told. But I will write it down for you.

First, however, I must mention another thing. The people of this country have a custom, that as soon as a child is born they write down the day and hour and the planet and sign under which its birth has taken place; so that every one among them knows the day of his birth. And when any one intends a journey he goes to the astrologers, and gives the particulars of his nativity in order to learn whether he shall have good luck or no. Sometimes they will say _no_, and in that case the journey is put off till such day as the astrologer may recommend. These astrologers are very skilful at their business, and often their words come to pass, so the people have great faith in them.

They burn the bodies of the dead. And when any one dies the friends and relations make a great mourning for the deceased, and clothe themselves in hempen garments, and follow the corpse playing on a variety of instruments and singing hymns to their idols. And when they come to the burning place, they take representations of things cut out of parchment, such as caparisoned horses, male and female slaves, camels, armour suits of cloth of gold (and money), in great quantities, and these things they put on the fire along with the corpse, so that they are all burnt with it. And they tell you that the dead man shall have all these slaves and animals of which the effigies are burnt, alive in flesh and blood, and the money in gold, at his disposal in the next world; and that the instruments which they have caused to be played at his funeral, and the idol hymns that have been chanted, shall also be produced again to welcome him in the next world; and that the idols themselves will come to do him honour.

Furthermore there exists in this city the palace of the king who fled, him who was Emperor of Manzi, and that is the greatest palace in the world, as I shall tell you more particularly. For you must know its demesne hath a compass of ten miles, all enclosed with lofty battlemented walls; and inside the walls are the finest and most delectable gardens upon earth, and filled too with the finest fruits. There are numerous fountains in it also, and lakes full of fish. In the middle is the palace itself, a great and splendid building. It contains 20 great and handsome halls, one of which is more spacious than the rest, and affords room for a vast multitude to dine. It is all painted in gold, with many histories and representations of beasts and birds, of knights and dames, and many marvellous things. It forms a really magnificent spectacle, for over all the walls and all the ceiling you see nothing but paintings in gold. And besides these halls the palace contains 1000 large and handsome chambers, all painted in gold and divers colours.

Moreover, I must tell you that in this city there are 160 tomans of fires, or in other words 160 tomans of houses. Now I should tell you that the toman is 10,000, so that you can reckon the total as altogether 1,600,000 houses, among which are a great number of rich palaces. There is one church only, belonging to the Nestorian Christians.

There is another thing I must tell you. It is the custom for every burgess of this city, and in fact for every description of person in it, to write over his door his own name, the name of his wife, and those of his children, his slaves, and all the inmates of his house, and also the number of animals that he keeps. And if any one dies in the house then the name of that person is erased, and if any child is born its name is added. So in this way the sovereign is able to know exactly the population of the city. And this is the practice also throughout all Manzi and Cathay.

And I must tell you that every hosteler who keeps an hostel for travelers is bound to register their names and surnames, as well as the day and month of their arrival and departure. And thus the sovereign hath the means of knowing, whenever it pleases him, who come and go throughout his dominions. And certes this is a wise order and a provident.[26]

Today, Hangzhou is dwarfed by its neighbor, Shanghai, but retains its importance as a leisure center and is fast becoming one of China's most important tourist destinations, with visitors attracted by the tranquility of the West Lake, just as in the days of the Song Empire and the Yuan Dynasty. The Phoenix Temple, Hangzhou's mosque, is one of the most important Islamic sites in the country, though few realize that its beautifully preserved Chinese style domes were built in the days of Qubilai Khan.

TABRIZ AND MARAGHEH

Tabriz became the Mongols' capital in the west and their gateway to Europe, Africa, and the Arab world, an entrepôt between east and west. The North African traveler Ibn Battuta (1304–69) considered the grand bazaar in Tabriz to be among the finest he had ever encountered on his world travels. Marco Polo, who visited the city nearly half a century earlier, considered it the grandest city in that part of the world and lauded its flora and gardens. Hülegü Khan set up his first capital, Khariyat-i-Maragheh, 70 miles south of Tabriz in 1258. The full name of the town means "the village of the pastures." The terrain and climate of Azerbaijan reminded him of the Mongolian steppe, and his successors remained in the vicinity long after they had consolidated their hold on the Il-Khanid Empire. Abaqa Khan (ruled 1265–82) fixed the Mongols' Persian capital in Tabriz, and the city has remained politically and commercially important ever since. It is said that to rule Iran, Tabriz must first be conquered and controlled.

Tabriz lies some 30 miles east of Lake Urumiyeh in what is today the province of Azerbaijan in northwestern Iran. Maragheh is situated closer to the lake and in medieval times was more accessible to the fishing fleets that thrived on the salty waters of Lake Urumiyeh. Today Tabriz is a major industrial, commercial, and political center and is strategically placed on the major road link between Turkey, Iran, and the east. Maragheh, however, is now a sleepy, leafy market town, hidden away in the folds of

Mount Sahand, which towers above the lake to its west and Tabriz to its north.

> Tabriz is like a paradise, and its people are pure
> like a mirror pure from the detritus of rust.
> You say that they are not sincere in their friendship
> But the mirror does not reflect that which it doesn't find.
>
> Tabriz is paradise and its people are like angels,
> Angels act from consideration not from malevolence,
> They do not mingle with nobodies and nonentities,
> Because a stench and a perfume can never be united.

Hamdallah Mustawfī Qazvīnī, Nuzhat al-Qulūb

So said the fourteenth-century historian, geographer, government tax official, and notable Hamdallah Mustawfī Qazvīnī (1282–1344), to whom so much is owed concerning knowledge and understanding of events and conditions of Mongol rule in Iran and western Asia.

Until the ninth century Tabriz was a small village. Tradition says that Zubaydah, the wife of the illustrious ʿAbbāsid Caliph Hārūn al-Rashīd (died 809), laid the foundations of what would become a great city, and it is recorded that in 1213 on the eve of the Mongol invasions it was the chief town of Azerbaijan and famed for its fine Friday mosque, orchards, and its 'Attābī (tabby) silks, velvets, and woven material. Through negotiation and payment of tribute, the city escaped destruction by Mongol forces in 1221. When Hülegü arrived in about 1257, he chose Maragheh rather than Tabriz to base his administration, possibly because the town was more sheltered than its neighbor to the north. However, within years of Hülegü's arrival, Maragheh was transformed into an internationally renowned intellectual metropolis.

It was the construction of an observatory at the request of the Great Khan Möngke (died 1259) that put Maragheh on the world's map. It was soon realized that from the rubble left after the destruction, in 1256, of Alamut, the Assassins' last stronghold, a prize had been won. A particularly bright star lay subdued and ready to serve in the palm of his new masters, and so plans for the construction of a center of learning were immediately implemented. That star was Naṣīr al-Dīn Ṭūsī. He had served the Assassins, and now he was quite ready to serve the Mongols. Unlike the Sunni caliph of Baghdad, Ṭūsī was a Shi'ite Muslim.

Now the fame of the Khwāja Naṣīr al-Dīn's accomplishments had traversed the world like the wind, and accordingly Menggu Qa'an, when bidding farewell to his brother, had said: "When the castles of the Heretics have been captured send the Khwāja Naṣīr al-Dīn here."[27]

Naṣir al-Dīn Ṭūsī was an intellectual giant, and his works on philosophy, theology, astrology, and other diverse fields are still studied today. His

Tomb of fourteenth-century historian Mustawfi.
Courtesy of Abu Hajal Company

university ensured that Maragheh achieved international fame. Ṭūsī had gained the gratitude and support of his new master, Hülegü, after reassuring the Mongol prince that no harm would befall him if he went ahead and stormed Baghdad and executed the caliph. The stars were favorable toward Hülegü according to Ṭūsī's reading, and this was exactly what the conqueror wanted to hear.

The Rasadkhāneh of Maragheh was to prove a theater not only for Ṭūsī's many gifts but for a wide multicultural audience and cast of ethnically diverse players. The observatory was equipped with the best possible technical instruments, including those collected by the Mongol armies from Baghdad, Khorasan, Syria, and other Islamic centers of learning. The instruments included astrolabes, representations of constellations, epicycles, shapes of spheres, and one Ṭūsī himself had invented called the turquet, which contained two planes. The new astronomical tables, which he named Al-Zīj al-Ilkhānī and dedicated to the Il-khan (Hülegü Khan), were the result of 12 years of considerable work by himself and a dedicated gathering of notable scholars and scientists. Although Ṭūsī had contemplated completing the tables in 30 years, the time required for the completion of planetary cycles, he had had to finish them in 12 years on orders from Hülegü Khan. The tables were for the most part based on original observations, but they also drew upon the wide amount of existing astrological knowledge. Naṣīr al-Dīn pointed out several serious shortcomings in Ptolemy's astronomy and foreshadowed the later dissatisfaction with the system that culminated in the Copernican reforms. The Zīj al-Ilkhānī retained its position as most popular astrological table for at least 200 years. That its use was not confined to a closed circle of Persian and Muslim scholars is demonstrated by Ṭūsī's original introduction to his treatise. In this introduction, the extant manuscript of which is believed to have been made three years after Ṭūsī's death in 1277–8, various details suggest that the expected audience was not local. The language of the text was of a more straightforward Persian, the lingua franca of the empire, than Naṣīr al-Dīn Ṭūsī's usual scholarly writing. He also made extensive use of Chinese technical jargon in, for example, describing the three cycles of the sexagenary system and using the Chinese names for the 10 celestial stems and 12 earthly branches of the sexagenary cycle.[28] He translated the date 1203, the year of the Pig, not only to the Muslim calendar but also to the calendar of the Zoroastrians, the Eastern Christians, and the Chinese. He also saw it appropriate to provide his readers with a brief outline of the rise of Islam and felt it necessary to explain to his audience that Muhammad, the Prophet, was a native of Mecca.[29] Such explanations would not have been necessary for anyone with any meaningful contact with the Muslim world. In the environment he now found himself, Ṭūsī was able to cast off the sectarian parochialism that plagued so many of his contemporaries and cast his aspirations toward wider horizons. Ṭūsī adapted comfortably into this new intellectual milieu, with the rich and nourishing intellectual climate he helped create reflected in his work.

Naṣīr al-Dīn Ṭūsī was not the only recipient of Hülegü's largesse. The Syriac cleric Bar Hebraeus had long had dealings with the Mongols. Hülegü's wife Dokuz Khātūn was, like many Mongols, a Christian, and she made the welfare of the church in this new kingdom her special concern. When Bar Hebraeus's considerable intellectual and literary talents became known, he was invited to make use of the library that had been established in Maragheh.

I, having entered the Library of the city of Maragheh of Adhorbijan, have loaded up this my little book with narratives which are worthy of remembrance from many volumes of the Syrians, Saracens [Arabs], and Persians which are preserved here.[30]

Though not explicitly stated, it can be assumed that this magnificent library that apparently appeared out of nowhere in fact benefited from the pillaging of the renowned libraries of both Alamūt (1256) and Baghdad (1258). Scholars of the caliber of Naṣīr al-Dīn Ṭūsī and ʿAṭā Malik ʿAlā al-Dīn Juwaynī could not have sat idly by to witness the destruction of two of the medieval world's greatest collections of books. Their intervention was inevitable and accounts for the appearance of the library of Maragheh. Though Juwaynī claims only to have saved "copies of the Koran and [other] choice books," adding "as for the remaining books, which related to their [Ismāʿīlī] heresy and error . . . I burnt them all,"[31] his words do not ring true because he quotes at great length in his own history from the biography of Ḥasan-i-Ṣabbāḥ, founder of the Nizārī Ismāʿīlīs of Persia. The fact that he did not destroy this "iniquitous" book casts doubt on his claim to have destroyed all books concerning Ismāʿīlī thought and belief. The accusation of book burning and in particular the charge of willfully destroying the literary heritage of Baghdad have long blackened the reputation of Hülegü Khan, grandson of Chinggis Khan. Unfortunately, almost nothing remains today of the center of learning constructed on Hülegü's orders on the hills overlooking Maragheh, and there is no solid evidence that the contents of the two libraries were transported here after the cessation of hostilities. In later accounts of the destruction of Baghdad, reference is made to the burning of books and to the Tigris running black with the ink from the desecrated tomes, presumably after the reddened waters of blood had washed away. Such stories can safely be dismissed as anti-Mongol tirades. Even Chinggis Khan had shown the greatest respect for scholars and learning, and for Hülegü, who had been brought up with the learned elite from all over his family's empire and was surrounded by scholarly advisers, to order such wanton destruction is inconceivable. Ṭūsī, who was at Hülegü's side during the siege of Baghdad, might have had contempt for many of his fellow humans and thought little of spilling their blood, but he could never have countenanced the pillaging and devastation of a library.

Bar Hebraeus spent the last years of his life in Maragheh, the Il-Khanid capital. Maragheh had already established connections with the Syrian Orthodox Church when Rabban Simeon first entered Hülegü's service. Part of his annual 5,000 dinar income was provided for by Maragheh.[32] Bar Hebraeus had visited the city from Tabriz as early as 1268, in which year he had first been exposed to the books of Euclid, and again in 1273, when he studied the 13 astronomical volumes of the Almegest of Ptolemy.[33] He had early begun planning a program of church construction in western Azerbaijan. In 1279, the year of Bar Hebraeus's return to Maragheh, Qutai Khatun, the mother of Ahmad Tegudar (Il-Khan 1282–84), had revived the Christian procession of the Epiphany, which involved the blessing of the waters of the river Safi. The annual procession had ceased to be held because of conflicts between the Muslims and Christians, but the presence of one of the royal family ensured the success of the revived festival.

[Qutai Khatun] came in person to the city of Maragheh, and commanded the Christians to go forth according to their custom with crosses suspended from the heads of their spears. And having gone forth the Divine Grace visited them, and the strength of the cold diminished, and the grass prospered, and the winter possessed the characteristics [favorable] for herbage. And the Mongols had joy in keeping their horses in condition, and the Christians in the triumph of their faith.[34]

According to Assemani, in 1282, Ahmad Tegudar had granted Abu al-Faraj (Bar Hebraeus) a license to build churches in Azerbaijan, Assyria, and Mesopotamia,[35] and both Tabriz and Maragheh benefited from his industry. He had been reluctant to leave Mosul for the Mongol capital, knowing that the move might be his last. However, his brother, who feared lest the Maphrian's own prophecies foreseeing his death in his 60th year should come about at the hands of "thieves and robbers," had insisted that he should abandon the lawless marsh lands of Syria and seek the safety of the Il-Khanid metropolis where he could find sanctuary in his own church and monastery. So tranquil and conducive to intellectual activity was the Il-Khanid capital that the aging cleric was able to complete not only his great work, the *Ethicon,* but also a scientific work inspired and helped no doubt by the proximity of the Raṣadkhāneh of Naṣīr al-Dīn Ṭūsī, the *Book of the Ascension of the Intellect.*[36]

It is claimed that the remains of his church and monastery can still be seen today on the outskirts of the leafy town of Maragheh. This church on the western face of a hill overlooking the city would have been ideal for the aging cleric whose great interest in the stars has already been noted. The entrance to the caves that formed the body of this church lay only 30 or 40 meters beneath the famous observatory of Maragheh, the Raṣadkhāneh, which Hülegü had had constructed for his greatly respected advisor and friend of Bar Hebraeus, Naṣīr al-Dīn Ṭūsī.[37] That a new monastery and a new church existed at this time in Maragheh is attested to in Bar Hebraeus's *Chronicum Ecclesiasticum.*[38] Well aware that his time had come, for he had seen it in the night sky, the dying Abu al-Faraj (Bar Hebraeus) "never ceased from telling stories with laughter and a cheerful face. [Suddenly] he went out like a lamp."[39] The Uyghur catholicos of the Nestorians ordered the bazaars of Maragheh closed, and there was great mourning in all the communities when the news of the death became known.

Among the other historical monuments that litter Maragheh—and for such a small town there are quite a number—are two well-preserved tomb towers from the Mongol period. One is known locally as the tomb of Hülegü's mother, though there is no evidence other than this local tradition that supports this claim. The distinctively shaped and intricately tiled tower is hidden away down an anonymous buff side street behind the high metal gates of a girls' school. Hülegü's mother's tomb and the Round Tower, built in 1168, are situated side by side to the back of the school's playground, and to view these magnificent monuments permission and a key must be sought from the school's headmistress. More accessible than this supposed tomb to one of the Mongols' most illustrious women, the redoubtable Sorghaghtani Beki, is a square tomb tower nearer the center of the town named the Gharāfieh Tower and built (1325–28) for the Mongol regional commander Shams al-Dīn Qara Sonqur. The town's small museum contains the usual array of small artifacts of jewelry and pottery, but in addition the grounds contain a memorial to the poet Awḥādī Marāghī (1272–1338), who like many of the poets of that era would have enjoyed Mongol patronage.

Known as one of the Tabrizi poets, Awḥādī wrote glowingly of his Mongol master, Abū Saʿīd (died 1335), and the *ṣāḥib dīwān* (prime minister) Ghiyāth al-Dīn (ruled 1327–36), son of the justly renowned Rashīd al-Dīn (died 1318). The Tabrizi poets were Sufis who flourished under the Mongol regime of their time. Their principal *khāngāh* (Sufi-run hospice), mosque, and madrassa were located in the district of Tabriz built by the great vizier of Ghazan Khan (died 1304), Rashīd al-Dīn and called appropriately the Rab'-i-Rashīdī. Little remains today of this district of Tabriz built as a testament to the great man, and much of the area was damaged in rioting in 1218 following his fall from grace and ignoble execution. In a typically hyperbolic description from Awḥādī verse, the Rab'-i-Rashīdī was said to bestow "the golden light of divine fortune upon Tabriz" with its "ground made from musk, and its stone of marble; its breeze a scent from paradise and its waters from Kawthar [river in Heaven]." What this quarter did do was provide a home, haven, and meeting place for poets, Sufis, and artists, all of whom thrived under the patronage and benevolence of the Mongol regime in Iran, the Il-Khanate (1256–1335).

Tabriz attained its zenith under the rule of Ghazan Khan (1295–1304), the Mongol sultan who converted to Islam and made it the official religion of his empire, which spread from the Oxus River in the northeast to Egypt in the southwest. The city had replaced Baghdad as the principal commercial center in western Asia and formed the western hub of the arterial Silk Road. Abaqa (died 1282) moved his capital from Maragheh to Tabriz, and from that time until the advent of the Timurids toward the end of the fourteenth century Tabriz maintained its central role. Not only was it a commercial capital but it also became a center for literary, cultural, and spiritual pursuits. With the Mongol sultans generally practicing their traditional religious tolerance, Tabriz became the beating heart of what has been described as a spiritual and cultural anarchy. In the sultan's court there was intense rivalry between Christians, Buddhists, and Muslims. The seemingly draconian laws that were sometimes supposedly imposed on the country were never enforced in the court so that when Öljeitü (ruled 1304–16) ordered the closing of all wine shops and taverns, the drinking and merrymaking did not cease within the precincts of his palaces. Edicts were often issued more with an eye to the history books than on the moral welfare of the people. The cultural climate emanating from Tabriz during this period was dynamic, inventive, and creative, and the sobriquet Golden Age is richly deserved when applied to Il-Khanid Iran.

Tabriz with its lauded Sufi poets became widely regarded as another center of mysticism to rival Konya, the capital of the Saljuq sultanate of Rum, and praise for the city is common in many of the works of contemporary poets. "Go seek paradise, Oh pietist!! Kamāl prefers Tabriz and its Mount of Saints," "From the kingdom of heaven in God's glory and excellence to the town of Tabriz is but half a league." These words of Kamāl Khujandī (died 1400) also acknowledge the importance of the graveyards and cemeteries of Tabriz because its reputation created a sanctity for the dead and it became a desirable place to be buried. But Tabriz was also admired for its earthly beauty, and verses celebrating this are not difficult to find. "In Baghdad beside the Tigris, O Khwājū, there lies paradise, but pleasanter still I tell you, is the land of Tabriz," said another mystic poet of the time, Khwājū Kirmānī (died 1342).

The North African traveler Ibn Battuta visited Tabriz in the 1330s and left this evocative description.

> We arrived at the city of Tabriz after ten days' journey, and encamped outside it in a place called al-Sham. At that place is the grave of Qazan [Ghazan], king of al-'Iraq, and alongside it a fine madrasa and a hospice in which food is supplied to all way-farers, consisting of bread, meat, rice cooked in ghee, and sweetmeats. The amir arranged for my lodging in this hospice, which is situated among rushing streams and leafy trees. On the following morning I entered the city by a gate called the Baghdad Gate, and we came to an immense bazaar called the Qazan bazaar, one of the finest bazaars I have seen the world over. Each trade has its own location in it, separate from every other. I passed through the jewellers' bazaar, and my eyes were dazzled by the varieties of precious stones that I saw; they were [displayed] in the hands of beautiful slave-boys, wearing rich robes and their waists girt with sashes of silk, who [stood] in front of the merchants exhibiting the jewels to the wives of the Turks—while the women were buying them in large quantities and trying to outdo one another. What I saw of all this was a scandal—may God preserve us from such! We went into the ambergris and musk bazaar [also] and saw the like of this again, or worse. Afterwards we came to the cathedral mosque, which was founded by the vizier 'Ali Shah, known by the name of Jilan. Outside it, to the right as one faces the qibla' is a college and to the left is a hospice. The court of the mosque is paved with marble, and its walls are faced with [tiles of] *gashani*, which is like *zalij*. It is traversed by a canal of water and it contains all sorts of trees, vines and jasmines.[40]

A century later, in June 1404, Clavijo, the Spanish ambassador to Persia, special emissary of King Henry VII of Castille, arrived in Tabriz and was equally enthusiastic about its grandeur:

> On Wednesday the 11th of June at the hour of vespers we entered the great city of Tabriz, which lies in a plain between two high ranges of hills that are quite bare of trees.... Throughout the city there are fine roadways with open spaces well laid out: and round these are seen many great buildings and houses, each with its main doorway facing the square. Such are the caravanserais: and within are constructed separate apartments and shops with offices that are planned for various uses. Leaving these caravanserais you pass into the market streets where goods of all kinds are sold: such are silk stuffs and cotton cloths, crapes, taffetas, raw silk and jewelry: for in these shops wares of every kind may be found. There is indeed an immense concourse of merchants and merchandise here. Thus for instance in certain of the caravanserais those who sell cosmetics and perfumes for women are established and to be met with, the women coming here to these shops to buy the same, for they are wont to use many perfumes and unguents.
>
> Now the dress the women wear in the streets is that they go covered in a white sheet, and they wear over their faces a black mask of horsehair, and thus they are concealed completely so that none may know them. Throughout Tabriz many fine buildings may be seen, the Mosques more especially these being most beautifully adorned with tiles in blue and gold; and here they have glass bowls [for the lamps] even as we had seen in Turkish lands. Tabriz is indeed a very mighty city rich in goods and abounding in wealth, for commerce daily flourishes here. They say that in former times its population was even greater than it is now, but even at the present day there must be 200,000 householders within the city limits, or perhaps even more.[41]

Today, Tabriz has an air of brooding patience. War is brewing on its western horizon, while to the north Europe is getting progressively nearer. The continuing prosperity and democratization of Turkey is also a constant challenge to Iran's second capital. The presence of its past can be seen in the faces of its people. In the cool of the shaded, ancient bazaars, it is often oriental eyes that peer out from beneath the covering chadors or the shadowy archways. Tabriz continues to be a gateway, and much continues to pass through its portals.

NOTES

1. Giovanni DiPlano Carpini, *The Story of the Mongols Whom We Call the Tartars: Historia Mongalorum,* trans. Erik Hildinger (Boston: Branden, 1996), 41.

2. The text here is the translation by W. W. Rockhill, *The Journey of William of Rubruck to the Eastern Parts of the World, 1253–55, as Narrated by Himself, with Two Accounts of the Earlier Journey of John of Pian de Carpine*, trans. from the Latin and ed., with an introductory notice, by William Woodville Rockhill (London: Hakluyt Society, 1900), 73.

3. William of Rubruck, *The Journey of William of Rubruck.*

4. Carpini, *The Story of the Mongols*, 41.

5. Marco Polo and Rustichello of Pisa, *The Project Gutenberg EBook of The Travels of Marco Polo*, vols. 1 and 2, http://www.gutenberg.net

6. Charles Melville, "The Itineraries of Sultan Oljeitu: 1304–16," *Iran: Journal of the British Institute of Persian Studies* 28 (1990): 64.

7. Ala-ad-Din 'Ata-Malik Juvaini, *The History of the World Conqueror,* trans. John Andrew Boyle, intro. David Morgan (Manchester, U.K.: Manchester University Press, 1997), 616.

8. Ibid, 610–11

9. Rashīd al-Dīn, *Compendium of Chronicles*, 328–29.

10. Rashid al-Din, *The Successors of Genghis Khan*, trans. John Andrew Boyle (New York: Columbia University Press, 1971), 61.

11. Ibid.

12. Juvaini, *World Conqueror*, 237–38.

13. Carpini, *The Story of the Mongols,* 109.

14. Juvaini, *World Conqueror*, 237.

15. William of Rubruck, *The Mission of Friar William of Rubruck*, trans. and ed. Peter Jackson with David Morgan (London: Hakluyt Society, 1990), 231.

16. Ibid, 221.

17. Ibid, 210.

18. Rashid al-Din, *The Successors of Genghis Khan*, 274.

19. Marco Polo and Rustichello of Pisa, *The Project Gutenberg EBook of The Travels of Marco Polo*, vols. 1 and 2, http://www.gutenberg.net.

20. Ibid, Chapter XVIII.

21. Friar Oderic of Pordenone, "The Travels of Friar Oderic," in Henry Yule, ed., *Cathay and the Way Thither,* 3 vols. (Reprint, Millwood, N.Y.: Kraus Reprint [1914] 1967), 217–22.

22. Marco Polo, *The Travels of Marco Polo,* trans. Teresa Waugh (London: Sidgewick and Jackson, 1985), 72–73, 1985.

23. Marco Polo and Rustichello of Pisa, *The Project Gutenberg EBook of The Travels of Marco Polo*, vols. 1 and 2, http://www.gutenberg.net

24. Rashīd al-Dīn, *Jāmi' al-Tavārīkh,* eds., Mohammad Roushan and Mustafah Mūsavī (Tehran: Nashr albaraz, 1994), translation by George Lane.

25. Marco Polo and Rustichello of Pisa, *The Project Gutenberg EBook of The Travels of Marco Polo*, vols. 1 and 2, http://www.gutenberg.net.

26. From *The Book of Ser Marco Polo the Venetian concerning the Kingdoms and Marvels of the East,* trans. and ed. by Henry Yule, 3rd ed. revised by Henri Cordier (London: John Murray, 1903), vol. 2, 185–93, 200–205, 215–16.

27. Rashīd al-Dīn, *Jāmi' al-Tavārīkh,* 1024; Rashīd al-Dīn, *Rashiduddin Fazlullah Jami 'u' t-Tawarikh,* 501–2.

28. Thomas Allsen, *Culture and Conquest in Mongol Eurasia* (Cambridge: Cambridge University Press, 2001), 162–65.

29. J. A. Boyle, *The Mongol World Empire, 1206–1370* (Aldershot, U.K.: Variorum Reprints, 1977); Nasir al-Din Tusi, "The Longer Introduction to the Zij al-Ilkhānī

of Naṣ ir-al-Dīn Ṭ ūsī," trans. and intro. John Andrew Boyle, *Journal of Semitic Studies* 8.

30. Bar Hebraeus, *The Chronography of Gregory Abu'l-Faraj Bar Hebraeus' Political History of the World, Part I*, trans. Ernest A. Wallis-Budge (London, 1932), 2.

31. Juvaini, *The History of the World Conqueror*, 719.

32. Bar Hebraeus, *The Chronography of Gregory Abu'l-Faraj Bar Hebraeus' Political History of the World, Part I*, 437.

33. J. M. Fiey, *Chrétiens Syriaques sous les Mongols* (Louvain, 1975), 99.

34. Bar Hebraeus, *The Chronography of Gregory Abu'l-Faraj Bar Hebraeus' Political History of the World, Part I*, 460; cf. Fiey, *Chrétiens Syriaques sous les Mongols*, 38.

35. *Bibliotheca Orientalis*, vol. 2, 258, cited in John Bowman and J. A. Thompson, "The Monastery-Church of Bar Hebraeus at Maragheh in West Azerbaijan," *Abr-Nahrain*, vol. 5 (Leiden, Netherlands: Brill, 1966), 38.

36. F. Nau, ed. and trans., *Le Livre de l'Ascension de l'Esprit sur la Forme du ciel et de la Terre*, Bibliotheque de l'Ecole des Hautes Etudes, Sciences philologiques et historiques, 2 vols. (Paris, 1899–1900), 121.

37. For a description and explanation of this "church," see Bowman and Thompson, "The Monastery-Church of Bar Hebraeus," 35–61. For an alternative view as to the nature of these caves see Warwick Ball, "Two Aspects of Iranian Buddhism," *Bulletin of the Asia Institute of Pahlavi University* 1–4 (1976): 103–63; "The Imamzadeh Ma'sum at Vardjovi: A Rock-cut Il-Khanid Complex Near Maragheh," *Archaeologische Mitteilungen aus Iran* 12 (1979): 329–40.

38. *Chronicum Ecclesiasticum*, III, 443; cited in Gregory Bar Hebraeus, *Ethicon*, trans. Herman Teule, vol. 2 (Louvain, Belgium: E. Peeters, 1993): xi, n. 12.

39. Bar Hebraeus, *Chronography*, xxix.

40. Ibn Battuta, *The Travels of Ibn Battuta* A.D. *1325–1354*, trans. H.A.R. Gibb, vols. 1–3 (New Delhi: Munsharim, 1999), 344–45.

41. Guy Le Strange, *Clavijo. Embassy to Tamerlane 1403–1406* (New York and London: Harper, 1928), http://depts.washington.edu/uwch/silkroad/texts/clavijo/cltxt1.html.

5

THE ARMY

The army was the backbone of Mongol rule during its days of empire. In the days when the empire was still confined to the steppe, the army was the backbone and body, limbs, and head. Everyone was part of the army, and everyone was involved in any military campaigns and battles. To be a Mongol man was to be a Mongol warrior. Juwaynī, the historian and one-time governor of Baghdad, described the army thus:

In time of action, when attacking and assaulting, they are like trained wild beasts out after game, and in the days of peace and security they are like sheep, yielding milk, and wool, and many other useful things.... It is an army after the fashion of a peasantry, being liable to all manner of contributions and rendering without complaint whatever is enjoined upon it.... It is also a peasantry in the guise of an army, all of them, great or small, noble and base, in time of battle becoming swordsmen, archers and lancers and advancing in whatever manner the occasion requires.

When the army moved, the tribe moved with it. Immediately after the Great *Quriltai* (grand assembly of the Mongol nobility) of 1206, which confirmed him as Qa'an (Great Khan), Chinggis Khan began to consolidate power and reorganize his army in anticipation of expansion from the steppe into the sown, the settled lands southeast and west of his homelands. He knew that henceforth the nature of his military campaigns would change and that if he hoped to maintain the tribal unity that he had achieved he would have to strengthen and develop his armies.

EARLY REFORM

In order to strengthen and develop his armies he introduced the process of decimalization in which military units were divided into decimal units of 10, 100, 1,000, and 10,000, with the *tümen* of 10,000 being the major fighting unit. In addition, where possible he broke up tribal structures and rewarded with command postings those who had been loyal to him during the lean years of his rise to power. The breakup of the tribal composition of his fighting force was to have profound effects on the loyalty, discipline, and effectiveness of his army. Family and clan had been replaced by unit, and loyalty was given first to the unit and its commander and indeed ultimately to the Qa'an himself. The new decimal military structure completely undermined the old Turco-Mongol social setup, and a fundamental realignment took hold. Old tribal identities did not completely disappear, and those tribes such as the Önggüt and Qongirrat who had remained loyal to Temüjin throughout the hard years retained some integrity and sense of continued identity, whereas the Tatars, Merkits, Keraits, Naimans, and other former enemy clans were more forcefully and thoroughly broken up. Hence there existed examples of Önggüt *tümen* but never Tatar *tümen*. Tribal loyalty had been replaced with unit loyalty and obedience to the *tümen* commander. Ultimately, of course, loyalty and allegiance were awarded to the royal Golden family, the Chinggisids. As long as wealth and prosperity continued to roll in, that loyalty and allegiance did not waiver. Strict discipline and a well-defined chain of command with duties and responsibilities itemized and standardized gave every soldier a position in the brave new world that the Mongols were carving out for themselves.

The *ordu* (base camp) was a tightly regulated unit, and its layout and organization were often uniform so that newcomers and visitors would immediately know where to find the armory, the physician's tent, or the chief. The fighting men, which included all males from 14 to 60, were organized into the standard units, named *arbans* (10 men), *jaguns* (100 men), *minghans* (1,000 men), and *tümens* (10,000 men), and these units were overseen by the *tümen* quartermaster, called the *jurtchi*. Such an organization meant that no order would ever have to be given to more than 10 men at any one time. Transfers between units were forbidden. Soldiers fought as part of a unit, not as individuals. Individual soldiers, however, were responsible for their equipment, weapons, and up to five mounts. Their families and even their herds would accompany them on foreign expeditions.

KESHIG

Above all these various groupings, Chinggis created an elite force originally formed from his most loyal and longest serving companions. This bodyguard, whose size reflected the Great Khan's prestige and power rather than any imminent danger to his life, numbered 10,000 men at the time of the 1206 *quriltai*. The *keshig*, or imperial guard, were recruited from across all tribal barriers, and the unit's tasks multiplied as it increased in size. Membership in the *keshig* was regarded as a supreme honor, and as such, enlistment in its ranks was an alternative to the necessity of hostage taking for the highborn. The powerful nobility would be honored rather than shamed by the presence of their offspring in the imperial household. In addition, service in the royal household constituted military and administrative training. The *keshig* formed the breeding ground for the new elite and the future ruling classes. The children of any potential rival or source of conflict could therefore serve honorably at court and be painlessly co-opted into the ruling establishment.

The *keshig* were handsomely equipped and armed. An ordinary soldier in the imperial guard had precedence over a commander in the rest of the army. It was from this unit's ranks that the future generals and top commanders were selected. It was early recognized as a military academy as well as an administrative training school.

The training of the rest of the army was the responsibility of its officers. Officers were expected to inspect their troops regularly while on active service and to ensure that they were all fully equipped. This extended to such details as ensuring that each soldier had his own needle and thread, and if it were found that a soldier was underequipped or lacking in any item of clothing, armor, or weaponry, his commanding officer was deemed responsible and would be liable for punishment. During military engagement if any soldier lost or dropped any item of his personal gear or equipment, the man behind him would have to retrieve and return the lost item to its owner or suffer punishment, which could mean death. Death was also meted out to anyone who fled before the order to retire had been

issued, anyone looting before permission had been granted, and for desertion. Discipline was exceptionally strict in the Mongol army.

APPEARANCE

Descriptions of the Mongol troops all mentioned the heavy coats,
boots, and hats, which together added to their characteristic stockiness.
"They had broad faces, flat noses, prominent cheek bones, slit eyes, thick
lips, sparse beards, and straight black hair; swarthy skins, tanned by the
sun, wind and frost, they were short of stature and their stocky heavy
bodies were supported by bow legs."[2] The Persian poet Amir Khosrow
Delhavi (1253–1324), writing from outside the Mongol Empire, gave a
vivid description of a group of Mongol prisoners captured by the army
of the sultan of Delhi. Amir Khosrow's father had had to flee for his life
after the Mongols invaded his hometown of Balkh, and consequently the
son felt no great love for the Mongols.

Their eyes were so narrow and piercing that they might have bored a hole in a
brazen vessel, and their stench was more horrible than their colour. Their heads
were set on their bodies as if they had no necks, and their cheeks resembled leather
bottles full of wrinkles and knots. Their noses extended from cheekbone to cheekbone. Their nostrils resembled rotting graves, and from them the hair descended
as far as the lips. Their moustaches were of extravagant length, but the beards
about their chins were very scanty. Their chests, in colour half-black, half-white,
were covered with lice which looked like sesame growing on a bad soil. Their bodies, indeed, were covered with these insects, and their skins were as rough-grained
as shagreen leather, fit only to be converted into shoes.[3]

BASIC COSTUME

The basic costume of the Mongol fighting man was his everyday apparel.
It consisted of a heavy coat fastened at the waist by a leather belt. From
the belt would hang his sword, dagger, and possibly an ax. This long robe-
like coat would double over, left breast over right, and be secured with a
button a few inches below the right armpit. The coat might be lined with
fox, wolf, or lynx fur. Pockets in the coat could contain a stone for sharpening his weapons and arrowheads. Dried meat and curd wrapped in cloth
might also be found in this pocket. Underneath the coat, a shirtlike under-
garment with long, wide sleeves was commonly worn. Materials such as
silk and metallic thread were increasingly used. The richer soldiers would
wear garments fashioned from the skins of wolves, foxes, and even monkeys, whereas the poorer soldier would make do with dog or goat skins.
Lining was made from silk stuffing, which proved a very effective form of
insulation. The poor would line their outer garments with cotton cloth or
with the fine wool picked from the coarser wool used in making felt. Silk
became more and more common as the conquest of China proceeded.

The boots were made from felt and leather and though heavy would be comfortable and wide enough to accommodate the trousers tucked in before lacing tightly. They were heelless, though the soles were very thick and lined with fur. Worn with felt socks, the feet were unlikely to get cold. The characteristic Mongol hat was made of felt and fur.

Lamellar armor would be worn over the thick coat. The armor was composed of small scales of iron, chain mail, or hard leather sewn together with leather thongs and could weigh 10 kilograms if made of leather alone and more if the cuirass was made of metal scales. The leather used in armor was first softened by boiling. It was then coated in a crude lacquer made from pitch, which rendered it waterproof. Sometimes the soldier's heavy coat was simply reinforced with metal plates. Friar Giovanni DiPlano Carpini, an intelligence agent, reported in some detail on all aspects of the soldiers' apparel and equipment.

Mongol warrior's helmet, Hohhut Museum. Courtesy of Xinjiang Qinshan Culture Publishing

Helmets were cone shaped and composed of iron or steel plates of different sizes and included iron-plated neck guards. The Mongol cap was also conical in shape and made of quilted material with a large turned-up brim, reversible in winter, and earmuffs.

Combatants wore protective heavy silk undershirts, a practice learned from the Chinese. Even if an arrow pierced their mail or leather outer garment, the arrowhead was unlikely to completely pierce the silk. In this way, though a wound might be opened in the flesh, the actual metal would be tightly bound in the silk and so would be prevented from causing more extensive harm and would also be easier to withdraw later. The silk undershirt would be worn beneath a tunic of thick leather, layered armor plate or mail, and sometimes a cuirass of leather-covered iron scales. Whether the helmet was leather or metal depended on rank. Contemporary illustrations depict helmets with a central metal spike bending backward and others ending in a ball with a plume and wide neck guard shielding the shoulders and the jaws and neck.

HORSES

The Mongols protected their horses in the same way as they did themselves, covering them with lamellar armor. Horse armor was divided into five parts and designed to protect every part of the horse, including the forehead, which had a specially crafted plate which was tied on each side of the neck.

The Mongols' horses were small but powerful. During infancy all Mongols learned to ride and so became inseparable from their horses. It

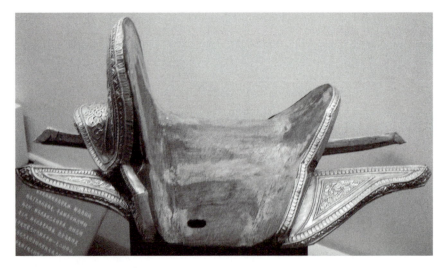

A Mongol saddle, wood coated in gold leaf, Hohhut Museum. Courtesy of Lan Tien Lang Publications

is estimated that each man had between 2 and 18 horses, with 5 or 6 being the norm. The horses were watered once a day and for the most part fed on grass. They were not ridden until they reached the age of three, and after they were broken in they never strayed, and several thousand could be assembled without problem. The horses were renowned for their stamina, and it is on record that one horse could cover 600 miles in nine days. It is unlikely that the horses were fitted with horseshoes at the time of the initial conquests, and Rashīd al-Dīn mentioned horseshoes as a "special precautionary measure." Thomas de Spalato, an eyewitness of the European campaigns, noted that Mongol horses "run around on rocks and stones without horseshoes as if they were wild goats." However, horses did wear saddles for their riders. They were made from oiled wood, high in the back and front so as to provide a tight fit for an archer to turn in the saddle and fire behind

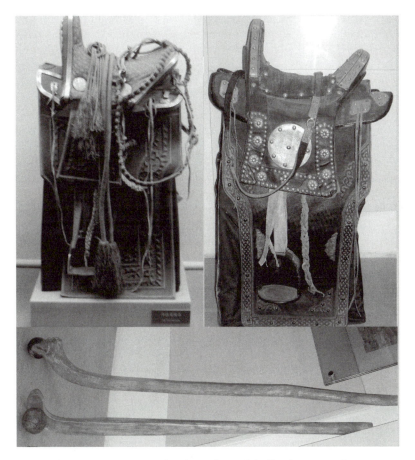

Mongol military saddles and polo sticks with balls. Courtesy of Xinjiang Qinshan Culture Publishing

as he continued to gallop forward, a maneuver for which the Mongols were famous. The efficiency of the postal system, the *yam*, bore testimony to the high quality of the Mongols' horses.

WEAPONS

The Mongols were famous for their mastery of firing their arrows in any direction while mounted and galloping at full speed. Strapped to their backs, their quivers contained 60 arrows and two bows made of bamboo, sinew, and yak horn. These composite reflex bows were first glued together and then bound in such a way that they set into a solid, extremely strong and durable piece. The bow was strung against its natural curve, which gave an exceptionally strong pull and enabled the archer to deliver a very accurate and deadly shot. The bow had a pull of 166 pounds and a destructive range of between 200 and 300 yards. A mounted archer would keep two or three bows accessible in a large protective bow case along with quivers containing 30 arrows with an assortment of arrowheads. The arrowheads were hardened by first heating over fire and then plunging the red-hot metal into brine. Such arrows were capable of piercing armor. Sometimes poison was added to the arrows. Eagle feathers were used for the fletching and could be made to whistle if needed for signaling purposes.

In hand-to-hand combat the soldier's best protection was the shield. It was usually small, round, and made of wood, osier, or wicker. It had to be light enough for the fighter to also wield his saber-shaped sword and ax. Carpini claimed that the shields were only employed by camp guards. Spears and maces of various designs, shapes, and weights would also be employed. If carrying and also using these weapons was not enough, the Mongol warrior was also weighed down with a lasso, a file, an iron cooking pot, two leather bottles, and a leather bag to keep equipment and clothes dry when crossing rivers. A tent, shared by 10 men, also had to be carried.

The light cavalry were armed with a small sword and two or three javelins, whereas the heavy horsemen carried a long lance (4 meters) fitted with a hook, a heavy mace or ax, and a scimitar (an oriental sword with a curved blade broadening toward the point). The hooks on the lance were used to drag an opponent from his horse.

The Franciscan Friar Giovanni DiPlano Carpini (1180–1264) traveled to the court of the Great Khan Güyük between 1245 and 1247 as a representative of the Pope Innocent IV. He was essentially a spy, though an extremely unlikely candidate at well over 60 years old and somewhat obese. He had knowledge of languages other than Latin, however, and as a friar he had experience with dealing with both the high and mighty and with the common rabble. His brief was to find out as much as possible about the dreaded Tatars, and this he succeeded in admirably. His report is particularly interesting where he reports on military matters. The following extract concerns soldiers' weapons.

Everyone must have at least these weapons: two or three bows or at least one good one, and three large quivers filled with arrows, a battle-axe and ropes for dragging machines. The rich, however, have swords which are sharp at the tip and honed on only one edge and somewhat curved, and they have horse armor, leg armor and a helmet and cuirass. Their cuirasses and horse armors are of leather and made this way: they take strips of cowhide or other animal hide of one hand's width wide, and they glue three or four of these together and tie them to each other with laces or cords. In the top strip they put the cords at the edge, in the one below they put them in the center and they do this until the end. Therefore, when the soldiers bend, the lower strips slide up over the upper ones and so they are doubled or even tripled over the body.

The Tartars make horse armor in five parts: they put one piece along each side of the horse which protects it from the tail to the head and is tied to the saddle, behind the saddle on the back, and at the neck. Over the horse's back they put another piece where the two parts of the harness are joined and they make a hole in this piece through which they expose the tail, while in front of the chest they place a piece that protects everything from the knees or the knee joints. On the forehead they put an iron plate which is tied on each side of the neck.[4]

On campaign all fighting men were expected to carry their equipment and provisions as well as their weaponry. A horsehair lasso, a coil of stout rope, an awl, needle and thread, cooking pots, leather water bottles, and a file for sharpening arrows would be among the utilities possibly carried in an inflatable saddlebag fashioned from a cow's stomach. When fording rivers, this saddlebag, if inflated, could double as a float.

When not on campaign life was not so very different. War simply entailed some modifications to the Mongols' daily life. As nomads, the Mongols continued to practice seasonal migration from the open plains of summer to the sheltered valleys of the winter months. Distances were not great, with a typical route encompassing 100 miles. To adapt to a war footing would not necessarily have to entail a great change in routine, though careful planning and preparation would be an essential part of such military migration.

BATTLE

The Mongol army operated according to the dictum march divided, attack united. They traveled in widely dispersed columns, though at all times good communications were maintained. Messengers with fresh, ready, saddled horses were kept with every unit, and smoke signals were also employed to keep constant contact. This high level of communication meant that the dispersed columns of the army could be reunited very rapidly and also enabled the Mongols to utilize one of their favorite military tactics, the feigned retreat. Countless times the unwitting enemy was drawn into pursuit of a retreating Mongol column only later to find itself surrounded in a deadly trap.

Before entering into battle the Mongols employed their vast intelligence network of spies and scouts. The physical landscape was scoured for information advantageous to an advancing army. Grazing ground, water supplies, food sources, secure camping ground, possible battle sites, and lookout points all had to be assessed and considered before the army moved. In addition human intelligence was gathered in order to maximize any advantages to be gained from an enemy's weaknesses. To gathering intelligence, the spies and scouts would also sow disinformation and cast doubt in order to weaken enemy morale. Nobody ever surprised the Mongols. The Mongols valued intelligence highly and early appreciated the advantages to be gained from a thorough knowledge of the enemy terrain, brain, and any rivalries and splits within the enemy ranks, especially those that they could exploit. Psychological warfare was a key component of their expanding repertoire.

Once contact had been made with the enemy, usually through scouts sent up to 70 miles ahead of the main army, the main body of the army would begin to extend its front, stretching it so as to envelop the enemy forces. Skirmishes would be initiated in order to test the enemy's fortitude, but full-scale clashes were avoided until the Mongols were ready. If the enemy was weak and small, the Mongol vanguard might deal with the situation itself, but if it was larger and more formidable, the advance party would attempt to lure the enemy troops back into the waiting arms of the main army. Once the trap had been sprung there was no escape.

The scenario had been rehearsed many times before during the *nerge*, in which all Mongols partook. Standard battle formation consisted of five *jaguns* separated by wide intervals. The front two *jaguns* were made up of heavy cavalry armed with maces, swords, lances, and armored horses. Behind them the other three *jaguns* were composed of light cavalry wearing little if any armor and armed with bows and javelins. The light cavalry would advance through gaps in the ranks of heavy cavalry and pour volleys of arrows and spears into the enemy ranks while at the same time advancing the flanks on either side and thereby initiating an encircling movement known as the *tulughma*. If the original attack was forced back, the archers would calmly withdraw shooting as they did so, and their positions would simply be replaced by fresh light cavalry. As soon as the enemy became sufficiently weakened and disheartened, the heavy cavalry would be sent in to deliver the *coup de grâce*.

All the battle formations and tactics performed before the charge of the heavy cavalry were carried out in silence, with orders and communication transmitted wordlessly using black and white flags and, at night, lanterns. As soon as the signal for the charge of the heavy cavalry was given, a mighty roar went up, and the pounding roll of the *naccara* war drums carried on a Bactrian camel unleashed the screaming hordes of mongols. Simultaneously, the light cavalry poured in from either side, quickly closing the pincer movement. However, Mongol cunning dictated that this pincer movement should never completely close and so force the enemy to fight in desperation to the last man. Such desperation would cost the Mongols lives, which they were keen to avoid. Instead, they would allow a means of escape for which the desperate enemy would scramble. These fleeing stragglers could then be picked off in the open at the Mongols' convenience and leisure. A beaten and demoralized army could be pursued for days, providing not only sport for the Mongol soldiery but excellent propaganda as the harassed and hungry enemy terrorized the countryside, plundering and pillaging in their desperation and earning the contempt and hatred of the people. The Khwārazmshāh's army spent years after 1220 spreading fear and mayhem around Iran after their routing by the Mongols. Eventually they were more feared and despised than the Mongols themselves.

Even though the Mongols' tactic of a feigned retreat was well known, it continued to work whenever they used it. One famous example of the feigned retreat was prolonged over nine days. This occurred during the legendary reconnaissance trip of the *noyans* (generals) Subodai and Jebe circa 1222 in a confrontation with Russian princes and their Cuman Turk allies. The Mongols retreated before the pursuing enemy, but at the same time they slowly spread their forces wide so that eventually they were able to turn and snare in a pincer movement the rapidly advancing vanguard of the Russian-Cuman forces, which had become separated from the main body of their army. The Franciscan spy Carpini warned his readers of this tactic in his report to the pope. "Even if the Tatars retreat our men ought not to separate from each other or be split up, for the Tatars pretend to withdraw in order to divide an enemy." Carpini recommended the use of crossbows against the Mongols, noting that they were very afraid of them, and also lances with hooks with which to pull them from their saddles. Carpini reckoned that Mongols could easily be pulled from their horses by means of these lances and hooks.

The following extract from Mustawfī's epic, the *Zafarnāmeh*, is an account of a very unequally pitted battle, which was valiantly fought by the losers. Though he wrote the poem more than a century after the battle Mustawfī would have known relatives and acquaintances of eyewitnesses to the terrible events because his family of notables had played an important role in the affairs of Qazvin for a great many years and Mustawfī had sought out eyewitnesses whenever possible for many of the events he was to relate in his histories.

> Thence [from Zanjan] to the town of Qazvin, Subutay
> Like raging tiger came right speedily.

The tale of years at six, one, seven stood
When that fair town became a lake of blood,
And Sha'ban's month had counted seven days' [7th Sha'bān, 617 AH = 7 Oct.
     1220 CE]
When it was filled with woe and sore amaze.
The governor who held the ill-starred town
Muzaffar named, a ruler of renown,
Was, by the Caliph's most august command,
Set to control the fortunes of the land.
When came the hosts of war and direful fate
Firm as a rock they closed the city gate.
Upon the wall the warriors took their place,
And each towards the Mongols set his face.
Three days they kept the ruthless foe at bay,
But on the fourth they forced a blood-stained way.
Fiercely the Mongols entered Qazvin Town
And heads held high before were now brought down.
No quarter in that place the Mongols gave:
The days were ended of each chieftain brave.
Nothing could save the townsmen from their doom,
And all were gathered in one common tomb.
Alike of great and small, of old and young,
The lifeless bodies in the dust they flung:
Both men and women shared a common fate:
The luck-forsaken land lay desolate.
Many a fair one in that fearful hour
Sought death to save her from the invaders' power:
Chaste maidens of the Prophet's progeny
Who shone like asteroids in Virtue's sky,
Fearing the lust of that ferocious host
Did cast them down, and so gave up the ghost.
Much in that land prevails the Shafi'ite [Muslim sect];
One in a thousand is a Hanafite [Muslim sect];
And yet they counted on that gory plain
Twelve thousand Hanafites amongst the slain !
In heaps on every side the corpses lay,
Alike on lonely path and broad highway.
Uncounted bodies cumbered every street:
Scarce might one find a place to set one's feet.
In terror of the Mongol soldiery
Hither and thither did the people fly,
Some seeking refuge to the Mosque did go,
Hearts filled with anguish, souls surcharged with woe.
From that fierce foe so sore their straits and plight
That climbing forms the arches hid from sight
The ruthless Mongols burning brands did ply
Till tongues of flame leapt upwards to the sky.
Roof, vault and arch in burning ruin fell,
A heathen holocaust of Death and Hell![5]

THE *NERGE*

The *nerge,* or hunt, was not only a source of entertainment and food but was vital in the training of the Mongol army as a disciplined and coordinated fighting force. The preparation and logistics required for the *nerge* could be transferred to a war footing if the army were needed for combat. The *nerge* was a regular part of Eurasian life and culture in which the whole extended tribe took part. Everybody was involved in the various tasks, duties, and demands of the *nerge* so that if instead of the hunting of animals the action was the hunting of men, the disruption was of the same order.

From an early age all Mongol children learned horsemanship and archery. This was prescribed by law. The maneuvers and battlefield tactics were drilled into the Mongol citizenry by constant practice. Chinggis Khan formalized the Great Hunt, the *nerge,* as a military training exercise. The *nerge* was a vast, highly organized, and strictly regulated hunt that at its most basic replenished the tribe's meat supplies for the coming winter. However, as Juwaynī (died 1282), an eyewitness historian and later governor of Baghdad for the Mongol Il-Khans, was quick to note, this chase was far more than a Mongol shopping trip.

Now war—with its killing, counting of the slain and sparing of the survivors—is after the same fashion, and indeed analogous in every detail, because all that is left in the neighbourhood of the battlefield are a few broken-down wretches.[6]

The *nerge* was training practice for war and battle. Stealth, tight communications, horsemanship, and coordination were all essential skills honed and perfected during the *nerge.* The Mongols learned the disciplined teamwork for which they were both admired and feared from these annual events. The *nerge* would be held in winter and would last three months, and every soldier and most of the tribe would participate. It would be a morale booster and excellent practice for the real thing. All military skills would be honed during the course of the Great Hunt, particularly discipline, coordination of units, and most essentially close, effective communications.

The overall strategy and development of the hunt was usually the same. A starting line, possibly 80 miles long, would be established by huntsmen, who would plant flags at various assembly points to position the *tümens* (units of 10,000) that would be taking part in the *nerge.* Another flag, hundreds of miles distant, would be planted to mark the suitable finishing point. On a signal from the khan this vast line of fully armed, battle-ready troops would begin to move forward, and before them all wildlife would flee. Over the next few weeks as the amount of game and other animals increased, the two flanks of this vast army would move ahead and slowly close in on their prey. The two wings would aim to pass the finishing flag and then move closer in order to eventually meet up with each other, thereby trapping the increasingly frantic animals in a circle. The hunters would form a vast ring over a huge expanse of land. This human ring would then slowly contract, driving every living beast within its circumference toward its center. Shifts would be employed to ensure that a vigil was kept at all times, with even the sleeping troops fully clothed and ready for action. Any hunter who allowed any game to escape the diminishing circle could expect severe punishment, as could anyone who killed any animal before the allotted time.

And if, unexpectedly, any game should break through, a minute inquiry is made into the cause and reason, and the commanders of thousands, hundreds, and tens are clubbed therefore, and even put to death. And if ... a man does not keep to the line ... but takes a step forwards or backwards, severe punishment is dealt out to him and is never remitted.[7]

The initial line of fully armed, mounted men, which might have been as long as 130 kilometers before the flanks had formed, would now be compressed into a tightly knit human stadium with an arena of hysterical and highly dangerous animals at its core. The khan would be waiting with his own smaller line of troops at a predetermined spot chosen for its suitability for the final entrapment, possibly hundreds of kilometers from the starting line.

Here there becomes massed together an extraordinary multitude of wild beasts, such as lions, wild oxen, bears, stags, and a great variety of others, and all in a state of the greatest alarm. For there is such a prodigious noise and uproar ... that a person cannot hear what his neighbour says; and all the unfortunate beasts quiver with terror at the disturbance.[8]

When the frantic roaring and screeching horde of terrified animals was finally massed together, the khan would make the first kill, and this would be the signal for the massacre to commence. Animals destined for the kitchens and cookhouses might be cleanly and swiftly killed, whereas others would have to earn their deaths. Sometimes the Great Khan and some of his retinue would disport themselves killing game before the lesser princes would be allowed to start. When these princes in turn had tired of their sport, the ordinary soldiers would be let loose on the unfortunate captives. All knew that the Great Khan and commanders were present and witnessing the fun, and therefore the *nerge* was seen as an opportunity for the soldiery to demonstrate their skills and valor against often very ferocious animals. Unarmed combat, sword and knife fighting, on foot and on horseback, and other martial skills would all be demonstrated in the hope of attracting the attention of the commanders to the dexterity and talents of the individual soldier.

Some animals would be retained for breeding, and some would be symbolically released, though most would end up with the kitchen staff. A Mongol tradition had young princes and old soldiers come before the khan to plead for the life of remaining animals, and the khan's subsequent act of clemency signaled the end of the hunt. After the *nerge,* nine days of feasting and revelry would ensue. The remaining food would be distributed throughout the various units to ensure that all who had participated in the great event had their due share of the booty.

The *nerge* perfected the Mongols' communications system, which utilized frequent couriers, flag waving, torch burning, and an efficient, highly effective network of staging posts called the *yam,* for which history has long recorded its admiration. It provided provisions for the tribe and entertainment for all. Most important perhaps was the *nerge's* ability to provide battle experience for the troops the worth of which has been proved many times.

The *nerge* attracted the imagination of not only travelers who journeyed east and witnessed it firsthand, such as Friar Odoric of Pordenone (traveled 1316–1330), but also of those who heard tales of the chase back in Europe. Edward Gibbons gave a vivid account of the *nerge* in his epic history the *Decline and Fall of the Roman Empire.*

The pastoral life, compared with the labours of agriculture and manufactures, is undoubtedly a life of idleness; and as the most honourable shepherds of the Tartar race devolve on their captives the domestic management of the cattle, their own leisure is seldom disturbed by any servile and assiduous cares. But this leisure, instead of being devoted to the soft enjoyments of love and harmony, is usefully spent in the violent and sanguinary exercise of the chase. The plains of Tartary are filled with a strong and serviceable breed of horses, which are easily trained for the purposes of war and hunting. The Scythians of every age have been celebrated as bold and skilful riders, and constant practice had seated them so firmly on horseback that they were supposed by strangers to perform the ordinary duties of civil life, to eat, to drink, and even to sleep, without dismounting from their steeds. They excel in the dexterous management of the lance; the long Tartar bow is drawn with a nervous arm, and the weighty arrow is directed to its object with unerring aim and irresistible force. These arrows are often pointed against the harmless animals of the desert, which increase and multiply in the absence of their most formidable enemy—the hare, the goat, the roebuck, the fallow-deer, the stag, the elk, and the antelope. The vigour and patience both of the men and horses are continually exercised by the fatigues of the chase, and the plentiful supply of game contributes to the subsistence and even luxury of a Tartar camp. But the exploits of the hunters of Scythia are not confined to the destruction of timid or innoxious beasts: they boldly encounter the angry wild boar when he turns against his pursuers, excite the sluggish courage of the bear, and provoke the fury of the tiger as he slumbers in the thicket. Where there is danger, there may be glory; and the mode of hunting which opens the fairest field to the exertions of valour may justly be considered as the image and as the school of war. The general hunting matches, the pride and delight of the Tartar princes, compose an instructive exercise for their numerous cavalry. A circle is drawn, of many miles in circumference, to encompass the game of an extensive district; and the troops that form the circle regularly advance towards a common centre, where the captive animals, surrounded on every side, are abandoned to the darts of the hunters. In this march, which frequently continues many days, the cavalry are obliged to climb the hills, to swim the rivers, and to wind through the valleys, without interrupting the prescribed order of their gradual progress. They acquire the habit of directing their eye and their steps to a remote object, of preserving their intervals, of suspending or accelerating their pace according to the motions of the troops on their right and left, and of watching and repeating the signals of their leaders. Their leaders study in this practical school the most important lesson of the military art, the prompt and accurate judgment of ground, of distance, and of time. To employ against a human enemy the same patience and valour, the same skill and discipline, is the only alteration which is required in real war, and the amusements of the chase serve as a prelude to the conquest of an empire.[9]

The *nerge* formed an essential element in Mongol life. The following four writers deal with aspects of this activity, by which no visitor to the Mongol court could fail to be impressed. Juwaynī, the writer of the first account, was brought up in the Mongol court and later became governor of Baghdad under the Il-Khan Hülegü, and he must have witnessed, if not taken part in, the *nerge* many times. Friar Odoric of Pordenone traveled eastward between 1316 and 1330, and he was witness to the great chase in China under the rule of the Yüan dynasty. William of Rubruck traveled through Russia and Eurasia to reach Qaraqorum between 1253 and 1255, and he too remarks on the importance of the chase. Rashīd al-Dīn, credited with being the first man to compose a true world history, became prime minister of the Persian Empire under Ghazan Khan. He also forged ever closer trade and cultural links with China, cemented with his close links with the Mongol renaissance man Bolad Chinksank.

[Chinggis Khan] took the business of the chase very seriously and would say that the hunting and corralling was a suitable occupation for the commanders of armies; and that instruction and training was obligatory on warriors and men-at-arms, [who should learn] how the huntsmen come up with the prey, how they hunt it, how they adorn themselves and in what way they encircle the prey depending whether it is great or small. For when the Mongols wish to go hunting, scouts are first dispatched to determine what kinds of game are available and whether it is limited or abundant. And when they are not busy in the affairs of the army, they are always eager for the chase and their armies are encouraged as such to engage themselves [in hunting]; not only for the hunt, but also in order that they may become accustomed and hardened to hunting and familiarized with the use of the bow and the endurance of hardships. Whenever the Khan sets out on the great hunt which takes place at the start of the winter season, he issues orders that the troops stationed around his headquarters and in the neighbourhood of the *ordus* should prepare for the hunt, saddling up several men from each unit of ten according to instructions and distributing equipment such as arms and other things which are appropriate for the location where it is intended to hunt. The right wing, left wing and centre of the army are drawn up and put under the command to the great emirs; and they set out together with the Royal Ladies *(khavātīn)* and the concubines, and also provisions of food and drink. For a month, or two, or three they form a hunting ring and drive the prey slowly and gradually before them, taking care that none escape from the ring. And if, by chance, any game should break through, an investigation is carried out into the causes and reasons, and the commanders of thousands, hundreds and tens are beaten, and often killed. And if, for example, a man does not keep to the line which they call *nerge*, but takes a step forwards or backwards, he is severely punished and is never excused. For two or three months, by day and by night, they drive the game in this manner, like a flock of sheep, and envoys are sent to the Khan to inform him of the condition of the hunt, its scarcity or plenty, where it has reached and from where it fled. Finally, when the ring has been contracted to a diameter of two or three parasangs, they tie ropes together and cover them in felts. Meanwhile the troops come to a halt around the circle, standing shoulder to shoulder. The ring is now filled with the cries and commotion of every manner of game and the roaring and tumult of every kind of ferocious beast; all thinking that the appointed hour of "And when the wild beasts shall be gathered together" is come; lions becoming familiar with wild asses, hyenas friendly with foxes, wolves intimate with hares. When the circle has been so much contracted that the wild beasts are unable to stir, first the Khan rides in together with some of his retinue; then, after he has wearied of the sport, they dismount upon high ground in the centre of the *nerge* to watch the princes entering the ring in the same way, and after them, in due order, the noyans, the commanders and the troops. Several days are spent in this manner; then, when nothing is left of the game but a few wounded and emaciated stragglers, old men and greybeards humbly approach the Khan, offer up prayers for his well-being and plead for the lives of the remaining animals asking that they be allowed to depart to some place nearer to grass and water. Finally, they collect together all the game that they have bagged; and if the counting of every species of animal proves impracticable they count only the beasts of prey and the wild asses.[10]

Ship from Rashīd al-Dīn's *Jami' al-Tavarikh*. Courtesy of Lan Tien Lang
Publications

**The Hunt as
Witnessed by
Friar Odoric**

The Franciscan Friar Odoric was born in 1286, though
some claim 1274 more probable, and died in January
1331. He set out on his missionary travels to China and
India sometime between 1316 and 1318 and returned
in 1330. Before his travels began he had earned himself
a reputation for sanctity and miracles. His travels commenced in Constantinople from where he headed for the lands of the Il-Khanate. He traveled
extensively in Iran before boarding a ship bound for India. He embarked
at Malabar before continuing by sea eastward via Ceylon (Sri Lanka),
Sumatra, Java, Champa (Vietnam), Guangzhou, Hangzhou, and sailed
up the grand canal to the Yüan capital, Khan Baliq (Beijing). He returned
home overland, passing through Kabul and Tabriz en route back to Venice.
He was accompanied on this epic journey by an Irishman, Friar James. His
account of the hunt is interesting in that he describes the practice in China
more than 50 years after the Persian Juwaynī's report.

When the Great Khan goes hunting 'tis thus ordered: At some twenty days'
journey from Cambalech [Khan Baliq, Beijing, Ta-tu, Daidu], there is a fine
forest of eight days' journey in compass; and in it are such multitudes and

varieties of animals as are truly wonderful. All round this forest there be keepers posted on account of the Khan, to take diligent charge thereof; and every third or fourth year he goeth with his people to this forest. On such occasions they first surround the whole forest with beaters, and let slip the dogs [and lions and lionesses and other tamed beasts trained to this business] and the hawks trained to this sport, and then gradually closing in upon the game, they drive it to a certain fine open spot that there is in the middle of the wood. Here there becomes massed together an extraordinary multitude of wild beasts, such as lions, wild oxen, bears, stags, and a great variety of others, and all in a state of the greatest alarm. For there is such a prodigious noise and uproar raised by the birds and the dogs that have been let slip into the wood, that a person cannot hear what his neighbour says; and all the unfortunate wild beasts quiver with terror at the disturbance. And when they all have been driven together into that open glade, the Great Khan comes up on three elephants and shoots five arrows at the game. As soon as he has shot, the whole of his retinue do likewise. And when all have shot their arrows (each man's arrows having a token by which they may be discerned), then the Great Emperor causeth to be called out "*Syo!*" which is to say as it were "*Quarter*" to the beasts (to wit) that have been driven from the wood. Then [the huntsmen sound the recall and call in the dogs and hawks from the prey and] the animals which have escaped with life are allowed to go back into the forest, and all the barons come forward to view the game that has been killed and to recover the arrows that they have shot (which they can well do by the marks on them); and everyone has what his arrow has struck. And such is the order of the Khan's hunting.[11]

They obtain a large proportion of their food by the chase. When they intend to hunt wild animals, they gather in great numbers and surround the area where they know wild beasts are to be found, gradually converging until the animals are enclosed in the middle in a kind of circle; then they shoot them with their arrows.[12]

The *Nerge* and William of Rubruck

Rashīd al-Dīn

He had ordered that at [Ögödei Qa'an's] winter quarters in Ong Qin a two-day-journey-long wall made of wood and clay be constructed. Gates were put into it and it was named a *chihik*. When a hunt was held [*ulām*], soldiers from all sides would be informed so that all of them would form a circle and head for the wall, driving the game toward it. From a one-month's journey away, taking the utmost precautions and exchanging intelligence at all times, they drove all the prey to the *chihik,* and then the soldiers would form a circle standing shoulder to shoulder. First

[Ögödai] Qa'an and his elite would enter the circle, amuse themselves for a time killing the animals. When he grew weary, he would go to some high ground within the circle and the princes and amirs in their turn would enter. Then the commoners and soldiers would take their turn to hunt. Then they would release some [of the animals] for breeding [*uruqlamishi*] and the *boka'uls* [*bökä'ül;* court taster, officer in charge of army provisions] would distribute all the game among the princes, amirs, and army so that no one was without a share. Then all that assembly would perform the ceremony of *tigishmishi* [presentation of gifts], and after nine days of banqueting every tribe would return to its yurt and home.[13]

In modern-day Afghanistan, the game of *buzkashi* (goat killing or goat pulling) is still played and continues to draw large, very enthusiastic crowds to watch. It is commonly believed that this game is based on sports practiced by the Mongols.

SIZE

Though speaking generally, in the medieval period size did matter, and as a rule large armies defeated small armies. This truism proved false, however, in the case of Mongol armies. It was Mongol discipline, training, and battle strategy that often won the day rather than just brute force of numbers. So thorough was the training, preparation, and discipline that few medieval armies stood much of a chance when confronted with a Mongol formation. Robert of Spolato, who witnessed firsthand the Mongol invasion of Europe, considered them to be invincible on the open field, such were their martial skills. When the Mongols were famously defeated in 1260 at 'Ain Jālūt it was because in the Mamluk army riding out of Egypt they confronted what could have been a reflection of themselves. The Mamluk army was composed of Turks, Mongols, and Caucasian troops, much the same as the composition of the Mongol army itself.

The Mongol army was often believed to be larger than it actually was due to their mobility and their technique of envelopment. It was organized into two wings and a central body that would often be composed of the imperial guard or elite troops and it was able to fan out into a pincer formation with a deadly sting at its center. *The Secret History of the Mongols* suggests an army of 105,000 at the time of the Great *Quriltai* of 1206. At the time of Chinggis Khan's death Rashīd al-Dīn put the army at 123,000 men with 62,000 assigned to the left wing, 38,000 to the right wing, and 23,000 to the center. As the armies moved southward, eastward, and westward absorbing manpower from captured territory, these figures would have increased accordingly, and by the time of Ögödei's death in 1241 the Mongol army was considerably larger. Jūzjānī, writing

The national sport of Afghanistan, Buzkashi, originates from the Mongols.
Courtesy of Abu Hajal Company

Buzkashi. Courtesy of Abu Hajal Company

outside the Mongol area in Delhi, claimed that the forces that attacked the Khwārazmshāh numbered 700,000 or 800,000, whereas the Mamluk fourteenth-century chronicler al-'Umarī reckoned the Il-Khans had an army of between 200,000 to 300,000. He claims that the Golden Horde sent an army of 250,000 to invade Transoxiana at the end of the thirteenth century.

Most of the Mongol army would have been mounted, with up to five horses assigned to each soldier. Add to this other provisions, which might include a slave or two, a weapons wagon, and a small herd of sheep and goats, it was not only a logistical nightmare in the making for the army commanders but a major calamity waiting to strike the towns, villages, and lands through which this martial storm intended to pass. Some contemporary historians have calculated the Mongol army as many as 800,000 in 1220, in which case a storm of 4 million horses and 24 million sheep and goats in addition to the highly armed troops would have swept across central Asia and Khorasan after the sacking of Bokhara. Such an invasion would have been devastating even without the military aspect. However the matter of the actual numerical size of the Mongol armies has still not been decided by historians.

One reason for the uncertainty and confusion is that contemporary sources often quote the number of army units or the number of commanders of *tümens,* for example. However, though theoretically a *tümen* consisted of 10,000 men and a commander of a *tümen* had 10,000 men under his command, this was rarely the case, and in reality numbers could be very considerably less. To observers of the army on the move, especially on maneuvers or on the attack, numbers were made deliberately difficult to calculate. Dummies were placed on spare horses and branches were pulled behind the mounted cavalry as a means to create the impression of a larger force.

The Mongol historian David Morgan has argued convincingly that the exaggerated figures given in the sources for the size of the Mongol forces cannot be taken literally simply because the land would not have been able to sustain such a large force. Juwaynī has shown how the Mongols, and Hülegü in particular, were able to deal with the logistical problems of maneuvering and supplying a huge army with considerable expertise. But whatever the level of competence, if the land itself was arid no amount of expertise could extract sufficient sustenance for an army of the size suggested by some contemporary sources, particularly the Mamluk sources from Egypt. Morgan believes that the Mongol's failure to conquer Syria was due primarily to the lack of pastures there.

The only conclusion that can safely be made is that Mongol armies were far larger than European armies of that time but probably smaller than the armies that could be raised by either the Chinese Song or Chin emperors or by the Khwārazmshāh. All three were soundly defeated despite their numerically stronger armies, which proved that in the case of the Mongols size did not matter.

PROPAGANDA

Propaganda and terror were also tools of the Mongol army. So terrible was their reputation that victory was often achieved without actual fighting. They deliberately exaggerated and encouraged the horror stories that circulated about them and preceded their arrival in order to ensure an unhesitating surrender of the cowed population. This ploy was so effective that it is this element of their conquests that shapes their reputation to this day. The Mongols encouraged the stories of slaughter, brutality, and cruelty. It was a fundamental edict of the Great *Yasa* (law) of Chinggis Khan that any opponent, enemy, or rival should first be offered the opportunity to surrender before military might be brought to bear. This escape clause was offered verbally or in writing. However, in its stark simplicity, it remained chilling, the menace of those few words, heavy. "And if ye do otherwise [than surrender], what do we know? God knoweth."[14] The words of Ibn al-Athir have been responsible for much of the negative propaganda spread throughout the Islamic world and hence into Europe. His harrowing words sent a chill through every mosque and every madrassa and tea house in which they were read. "Oh that my mother had not born me, or that I had died and become a forgotten thing ere this befell!" And yet, Ibn al-Athir was not an eyewitness but was only repeating the stories that refugees from the east, all in need of charity and aid, had reported to him and the crowds that gathered to listen to their tales of woe. The result of such rumor mongering Ibn al-Athir acknowledges himself in the following extract from his chronicle.

"Stories have been related to me," he says, "which the hearer can scarcely credit, as to the terror of them [the Mongols] which God Almighty cast into men's hearts; so that it is said that a single one of them would enter a village or a quarter wherein were many people, and would continue to slay them one after another none daring to stretch forth his hand against this horseman. And I have heard that one of them took a man captive, but had not with him any weapon wherewith to kill him; and he said to his prisoner, 'Lay your head on the ground and do not move'; and he did so and the Tartar went and fetched his sword and slew him therewith." Another man related to me as follows; "I was going," said he "with seventeen others along a road, and there met us a Tartar horseman, and bade us bind one another's arms. My companions began to do as he bade them, but I said to them, 'He is but one man; wherefore, then, should we not kill him and flee?' They replied, 'We are afraid.' I said, 'This man intends to kill you immediately; let us therefore rather kill him, that perhaps God may deliver us.' But I swear by God that not one of them dared to do this, so I took a knife and slew him, and we fled and escaped. And such occurrences were many."[15]

News that a Mongol advance was imminent was enough to cause panic at worst but more often surrender. This suited the Mongols, who were enjoying the fruits of their conquests and earlier ruthlessness. This terror saved lives, Mongol lives in particular, and as the Mongols became increasingly aware of the paucity of their numbers as their empire expanded, they tried to avoid bloody confrontation if it were possible. They were quite prepared to commit the strategic atrocity if by so doing would result in a speedy end to hostilities. Even Hülegü, who entered Iran in triumph and was generally welcomed on his arrival in the 1250s, perpetrated acts of dreadful barbarity, possibly to stoke the embers of fear and dread of the ire of the Mongols. He showed no mercy when his vassals attempted to defy his will.

The following account, taken from Mustawfi's *Zafarnāmeh*, reminds us that the medieval world was a cruel and unforgiving age. Hülegü was not

Tusi's observatory, built on Hulegu's orders.
Courtesy of Abu Hajal Company

noted for his cruelty, but the uniquely ugly form of torture is particularly shocking.

Then King Gamil was taken prisoner at the hands of the army, and the Turks bore him and his brother quickly to the prince, and from the city the prince sent them to Hulegu's high throne. When his eyes fell on them anger surged in Hulegu's heart, and animosity overcame him, and his heart became warlike against Gamil. He recounted Gamil's offences, and his heart and soul grew faint. His lion like spirit left him, and helplessly he trembled in fear for his life, like a willow. Hülegü said to the executioner, "Quickly put him to a painful death." They severed the flesh from his body and put it in his mouth, and he died in agony. In this way, the day became black for him. After this, his brother was cut in two, and people's hearts were filled with fear as a result.[16]

Shortly after this Hülegü had cause to deal harshly with a noble who had not only acted treasonably toward his new king but had badly treated

Tusi's observatory. Courtesy of Abu Hajal Company

a wife that Hülegü had personally chosen for and awarded to him. Though Salih Malik pleaded for mercy and invoked the many years of loyal service of his father ,the Mongol king remained implacable and merciless.

> But the amir immediately sent him to the ruler of the world. Hulegu was fiercely angry with him, for he had broken his pledge with open impudence. He ordered that he should be stripped naked, and the courage of the oath breaker put to the torture. They made a hoop from an animal's tail and tied it round him with felt, like a rope girdle. They thus dressed him with the robe of honour of an enemy, and, full of hate, took him to the plain, following the order quickly. They tied him there in the sun and left him there, until the pain and lamentation of his soul brought that man to his end. It was so warm in that month of Murdad, for the sun was in the sign of Leo, an auspicious one. Notice how fate arranged it, that the heat brought doom to that man. They tied that man down on that wretched plain and left him there at the command of the shah. When the heat passed through the animal's tail, it putrefied and worms grew in it. After a month of putrefaction in the heat the soul of that ruler longed for death, for when the worms had eaten all of the tail, then the man's body became their food. They began to eat him completely, and the agony of the worms feeding on him, gave him a terrible death. He died from the pain and agony and distress. In that place he gave over his soul to good. What evil is done in the world, you might ask, when this kind of retribution comes to a man? Anyone who does not oppress another does not see the reality of pain and sorrow. Salih had a son of three years old, and heaven sent a letter of retribution to him too. The prince sent him to Mosul, and there they cut his body into two pieces. They hung the two pieces of his body on each side of the river, until there was nothing left of his body but warp and woof. The flesh putrefied, and sometimes dripped, and in this way calamity caused his stock to meet the dust. The hearts of the people of the world were pleased that his race had come to an end, in this way.[17]

THE *YAM*

The *yam* and *barīd*, which became the communications network for the empire, are first mentioned during Ögödei Khan's reign. It must be assumed that it developed during the expanding years of his father's rule, and then in 1234 Ögödei set up a properly organized network that in future years was to so impress visitors and merchants to the Mongol Empire. *Yam* is a Mongol term and the term most commonly employed in the Persian sources of the time, whereas *barīd* is an Arabic term used to describe the horse relay stations of the cAbbāsids (749–1258) and the later communications network of the Mamluks of Egypt, which in fact was a development of the Mongols' *yam* system. Much of what is known of the functioning of the *yam* is from later sources that detail various reforms of the system and often lambaste the failings of the operation under former rulers. Praise comes from many sources, however, including Marco Polo, who claims that distances of between 200 and 250 miles a day could be covered by the Great Khan's couriers, adding that "these strong, enduring messengers are highly prized men."[18] The *yam* operating in China, from where it originated, seems to have been more effectual than the Persian system, but whatever the criticisms of the sources whose authors so often had their own agendas, this network of fresh horses, couriers, supply houses, and escorts succeeded in establishing a remarkable degree of cohesion and communication over such a vast empire.

The network was run by the army, and therefore it crisscrossed the whole expanse of Mongol controlled territory from Eastern Europe to the Sea of Japan. Posthouses were established every three or four *farsangs* (*farsang, parsang, farsakh* = three to four-and-a-half miles), and each *yam* had at least 15 horses in good condition and ready to go or if Marco Polo is to be believed between 200 and 400 ready mounts. Rashīd al-Dīn put the figure at 500 mounts, but it can be assumed that different routes would have different requirements. *Ilchis* (messengers, representatives) would be authorized to make use of these waiting horses as well as replenish their supplies or seek shelter if their journey was to be continued by another waiting *īlchi*. Though the army was entrusted with operating and replenishing these numerous *yam* stations, it was the local peasantry who supplied the food, fodder, and generous provisions that were made available to the *īlchīs* and others passing through. One of the abuses of the *yam* system that was rectified by later reforms was the frequent use made of these facilities by merchants. Officially, only persons on official business and in possession of a tablet of authority, a *paiza,* made of wood, silver, or gold and engraved in the Uighur script with a tiger or gyrfalcon at its head were permitted to make use of the *yam* services. However, the heavy burden the *yam* stations inflicted on the locals suggests that many others benefited from the free horses, food, and provisions. The frequent references in the sources to reforms of the system to curb misuse imply that such exploitation was widespread. Particularly urgent messages or documents could also be sent with runners, who would also be on hand at the *yam* stations and at regular short intervals of a *farsang* or less in between. According to Marco Polo they would wear belts of bells so that the runner at the next village would hear their approach and be able to make preparations to continue the relay. He further claimed that not only did they carry urgent messages for the Great Khan but also fresh fruit. These runners, or *paykān,* would relay their packages from station to station, village to village, and they could cover between 30 to 40 *parsangs* in 24 hours. As with most figures recorded in medieval sources, numbers differ widely and cannot be relied on for accuracy. However that the *yam* was a major institution and that is was crucial for the smooth and effective running of the empire cannot be questioned. The fact that someone of the prestige and status of Rashīd al-Dīn, the grand vizier to the Il-Khan of Persia, Ghazan Khan (1295–1304), was put in charge of the *yam*'s operation and reform program speaks of the significance attached to this institution. Rashīd al-Dīn took responsibility for the *yam* stations away from the army and the burden of their financial upkeep from the local people and entrusted each *yam* to a great emir. Generous funds were allotted for maintenance, and strict regulations were laid down detailing exactly who was permitted use of the facilities. Documents requiring stamps and seals were issued to control unauthorized use of the horses, runners, and provisions of the *yam* stations. The *yam* under Ghazan Khan was a far more sophisticated institution than the improvised relay system that Chinggis Khan began adapting to his needs as his steppe empire began to emerge from its pastoralist past. It was certainly one of the more effective of the Mongols' imperial institutions, and it lived on in the *barīd* of the Egyptian Mamluks, the courier system found in the Delhi Sultanate, and even in the *ulak* system of the Ottoman Turks.

MILITARY HEROES

All the major figures in the emerging Mongol Empire owed their prominence and dominance to successful military careers. Mongol society was a military machine and there was no distinction between the army and civilians. As the great Tuluid empires based in Iran and China emerged so too did a distinction between the men of the sword and the men of the pen. Indeed the concept of the men of the pen did not exist in traditional Mongol society. Prior to 1300, by which time both the Yüan dynasty and the Il-Khanid state were solidly established, almost any Mongol hero had achieved fame and glory at least partially though military prowess. One notable exception remarkable because of his lack of martial mettle was the Mongol administrator and "man of the pen" Arghun Aqa (1210–75). More in keeping with the traditional ideal of a Mongol hero was *noyan* (general or noble) Subodai, immortalized as one of the duo of *noyans*, Subodai and Jebe, whose legendary reconnaissance trip around the Caspian Sea circa 1222 earned them an honored position in the annals of military history.

Noyans Subodai and Jebe

The reconnaissance trip that ensured their place securely in the annals of military history commenced when Subodai and Jebe abandoned the search for the dying Khwārazmshāh. On the island of Abaskun in the southeastern corner of the Caspian Sea, Mohammad Khwārazmshāh was left to slowly die from his ills. He had brought terrible tragedy on his divided people and the people of western Asia, and he had opened the legendary gates of Īrānzamīn to the mythical hordes of Tūrān. Chinggis Khan had unleashed his armies to wreak vengeance-fed death and destruction on an unprecedented scale after the Khwārazmshāh had allowed, if not ordered, the unprovoked murder of a trade delegation composed mainly of Muslim merchants. In Bokhara Chinggis Khan addressed the assembled citizens to explain his presence: "I am the Punishment of God. If you had not committed great sins, God would not have sent a punishment like me upon you."[19] If this had been the verdict on the people of Bokhara, there must have been countless other people in the environs of the Caspian Sea and the Qipchaq Steppes who thought those words should apply equally to them after being visited by the two *noyans*, Subodai and Jebe.

Subodai Bahadur (1176–1248) was the son of a blacksmith of the Uriangqadai clan and joined Temüjin as a youth in 1190. By the age of 25 this large and imposing man had been appointed commander of cavalry. He was so large that the slight Mongol horses sometimes had problems carrying him, and he is recorded as being carried to battle in various forms of carriage. Subodai was utterly loyal to his master, and in mopping up operations before the Great *Quriltai* of 1206, it was Subodai who pursued and terminally disposed of Kutu and Chila'un, sons of Chinggis's arch enemy, the defeated Merkit leader Tokhto. Such service and loyalty was rewarded. Subodai was made commander of a *tümen* (10,000) in the devastating wars against the Xixia (1209). Subodai's great claim to fame arose from his legendary reconnaissance trip around the Caspian Sea with his fellow general, Jebe. In 1221, charged with hunting down the fleeing Khwārazmshāh, the two Mongol *noyans* found themselves in western Iran. They did not linger, and their bloody visits enshrined the reputation of the Mongols for barbarity and bloodletting for all time. Though Tabriz managed to bribe the approaching army in time to avert catastrophe, other towns were not so fortunate, and the human wave of destruction engulfed them before they knew what was upon them. The pair did not linger so much so that the Georgian army under George IV was able to claim victory from their total defeat. After engaging the Mongol forces of 20,000 men and suffering calamitous defeat, the Caucasians fled in terror back to their capital, Tiflis, to await the inevitable siege. However, that siege never came, and the Mongols merely continued on their way northward, the encounter being merely another skirmish for them on their circumnavigation of the Caspian. George IV, seeing the Mongols in retreat, was able to convince himself that his decimated forces had in fact so impressed the invaders that they had fled rather than risk another encounter. Few believed his boasts.

The generals continued their unstoppable march northward through the rugged Caucasus, cleaving asunder at Derbent the biblical barrier restraining Gog and Magog,[20] and into the open plains beyond, encountering and defeating Cuman Turks from the Qipchaq steppe lands and Rus armies from what is today Russia. In the *Chronicle of Novgorod* the impact of their coming in 1224 is poignantly expressed in the few startling words of an observer.

The same year, for our sins, an unknown tribe came, whom no one exactly knows, who they are, nor whence they came out, nor what their language is, nor of what race they are, nor what their faith is; but they call them Tartars.... God alone knows who they are and whence they came out.[21]

Their army was to meet up with the main Mongol armies in Khwarazm and leave it to others to consolidate their gains. In these two short years they had expanded the reach of the Great Khan's writ as far as the borders of Eastern Europe and the heartlands of the Islamic world. The tales of horror, heroism, cunning, blood and gore, desperation, and bravery have filled the pages of many chronicles in almost as many languages associated with this epic journey and are too numerous to recount here. However, the famous battle of Kalka (1223),[22] fought on the river of the same name in the Crimea, deserves special mention. It was carried out with great tactical skill and classic Mongol cunning, and it left the alliance between the Qipchaq, Cuman, and Polovtsian Turks and the Rus princes shattered and their armies routed. The victory feast was celebrated literally on top of the still-living bodies of the vanquished foes. After the remnants of the defeated Kievan army surrendered to the Mongols, a heavy wooden platform was placed on top of the bodies of the tightly bound Russian generals. As the joyful Mongol leaders celebrated their hard-won victory, their helpless foes slowly suffocated to a horrible death.

THE STORY OF THE COMING OF JEBE AND SUBEDA'I TO THE PROVINCE OF IRAQ AND AZERBAIJAN AND ARAN AND THE KILLING AND PILLAGE IN THIS LAND, AND THE PASSING FROM THE ROAD TO DARBAND, QIPCHAG, TO MOGHULISTAN

When Sultan Jalāl al-Dīn fled from Nishapur and turned his thoughts to Ghaznin, Jebe and Subeda'i sent a messenger to Chinggis Khan to say, that Sultan Muhammad was no more and his son Jalāl al-Dīn had fled and was coming in that direction. "We are no longer worried about him, and in accordance with your command we will spend a year or two conquering as many lands that lie before us as we can and then we will be able to return via Derband, the Qipchaq Gates to the rendezvous point as commanded in Mongolia, God willing and through Chinggis Khan's fortune. The authority of the Great God and the fortune of Chinggis Khan know that." After that, as always for all eventualities [to ensure] obtainable materials, he dispatched envoys and since provinces had still not been secured, no fewer than three or four hundred envoys went. In short, when they began the conquest of Iraq [Persia], they first took Khwar and Simnan. From there they came to the city of Ray, where they killed and plundered. Then they went to Qum, and they killed all the people there and took the children captive. And from there they went to Hamadan. Sayyid Majd al-Dīn

Ala' al-Dawla surrendered, sending tribute in steeds and garments and accepting to have a *shahna*. And from there when they had heard that a large number of soldiers from the sultan's army had assembled in Sejās under the command of Beg-Tegin Silahi and Kuch Buqa Khan, they turned their attention upon them and "nothinged" [*nīst gardānīdan*] or annihilated them. From there they came to Zanjan, where they massacred many more times than they had done in other towns. They had never done [such atrocities] in other regions as they did in that region. They returned to Qazwin where they engaged in a fierce battle with the Qazwinis and took the city by force. The Qazwinis, as usual, fought inside the city with knives until nearly fifty thousand men had been killed on both sides. They massacred and plundered throughout the whole land of Iraq [Persia].

When winter set in, they engaged in a great battle in the vicinity of Ray. At that time Chinggis Khan was in the region of Nakhshab and Termez. That year the cold was extreme and sudden. They headed for Azerbaijan, any place they encountered a hindrance [*godāz;* gorge, ford], they indulged in killing and looting in the customary manner, along the way. When they reached Tabriz, the governor, who was Atabeg Ozbeg, son of Jahan Pahlavan, hid himself and sent someone to ask for a truce. He also sent much tribute and many animals. Under the truce they turned back to spend the winter there before setting out for Arran on the way to Georgia.

Ten thousand Georgians faced them and engaged them in battle. The Georgians were defeated, and most were killed. Since most of the roads in Georgia were narrow and they saw extremely wild and overgrown terrain, they turned back and set out for Maragheh. When they returned to Tabriz, the governor, Shams al-Dīn Tughra'i, sent out enough tribute to satisfy them, and they passed on. They laid siege to the city of Maragheh, and because at that time the ruler was a woman who ruled from Royindiz, there was no one in the city who could offer resistance or devise a strategy. They [therefore] turned their hands to war.

The Mongols put the Muslim prisoners out in front in order to attack the walls, and they killed anyone who turned back. They fought in this fashion for several days. In the end, they seized the city by force and put [both] high and low to death. Anything that could be easily carried they took away, and the rest they burned and smashed. Then they set out for Diyarbakr and Arbela, but when they heard the great fame of the army of Muzaffar al-Dīn Kok-Bori, they turned back.

Because Jamāl al-Dīn Aybeh, one of the Khwārazmshāh's slaves, had stirred up sedition again with a group of people, killed the *shahna* of Hamadan, seized Ala' al-Dawla for having submitted, and imprisoned him in the castle of Girit, a dependency of Lur, they [Mongols] went again toward Hamadan. Although Jamāl al-Dīn Aybeh came forth to surrender, it did him no good. He and his *nokers* [vassals, lieutenants] were martyred and the Mongols laid siege to the city and carried out a general massacre in Rajab 618 [August–September 1221].

After devastating Hamadan, they set out for Nakhchivan, which they captured and [in which] they massacred and looted. In the end Atabeg Khāmūsh surrendered and they gave him a royal seal [*āl-tamqā*] and a wooden *pāīza*. From there they set out for Arran. [First] they took Saraw [Sarāb] and massacred and looted and [then] Ardabil in the same way. From there they went to the city of Baylaghan, which they seized by storm, killing old and young [alike]. After that, they attacked Ganja, which was the greatest of the cities of Arran. They seized it and totally devastated it too. From there they headed for Georgia, where [the people] had organised an army and had prepared for battle. While they were facing off against each other, Jebe hid himself with five thousand soldiers in a secret recess, and Subeda'i advanced with the army. At the beginning of the battle the Mongols retreated with the Georgians coming behind. Jebe leapt from ambush and caught [the Georgians] in a trap. In an instant thirty thousand Georgians were killed. From there they headed for Derbent and Shirvan. Along the way they took the city of Shemakhī by siege, massacring the people and taking many captives. Since it was impossible to pass through Derbent, they sent a few people to the Shirvanshah to agree a truce. He dispatched ten of his nobles. The Mongols killed one of them and said to the others, "If you show us the way through Derbent, we will spare your lives; otherwise we will kill you too." They guided them out of fear for their lives and [the Mongols] passed through.

When they reached the province of the Alans, a multitude of people were there, and together with the Qipchaqs they engaged the Mongol army in battle and not one [managed to] escape. Afterwards the Mongols sent a message to the Qipchaqs, saying, "We and you are one tribe and of one sort. The Alans are aliens to us. We have made a pact with you not to harm one another. We will give you whatever gold and vestments you want. Leave them with us." And they dispatched a large quantity of goods.

The Qipchaqs turned back, and the Mongols achieved victory over the Alans, exerting themselves as much as they could in massacring and looting. The Qipchaqs, in hopes of peace, dispersed in safety in their own territory. Suddenly the Mongols attacked them and killed everyone they found, taking double that which they had given [the Qipchaqs] before turning back. Some of the Qipchaqs who remained fled to the lands of the Rus. The Mongols wintered in that area, which was all pasture lands.

From there they went to the city of Sudāq on the coast of the sea that is connected to the Gulf of Constantinople. They took that city, and the people scattered. After that, they resolved to attack the land of the Rus and the Qipchaqs who had gone there. They [the Rus and Qipchaqs] got ready and assembled a large army, and when the Mongols saw their formidable size they retreated.

The Qipchaqs and Rus supposed they were retreating out of fear and pursued them at a distance of twelve-days. Then, without warning, the Mongol army turned around and attacked them, and before they could re-group many were killed. They fought for a week, but finally the Qipchaqs and Rus were routed. The Mongols went in pursuit and destroyed their towns. A great part of their province was emptied of people. From there they travelled until they rejoined Chinggis Khan, who had returned from the lands of the Tajiks.[23]

Subodai continued a celebrated military career, and his descendants added to his illustrious legacy. His last campaign was in Hungary, where he decimated the Hungarian troops after luring the already defeated army into a trap that enabled the Mongol archers to pick off the fleeing enemy one by one. Reports claim that bodies littered the region for a distance of two days' march. By late 1241 Subodai was discussing plans with his generals for the invasion of Austria, Italy, and Germany. It was the death of the Great Khan, Ögödei, and the subsequent recall of all the leaders of the clans to Qaraqorum that saved Europe from the Tatar yoke.

Subodai was dead by 1248, but his progeny continued in his military footsteps. His son, Uriyangkhadai, led Mongol armies into the jungles of what is today north Vietnam, and his grandson Bayan earned a reputation of which his grandfather would have been proud. He is credited with finally defeating the Song armies of southern China in 1276.

Qaidu Khan Chinggis Khan succeeded in transforming a disparate group of feuding bandit tribes into a united and mighty fighting force by revolutionizing steppe society and regulating and controlling those skills his people excelled in, namely horsemanship, archery, mounted warfare, and battle discipline. Later he added the military skills and techniques of the people he had conquered, and it was an international force that his sons led to further conquests. His reforms were unavoidable, and, recognizing this, his successors continued to reform and change all aspects of Mongol life. This was not universally popular, and many Mongols strongly disapproved of what the Mongol Empire was developing into. Much of the ire and disapproval of these traditionalists was directed at the House of Tolui and the Yüan dynasty and the Il-Khanate in particular. Qaidu Khan (1236–1301), a survivor of the House of Ögödei, became the champion of those who yearned for the traditional values of the steppe and the days when the Mongols were true nomads, unfettered with the trappings of the sedentary life and the malign influences of the Chinese and Persians. He rose in revolt against Qubilai Khan, emperor of China and Great Khan of the Mongols, and his revolt also brought him into conflict with Abaqa, the Mongol Emperor of Persia.

Qaidu's driving motivation, however, was not, as some would have it, to acquire the mantle of the Qa'an or Great Khan. His motivation was partly to promote the return to the traditional values of the nomadic lifestyle and culture of the steppes in contrast to the so-called progressive sedentary regimes of the Il-Khans and the Yüan dynasty and to redress the wrongs done to his own branch of the royal family, the Ögödeids, by the Toluids during Möngke Khan's rise to power in 1250–51. When the Toluids under Möngke seized power from the descendants of Güyük (1246–48), they initiated a massacre of any Ögödeid and Chaghedaid princes who might have posed a threat. The House of Ögödei had been decimated and had lost their leaders and their lands, and it was this wrong that Qaidu felt compelled to right. He did not seek the Mongol throne, but he wanted his ancestral lands restored to him and his family. He sought to establish a state representing the house of Ögödei that was at least equal in status to and commensurate with the other Mongol states. In 1271, following the defeat and death of the Chaghedaid Baraq Khan by Abaqa Khan at the Battle of Herat, Qaidu assumed control of central Asia and oversaw the establishment of an Ögödeid state. Such was his stature and political dexterity, backed by military aptitude, that he was able to achieve to some degree his aims in his own lifetime. However, lacking their father's prestige and genius his sons were unable to sustain these considerable achievements, and within 10 years of his death in 1301 they had lost much of their political power, and the Mongol state over which they ruled became known to history as the Chaghadaid Khanate.

Qaidu remains a military hero and a champion of Mongol tradition, and though he is a marginal figure in most accounts of Mongol history he epitomizes Mongol values and the Mongol warrior. Myths and legends surrounded and contributed to his fame and stature, not least of which are the stories told of his remarkable daughter, Qutulun, who is mentioned elsewhere in this book.

THE MONGOLS AT WAR: MONGOLS AND MAMLUKS[24]

A wise man once said, "When the sun rises, the stars have no heat to compare with it." Just as the ocean becomes turbulent, so the hearts of the enemy were agitated by lamentation. What was Nasir [Mamluk Sultan of Egypt, ruled 1299–1341] compared with Ghazan [Il-Khan, ruled 1295–1304], at this time? What is an ant compared with a destroying elephant?

Two princes of the Egyptians came to meet him [Ghazan Khan] and engage him in battle. He killed them with the spear, which was like a gnat in his hands. The noble Audai said to him, "If you must seek battle, why must it be with this vast army? It is not right that the shah should bathe his hands in blood. You must not be our example any longer."

Boldly he left his place in the battle and brought the shah back before the army, and did not again allow him to enter the battle, and he showed his love for the shah. When the army saw what Ghazan had done, they recovered their courage and rushed to attack the enemy, calling on the name of God.

First the advance guard attacked the enemy like lions, led by the amir Choban, roaring like a lion. The Egyptians were unacquainted with his bravery, and they came to meet him. When they met him, they met death too, and they grew to fear him. He raised his hand in battle, and the Egyptians were destroyed. When they saw his attack, none dared to meet it, and they had cause to remember his bravery, for he rended that great army like a lion or a wolf. Another amir, the Sultan Yasawal attacked like a lion, and the arrows rained down, even as the hail flows from the clouds, while Barandaq fought until the enemy lives were wasted.

The right wing also attacked, under Qutluh-shah, who attacked like a lion, and killed and took prisoners. The handsome Sulamish, who was as brave as he was beautiful, killed an Arab with every arrow that he loosed, while Mulai hurled himself into the midst of the battle [500] and split the enemy ranks. When Abashgai saw his fury and his bravery, he hurried to support him, and Binaq assaulted the Egyptians like a rutting elephant.

When Sultan Takfur joined the battle, the colour left the faces of the enemy. There was no escape for enemy heads from the arm of the battle-tried Ya'uldar. Boladqiya was so fierce in battle, that he became black with blood, and by his attack, the enemy were put to flight. The world was made black for the shah's enemies by Qipchaq, while disaster struck their ranks from Taghilchah. Baman hurled himself into the attack and from his deeds, the enemy met the day of judgement; so hotly did that war-like man attack them, that death took their bodies. The left wing poured arrows on the enemy like hail. Qurumshi's only desire was to fight, and neither coats of mail nor armour were of any use against his arrows. Gurkan Jaijaq brought down destruction on the enemy, and Ramadan toppled enemy heads. Although the fierce enemy were bigger than mountains before Tuq-Timur, they became less than straw. When Altamish joined the fighting, the world became harsh for the Egyptians, and the battlefield was like a hunting ground on the day of the chase. Tughan and Hulachu caused the enemy's cheeks to blanch by their arrows. In the centre, the army leaders displayed their courage to the shah.

Enemy heads were lopped by Alghu, their hearts were filled with blood and their livers pierced. Through the bravery of Gur-Timur and Taramtaz, the hearts of the Egyptian people were filled with dismay, while Tashfarad and Ta'mtash made the world black for the Egyptian king. The lion-like Qutlugh-Qiya left the enemy with no glory, while Yusuf Buqa charged fiercely and the world shed the enemy's blood. Tughai, son of Sutai was like the fire which consumes the dry reeds. The youth fought bravely, like a lion, among the ranks of the Egyptians, and killed so many that the shah was pleased at his bravery.

NOTES

1. Het'um, *Flowers of History*, trans. Robert Bedrosian, *Sources for the Armenian Tradition*, available at: http://rbedrosian.com/kg1.htm.

2. Kulliyat-i-Amīr Khosrow.

3. S.R. Turnbull and A. McBride, *The Mongols*, Men-at-Arms Series, no. 105 (Oxford, U.K.: Osprey Military, 2000), 13–14.

4. Giovanni DiPlano Carpini, *The Story of the Mongols Whom We Call the Tartars: Historia Mongalorum*, trans. Erik Hildinger (Boston: Branden, 1996), 72.

5. Mustawfī, *Z̧ afarnāmeh*, quoted in E.G. Browne, *A Literary History of Persia*, vol. 3, *Persian Literature under Tartar Domination 1265–1502* (Cambridge: Cambridge University Press, 1920), 97–98.

6. Juvaini, 29.

7. Ibid., 28.

8. "The Travels of Friar Oderic," in Henry Yule, *Cathay and the Way Thither*, vol. 2 (Reprint, Millwood, N.Y.: Kraus Reprint, 1967), 235.

9. Edward Gibbons, *Decline and Fall of the Roman Empire* (London: Everyman's Library, 1910), vol. 3, 8–9.

10. Adapted from Ala-ad-Din 'Ata-Malik Juvaini, *The History of the World Conqueror*, trans. John Andrew Boyle, intro. David Morgan (Manchester, U.K.: Manchester University Press, 1997), 27–28.

11. "The Travels of Friar Oderic," in Henry Yule, *Cathay and the Way Thither* (Millwood, N.Y.: Kraus Reprint, 1967), 234–40.

12. "The Mission of Friar William of Rubruck, His Journey to the Court of the Great Khan, Möngke, 1253–1255," in William of Rubruck, *The Mission of William of Rubruck*, trans. and ed. Peter Jackson with David Morgan (London: Hakluyt Society, 1990), 85.

13. Rashīd al-Dīn, *Jāmi' al-Tavārīkh*, eds., Mohammad Roushan and Muṣ tafah Mūsavī, (Tehran: Nashr albaraz, 1994), translation by George Lane, 672.

14. Adapted from Boyle's translation of Juvaini, *History of the World Conqueror*, 26, Persian text of Juwaynī, 19–21.

15. Edward G. Browne, *A Literary History of Persia*, vol. 2, *From Firdawsi to Saᶜdī* (London: Unwin, 1915), 427–31.

16. Mustawfī, *Zafarnameh*, 140–41; cf. Rashīd al-Dīn, *Jāmi' al-Tavārīkh*, translation by George Lane, 1038.

17. Mustawfī, *Zafarnameh*, 179–80; cf. Rashīd al-Dīn, *Jāmi' al-Tavārīkh*, translation by George Lane, 1043.

18. Marco Polo, *The Travels of Marco Polo*, (Everyman edition, 1983), 212.

19. Ala-ad-Din 'Ata-Malik Juvaini, *The History of the World Conqueror*, trans. John Andrew Boyle, intro. David Morgan (Manchester, U.K.: Manchester University Press, 1997), 105.

20. In the Bible, a hostile power that is ruled by Satan and will manifest itself immediately before the end of the world (Revelation 20). In the biblical passage in Revelation and in other Christian and Jewish apocalyptic literature, Gog is joined by a second hostile force, Magog, but elsewhere (Ezekiel 38, Genesis 10:2) Magog is apparently the place of Gog's origin.

21. R. Michell and Nevill Forbes, *The Chronicle of Novgorod 1016–1471*, Camden Third Series, vol. 25 (London: Offices of the Society, 1914), 64.

22. D. Nicolle and V. Shpakovsky, *Kalka River 1223* (Oxford, U.K.: Osprey Publishing, 2001).

23. Rashīd al-Dīn, *Jāmi' al-Tavārīkh,* translation by George Lane, 531–35.

24. Mustawfī, *Zafarnāmeh,* trans. L. J. Ward, 499–500.

APPENDIX A: HOW THE TARTARS CONDUCT THEMSELVES IN WAR

Friar Giovanni DiPlano Carpini

Genghis Khan divided his Tartars by captains of ten, captains of a hundred, and captains of a thousand, and over ten millenaries, or captains of a thousand, he placed one colonel, and over one whole army he authorized two or three chiefs, but so that all should be under one of the said chiefs. When they join battle against any other nation, unless they do all consent to retreat, every man who deserts is put to death. And if one or two, or more, often proceed manfully to the battle, but the residue of those ten draw back and follow not the company, they are in like manner slain. Also, if one among ten or more be taken, their fellows, if they fail to rescue them, are punished with death.

Moreover they are required to have these weapons: two long bows or one good one at least, three quivers full of arrows, and one axe, and ropes to draw engines of war. But the richer have single-edged swords, with sharp points, and somewhat crooked. They have also armed horses, with their shoulders and breasts protected; they have helmets and coats of mail. Some of them have jackets for their horses, made of leather artificially doubled or trebled, shaped upon their bodies. The upper part of their helmet is of iron or steel, but that part which circles about the neck and the throat is of leather. Some of them have all their armour of iron made in the following manner: they beat out many thin plates a finger broad, and a hand long, and making in every one of them eight little holes, they lace through three strong and straight leather thongs. So they join the plates one to another, as it were, ascending by degrees. Then they tie the plates to the thongs, with other small and slender thongs, drawn through the holes, and in the upper part, on each side, they fasten one small doubled thong, that the plates may firmly be knit together. These they make, as well for their horses as for the armour of their men; and they scour them so bright that a man may behold his face in them. Some of them upon the neck of their lance have a hook, with which they attempt to pull men out of their saddles. The heads of their arrows are exceedingly sharp, cutting both ways like a two-edged sword, and they always carry a file in their quivers to sharpen their arrowheads.

They are most efficient in wars, having been in conflict with other nations for the space of these forty-two years. When they come to any rivers, the chief men of the company have a round and light piece of leather. They put a rope through the many loops on the edge of this, draw it together like a purse, and so bring it into the round form of a ball, which leather they fill with their garments and other necessaries, trussing it up most strongly. But upon the midst of the upper part thereof, they lay their saddles and other hard things; there also do the men themselves sit. This, their boat, they tie to a horse's tail, causing a man to swim before, to guide over the horse, or sometimes they have two oars to row themselves over. The first horse, therefore, being driven into the water, all the others' horses of the company follow him, and so they pass through the river. But the common soldiers have each his leather bag or satchel well sewn together, wherein he packs up all his trinkets, and strongly trussing it up hangs it at his horse's tail, and so he crosses the river.

Source: John de Plano Carpini, *The long and wonderful voyage of Frier Iohn de Plano Carpini,* http://etext.library.adelaide.edu.au/h/hakluyt/voyages/carpini/complete.html

APPENDIX B: OF THEIR SPIES AND HOW THEY MAY BE RESISTED

No one kingdom or province is able to resist the Tartars; because they use soldiers out of every country of their dominions. If the neighbouring province to that which they invade will not aid them, they waste it, and with the inhabitants, whom they take with them, they proceed to fight against the other province. They place their captives in the front of the battle, and if they fight not courageously they put them to the sword. Therefore, if Christians would resist them, it is expedient that the provinces and governors of countries should all agree, and so by a united force should meet their encounter.

Soldiers also must be furnished with strong hand-bows and cross-bows, which they greatly dread, with sufficient arrows, with maces also of strong iron, or an axe with a long handle. When they make their arrow-heads, they must, according to the Tartars' custom, dip them red-hot into salt water, that they may be strong enough to pierce the enemies' armour. They that will may have swords also and lances with hooks at the ends, to pull them from their saddles, out of which they are easily removed. They must have helmets and other armour to defend themselves and their horses from the Tartars' weapons and arrows, and they that are unarmed, must, according to the Tartars' custom, march behind their fellows, and discharge at the enemy with longbows and cross-bows. And, as it has already been said of the Tartars, they must dispose their bands and troops in an orderly manner, and ordain laws for their soldiers. Whosoever runs to the prey or spoil, before the victory is achieved, must undergo a most severe punishment. For such a fellow is put to death among the Tartars without pity or mercy.

The place of battle must be chosen, if it is possible, in a plain field, where they may see round about; neither must all troops be in one company, but in many, not very far distant one from another. They which give the first encounter must send one band before, and must have another in readiness to relieve and support the former in time. They must have spies, also, on every side, to give them notice when the rest of the enemy's bands approach. They ought always to send forth band against band and troop against troop, because the Tartar always attempts to get his enemy in the midst and so to surround him. Let our bands take this advice also; if the enemy retreats, not to make any long pursuit after him, lest according to his custom he might draw them into some secret ambush. For the Tartar fights more by cunning than by main force. And again, a long pursuit would tire our horses, for we are not so well supplied with horses as they. Those horses which the Tartars use one day, they do not ride upon for three or four days after. Moreover, if the Tartars draw homeward, our men must not therefore depart and break up their bands, or separate themselves; because they do this also upon policy, namely, to have our army divided, that they may more securely invade and waste the country. Indeed, our captains ought both day and night to keep their army in readiness; and not to put off their armour, but at all time to be prepared for battle. The Tartars, like devils, are always watching and devising how to practice mischief. Furthermore, if in battle any of the Tartars be cast off their horses, they must be captured, for being on foot they shoot strongly, wounding and killing both horses and men.

Source: John de Plano Carpini, *The long and wonderful voyage of Frier Iohn de Plano Carpini,* taken out of the 32. booke of Vincentius Beluacensis his *Speculum historiale,* available on the Internet at http://etext.library.adelaide.edu.au/h/hakluyt/voyages/carpini/

1237 THE MONGOL ATTACK ON
THE LANDS OF THE RUS PRINCES

The princes of Riazan, Murom, and Pronsk moved against the godless and engaged them in a battle. The struggle was fierce, but the godless Mohammedans [non-Christian] emerged victorious with each prince fleeing toward his own city. Thus angered, the Tartars now began the conquest of the Riazan land with great fury. They destroyed cities, killed people, burned and took [people] into slavery. On December 6, [1237,] the cursed strangers approached the capital city of Riazan, besieged it, and surrounded it with a stockade. The princes of Riazan shut themselves up with the people in the city, fought bravely, but succumbed. On December 21, [1237,] the Tartars took the city of Riazan, burned it completely, killed

Prince Iurii Igorevich, his wife, slaughtered other princes, and of the captured men, women, and children, some they killed with their swords, others they killed with arrows and [then] threw them into the fire; while some of the captured they bound, cut and disemboweled their bodies. The Tartars burned many holy churches, monasteries, and villages, and took their property.

Then the Tartars went toward Kolomna. From Vladimir, Grand Prince Iurii Vsevolodovich sent his son, Prince Vsevolod, against them; with him also went Prince Roman Igorevich of Riazan with his armies. Grand Prince Iurii sent his military commander, Eremei Glebovich, ahead with a patrol. This group joined Vsevolod's and Roman Igorevich's forces at Kolomna. There they were surrounded by the Tartars. The struggle was very fierce and the Russians were driven away to a hill. And there they [the Tartars] killed Prince Roman Igorevich Riazanskii, and Eremei Glebovich, the military commander of Vsevolod Iurievich, and they slaughtered many other men. Prince Vsevolod, with a small detachment, fled to Vladimir. The Tartars [then] went toward Moscow. They took Moscow and killed the military commander Philip Nianka, and captured Vladimir, the son of Prince Iurii; they slaughtered people old and young alike, some they took with them into captivity; they departed with a great amount of wealth.

Source: Polnoe Sobranie Rossiiskikh letopisei (Complete Collection of Russian Chronicles), in Basil Dmytryshyn, Medieval Russia: A Source Book 900–1700 (New York: Holt, Rinehart, and Winston, 1973), 108.

6

HEALTH AND MEDICINE

For a people who regularly indulged in decidedly unhealthy habits, the Mongols were surprisingly concerned with their health and medicine. At the height of their empire in the late thirteenth early fourteenth centuries, the Mongols had access to and use of the major medical systems of Eurasia, namely Chinese, Korean, Tibetan, Indian, Uighur, Islamic, and Nestorian Christian. Individual princes on their journeys around the empire or out on the campaign trails were accompanied by their own retinue of medical teams selected from this pool of medical expertise and learning. Though they also retained their traditional shamans (holy men) whose role included treatment of disease and physical ailments, the Mongols differentiated between the various medical practitioners and the native shamans. The term *otochi* was applied to the foreign doctors, and they were identified as using herbs and drugs, *em*, whereas the Mongol witch doctors (shamans) relied on spiritual powers and magic to treat and cure.

EARLY PRACTICES

On the steppe it was the shaman whose skills were called upon in cases of sickness and disease, and one of his (or her) first functions was to establish whether the affliction had its origin in natural sources or in malevolent witchcraft. These medieval shamans were sometimes referred to as physicians *(tabīb)*, though their main skill remained in prophecy. Some of their practices seem not only bizarre but suspiciously barbaric.

Now the chief who called himself the brother of God came into the midst of the country and mercilessly trampled the miserable Christians; and they burned all the wooden crosses wherever they came upon them erected on the roads and in the mountains. Yet nothing satisfied them. Indeed, they plundered even more those monasteries they came upon in the country by eating and drinking. They mercilessly hung up the venerable priests and beat them.

A chief from Xul's cavalry went to a monastery called Geret'i. Its abbot was named Step'annos, white-haired and old, very select, holy and virtuous in behavior and accomplished in good deeds. When he saw the chief of the T'at'ars coming toward him at the monastery, he took a vessel of wine and went before the T'at'ar holding tzghu, as is the T'at'ar custom. After this, [Step'annos] took them to the monastery and seated them together with other cavalrymen who were following their chief. He slaughtered a sheep, opened other wine and satiated them all with eating and drinking to the point that [the Mongols] could barely stay on their horses. At night, drunk, they went to their dwellings, since the T'at'ars' camp was close to the monastery.

After reaching home and sleeping the night, in the morning they saw that their chief was very ill. When they asked him the cause of the sickness, the chief replied that "the priest drugged me last night." The priest was innocent of this; rather it was from their wicked, insatiable eating and drinking that he had become ill. They immediately went [to the monastery] and brought back the marvellous old father Step'annos, shackled. After much questioning and probing, [the Mongols] did not believe him. They put four wooden stakes into the ground and mercilessly tied the blameless man to them, some distance off the ground. Then they lit a fire and roasted his entire body until the marvellous old Step'annos expired. They clearly saw a sign and column of light over the venerable father Step'annos who was so innocently and pointlessly martyred, crowned among the blessed martyrs.

Now that obscene and merciless chief, aside from the pain he had, was possessed by a dew such that in frenzy he devoured his own vile flesh. And thus did he perish, with torments and bitter blows. Similarly, the entire army fell to the wicked illness and many of them perished from it. Although this is what happened, [the Mongols] did not fear God but instead persisted in constantly working deeds of cruelty and bitter tears. Their great chief, Xul, the same one who immodestly claimed he was like unto and the brother of God, fell sick with gout. As a result of this illness, he committed an unmentionably evil and lamentable deed. They went and found an unbelieving Jewish doctor and brought him to Xul. When that impious and false doctor saw his illness, he stated the antidote: the stomach of a red-haired boy should be split open while [the boy] was still alive, and [Xul] should place his foot into the boy's stomach. [The Mongols] immediately sent horsemen into the country who entered Christian villages snatching boys off the streets then fleeing like wolves. The children's parents went after them screaming and shrieking loudly and shedding bitter, pitiful tears, but were unable to get them free. Instead, they turned back to their homes, with sorrowing hearts. If they forcibly seized their children, [the Mongols] shot arrows at the parents. Thus did this pitiful event occur by the hand of the impious Jew, until they reached the figure of thirty boys with stomachs torn open, and still he did not get better. Instead, when the impious Xul realized that he had committed such gruesome acts and nothing had helped, he then grew angry out of pity for the boys. He commanded that the Jewish hek'im be brought before him, have his stomach cut open and fed to the dogs. And [the Mongols] did so at once. But after this, Xul himself perished with an evil death. His son, Mighan, then sat in Xul's place.[1]

This story reported by the historian cleric, Grigor of Akanc must be viewed with some suspicion because his *History of the Nation of Archers* contains much that is biased and of questionable objectivity, and some tales and reports are obviously examples of his own wish fulfillment. However, whether the actual gruesome details reported are accurate or not, the practice of immersion of the body or body parts in warm entrails is widely attested to. The remedy for gout, a common illness among the Mongols, that the Persian doctor prescribed, slitting open the belly and placing the afflicted foot inside, must have been learned from Turco-Mongol sources. In other sources, there are no references to this practice being connected with Jewish medicine or medical tradition, nor can the necessity of a red-haired boy or indeed only in one isolated case the need for any human be traced. Other sources do refer to the Turco-Mongol practice of immersing or covering diseased or injured body parts in the fresh entrails of animals.

This practice of employing the fresh entrails of animals to treat a variety of ailments appears to have been quite common judging by the number of references that occur in the literary sources. A Chinese source reports that, in a state of shock, a patient was placed wholly in the belly of an ox where after soaking in the hot blood he would recover. References to this practice, though hardly commonplace, are not rare, suggesting the practice was well known. In the *Yuan Shih*, the official record of the Yüan dynasty written by the succeeding Ming historians and chroniclers, the following story is recorded:

Under Chinggis, Bujir [a Mongol general] campaigned against the Hui-hui [Muslims], Russians, and other countries. When in battle, Bujir launched and fought ferociously. [Once] his body was hit by a number of arrows. Blood was flowing. Chinggis Khan went personally to see him. He had somebody pull out the arrows. Blood was flowing all over his body, he fell prostrate in a faint and was almost dead. Chinggis Khan commanded that one take an ox and cut open its belly and put Bujir in the ox belly. [Thus] having soaked in the hot blood, after a short while, then, he revived.[2]

Other examples can be found in the *Yuan Shih* recorded at different times and various places. "An arrow went through his breast and he was about to expire. Bayan commanded that one cut open the belly of a water-buffalo and put him in the inside of it. After a good while, then, he revived." "They put him in the belly of an ox and he re-gained life." "Ögödei Qa'an commanded an army officer to draw out the arrows and, binding an ox [tightly], to cut out its intestines and, stripping Mu-huan naked, to put him in the belly of the ox. After a good while, then, he revived."[3]

It was not always necessary to take such drastic measures as total immersion in the belly of a beast, and sometimes the application of a poultice made from the skin of a freshly killed ox or the masticated grasses from an animal's stomach sufficed for the treatment of wounds. In fact there are cases known in which Kazakhs of more modern times have used the extracted stomach of a colt to wrap around wounds and injuries. They believe that the stomach and its fat can absorb bad blood. The remedial agent in all these various reports is the belly and stomach of a freshly killed beast.

With increasing contact with the sedentary world, however, the influence of the shamans, particularly in medical matters, decreased.

CHINESE MEDICINE

Chinese medicine was pervasive in the Mongol Empire even though evidence of other systems was certainly widespread. With their westward spread the Mongol commanders took with them Chinese physicians who spread their influence to the local population. Records reveal that all the Mongol rulers who traveled westward retained physicians trained in eastern Asian medicine. The Persian sources from the Il-Khanid period (1256–1335), when the Mongols ruled Iran, clearly demonstrate the penetration of Chinese medicine into western Asia. The chief minister for Ghazan Khan (died 1304) and Öljeitü Khan (died 1216), the historian and statesman Rashīd al-Dīn, started his career as both a chef and a physician. Both occupations were held in great esteem at this time, and Rashīd al-Dīn's interest in medicine is reflected both in his writings and in his successful efforts to introduce Chinese medicine to his homeland, Iran. He is commonly known as Rashīd al-Dīn Ṭabīb (the Physician), and among his greatest achievements was the establishment of the Rabᶜ-i Rashīdī quarter of Tabriz (in northwestern Iran), which contained a famous house of healing.

The Chinese introduced various medical practices to the Mongols and hence to their subjects in other parts of the empire. These included the use of drugs; various folk medicines and potions; acupuncture, which utilizes needles to stimulate power points and energy channels in the body; and moxibustion, which achieves the same results through the utilization of heat, applied through the dried, powdered, and burned leaves of the tree *artemisia moxa*.

ACUPUNCTURE AND MOXIBUSTION

Both acupuncture and moxibustion were used extensively in the Chin-Yüan period. Various acupuncture points and their corresponding therapeutic virtues were validated throughout this period. Procedures in applying acupuncture and moxibustion to these points had been developed differently over the centuries. Four books of acupuncture and moxibustion (*Zhenjiu Sishu*), published by Dou Guifang in 1331, and important works on acupuncture written during the Song and Chin dynasties were compiled. For example, an acupuncture point known as *jiuwei* mentioned in the *Huangdi Mingdang Jiujing*, one of the four books, was used in the treatment of palpitations and epilepsy and has been used from that time until the present.

Zhu Zhenheng (1281–1358), known as Master Danxi from Zhejiang province, achieved renown for his medical research and theories into the generation of internal heat during physiological and pathological change in the body, expounded in his work *Gezhi Yulun* (*Theories of In-depth Research*). As with so much Chinese medical theory, his ideas centered on the balance between the yang elements and the yin. Yang energy, or minister-fire, vital for the body to function, exists mainly in the kidneys and liver from where it cooperates with heart-fire or master-fire to promote the stable function of the organs. Zhu Zhenheng believed that during periods of illness the body's yang elements increased at the expense of the yin, and as a result fire in the body increased as the disease developed. Treatment consisted of nourishing the yin, which had been consumed by minister-fire, and quenching the fire. Recommended were strict diet and regulated sexual activity, which were believed to preserve the yin. The theories surrounding minister-fire are still observed today.

The Mongols contributed to medical knowledge regarding acupuncture and moxibustion (the burning of herbs over certain points on the skin). Therapeutic methods like Mongolian moxibustion and bloodletting were very popular at the time. The Mongolian tradition of moxibustion was later integrated into the Tibetan medical system and became known as *Horgi Metzaí* or *Sogpo Metzaí* (Mongolian fire burning). Bonesetting, traumatic surgery, and the development of external medicine were fields in which the Mongols excelled due to the nature of their nomadic lifestyle, which involved often continuous military activity. Surgery and anatomy were also well known to the Chinese and Mongols for this same reason and also because of the Chinese habit of using the bodies of executed criminals for dissection and anatomical investigation.

BONESETTING

Bonesetting after a fracture or a dislocation was performed by a *Bariachi*, a bonesetter, without medicines or surgical instruments. The *Bariachi* would hold the fractured or dislocated part of the sufferer's body with his or her own hands, twisting it freely for some time, without any apparent pain to the patient. These bonesetters could reputedly cure bone disorders perfectly through a gift with which they were born. After the treatment, there would be no complaints at all, however serious the injury might have been. These healers had neither medical knowledge nor knowledge of any charms or magic. The *Bariachi* had the bonesetting secret in their blood, and the art was passed on through generations.

A manual, *Shiyi Dexiaofang (Efficacious Remedies of the Physicians)*, cemented the fame of Yüan physician Wei Yilin (circa 1277–1347) as an orthopedic surgeon in particular for his work in setting fractures and in treating dislocations of the shoulder, hip, and knee. He pioneered the suspension method for joint reduction, finally adopted into Western medicine in 1927, and employed anesthetics during his operations. A contemporary of Wei Yilin under the Yüan was Qi Dezhi, known for his book *Waike Jingyi (The Essentials of External Medicine)*, compiled from 1335 c.e. As well as describing various methods of therapeutic minor surgery, the book lists decoctions, tablets, pills, powders, and ointments used in the treatment of skin disorders. Qi Dezhi explained in his treatise on dermatology that imbalances within the body, disharmony between the yin and the yang invariably resulted in skin ailments. Herbal remedies and phytotherapy (use of herbs) were an integral part of his work.

DIET

A Mongol physician who realized the link between health and diet was Hu Sihui, whose book *Yinshan Zhengyao (Important Principles of Food and Drink)* written in 1330 exhorted the importance of the balanced diet and moderation in both eating and drinking. In his book he listed the beneficial properties of 230 cereals, fish, shellfish, meat, fruit, and vegetables. He warned against distension caused by eating too many apples and liver disorders brought on by overindulgence in oranges, but he recommended grapes for strengthening character and sustaining energy and claimed that dog meat, though salty, was nontoxic and calmed the *zang* organs (liver, spleen, heart, lungs, kidneys, and pericardium). Other notable physicians from the Yüan period include Ge Keijiu (1305–52) whose work on tuberculosis is detailed in his *Shiyao Shenshu*, and Zeng Shirong who built on the study of pediatrics, begun in the Song dynasty, in his book *Houyou Xinshu*, completed in 1294.

PULSE DIAGNOSIS

In western Asia and Iran in particular, however, it was the ancient Chinese technique of pulse diagnosis that was most admired, and its introduction to the Islamic west can be traced to the Mongols. Various books on the technique were translated into Mongolian and were highly esteemed, including the standard book on the pulse, the *Mai-ching* of Wang Shu-ho. The pulse, the heartbeat, and the blood flow were all interconnected and were considered crucial for monitoring and manipulating general health. The papal envoy William of Rubruck spoke highly of the Chinese herbalists and practitioners of pulse diagnosis on his visit (1253–55) to the Mongol capital, Qaraqorum, though he criticized them for their ignorance of the diagnostic importance of urine samples. In fact, the Chinese valued urine highly, but for its remedial properties rather than for its diagnostic uses.

The *Yuan Shih* recounts how in 1241 Ögödei Qa'an fell seriously ill with an irregular *mai* (pulse). On Ögödei's orders, a general amnesty was proclaimed, and soon afterward the Qa'an's physicians again checked his pulse and found that it had returned to normal. This story, whatever its historical accuracy, is revealing because it demonstrates the Mongol belief in an intimate connection between physical health and the moral order.

Pulse-based medicine was put firmly in the forefront of Mongol medical practice when Qubilai ordered the Uighur scholar An-ts'ung to translate the ancient Chinese manual of pulse scholarship, the *Nan-ching*, into Mongolian, and then in 1305 his successor, Temür, made pulse diagnosis for adults and for children top of the list of 10 compulsory subjects on which medical students at the Imperial Academy of Medicine (T'ai-i yuan) were to be examined. The Iranian prime minister, Rashīd al-Dīn, included some of the set texts on pulse diagnosis among the texts he translated for use within the Persian Il-Khanid administration.

CHINESE MEDICINE IN THE IL-KHANATE

Hülegü had Chinese physicians with him when he came west, and they continued to treat him, including treatment with purgatives, until he succumbed to his final illness in 1265. Hülegü's grandson, Arghun, though raised in western Asia, continued to rely mainly on east Asian medicine. It is widely believed that it was the medical treatment he received that killed him. Though the actual physicians who were treating him were Uighur or Indian, they fed him a concoction of Chinese medicine that included cinnabar, a source of mercury sulfide, sometimes considered an elixir of life. Despite its history of fatalities and an impressive list of noble and elite victims, mercury and cinnabar continued to be popular with Taoist alchemists. Ghazan continued the Il-Khanid attachment to Chinese medicine, and when local Muslim doctors proved unable to relieve his affliction with ophthalmia he sought help from Chinese physicians in Tabriz who

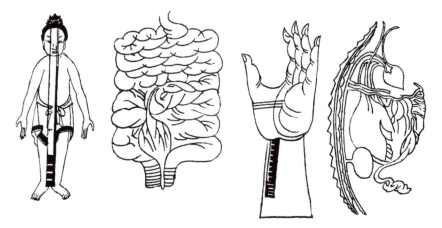

From Rashīd al-Dīn's *Tanksūq-nāmeh*. Courtesy of Lan Tien Lang Publications

employed moxibustion to treat the Mongol sultan. It is probable that the continuing popularity of Chinese medicine in Il-Khanid Iran owes much to the open-mindedness and intellectual and scientific curiosity of Rashīd al-Dīn, who actively encouraged eastern Asian medical practices and also disseminated the science in his extensive writings. Much of the secrets of Chinese medicine have been preserved in Rashīd al-Dīn's *Tanksūq-nāmeh īl-khānī (The Treasure Book of the Il-Khans)*. Prominent in the descriptions and explanations of eastern medical practice in this learned book are those subjects related to pulse diagnosis, a branch of medicine particularly admired by the Iranians.

WESTERN MEDICINE IN CHINA

Though Chinese medical influence was pervasive, there is evidence that the western half of the Mongol Empire also contributed to the health of the Mongol lords and their subjects. In fact, even medical practitioners from Europe are recorded as being in Khan Baliq (Beijing). Friar John of Montecorvino claimed that "a certain Lombard leech and chirurgeon" appeared in Timür Khan's Yüan court in 1303.

Nestorian Christians had long had an influential presence in East Asia and long-established links with the medical world. Some of the main Mongol tribes were adherents of the Nestorian creed. The Kereyid, Naiman, and Önggüt were heavily Nestorian, and even the Tatars were influenced by these eastern Christians. Indeed, Dokuz Khātūn, the wife of Hülegü Khan (died 1265), ruler of Iran (ruled 1256–65) was a devout Nestorian Christian. Urban and settled centers such as Semirechie, the Tarim Basin, Uyghuristan, and other scattered towns and villages throughout China had thriving Nestorian communities. Just as in the Muslim west, the Nestorians in the east had a tradition of involvement in the medical profession. They are credited with being the conduit of the Galenic tradition (Galen of Pergumum; died 217 C.E.) to the Arabs. The presence of their communities in central Asia and the east facilitated the flow of Western medicine to China and the Turco-Mongol steppe lands. Many central Asian Uighurs were Nestorians, and it was the Uighurs in particular who formed such an influential part of the Mongol administration. A considerable body of Syriac literature, including medical texts, has been recovered in central Asia. West Asian Nestorians received a warm welcome in the Mongol courts. Many Nestorians achieved high office in the service of the Mongols as Chinqai, chief advisor to Ögödei, Qadaq, *atabeg* (tutor) to Güyük, and Bulghai, senior administrative officer under Möngke, aptly testify. The Nestorians' fortunes seemed tied to those of the Mongol Empire, and when the empire declined so too did the fortunes of the Nestorians of the east.

The physician Simeon, named Rabban Ata by the Great Khan Ögödei, used his medical skills to gain political influence at the Mongol court, which he then used to advance Christian communities in the Muslim west. Simeon was a native of Rum Qal'a on the upper Euphrates River who sought his fortune in Mongolia in the 1230s and '40s. He achieved high office and was well regarded by the Mongol elite. He later served Hülegü as a physician and was reputedly also very astute commercially. Bar Hebraeus speaks warmly of this Nestorian physician who early realized the value that the Mongols gave to medics.

And in those days Rabban Simeon the Elder and physician... who was a native of Kal'ah Rhomaita, was taken into service of the King of Kings, Hûlâbû. And he flourished and prospered greatly, and he was beloved by all the sons of the kings and by the queens. And he possessed dwellings like those of kings, and gardens, and plantations, and towers in the meadows, and his income yearly was five thousand dinars, from Baghdad, and Assyria, and Cappadocia, and from Maragheh. The remnant of our people obtained through him help, and great lifting up of the head, and honour. And the Church acquired stability and protection in every place.[4]

Nestorians became prominent in medical circles under the Yüan dynasty (Mongol China, 1260–1370). Often their practices, innovations, and infusions were known locally and generically as Muslim (Hui-hui) medicine, and they would certainly have incorporated the teachings and traditions of the Persian physician Ibn Sina (Avicenna; died 1037) into their practices. Travelers from Europe recognized that Muslim, or Hui-hui, medicine was in fact usually practiced by and probably introduced by Nestorian Christians. Odoric of Pordenone observed circa 1320 that of those charged with safeguarding the Great Khan's health, 400 were idolaters, presumably Chinese, 8 were Christian, and only 1 was Muslim (Saracen).[5]

Jesus (ʿIsā) the Interpreter, was another Nestorian physician, and he so impressed Qubilai with his many skills, his plain speaking, and his medical knowledge that he accompanied the emperor to his new political base in north China and in 1263 established an office of west Asian medicine, the Medical Bureau of the Capital *(Ching-shih i-yao yuan)*. In 1273 this organization was renamed the Broadening Benevolence Office *(kuang-hui ssu)* or more commonly as the Muslim Medical Office. This ʿIsā is thought to be the same worthy physician who administered to the medical needs of the Armenian King Het'um (ruled 1226–69) and is mentioned by Bar Hebraeus.[6] It is believed that ʿIsā (Ai-hsieh in Chinese) traveled east with Het'um's brother Smbat the Constable in 1247 to the court of Güyük Khan (ruled 1247–49) and took up official duties on the recommendation of Rabban Simeon, who left to return to the west about that time. Chinese sources speaking of ʿIsā claim that Güyük was impressed by his reputation. "Regarding the various languages of the Western Region, their astronomy, and medicine, there were none he did not study and practice."[7] An educated Nestorian serving the Mongol court could be expected to speak his native Syriac, Greek, Arabic, Armenian, Persian, Mongolian, and Chinese. Until he left China with Bolad, Qubilai's envoy to Iran, in the mid-1280s, ʿIsā was director of the Muslim Medical Office, "charged with the preparation of Muslim medicine for imperial use and with mixing medicine to relieve the members of the imperial guard [*kesig*] and the orphaned and poor in the capital."[8] ʿIsā's successor is recorded in 1334 to be Nieh-chih-erh, who is described as a Christian, which suggests that the Nestorians remained in charge of Muslim and Western medicine throughout the period of Mongol rule.

LACK OF TRANSLATIONS

As far as is known, west Asian medical works were not translated into Chinese during the Mongol period. However, in 1273 at least one Western medical tome was available in the imperial library where it was cataloged as a medical classic, or *i-ching*. It is thought to have been Ibn Sina's *The Canon on Medicine* because Ibn Sina, who synthesized Greek and Perso-Arabic medical traditions, was highly regarded in western Asia. The physicians at the Mongol court traveled with their own books, which possibly explains this apparent omission from the official libraries. They also traveled with their own collection of medicines and had their own diagnostic and therapeutic techniques. The Mongols had a long tradition of herbalist medicines, and they took a keen interest in the herbal remedies used by others in their empire. William of Rubruck had commented positively on Mongol physicians as being "well versed in the efficacy of herbs." Qubilai had Chinese pharmacopoeias translated into Mongolian.

DRUGS AND MEDICINE: EAST–WEST EXCHANGE

As a result of the Mongols' great enthusiasm for medicine and herbal remedies, there was a great deal of traffic and exchange between the east and west of their vast empire of *materia medica*. Rhubarb traveled westward from China to Iran where it became an important component in Persian medicine. The Mongols seem to have rediscovered it, and during their raids against the Tanguts in addition to seizing gold, maidens, textiles, and valuables, the famed statesman Yeh-lü Ch'u-ts'ai, "took only some books and two camel-loads of rhubarb."[9] Spices from the east with medicinal properties, such as cubebs, cinnamon, and white pepper, were much sought after by Persian pharmacists. Rashīd al-Dīn reveals an intimate acquaintance with Chinese and other eastern spices and herbs, due no doubt to his contacts with the Mongol statesman and envoy Bolad and the Chinese physicians who accompanied him to Iran. The *Yuan Shih* states clearly that in fact this international trade in drugs was a two-way traffic. In 1331, "The envoy of the imperial prince [Il-Khan of Iran] Abū Saʿīd [d.1335] returned to the Western Region to announce that [the Yüan court] repaid the tribute which they had presented with *materia medica* of equal value."[10] This trade was considerable and had been going on for some time as is indicated by another entry from the *Yuan Shih* for the year 1273, which states that Qubilai "dispatched envoys with 100,000 ounces of gold to imperial prince [Il-Khan of Iran] Abaqa in order to purchase drugs."[11]

The physicians of west Asia are thought to have introduced a number of medicines to the east through the agency of the Mongol courts. Two pharmaceutical bureaus (Hui-hui *yao-wu yuan*) were established by the Yüan court to manage the influx of Muslim medicines. Mastic (a resin of *Pistacia lentisus*), nux vomica (the seed of the fruit of the strychnine tree), the electuary sherbets, and the compound drug theriaca, used as an antidote for animal and insect venom and later a popular cure-all throughout the empire, are just the best-known examples of this west to east travel.

Sherbets were used as refreshment and restoratives, particularly popular with Il-Khanid envoys, and as vehicles to facilitate the ingestion of other medicines, and Rashīd al-Dīn mentions their widespread usage by west Asian physicians. They first appeared in China during the Yüan dynasty, and the Il-Khans of Iran became devotees of sherbet. Nestorians from Samarqand were the earliest recorded sherbet makers in China. Qubilai Khan created the office of official sherbet maker (*sherbetchi*), one holder of which was Marsarchis (Mar Sargis), whom Marco Polo encountered in Cinghianfu. Mar Sargis was an active Nestorian responsible for the construction of many churches and monasteries during a period when he was a Mongol overseer (*darughachi*) in Cinghianfu on the Lower Yangtze. As *sherbetchi* he made drinks and elixirs whose fame was widespread for their authenticity, the various ingredients from all parts of the empire being available to him in China. These concoctions were composed of citrus fruit, the juice of fresh berries, honey, sugar, rosewater, and even special Baghdadi lemons, all mixed by specially trained Chinese.

The popular cure-all theriaca, a mainstay of Muslim and eastern Christian pharmaceutical supplies, became a particular favorite with the Mongol elite. Various sources record large rewards given to suppliers and providers of theriaca by grateful Mongol rulers. One explanation for this attachment to theriaca by these Mongol rulers is probably the concoction's reputation as an antidote to all known toxins and venoms because Chinggisid princes had a well-founded fear of poisoning. The Muslim Il-Khan of Iran, Ghazan (ruled 1295–1304), had his own special antidote made up for him, which he honored with his name, *tiraq-i Ghāzānī*. Another reason for the widespread popularity of the theriaca supplied to the Mongol courts by their Muslim physicians was the fact that opium was a key component in its makeup.

MEDICAL BOOKS

One result of the Mongols' interest in medicine, their encouragement of various medical disciplines, and their willingness to act as the agency of cross-cultural interaction and exchange is the existence of a number of medical books and particularly pharmacopoeias. The two traditions— Galenic, based on the theory of humors, and Chinese, with its yin-yang and five agencies—remained deeply suspicious of each other, but mutual borrowing is evident, and of course the Mongols used freely of both traditions. This can be seen in their pharmacopoeias, which were enriched through the contacts made possible by political union. Scholars such as Rashīd al-Dīn and the Mongol statesman Bolad encouraged and enabled the exchange of medical knowledge, but it was the establishment of the Mongol Empire that created the agency for such an exchange. The Mongols with their emphasis on individuals and their nurturing of individual physicians over schools encouraged the emergence of medicine as a career profession of choice. Thousands were co-opted into the service of the Mongol courts, and medicine was a fast-track option. Evidence of the influence of the Mongols in the field of medicine after their demise is demonstrated by the translation into Chinese of Persian medical manuals by the Ming (1368–1644), the nationalists who succeeded the Mongols. The *Book of Muslim Medicine* was incorporated into the great Ming encyclopedia, *Yung-lo ta-tien,* and the *Muslim Medical Prescriptions* was a four-volume compilation of Persian medical drugs and plants.

NOTES

1. Grigor of Akanc, *History of the Nation of Archers*, trans. R. Blake and R. Frye (Cambridge: Harvard University Press, 1954), 10.

2. Francis Woodman Cleaves, trans., "The Biography of Bayan of the Barin in the Yuan Shih," *Harvard Journal of Asiatic Studies* 19 (1956): 433.

3. Francis Woodman Cleaves "A Medical Practice of the Mongols" in *Harvard Journal of Asiatic Studies* 17, Issue 3/4, (Dec 1954): 428–444.

4. Bar Hebraeus, *The Chronography of Gregory Abu'l-Faraj Bar Hebraeus' Political History of the World, Part I*, trans. Ernest A. Wallis-Budge, (Piscataway, N.J.: Gorgias Press, 2003), 437.

5. Henry Yule, *Cathay and the Way Thither,* 3 vols. (Reprint, Millwood, N.Y.: Kraus Reprint, 1967), 226.

6. Bar Hebraeus, *The Chronography,* 409–10.

7. Thomas Allsen, *Culture and Conquest in Mongol Eurasia* (Cambridge: Cambridge University Press, 2001), 150.

8. Ibid.; Yuan Shih cited in Allsen, *Culture and Conquest,* 221.

9. Allsen, 152.

10. Ibid., 153–54.

11. Ibid., 154.

7

DRINKING AND THE MONGOLS

Drinking was one of the distinctive traits of the Mongols. Heavy drinking was a defining characteristic of Mongol daily life. If modern genetic research is to be accepted, excessive drinking is part of the legacy the Mongols have bequeathed to their subject races. They lived and died drinking. In the case of a number of khans and even Great Khans this was literally true, and alcohol was openly admitted as the cause of death. The Armenian cleric and historian Kirakos observed firsthand that, "Whenever possible they ate and drank insatiably."[1] Heavy drinking and drunkenness were common and socially acceptable indulgences, and stories of alcohol-fueled excesses are numerous.

Drunkenness is honourable among the Tartars, and when someone drinks a great deal he is sick right on the spot, and this does not prevent him from drinking more.[2]

So observed the Friar Giovanni DiPlano Carpini (died 1252) who traveled to Mongolia between 1245 and 1247. A companion of the friar added that the Mongols were more given to drunkenness than any other people on earth, and their drinking bouts were not limited to one session a day but occurred several times throughout the day. Though it did not seem to have induced violence, excessive alcohol consumption has commonly been blamed for the early deaths of many of the leading Mongol rulers.

Drinking is one tradition the Mongols did not abandon when they assumed the trappings of imperial greatness and sophistication. Ögödei, Güyük, Qubilai, Abaqa, Geikhatu, Baidu, and Öljeitü were not the exceptions, just the most prolific. Though Chinggis lived into his 60s and Qubilai amazingly to the age of 78, the Mongol rulers were not noted for their longevity, rarely living beyond 50, and the cause of their truncated lives has usually been attributed to overindulgence in alcohol.

KOUMISS, *AIRAG*

Although the Mongols drank fresh milk, the favored beverage was a fermented dairy drink still made to day. This alcoholic concoction is known as koumiss, or *qumis,* and was generally fermented from mares' milk. Koumiss is in fact the Turkish name for the Mongolian alcoholic beverage *airag,* made from the milk of any one of the "five animals" (cow, sheep, horse, goat, yak). William of Rubruck was an unwitting initiate to the pleasures of koumiss, which upon swallowing for the first time brought him out in a sweat of

Utensil for making koumiss. Courtesy of Lan Tien Lang Publications

"alarm and surprise." However, he admitted to finding the drink very palatable. In preimperial times koumiss was the sole drink available to the Mongol tribes because, as Carpini noted, "[The Mongols] do not have wine, ale, or mead unless it is set or given to them by other nations."[3]

Rubruck devoted a short chapter of his travelogue to the making of koumiss.[4] He described how the foals of the tribe's horses were tethered to a stretched rope. The mares would seek out their young and then stand peacefully beside their offspring and allow themselves to be milked. If any mare should prove intractable, the foal would be allowed to initiate the milking process. The collected milk, "sweet as cow's milk," would be poured into a bag or large skin and then churned with a specially made club "as thick at the lower end as a man's head and hollowed out" until the mix began to bubble "like new wine" and to turn sour and ferment. Churning would continue until butter could be extracted. It was considered ready for drinking when it was moderately pungent. The taste had a sting on the tongue like sour wine but a very pleasant aftertaste like the milk of almonds. In addition it produced "a very agreeable sensation inside," a desire to urinate, and intoxication.[5]

Though mare's milk, which is particularly high in lactose (6% +), readily ferments into koumiss, the resulting liquor is not particularly high in alcohol, ranging from only 1.65 percent to 3.25 percent. Because the drink was not so potent, the Mongols had to consume large quantities of koumiss in order to achieve the desired intoxication, as Carpini again noted, "They drink mare's milk in very large quantities if they have it."[6] Rubruck claimed that in summer koumiss drinking was almost the sole occupation.

And when the master begins to drink, then one of the attendants cries with a loud voice, "Ha!" and the [minstrel] strikes his guitar, and when they have a great feast they all clap their hands, and also dance about to the sound of the guitar, the men before the master, the women before the mistress. And when the master has drunken, then the attendant cries as before, and the guitarist stops. Then they drink all around, and sometimes they do drink right shamefully and gluttonly. And when they want to challenge anyone to drink, they take hold of him by the ears, and pull so as to distend his throat, and they clap and dance before him. Likewise, when they want to make a great feasting and jollity with someone, one takes a full cup, and two others are on his right and left, and thus these three come singing and dancing towards him who is to take the cup, and they sing and dance before him; and when he holds out his hand to take the cup, they quickly draw it back, and then again they come back as before, and so they elude him three or four times by drawing away the cup, till he hath become well excited and is in good appetite, and then they give him the cup, and while he drinks they sing and clap their hands and strike with their feet.[7]

As well as this ordinary koumiss, sometimes dismissively described as white, cloudy, and sour tasting, a superior mare's milk beverage was also fermented. This was known as *qara kumis,* or black koumiss, and has been described as clear and sweet. Because their mares' milk did not curdle, the churning process was continued until everything solid in the milk sank to the bottom and the liquid that remained on top was very clear. The dregs, which were very white, were then separated and given to the slaves, and according to Rubruck, they had a highly soporific effect on them. The clear liquid, black koumiss, was presented to the Mongol lords for their consumption. This drink was very sweet and very potent. Distilled mare's milk is popular in both inner and outer Mongolia today.

Batu Khan (1255), lord of the Golden Horde of Russia and the Ukraine, was kept supplied with black koumiss by 30 men stationed one day's ride away from his *ordu* (camp). Each rider would supply the produce of 100 mares,

Vat used in the fermenting of koumiss, Hohhut Museum.
Courtesy of Xinjiang Qinshan Culture Publishing

which means a total of 3,000 mares daily servicing the needs of this Mongol prince. This figure does not include those mares producing the ordinary koumiss. Marco Polo claimed that Qubilai Khan (died 1294) of China needed 10,000 mares daily to satisfy his *ordu*'s demand for black koumiss.

Before the imperial age, the Mongols' drinking sprees and the perils of prolonged alcohol abuse were limited by certain practicalities. Mare's milk was generally available only in summer during the three to five months of the mares' lactation period, and as Rubruck suggests, it was in these months that the Mongols indulged their passion for koumiss. An exclusive diet of koumiss, at 2,000 calories a day, would demand a daily consumption of at least nine pints per person, which corresponds to the daily milk production of two mares (beyond the needs of their foals). An ordinary family would have kept two mares, and therefore the man of the family would have been able to devote himself to serious koumiss consumption during the five milking months of spring and summer.

Koumiss also played a part in religious ceremonies and observances. With horse- and cattle-breeding people their religious rituals often involve the animals that are central to their way of life, and the Mongols were able to honor both their sky god and their horses with ceremonies involving the sprinkling of koumiss and the consecration of their herds with this libation. Marco Polo witnessed one such ceremony.

The Lord abides at this Park of his, dwelling sometimes in the marble Palace and sometimes in the Cane Palace for three months of the year, to wit, June, July, and August; preferring this residence because it is by no means hot; in fact it is a very cool place. When the 28th day of [the moon of] August arrives he takes his departure, and the Cane Palace is taken to pieces. But I must tell you what happens when he goes away from this Palace every year on the 28th of the August [moon].

You must know that the Kaan keeps an immense stud of white horses and mares; in fact more than 10,000 of them, and all pure white without a speck. The milk of these mares is drunk by himself and his family, and by none else, except by those of one great tribe that have also the privilege of drinking it. This privilege was granted them by Chinghis Kaan, on account of a certain victory that they helped him to win long ago. The name of the tribe is HORIAD [Oyrat, Oirat].

Now when these mares are passing across the country, and any one falls in with them, be he the greatest lord in the land, he must not presume to pass until the mares have gone by; he must either tarry where he is, or go a half-day's journey round if need so be, so as not to come nigh them; for they are to be treated with the greatest respect. Well, when the Lord sets out from the Park on the 28th of August, as I told you, the milk of all those mares is taken and sprinkled on the ground. And this is done on the injunction of the Idolaters and Idol-priests, who say that it is an excellent thing to sprinkle that milk on the ground every 28th of August, so that the Earth and the Air and the False Gods shall have their share of it, and the Spirits likewise that inhabit the Air and the Earth. And thus those beings will protect and bless the Kaan and his children and his wives and his folk and his gear, and his cattle and his horses, his corn and all that is his.[8]

William of Rubruck provided a similar observation.

On the 9th day of the May Moon they collect all the white mares of their herds and consecrate them. The Christian priests also must then assemble with their thuribles. They then sprinkle new cosmos [*kumís*] on the ground, and make a great feast that day, for according to their calendar, it is their time of first drinking new cosmos, just as we reckon of our new wine at the feast of St. Bartholomew [August 24], or that of St. Sixtus [August 6], or of our fruit on the feast of St. James and St. Christopher [July 25].[9]

Chang Te-hui, a Chinese teacher, recounted the following, which occurred when he was summoned to Qubilai Khan's court in Mongolia some 12 years before that prince ascended the throne.

On the 9th day of the 9th Moon (October), the Prince, having called his subjects before his chief tent, performed the libation of the milk of a white mare. This was the customary sacrifice at that time. The vessels used were made of birch-bark, not ornamented with either silver or gold. Such here is the respect for simplicity.... At the last day of the year the Mongols suddenly changed their camping-ground to another place, for the mutual congratulation on the 1st Moon. Then there was every day feasting before the tents for the lower ranks. Beginning with the Prince, all dressed themselves in white fur clothing....On the 9th day of the 4th Moon (May) the Prince again collected his vassals before the chief tent for the libation of the milk of a white mare. This sacrifice is performed twice a year.

IMPERIAL SOPHISTICATION

Contact with the sophisticated urban centers of the Islamic west and the Chinese south led to more varied drinking habits though apparently no less excessive. Ibn Battuta, traveling across the lands of the northern Golden Horde, was served at a religious feast during the holy month of Ramadan, "mare's milk [and] afterwards they brought *buza* [fermented millet] and when the meal was done the Qur'an-readers recited with beautiful voices."[10] The Mongols drank rice mead, rice ale, honey mead (*bal*), fermented millet (*buza*), as well as red grape wine, which Rubruck compared to the French wine La Rochelle. It was the Mongols who facili-tated the popularity of grape wine to China. A colony of Muslim artisans originally from Samarqand settled in Sīmalī just north of Beijing, cultivated grapes, and provided wine for the imperial court throughout the thirteenth century. The Chinese introduced rice wine to the Persians, who called it *tarāsūn*. The Mongols drank both.

Friar Oderic of Pordenone, who traveled eastward between 1316 and 1330, noted the vast abundance of wine, known as *bigni*, in Kinsai (today's Hangzhou). It was said to resemble Rhenish wine in color, taste, and strength when kept for a year or so. This rice wine was made from rice first bruised and then compressed into cakes. These cakes were broken up and put into vessels with hot water where they were left to ferment. The wine produced could be made sweet or acidic and its color controlled with the addition of certain herbs during fermentation, and it was reputed to resemble grape wine in taste. In fact the word *bigni* used by Friar Oderic to describe the wine is said to be derived from the Persian *bigini,* which refers to malt liquor or beer. Hangzhou was famed for a date wine called *Mi-yin* or *Bi-im.*

HU SZU-HUI'S IMPERIAL DRINK

In 1330 the Yüan emperor Tuq Temür was presented with a magnificent cookbook, the *Yin-shan cheng-yao,* a new concept brought to the east from the Islamic west by Mongol cultural brokers. The author, Hu Szu-hui, probably an Uyghur, included a splendid array of dishes from throughout the empire. He also included a section on alcoholic beverages and their medicinal and nutritional properties. Apart from grape wine, popular since the time of the T'ang dynasty (618–907 c.e.), and a few rare fruit drinks, Chinese liquor is always brewed from grain. The medicinal concoctions described in the *Yin-shan cheng-yao* involved steeping various objects in liquor. Usually they were added to the grain mash and fermentation allowed to continue, or they were added to the finished spirit, such as the case with lamb wine. Lamb wine did not involve fermenting lamb meat. Tiger bone wine, still popular today for its supposed medicinal properties, is simply local vodka with a few grains of powered bone added. These various tinctures were and are referred to as *chiu,* which is translated rather inaccurately as "wine" and is misleading in that a *chiu* with an alcohol content of possibly more than 55 percent is far more potent than the average wine's alcohol content of 12 percent. The *Yin-shan cheng-yao* lists a number of alcoholic drinks that might be served at the imperial tables. Tiger bone liquor, wolfhornberry liquor, Chinese foxglove liquor, pine knot liquor, China root liquor, lamb liquor, *olnul* "naval" (penis and testes of the seal) liquor, Acanthopanax bark liquor, and pine root liquor are among the medicinal tonics recommended for a variety of needs. Also listed are some wines, such as grape wine, *qarakhodja* wine, Tibetan wine, and a brandy, *arajhi,* said to be sweet and piquant, and *sürmä* liquor, also known widely as *boza.*

Yuhuchun Yuan vase, Xi'an Museum. Courtesy of Lan
Tien Lang Publications

SPOUTING FOUNTAIN

With their growing sophistication and their acquaintance with liquors
other than those made from mare's milk, the Mongols also acquired more
refined implements to serve their drinks than the leather bags used for holding koumiss and *airag*. Rubruck described seeing an intricate contraption at
Qaraqorum, the capital of the Great Khan, Möngke (ruled 1251–58).

> In the entry of this great palace, it being unseemly to bring in there skins
> of milk and other drinks, master William the Parisian had made for him
> a great silver tree, and at its roots are four lions of silver, each with a
> conduit through it, and all belching forth white milk of mares. And four

conduits are led inside the tree to its tops, which are bent downward, and on each of these is also a gilded serpent, whose tail twines round the tree. And from one of these pipes flows wine, from another *cara cosmos*, or clarified mare's milk, from another *bal*, a drink made with honey, and from another rice mead, which is called *terracina*; and for each liquor there is a special silver bowl at the foot of the tree to receive it. Between these four conduits in the top, he made an angel holding a trumpet, and underneath the tree he made a vault in which a man can be hid. And pipes go up through the heart of the tree to the angel. In the first place he made bellows, but they did not give enough wind. Outside the palace is a cellar in which the liquors are stored, and there are servants all ready to pour them out when they hear the angel trumpeting. And there are branches of silver on the tree, and leaves and fruit. When then drink is wanted, the head butler cries to the angel to blow his trumpet. Then he who is concealed in the vault, hearing this blows with all his might in the pipe leading to the angel, and the angel places the trumpet to his mouth, and blows the trumpet right loudly. Then the servants who are in the cellar, hearing this, pour the different liquors into the proper conduits, and the conduits lead them down into the bowls prepared for that, and then the butlers draw it and carry it to the palace to the men and women.[11]

Marco Polo, who traveled from Venice with his father and uncle to Qubilai Khan's grand court in his summer capital, Shangdu (Xanadu) in 1271–75, also witnessed the alcoholic excesses for which the Mongols were so famous, and he noted that Qubilai was continuing this tradition of elaborate contraptions for serving their drinks. Qubilai Khan's banquets could accommodate up to 40,000 guests, and for such festivities he had constructed a

very fine piece of furniture of great size and splendour in the form of a square chest, each side being three paces [about 8 feet] in length, elaborately carved with figures of animals finely wrought in gold. The inside is hollow and contains a huge golden vessel in the form of a pitcher with the capacity of a butt [two hogshead of between 52 to 116 gallons each], which is filled with wine. In each corner of the chest is a vessel with the capacity of a firkin [a quarter of a 26.25 gallon barrel], one filled with mares' milk, one with camels' milk, and the others with other beverages.... From [the chest] the wine or other precious beverage is drawn off to fill huge stoups of gold, each containing enough to satisfy eight or ten men. One of these [stoups] is set between every two men seated at the table. Each of the two has a gold cup with a handle, which he fills from the stoup. And for every pair of ladies one stoup and two cups are provided in the same way.[12]

Marco Polo noted that the Mongols celebrated their birthdays as festivals, and because Qubilai had 4 wives and 22 sons and an unspecified number of daughters by them, various concubines who had given him a

Yuan period vase. Courtesy of Lan Tien Lang Publications

further 25 sons, plus his various relatives and top commanders with their families, there was limitless scope for celebration and partying.

IBN BATTUTA

Ibn Battuta was impressed with the gold and silver vessels that were brought in to serve the guests of the Muslim leader of the Golden Horde, Özbek Khan (ruled 1313–14), when he organized a banquet during the holy month of Ramadan for his top commanders, possibly numbering 187, religious leaders, and visiting dignitaries such as Ibn Battuta himself.

After [the meal], drinking vessels of gold and silver are brought. The beverage they make most use of is fermented liquor of honey, since, being of the Hanafite School of [Islamic] law, they hold fermented liquor to be lawful. When the sultan [Özbek Khan] wishes to drink, his daughter takes the bowl in her hand, pays homage ... and then presents the bowl to him. When he has drunk she takes another bowl and presents it to the chief [wife], who drinks from it, after which she presents it to the other [wives] in their order of precedence. The sultan's heir then takes the bowl, pays homage, and presents it to his father, then, when he has drunk, presents it to the [wives] and to his sister after them, paying homage to them all. The second son then rises, takes the bowl and gives it to his brother to drink paying homage to him. Thereafter the great [commanders] rise, and each one of [the 17 of] them gives the cup to the sultan's heir and pays homage to him, after which the [other] members of the royal house rise and each one of them gives the cup to this second son, paying homage to him. The [170] lesser [commanders] then rise and give the sons of the king to drink. During all this [ceremony], they sing [songs resembling the] chants sung by oarsmen.[13]

After these festivities, Ibn Battuta informed his readers, the sultan was so drunk that he could not make Friday prayers on time at the mosque. He did eventually appear but arrived swaying, and after the prayers were recited he retired once again to his tent to resume his drinking. Ozbak Khan was a generous host, and Ibn Battuta described seeing wagons laden with skins of koumiss stretching to the horizon waiting to be distributed to the sultan's guests. One wagon could hold 131 gallons of koumiss. Ibn Battuta informed his readers that he presented his Turkish neighbors with the wagon presented to him. As some kind of comparison Juwaynī claimed that Möngke's week-long *quriltai* in 1251 needed 2,000 wagon loads of koumiss and wine per day to keep the guests and his own people happy.

U.S. historian John Masson Smith Jr. came out with some interesting figures to elaborate both the Mongols' drinking and eating habits. Based on details provided by William of Rubruck, he calculated that at a great drinking festival organized by Möngke Khan on June 24, 1254, each guest would have been provided with the equivalent of 19 shots of whiskey. He assumed that the drink-laden wagons carried 1,000-pound loads and that each of the estimated 7,000 guests received two gallons of koumiss each.

WOMEN

It was not only the Mongol men who had a predilection for excessive drinking. The Mongol women who not only performed admirably on the battlefield also matched their men folk in the art of prodigious alcohol consumption. William of Rubruck faithfully noted that the women enjoyed getting as outrageously drunk as their men and that they joined in the "singing and loud shouting" because such drunken behavior was "not considered reprehensible in either men or women." It surprised Rubruck that though the women got very intoxicated they never became physically aggressive and they never came to blows or traded insults. He described being waited on by one of Möngke's wives at another of the Great Khan's banquets.

[She served us] rice ale, red wine... and [koumiss]. The lady, holding a full goblet in her hand, knelt down and asked a blessing, and all the priests sang in a loud voice and she drank it all. My companion and I were also obliged to sing another time when she wanted to drink. When they were all nearly intoxicated food was brought, [mutton and carp] and of this I ate a little. In this way they passed the time until evening. Then the lady, now drunk, got into a cart, while the priests sang and howled, and she went on her way.[14]

In Iran, the reformer Ghazan Khan (ruled 1295–1304), who was a Muslim convert and had made Islam the state religion of the Il-Khanate, attempted to curb the drinking excesses of the women at his court. Among the curbs he placed on the expenditure for the *ordus* (courts) of the princesses were restrictions on the purchases of clothing and provisions, including stocks for the *sharab-khāneh,* or wine cellars. Provisions for the *sharab-khāneh* were itemized separately, which suggests that this was a major and important item of expenditure and that the women's use of this provision was in need of control. Rashīd al-Dīn mentions other provisions Ghazan was making for reducing the cost of alcohol and wine and increasing the efficiency of its delivery. He also introduced legislation to punish public displays of drunkenness and rowdiness throughout his domains, something he apparently deplored.

INFAMOUS IMBIBERS: ÖGÖDEI

Stories of Mongol drinking bouts and excesses are legion. Ögödei (1241), the successor to his father, Chinggis Khan, officially died of excessive drinking, which his brother, Chaghatai (died 1242), had tried in vain to curb.

Qa'an [Ögödei] was extremely fond of wine, and [he] drank continuously and to excess. Day by day he grew weaker, and though his intimates and well-wishers sought to prevent him, it was not possible, and he drank more in spite of them. Chaghatai appointed an emir to watch over him [Ögödei] and not allow him to drink more than a specified number of cups. As he could not disobey his brother's command, he used to drink from a large cup instead of a small one, so that the number remained the same.[15]

Ögödei's death followed yet another night of excessive drinking. He was discovered dead in his bed the following morning. With the sudden death

of a mighty leader, the hand of conspiracy and intrigue is always suspected. Initially suspicion fell on the *ba'urchi* (cook) and his mother, Ibaqa
Beki, a former wife of the Qa'an, and the Qa'an's hostess and cupbearer
that night. However, reason prevailed, and those closest to the Great Khan
were in no doubt as to the real cause of Ögödei's untimely demise. The
accusations were dismissed.

"What nonsense [the accusations] is this? ... The Qa'an always drank too much. Why
must we bad-mouth our Qa'an by saying he was assassinated by others? His time
had come, that's all. No one should speak of this nonsense again." Since he [a gen-
eral] was an intelligent man, he realised that the death had been caused by drinking
too much. He also knew how serious the end of overindulgence in wine was.[16]

GÜYÜK

Güyük, Ögödei's successor, kept the family tradition alive, and friar
Carpini was witness to more alcoholic excesses on a grand scale. He
reported how during Güyük's prolonged enthronement banquets the
chiefs conferred over matters of state in a huge tent

until almost noon and then began drinking mare's milk and they drank it until
evening which was amazing to see. They called us inside and gave us ale because
we did not like mare's milk in the least: and so did us great honor. But still they
compelled us to drink so much that we could not stay at all sober, so we complained that this bothered us, but still they continued to force us.[17]

Rashīd al-Dīn claimed that the universally dreaded and widely detested
Güyük filled most of his hours, "from morning till evening and from dawn
to dusk with the quaffing of cups of wine and the contemplation of peri-
faced, sweet-limbed maidens."[18]

MÖNGKE KHAN

The Qa'an, Möngke, not only drank with his meals and during drinking
festivals, he also liked to mix his binging with business. The papal representative William of Rubruck claimed that the emperor often appeared intoxicated when he summoned the cleric for interviews, and that Möngke would
continue drinking during the course of these interviews, Rubruck recording
that the Great Khan imbibed four times during their last meeting.

ABAQA KHAN AND OTHERS

The Il-Khan of Mongol Persia, Abaqa Khan, famously died of delirium
tremens and hallucinations, which were recorded by Rashīd al-Dīn.

On Wednesday 18 March he arrived in Hamadan and stopped at the palace of
Malik Fakr al-Dīn Minuchehr where he was continuously occupied with *jirghamishi*

[celebration] and enjoying various pleasures. On the eve of Wednesday 1 April, 1282...past midnight, after excessive drinking, he came out on the demand of a call of nature. The Harbinger of Death revealed itself to him as a black bird perched on the branch of the trees that were there. [Abaqa] cried out, "What is this black bird!" He then commandeered his quiver-bearer to shoot an arrow at it. However much they searched they could find no [trace of] the bird. Suddenly he closed his eyes and from his golden throne surrendered his precious soul.[19]

Abaqa died a well-loved and widely admired king remembered for his justice and wisdom rather than his excessive drinking. A later Il-Khan, Geikhatu (ruled 1291–95), was remembered primarily for his drinking, debauchery, and other excesses.

Day and night, he sought his desires...in wine and drinking. His desire continued to be for wine, and he dismissed all fear. Whether he was faced by plain or mountain, he had no worldly concern for passing them. Mountain or plain were the same to him, as were strangers or intimate companions.[20]

Geikhatu was also known for his liberality and generosity, though there were some who attributed this generosity to drunkenness. It was in fact this very drunkenness coupled with a generous and forgiving spirit that sealed his fate. One evening, he was with his cousin Baidu drinking liberally, and "their heads were hot with the fumes of the wine."[21] Baidu let slip a particularly insulting suggestion against Geikhatu's father, Abaqa Khan. As a result, Baidu received a severe beating and was thrown from the court. Even though he apologized in the morning for the insult and begged for and was granted his cousin's, Geikhatu's, forgiveness, Baidu vowed revenge for the beating. Later, Geikhatu's drink-induced debauchery reached new depths of depravity and included the seduction of Baidu's son who was present at court. The emirs and courtiers at Geikhatu's court went to Baghdad, where Baidu was governor, and pleaded with him to seize the throne. A pitched battle ensued, and eventually Geikhatu met his end after being trapped as a refugee in the mountains.

ALCOHOLISM

All this heavy drinking came at a price. Premature death was, of course, common, but pervasive alcoholism had far-reaching affects on the health of the Mongols as a people. Gout and chronic obesity were common and were a direct result of overeating and overdrinking and effected both the "wondrous fat" women and the sometimes "grotesquely fat" men, as the observant William of Rubruck duly noted. Ibn Battuta observed the widespread occurrence of gout during his travels in the territories of the Golden Horde.

We went to visit...the sultan's daughter....Her husband...was present, and sat with her on the same rug. He was suffering from gout, and was unable for this reason to go about on his feet or to ride a horse, and so used to ride only in a wagon.... In the same state too, I saw the amir Naghatay, who was the father of the second [wife of the sultan], and this disease is widespread among the [Mongols].[22]

Chinggis Khan himself drank but was at the same time well aware of the dangers of heavy binge drinking. He moderated his own drinking, limiting himself to three drinking sessions a month at most, unwilling to cloud his judgment and mental faculties with chronic drunkenness. Most other Mongols were not so disciplined or clear thinking, and drunkenness continued to be socially acceptable, even an honorable condition. With foreign beverages containing a far higher alcohol content than traditional koumiss becoming increasingly available and common, coupled with the continued high volume and long-sessioned intake favored by the Mongols, incidents of early death and serious illness increased. The declining longevity is evident among the Il-Khans of Persia, with Hülegü and his son Abaqa making 48, but Ghazan died at 32, Öljeitü at 35, and Abū Saʿīd died without heir at 30. The deaths of the other Il-Khans were caused by direct human intervention rather than their apparent lifestyle. A similar pattern can be seen with the successors of Qubilai in China. Timur made 42, Qaishan reached only 31, Ayurbarwada Buyantu died at 35, Yestin Timur died at 35, Tugh Timur died at only 28, Irinjibal at 7, and Toghon Timur at 50.

As well as apparently having a dramatic influence on longevity, the alcoholism and binge drinking common among Mongol men and women also seemed to have had a marked effect on fertility. Again Qubilai seems to have defied the trend even though his overindulgences were well known and documented. He sired 47 sons and no doubt a similar number of daughters by four wives and numerous concubines. Hülegü managed a respectable 21 children with his five wives and a few concubines, but his successors did little to populate the Perso-Mongol gene pool. Abaqa's 15 women gave him 9 children; Arghun had 9 women and 7 surviving offspring; Ghazan's 7 women gave him only 2 children, 1 of whom died in infancy; Öljeitü produced only 3 surviving offspring, though he had 12 women to help him; and, of course, with 2 wives Abū Saʿīd had only 1 posthumous child. The figures both for the premature deaths and for the declining fertility coupled with what is known of the Mongols' drinking habits seems to suggest a strong linkage between the two. The sudden disappearance of the Mongols of Persia, the Il-Khans, has long baffled historians because the dynasty does not seem to have entered any period of decline. In fact Abū Saʿīd's reign could in some ways be seen as their climax. The answer may be their lifestyle and their excessive drinking in particular. Drink caused their early deaths, their declining fertility, and ultimately the end of the Persian line of Hülegü and the Chinggisids.

WORDS OF WISDOM

The acclaimed historian and prime minister of Mongol Iran Rashīd al-Dīn (died 1318) recounted some words of wisdom attributed to Chinggis Khan that seem to suggest that in old age the founder of this world empire was well aware of the dangers of the habit that had such a grip on his people.

When a man gets drunk on wine and *tarāsūn* [rice wine], he is just like a blind man who can't see anything, a deaf man who can't hear when he's called, and a mute who can't reply when he's spoken to. When a man gets drunk he is like someone in a state of death: he can't sit up straight even if he wants to. He's as dazed and senseless as someone who's been hit over the head.[23]

DRINKING TODAY[24]

Airag is still the drink of choice in Mongolia today, and the country's official newsletter has even claimed that *airag* is as integral to their culture as Coca-Cola is to the culture of the United States. It is produced throughout the summer in a specially made hide skin bag. First, fresh milk is used to initiate fermentation, and the mix is regularly stirred with a special wooden stick. Fresh *airag* is basically mild, but if kept for long enough it may turn sour and acidic. Old *airag* may contain up to 9 percent alcohol. It is usually served in very large bowls.

Medical features of *airag* have long been proven according to Mongolian sources. It clears any poisons and antioxidants, especially the consequences of overconsumption of fat during the long winter, and generally strengthens the body. It contains many types of vitamins and organic and mineral elements. *Airag* is widely used for treatment of many diseases.

Not all families make *airag* because it involves considerable time and effort. Mares should be milked every two hours during the hot summer days and every three hours in autumn. The amount of milk produced by one mare averages about 1.5 liters to 2 liters when milked six times per day. The remaining milk is needed for the colts. So, in order to make enough *airag* for the family as well as for their visitors, at least a dozen mares are needed. In addition, to get good-quality *airag* it is necessary to stir the milk mix no less than 1,000 times each day. All guests are expected to contribute and assist with churning the *airag*.

To get good-quality milk, mares should be grazed on the best pastures and in cool places near rivers and lakes. The best *airag* is produced in the Middle Gobi province, called the Land of Airag and Long Songs. What makes the taste of Gobi *airag* special is the unique mixture of desert grasses on which the mares feed. Another area famous for *airag* is Arkhangai province, or Northern Mountains, which is known for its beautiful landscapes and the beauty of the local girls skilled in making dairy products.

Recent research in Russia into alcoholism and drunkenness has come out with some surprising conclusions. Scientists say that they have found a genetic link between Russians' traditional weakness for drink and the marauding Mongol armies of Chinggis Khan and claim that genetic traces the Mongols left behind are partly to blame for Russia's traditional weakness for vodka.

As many as 50 percent of Muscovites are estimated to have inherited Mongol genes that make them absorb more alcohol into the bloodstream and break it down at a slower rate than most Europeans, they say. That means that they get more easily drunk and have worse hangovers and are more likely to become addicted to alcohol. "The difference is huge—in reaction speed, memory, hand tremor—and in how they recover," Vladimir Nuzhny of the Health Ministry's National Narcology Research Center said. "On average, 50 percent of people in Moscow have this Mongoloid gene. So this, we think, is part of the problem. The way they get drunk is completely different. They are also more likely to feel aggressive or depressed," Dr. Nuzhny said. "They do not necessarily look Mongolian, but the gene that governs how they metabolise alcohol is Mongoloid."

Scientists have long known that people of Mongol extraction, including Chinese, Koreans, and Japanese, have an enzyme for metabolizing alcohol that is different from that of Caucasian Europeans. Dr. Nuzhny claims that his study is the first to look at the effect of alcohol on Russians who have inherited Mongol genes. He says that the phenomenon can be explained partly by evolution. The nomadic Mongols, whose only indigenous form of alcohol was fermented mare's milk, evolved with a different enzyme compared to the settled Europeans, with their long tradition of producing stronger grape- and grain-based alcohol.

The gene, known as ADH2-2, is common in Asian countries but almost nonexistent among Europeans. "This gene is found in 41 percent of the population in Moscow," says Dr. Pavel Gurtsov, head of the center's medical department.

"We don't know exactly how it affects the way alcohol is absorbed, but our findings show that carriers of the gene are more susceptible to the effects of drinking and more likely to become alcoholics."

NOTES

1. Kirakos Ganjaks'i, *Kirakos Ganjaks'i's History of the Armenians,* trans. Robert Bedrosian, *Sources for the Armenian Tradition,* available at: http://rbedrosian.com/kg1.htm, 234.

2. Giovanni DiPlano Carpini, *The Story of the Mongols Whom We Call the Tartars: Historia Mongalorum,* trans. Erik Hildinger (Boston: Branden, 1996), 51.

3. Ibid., 17.

4. William of Rubruck, *The Mission of William of Rubruck,* trans. and ed. Peter Jackson with David Morgan (London: Hakluyt Society, 1990), 81–83.

5. Ibid., 80–83.

6. Carpini, *The Story of the Mongols,* 17.

7. W.W. Rockhill, *The Journey of William of Rubruck to the Eastern Parts of the World, 1253–55, as Narrated by Himself, with Two Accounts of the Earlier Journey of John of Pian de Carpine*, trans. from the Latin and ed., with an introductory notice, by William Woodville Rockhill (London: Hakluyt Society, 1900).

8. Marco Polo and Rustichello of Pisa, *The Project Gutenberg EBook of The Travels of Marco Polo,* http://www.gutenberg.net.

9. William of Rubruck, *The Mission of William of Rubruck,* trans. and ed. Peter Jackson with David Morgan (London: Hakluyt Society, 1990), ch. 35, para. 4.

10. H.A.R. Gibb, J.H. Kramer, J. Schacht, and F. Levi-Provençal, eds., *The Encyclopaedia of Islam,* new ed. (Leiden, Netherlands: Luzac and Brill, 1960), 477.

11. William of Rubruck, *The Mission of William of Rubruck,* 210.

12. Complete Yule-Cordier Edition of Marco Polo's travels by Marco Polo and Rustichello of Pisa, *The Project Gutenberg EBook of the Travels of Marco Polo,* available at: http://www.gutenberg.net, vol. 2, x.

13. Gibb, Kramer, Schacht, and Levi-Provençal, *Encyclopaedia of Islam,* 495–96.

14. William of Rubruck, *The Mission of William of Rubruck,* 191.

15. Rashīd al-Dīn, *The Successors of Genghis Khan,* trans. John Andrew Boyle (New York: Columbia University Press, 1971), 65.

16. Rashīd al-Dīn, *Rashiduddin Fazlullah Jami 'u' t-Tawarikh: Compendium of Chronicles,* 3 vols., trans. W.M. Thackston (Cambridge, MA: Sources of Oriental Languages & Literature 45, Central Asian Sources, Harvard University), 330; Rashīd al-Dīn, *Jāmi' al-Tavārīkh,* eds., Mohammad Roushan and Mustafah Mūsavī (Tehran: Nashr albaraz, 1994), 673–74.

17. Giovanni DiPlano Carpini, *The Story of the Mongols,* 108.

18. Rashīd al-Dīn, *The Successors,* 188.

19. Rashīd al-Dīn, *Jāmi' al-Tavārīkh,* 1118.

20. Mustawfī, *Zafarnāmeh,* trans. L.J. Ward, 348.

21. Ibid., 351–52.

22. Gibb, Kramer, Schacht, and Levi-Provençal, *Encyclopaedia of Islam,* 489.

23. Rashid al-Din, *Rashiduddin Fazlullah Jami 'u' t-Tawarikh: Compendium of Chronicles,* trans. W.M. Thackston (Cambridge, Mass.: Sources of Oriental Languages & Literature 45, 1998), 297.

24. *The Times* (U.K.) January 19, 2004.

8

FOOD

Food was also an important aspect of Mongol daily life, though it is not surrounded in the myths and tall tales and raucous humor that accompany the subject of their drinking. There was also a clear distinction between the cuisines of traditional Mongol life and the fabulous epicurean extravaganzas that were laid before the later Great Qa'ans of the maturing empire. The study of the medieval Mongol cuisine and the food consumed within the borders of the Mongol Empire is a subject worthy of a multitomed book in itself, so this present chapter will merely attempt to lift a corner of the sumptuous curtain enclosing this topic and provide a few tantalizing appetizers from the vast range of delicious dishes once found on the khans' exotic tables.

The grandsons of Chinggis Khan, the Toluids in particular, were exposed to a wide range of cultural and culinary influences, and for the most part they welcomed these diverse temptations. Their pride in their Mongol heritage remained strong, for it was a confidence that welcomed the cultural richness they were exposed to as rulers of half the world. Their kitchens were no exception to this rule, and there is ample evidence that Mongols were very willing to try, and to enjoy, a wide variety of dishes and foods, often in public displays of lavish and conspicuous consumption.

HU SZU-HUI'S COOKBOOK

A remarkable manual presented to the Yüan emperor Toq Temür (ruled 1328–32) in 1330 has survived to the present day, and it is this document that has provided unprecedented insight into not only the culinary habits of the Mongol Yüan court of China but also the Mongol dietary customs in general. The *Yin-shan cheng-yao (Proper and Essential Things for the Emperor's Food and Drink)* was written by Hu Szu-hui, who had been an imperial dietary physician to the imperial court since the early years of the fourteenth century. Appointed after Qubilai's death, Hu served a number of his short-lived successors. Despite his Chinese name, it is believed that Hu Szu-hui was possibly Turkish, from the former lands of the Hsi-Hsia in northwestern China. Scholarly opinion suggests that his native language might have been Uyghur but that he had early exposure to Chinese and received a good schooling in Chinese, evident from the fine quality of the language used in his book.

Northern China was probably less than 80 percent Chinese in the fourteenth century, and the Mongols remained in power because of the close and strong alliances they forged with elites and power wielders in the north. The Chinese in the north had far greater roots and contacts with non-Chinese elements than did those from the Song-dominated south. Hu Szu-hui's Chinese name is indicative of the close ties existing between the communities in the north. His great work, the *Yin-shan cheng-yao,* written in Chinese in a framework of Chinese dietary and medical theory, comfortably embodies elements of Chinese, Mongolian, Turkic, Turco-Islamic, Persian, and Islamic culinary practice intermingled to produce the composite Mongol taste. Hu Szu-hui's *Yin-shan cheng-yao* is a Mongol

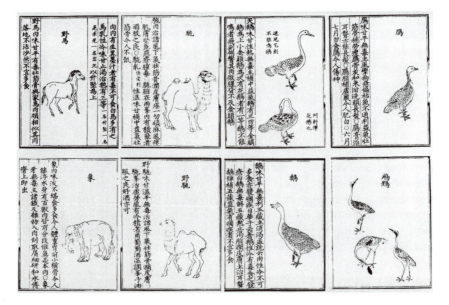

From Hu Szu-hui's *Yin-shan cheng-yao* (Mongol Cookbook). Courtesy of Lan Tien Lang Publications

cookbook. It was written for his Mongol masters, not for the Chinese. It reflects the tastes of the Mongol rulers, not those of their Chinese subjects. However, the Mongols of the Yüan dynasty were very different from those Mongols who had ridden thundering out from the steppe with Chinggis Khan 100 years previously. The fact that the descendants of those same rulers who rode out from the northern steppe lands were still in control attests to their ability to compromise and integrate. That process of cultural integration and assimilation is nowhere more succinctly expressed than in Hu Szu-hui's cookbook.

Even though the Mongols' dream of world domination had faded with the reality of the bitter internecine wars between the Golden clans, the pretense of universality could be maintained at the table. The eclectic culinary creations incorporated foods from all over the extended empire. Mongol medicine appears with west Asian cures in a main course of Chinese remedies, for much of the fare was chosen for its curative and health-strengthening properties.

Tales of the indolent luxury and indulgence of Qubilai Khan and the Yüan court over which he presided spread far beyond the confines of his empire, and even in faraway England there were whispers of the terrible opulence to be witnessed there. "And close your eyes in holy dread, / for he on honeydew has fed / and drunk the milk of paradise."[1] In fact, the Mongols like the Chinese were obsessed with the nutritional and medical aspects of food and their diet, and these health-conscious elements figured greatly in the choice and preparation of their food. Much of the *Yin-shan cheng-yao* was concerned with the medicinal value of food and recipes, and the overall presentation is in tune with medieval Chinese nutritional therapy.

Two traits, clearly discernable, mark this cookbook as unmistakably Mongol and not Chinese. First, sheep, the staple of the pastoralist nomad from the steppe, remains paramount, and all parts of this favorite animal of the Mongols were used in their broths and meat dishes. Second is the absence of pig, the staple of the Chinese but not so beloved of the Mongols. Wild game also figures in the recipes, as does the meat of other herd animals. The Mongols were no longer dependant on these herd animals, however, and they were eager that their kitchens should reflect their new reality and their desire and willingness to experiment with the new and the exotic. Their kitchens reflected their new cosmopolitan identity as well as their exotic and eclectic guest lists and the varied and unusual fare introduced to welcome those that they invited to sit at table with them.

TRADITIONAL MONGOL CUISINE

The nature of Mongol cuisine and eating habits changed considerably since the early days of the empire, as indicated in this report, circa 1240s, from Simon de Saint-Quentin's *Histoire des Tatares:*

Furthermore, they are the most unclean and filthy in their eating. They use neither tablecloths nor napkins, nor do they have bread [to use as a plate], or pay any attention to it, and scorn to eat it. They have not vegetables or even legumes; and nothing other than meat to eat, and they eat so little meat that other peoples could scarcely live from it. And further they eat all kinds of meats except for that of the mule, which is sterile, and this they do disgracefully and rapaciously. They lick their greasy fingers and wipe them dry on their boots. The great ones are wont to have little cloths with which they wipe their fingers carefully. They do not wash their hands before eating, nor their dishes afterwards; and if perchance they wash them in meat broth, they put the dish they have washed back into the pot along with the meat. Otherwise they do not wash pots or spoons or utensils of any kind. They like horsemeat more than any other meat. They even eat rats and dogs and dine on cats with great pleasure. They drink wine with great pleasure whenever they have it. They get drunk every day on the mare's milk which they call *kaumous* [koumiss], just as others get drunk on strong wine. And when they celebrate holidays and the festivals of their forefathers, they spend their time in singing, or rather shrieking, and in drinking bouts; and as long as such drinking bouts last, they attend to no business and dispatch no envoys. This is what the brothers of the Order of Preaching Monks, sent to the Mongols by the Pope and staying in their camp, experienced continuously for six days. They eat human meat like lions; devouring it roasted on the fire and soaked with grease. And whenever they take someone contrary or hostile to themselves, they come together in one place to eat him in vengeance for the rebellion raised against them. They avidly suck his blood just like hellish vampires.[2]

The Mongols in preimperial times ate a simple, calorie-sufficient, but poorly balanced diet. The average family unit possessed a herd of sheep, with some goats, plus a few cattle and camels. Horses were also kept for military duties, including the annual call to the *nerge* (hunt), and for koumiss. According to John Mason Smith, at least 100 sheep were required for nutritional needs, at least five (gelding) ponies for military duties, and in addition for transportation possibly three more ponies and some oxen and camels and of course a mare or two for milking. These animals provided the sustenance for the family because for most of the time they were not in contact with the settled world where vegetables and other foodstuffs might be available for sale or barter. Imported food was rare and considered a luxury.

Horse meat was the favorite, but it was beyond the means of most, who had to content themselves with mutton and lamb. In addition to meat, milk and milk products were the other main type of food for the majority of

Fresh food stall: fish, fowl, and flesh. Courtesy of Xinjiang Qinshan Culture Publishing

Mongols. Interestingly, the poorer Mongols probably had a better, more balanced diet. Temüjin and his family, thrown on hard times after the murder of his father and the theft of their herd, often could not afford meat and were forced to eat wild plants for sustenance. The *Secret History of the Mongols* claims that the boys grew up into fine men despite a diet of what was considered second-rate food. Forced to forage in the wild to feed her family, Hö'elün made them meals containing very nutritious wild pears, bird cherries, garden burnet root, cinquefoil root, wild onion, shallot, lily root, and garlic chives.

Carpini, the papal envoy and intelligence gatherer, painted an unappealing picture of squalor and the crudest food preparation imaginable, an impression reinforced by other contemporary reports, and unfortunately an impression that, like their early reputation for blood-thirsty depravity, attached itself to their name in perpetuity. Carpini witnessed

his Tatar escorts discovering the bodies of some unidentified dead animals
on their journey. "They found the fresh entrails of a beast. They took them
and cooked them, discarding only the dung."[3] Carpini also claimed that
the Mongols practiced cannibalism and ate wolves, dogs, foxes, mice, and
even lice. He claimed that in desperation they were even known to eat a
mare's afterbirth.

The Armenian cleric Kirakos had intimate contact with the Mongols
over a number of years, and he witnessed the transformation of their social
habits and customs over the decades. He recorded his first impressions of
these barbarians from the steppe, but by the end of his chronicle his views
on the Mongols mellowed considerably.

Whenever possible they ate and drank insatiably, but when it was not possible,
they were temperate. They ate all sorts of animals both clean and unclean, and
especially cherished horsemeat. This they would cut into pieces and cook or else
roast it without salt; then they would cut it up into small pieces and sop it in salt
water and eat it that way. Some eat on their knees, like camels, and some eat
sitting. When eating, lords and servants share equally. To drink *kumiss* or wine,
one of them first takes a great bowl in his hand and, taking from it with a small
cup, sprinkles the liquid to the sky, then to the east, west, north and south. Then the
sprinkler himself drinks some of it and offers it to the nobles. If someone brings
them food or drink, first they make the bearer eat and drink of it, and then they
themselves [will accept it] lest they be betrayed by some poison.[4]

The steppe lands were rich in water and grass and, hence, ideal for
sheep and horses, which became the main ingredients of the Mongols' diet.
Mares became the source of their chief pleasure in life, namely the drinking of koumiss, which relieved them body and soul. A Chinese observer
in the first decade of the empire noted that Chinese and other non-Mongol
slaves kept in the Mongol camps encountered considerable hardship as a
result of the meat-only diet forced on them. These slaves ate rice whenever
possible to ease the hunger they experienced with the monotonous menu.
As a result, the Mongols took to seizing rice and wheat in their raids and
to modifying their dishes to please the palates of their slaves. Another
Chinese source writing in the 1230s notes:

Their food is meat and not grain. Animals captured in hunting are the hare, deer,
wild pigs, the marmot, wild sheep, the dseiren antelope, wild horses, and fish
from rivers and springs. The animal normally raised to be eaten is the sheep. The
ox is second. They do not slaughter horses unless it is a major feast or assembly.
Meat is almost always roasted. Only rarely is it cooked in a pot. One cuts of a piece
of meat and eats. Afterwards the meat is given to others to eat. During the month
that I, T'ing, was in the steppe, I did not see the Tatars kill an ox to eat.[5]

Carpini noted that the Mongols with whom he traveled drank a kind
of millet broth. A couple of cupfuls of this millet soup in the morning sufficed until the evening when a portion of meat washed down with a meat

broth constituted the day's nourishment. This millet soup was allowed to be thickened, and eventually it became bread, and so it was that the revolution in the Mongols' diet and palate began. Just as their food developed, so too their drinking, and by the reign of Ögödei the Mongols had a taste for a variety of alcoholic beverages, including beers, wines, and liquors.

DEVELOPMENTS

Within a few decades, that simple step from millet soup to bread gave rise to recipes such as the following for honeyed stuffed crab given by Ni Tsan, author of another cookbook for the kings. The crabs were to be cooked in salted water until the color began to change to red, when they were be taken out and broken up so that the meat could be taken from the claws and legs. The meat should then be chopped up and stuffed into the shell. An egg was then to be mixed with a little honey and stirred into the meat within the shell. Fat would now be spread on the egg and the whole then steamed until the egg just started to solidify, taking care not to overcook. For eating, Ni Tsan suggested dipping it into ground orange peel and vinegar.

Another recipe instructed the cook to cut a carp into chunks before cooking it in a mixture of half water and half wine. Meanwhile, a fresh ginger should be peeled and sliced before grinding. This should be mixed with flower pepper before grinding again and then gently stirred into wine until liquid. Pour soy sauce into a pan before adding the fish. It should be brought to the boil three times before the ginger-pepper mix is added and the whole brought to the boil for a final time.

Marco Polo was witness to many of the sumptuous feasts common among the Mongol elite in the later years of the thirteenth century, and he wrote in startling contrast to Carpini a few decades earlier. Carpini traveled through the northern climes, however, which in later years remained more wedded to traditional Mongol values than did the more southern climes where Marco Polo traveled. Even today, West Lake, at the heart of fashionable and cosmopolitan Hangzhou, is famous for the restaurants and food stalls crowding its shores and even spilling onto the boats on the lake itself.

WEST ASIAN INFLUENCE

Safarjaliya was a recipe found in medieval Arabic cookbooks that closely resembled dishes found in Hu Szu-hui's manual. The fatty meat of the sheep's tail is thinly sliced and then cooked in the dissolved sheep's tail fat. A dirham of salt, two dirham of finely-ground coriander, cinnamon bark, and a pinch of mastic should be added to flavor. Water must now be added, and when nearly done add seasoned, minced kebab. The meat is next cooked in a broth. Meanwhile some large, ripe, bitter quinces should be peeled and the seeds removed and then cut and placed on top of the cooked meat. Other quinces must be pummeled in a mortar in order to extract their juices, which after straining should be added to the meat. Also add 5 dirham of wine vinegar and 10 dirham of sweet almonds, finely chopped and soaked in water. Saffron can be employed as food coloring. Finally, the sides of the pan should be wiped clean before placing over a gentle heat.

Cookbooks had been common in the Islamic world for centuries, but in China and eastern Asia Hu Szu-hui's *Yin-shan cheng-yao* and Ni Tsan's *Yün-lin-t'ang yin-shih chih-tu-chi* broke new ground. Even though they were both medicinal and nutritional in intent, they were effectively practical cookbooks, and it was the Mongols' demands for the kind of cooking manuals they encountered in the west that led to the inspiration and creation of Hu's and Ni Tsan's works. Just as the Mongols were cultural brokers in other fields, so they were responsible for the introduction of the cookbook to China.

One section of *Yin-shan cheng-yao* is devoted to recipes for strange delicacies of combined flavors. This section in particular revealed the influence of the Islamic world on Mongol gastronomy. The opening recipe for *mastajhi* [mastic] soup is an example of the adaptation of a basic Mongol dish, cauldron cooked mutton soup, to west Asian refinement. The ingredients included leg of mutton, chopped and boned; five cardamoms; cinnamon; and skinned and ground chickpeas, or what is essentially hummus. Boil all together to form a soup before straining to separate the meat, which should then be cut up and put aside. Add the cooked chickpeas and some aromatic nonglutinous rice along with a little *mastajhi* before adding the meat. Garnish with coriander leaves.

Foreign influence is often marked by the addition of herbs, spices, and other forms of flavoring to traditionally eastern dishes. Fenugreek[6] has long been a common ingredient of Mediterranean, Palestinian, and Anatolian cooking, and the condiment asafetida is indicative of Iranian influence. The presence of both in a popular broth suggests a strong Western influence. A recipe for deer head soup, a Mongolian dish, recommends the addition of black pepper, long pepper, the juice of sprouting ginger, and asafetida *(kasni)*, which would impart an Iranian flavor. Three dishes are mentioned using euryale, a Chinese water lily, the starchy fruit of which is ground for flour. Euryale is usually found only in Chinese dishes, but Hu Szu-hui cited three dishes originating from the Azerbaijan region in which euryale is added to the mutton-and-bone based recipes.

DIVERSE DISHES AND INGREDIENTS

Most of the delights recommended for the Great Khan's table seem to be a mixture of different gastronomic strains, perhaps deliberately so. The

Mongols enjoyed their emerging image of sophistication and worldliness and the reputation of their kitchens for exotic dishes from around the globe. A turtle soup was given a Mongolian flavor by the addition of mutton on the bone. The instructions indicate boiling the chopped mutton and bone together with five cardamoms into a broth. Five or six turtles should then be cooked, and when done they should be skinned, boned, and cut into lumps before adding to the soup. Fine vermicelli should be made and then roasted with the juice of a sprouting ginger and black pepper. This should then be added to the soup and the final taste adjusted with onions, salt, and vinegar.

Some delights found in Hu's collection can be discovered in a Middle Eastern pastry shop today. Poppy seed buns seem indistinguishable from the buns served in any modern Turkish, Arab, or Iranian bakery, with cow's milk used specifically and the poppy seeds sprinkled on the outside.

The steppe was not completely forgotten, and the presence of roast wolf soup attests to the influence of some nomadic diehards at the Qa'an's table. However, it is interesting to note that the wolf is flavored with some distinctly Persian, non-Mongol spices, namely saffron, asafetida *(kasni)*, turmeric, and others.

In complete contrast to the wolf soup, sheep's head dressed in flowers was also offered. This interesting gastronomic novelty combined "all that was most creative in Sino-Mongol-Turkic cuisine," in the view of Paul Buell, editor of Hu Szu-hui's cookbook, who bravely tried as many of these dishes as he was able to cook. The three sheep's heads were cut up and cooked with four sheep's loins, a set of sheep's stomach, and lungs. They were then deboned, dyed with safflower, and mixed with sprouting ginger, pickled ginger, five eggs, and three Chinese radishes cut into flower shapes. Flavor was adjusted to taste with onions, salt, and vinegar.

Wild animals remained a favorite with the Mongols. Every possible animal and every possible animal part, internal and external, seems to have found its way to the table. Elephant meat is apparently insipid to taste, and overindulgence can make the eater feel heavy in the body. Camel is recommended more for its fermented, slightly sweetish milk than for its meat found in the humps, and wild camel is preferable. On a diet of bear's paw, wind and cold can be effectively resisted. Donkey meat controls "wind mania and chronic depression." Wild donkey, the *kulan,* can control "dizziness due to an evil wind." Deer was an obvious favorite and was believed to cure a number of ailments. The medullas, head, hooves, penis, horn, fat, flesh, velvet (furry covering of the antlers), and viscera of deer all found some role in the Mongols' kitchen. Deer features prominently in modern Chinese medicinal cooking, and deer genitalia are considered to have restorative value for the human sexual function. Like deer, every part and organ of the sheep ended up in the Mongol hot pot. Wild sheep were common on the steppes in the thirteenth and fourteenth centuries, and they were popular as a source of nutrition. Head, heart, liver, blood, the five viscera, kidneys, bone, medullas, brain, and milk were all used in the dishes of the time.

Monkeys, weasels, badgers, wildcats, tigers, leopards, otters, dogs, wild boars, Yangtze porpoises, foxes, and even rhinos all fell to the chef's cleaver and were included as the main ingredients of specific dishes. As well as being recommended as plain food, these more exotic dishes became components in tonics, liquors, and balms. Some were suggested for physical application, including wolf throat's skin, which when wound around the head alleviated headache. A wolf's tooth warded off evil if worn, and a wolf's tail, hung before the breast of a horse, warded off evil influences and made the horse impervious to fear.

Fowl and poultry were traditional Mongol fare, particularly those hunted on the vast inland lakes high in the mountain stillness of Eurasia. Many varieties of swans were found in Mongolia but were unknown in China, therefore their presence in Hu's cookbook attests to the strong Mongolian traditions undaunted by the sophisticated cuisines dominant in their newly acquired lands. Swans, geese, cranes, curlew, wild hen, wild roosters, pheasants, many varieties of duck, pigeon, doves, quails, sparrows, and bunting were all eaten. Even the great bustard, described as sweet but coarse, ended up on the kitchen table. For cough and "hectic fever" the collard crow, despite its sour and salty flavor, was recommended.

As well as fowl, the freshwater lakes of the high mountains and the rolling steppe lands yielded abundant fish, and the Mongols added innumerable varieties of fish to their menus. Carp has been the favorite fish of the Chinese for centuries, and the Mongols gladly added this domesticated fish to their dishes. The Mongols were quick to take advantage of the fish culture of the Chinese, who had been domesticating and cultivating fish for thousands of years. Carp was introduced to the world by the Chinese. Bream, puffer fish, mud eels, sawfish, sheatfish, sturgeon, crab, shrimps, turtles, and mussels are just a few of the varieties of seafood and fish that could be found in the dishes served at Yüan courts.

The Yüan court is mentioned in particular because Qubilai and his successors came to epitomize the opulence and lavishness of the medieval world. There is evidence that other parts of the Mongol Empire hosted banquets, though not as sophisticated and bountiful as those witnessed in China, that were also demonstrative of an advanced gastronomic culture.

In the northern lands of the mountains and steppe a leg of raw lamb washed down with koumiss was no longer sufficient to serve the khan. A meal would occupy many courses.[7] Appetizers might have included *momo shapale* with *sipen mardur* sauce, delicate steamed Tibetan mushroom ravioli smothered in a creamy, spicy yogurt sauce. A salad of Bhutanese chili and cheese might have followed. The main course, *shabril* with *dresil*, comprised Tibetan meatball curry with nutted saffron rice, honey, and currants. Himalayan steamed bread with turmeric and barley beer with honey would have accompanied the main food, and also as a dessert

Chinese chestnut mound with cream and glazed fruit would have found favor. *Momo* is a traditional Tibetan dish using yak's meat, and mushrooms are a perfect complement and filler. In the Il-Khanate a more usual starter might have been hummus. The recipe for thirteenth-century hummus is basically the same as that found in Syria or Lebanon today. Fresh lemon juice, garlic, chickpeas, tahini, olive oil, paprika, and a touch of salt. The Koreans would have favored some hotter appetizer, and traditional *bulgogi* would have been popular. A steak was cut into cubes before frying in a very hot, spicy paste. After marinating, it was slowly and thoroughly grilled and served with chopped onions.

The fame that the opulence and abundance of Qubilai Khan's court enjoyed in Europe and that inspired such English poets as Samuel Taylor Coleridge was engendered to a great degree by the words of Marco Polo. He devotes much of his narrative to evoking the lavishness of the Great Khan's tables and praising the hospitality and generosity he spread before his guests and visiting envoys. Marco Polo also had an eye for detail and for the historian he has provided a wealth of fascinating minutiae in his descriptions of daily life in the Mongol palaces.

THE FASHION OF THE GREAT KAAN'S TABLE AT HIS HIGH FEASTS

And when the Great Kaan sits at table on any great court occasion, it is in this fashion. His table is elevated a good deal above the others, and he sits at the north end of the hall, looking towards the south, with his chief wife beside him on the left. On his right sit his sons and his nephews, and other kinsmen of the Blood Imperial, but lower, so that their heads are on a level with the Emperor's feet. And then the other Barons sit at other tables lower still. So also with the women; for all the wives of the Lord's sons, and of his nephews and other kinsmen, sit at the lower table to his right; and below them again the ladies of the other Barons and Knights, each in the place assigned by the Lord's orders. The tables are so disposed that the Emperor can see the whole of them from end to end, many as they are. [Further, you are not to suppose that everybody sits at table; on the contrary, the greater part of the soldiers and their officers sit at their meal in the hall on the carpets.] Outside the hall will be found more than 40,000 people; for there is a great concourse of folk bringing presents to the Lord, or come from foreign countries with curiosities.

In a certain part of the hall near where the Great Kaan holds his table, there [is set a large and very beautiful piece of workmanship in the form of a square coffer, or buffet, about three paces each way, exquisitely wrought with figures of animals, finely carved and gilt. The middle is hollow, and in it] stands a great vessel of pure gold, holding as much as an ordinary butt; and at each corner of the great vessel is one of smaller size [of the capacity of a firkin], and from the former the wine or beverage flavoured with fine and costly spices is drawn off into the latter. [And on the buffet aforesaid are set all the Lord's drinking vessels, among which are certain pitchers of the finest gold,] which are called *verniques*, and are big enough to hold drink for eight or ten persons. And one of these is put between every two persons, besides a couple of golden cups with handles, so that every man helps himself from the pitcher that stands between him and his neighbour. And the ladies are supplied in the same way. The value of these pitchers and cups is something immense; in fact, the Great Kaan has such a quantity of this kind of plate, and of gold and silver in other shapes, as no one ever before saw or heard tell of, or could believe.

There are certain Barons specially deputed to see that foreigners, who do not know the customs of the Court, are provided with places suited to their rank; and these Barons are continually moving to and fro in the hall, looking to the wants of the guests at table, and causing the servants to supply them promptly with wine, milk, meat, or whatever they lack. At every door of the hall (or, indeed, wherever the Emperor may be) there stand a couple of big men like giants, one on each side, armed with staves. Their business is to see that no one steps upon the threshold in entering, and if this does happen, they strip the offender of his clothes, and he must pay a forfeit to have them back again; or in lieu of taking his clothes, they give him a certain number of blows. If they are foreigners ignorant of the order, then there are Barons appointed to introduce them, and explain it to them. They think, in fact, that it brings bad luck if any one touches the threshold. Howbeit, they are not expected to stick at this in going forth again, for at that time some are like to be the worse for liquor, and incapable of looking to their steps.

And you must know that those who wait upon the Great Kaan with his dishes and his drink are some of the great Barons. They have the mouth and nose muffled with fine napkins of silk and gold, so that no breath nor odour from their persons should taint the dish or the goblet presented to the Lord. And when the Emperor is going to drink, all the musical instruments, of which he has vast store of every kind, begin to play. And when he takes the cup all the Barons and the rest of the company drop on their knees and make the deepest obeisance before him, and then the Emperor doth drink. But each time that he does so the whole ceremony is repeated.

I will say nought about the dishes, as you may easily conceive that there is a great plenty of every possible kind. But you should know that in every case where a Baron or Knight dines at those tables, their wives also dine there with the other ladies. And when all have dined and the tables have been removed, then come in a great number of players and jugglers, adepts at all sorts of wonderful feats, and perform before the Emperor and the rest of the company, creating great diversion and mirth, so that everybody is full of laughter and enjoyment. And when the performance is over, the company breaks up and every one goes to his quarters.[8]

NOTES

1. Samuel Taylor Coleridge, "Kubla Khan."

2. Simon de Saint Quentin, *Histoire des Tartars,* ed. Jean Richard (Paris: Libraire orientaliste, 1965), 40–41; Hu Szu-hui, *Yin-shan cheng-yao* [Proper and essential things for the emperor's food and drink], trans. Buell, Paul D., and Eugene N. Anderson, 2000, 46–47.

3. Hu Szu-hui, *Yin-shan cheng-yao,* 44.

4. Ganjaks'i Kirakos, *Kirakos Ganjaks'i's History of the Armenians,* trans. Robert Bedrosian, *Sources for the Armenian Tradition,* 1986, available at: http://rbedrosian. com/kg1.htm.

5. P'eng Ta-ya, *Hei-ta Shih-lüeh,* Wang, 1962, 475–76, cited in Hu, *Yin-shan cheng-yao,* 45–46.

6. Fenugreek *(Trigonella foenum-graecum)* is the slender annual herb of the pea family (Fabaceae) or its dried seeds, used as a food, a flavoring, and a medicine. The seeds' aroma and taste are strong, sweetish, and somewhat bitter, reminiscent of burned sugar. They are farinaceous in texture and may be mixed with flour for bread or eaten raw.

7. Suggested by Marc Cramer, *Imperial Mongolian Cooking: Recipes from the kingdoms of Genghis Khan* (New York: Hippocrene Books, 2003).

8. Complete Yule-Cordier Edition of Marco Polo's travels by Marco Polo and Rustichello of Pisa, *The Project Gutenberg EBook of the Travels of Marco Polo,* available at: http://www.gutenberg.net, vol. 1.

9

RELIGION AND THE MONGOLS

LIBERALITY

In the Mongol empire religious orders generally thrived. The Mongols were known for their liberality as regards the faiths of those under their rule, and the treatment of clerics and divines who fell into their hands was usually respectful. The Mongols did not adhere to any one particular faith, and in later years though different faiths had officially been proclaimed in the main Mongol states, religion was not the basis of hostilities even though occasionally used as an excuse. Within and without their frontiers the Mongol rulers adapted a laissez-faire attitude to people's beliefs. However, this attitude may not have been entirely altruistic. The Mongols were probably hedging their bets and playing spiritually safe. In addition to this liberal attitude, it was the wish of the Great Khan that all his subjects should pray for him and his well-being, and to this end the Mongol rulers courted the religious classes. The Mongols were determined to keep the goodwill of whatever god was ruling in the heavens. As a result of this policy, Islamic judges, clerics, and foundations; Christian priests and monks; and Buddhist lamas and monks were all exempted from forced labor and taxes.

Evidence of the Mongols' special regard for religion was evident from the early years of conquest. During Chinggis Khan's devastating advance on the Islamic lands of central Asia in 1218–22, he halted outside the gates of Khwārazm not only to give the traditional Mongol, spine-chilling ultimatum to the citizens of the besieged city but also to offer safe passage to the Sufi leader, Sheikh Najm al-Dīn Kobra [1145–1221], whose name and reputation were well known to the Great Khan. The holy man declined the offer, however, though he did accept safe passage for 70 of his disciples.

"I have lived for seventy years in Khwārazm with these people through both bitter and sweet times and now a time of calamity has befallen [us]. If I were to flee and go from amongst them, such behaviour would be far from [the spirit of] manly honour and magnanimity." Subsequently, after much searching, his body was found amongst the slain.[1]

This was not an exception but the rule. Thirty years later his grandson, Hülegü, stood before the gates of the Islamic capital, Baghdad, and openly worried about the consequences of the actions he was then contemplating. In the end, on the advice of his Islamic advisor and spokesman, Naṣīr al-Dīn Tūsī (1201–74), he had arrows shot into the besieged city offering safe conduct to various groups but with clerics of different creeds included prominently. "The class of *sayyids* [supposed descendants of the Prophet's family], *dānishmands* [for Mongols this meant Muslim clerics], *erke'ün* [Christian priests], *sheikhs* [well-respected community leaders, often clerics] and such as are not fighting us are safe from us."[2]

SHAMANISM

The religion that many Mongols traditionally practiced has been described as shamanism. Shamanism believes in the existence of various spirits that interact with the temporal world and can be contacted and influenced by holy men, or shamans. However, shamanism was in essence a practical religion concerned with the material needs of its adherents. The shaman was there to advance the material well-being of the tribe and the individual. As such he held a very powerful position in Mongol society and was respected and often feared by the whole tribe, in some cases more so than the tribe's own khan or chief. The shaman was given a certain amount of autonomy; therefore, some degree of rivalry between khan and shaman was inevitable when their interests coincided. Political rivalry between the shaman and the khan frequently erupted when the former formed a power base or became too identified with the khan's opponents or other factions within the clan. Chinggis Khan confronted this situation during his rise to power with his dealings with the shaman Teb-tengri, who sought to challenge the new emperor's authority.

The clash between Temüjin and Kököchu (Teb-tengri, "Most Heavenly"), the son of Mönglik, illustrates well the role and influence of the shaman in traditional Mongol society. Chinggis realized that this power and influence had to be curbed if he were to have any chance of putting his reforms into effect because Teb-tengri was opposed to any change or reform, which invariably meant restrictions on his authority. Chinggis owed his life to Teb-tengri's father, Mönglik, once when he escorted Temüjin back to camp following the death of his father, Yesügei, and when he uncovered a plot against Temüjin by Senggum. Mönglik was held in such great esteem that he was given Temüjin's mother, Hö'elün, for his wife on Yesügei's death. Teb-tengri supported Temüjin in the early years, and for this he earned Chinggis's unequivocal gratitude. As tribal shaman with a strong following and universal respect on his own merits he endorsed Temüjin's claim to kingship. After wandering naked through the barren steppe and mountains during a particularly bitter winter, Teb-tengri returned to proclaim, "God has spoken with me and has said: 'I have given all the face of the earth to Temüjin and his children and named him Chinggis Khan. Bid him administer justice in such and such a fashion.'"[3] Aware of the gratitude that his leader held for both him and his father, Teb-tengri grew not only arrogant but also hungry for power. He still held great influence over Temüjin, who sought his advice on all matters, and people were aware of his power. He sought to further his ambitions by sowing dissention and dissatisfaction within the royal family, particularly between Temüjin and his brother Kasar, a plot that almost succeeded. As soon as Chinggis realized Teb-tengri's role in the matter and understood the direction of his ambition he acted decisively. Chinggis's brother Temuge-Otchigin picked a fight with Teb-tengri, and as the two wrestled among the guests, the Great Khan ordered them outside to continue their fight away from his guests. When Temuge-Otchigin returned to announce that Teb-tengri had broken his back and died during the course of their fight there were few who did not guess that he had in fact been murdered in a prearranged plot. The father, Mönglik, was pardoned but warned against seeking revenge, and Chinggis Khan emerged the stronger from this ordeal. He appointed a new shaman, Usun of the Ba'arin tribe, who was devoted to him and his cause, and thus was established the supremacy of imperial power over the priests.

William of Rubruck had a particular interest in religion, and he recorded in detail the position of religion at Möngke's court. Shamans still had a major role to play, and William was able to elicit the attitude of the Great Khan toward shamans.

Their diviners are, as (Mangu Chan) confessed to me, their priests; and whatever they say must be done is executed without delay. I will tell you of their office, as well as I could learn about it from master William and others who used to speak truthfully to me. They are very numerous and always have a captain, like a pontiff, who always places his dwelling before the principal house of Mangu Chan, at about a stone's throw from it. Under his custody are, as I have previously said, the carts in which the idols are carried. The others come after the *ordu* in positions assigned to them; and there come to them from various parts of the world people who believe in their art. Some among them know something of astronomy, particularly the chief, and they predict to them the eclipses of the sun and moon; and when one is about to take place all the people lay in their food, for they must not go out of the door of their dwelling. And while the eclipse is taking place, they sound drums and instruments, and make a great noise and clamor. After the eclipse is over, they give themselves to drinking and feasting, and make great jollity. They predict lucky and unlucky days for the undertaking of all affairs; and so it is that they never assemble an army nor begin a war without their assent, and long since (the Moal) would have gone back to Hungary, but the diviners will not allow it.

All things which are sent to the court they take between fires, and for this they retain a certain portion of them. They also cleanse all the bedding of deceased persons by taking them between fires. For when anyone dies, they put aside all that belongs to him, and they are not allowed to the other people of the *ordu* until they have been purified by fires. This I saw in connection with the *ordu* of that lady who died while we were there. On account of this (custom) there was a double reason why Friar Andrew and his companion should have gone between fires; they bore presents, and they were destined for one who was already dead, Keu Chan [Guyuk Khan d.1248]. Nothing of the sort was required of me, because I brought nothing. If any animal or any other thing falls to the ground while passing between the fires, it is theirs.[4]

The Mongols believed in a sky god, Tenggeri, who resided in heaven, and an earth goddess, Itügen, who represented fertility. However, much of the practice of their religion revolved around ancestor worship and contacts with the spirits of the dead. The family often kept expensively dressed effigies of their ancestors in specially assigned places in their yurts. When they traveled, the effigies, which the Mongols called *ongghot*, were placed in a special wagon under the supervision of the shamans. No one other than the shamans was allowed access to these wagons containing the ancestors' effigies. These *ongghot* were made of felt. Both the master and mistress of the tent had an *ongghot* hung on the wall of the yurt above their designated position, and other smaller effigies would be placed nearer the entrance on a cow's and mare's udder in recognition of the importance of the milk from these animals. The *ongghot* always received sprinklings of drink and genuflections before drinking sessions commenced.

FUNERAL RITES

Public religious worship played no part in Mongol society, though various social formalities, practices, and taboos held religious significance. The common assertion that the Mongols were godless and irreligious originated because of the absence of religious services in Mongol society. Funeral services were an exception, and legends and myths have surrounded this subject, especially where the funerals of their leaders were concerned.

When one of them dies or they kill him, they do as follows: some they take around with them for many days since [they believe that] a devil entered the body and would say frivolous things; and there were those that they burned. Others they buried in the ground in deep ditches, placing with the deceased his weapons and clothing, gold and silver, whatever was his share. And if the deceased was one of the great ones, they place some of his servants and maids in the grave with him so that, they say, they will serve him. They also put the horse in since, they say, warfare there is fierce. If they want to recall the dead, they cut open the belly of a horse and pull out all the flesh without the bones. Then they burn the intestines and bones and sew up the skin of the horse as though its body were whole. Sharpening a great piece of wood, they pierce the horse's abdomen and draw it out of the mouth, and so erect it on a tree or in some elevated spot.[5]

The mystery that surrounds the funerals of Chinggis Khan and other of the great leaders has persisted to the present day and is liable to endure for as long as the burial sites remain undiscovered. The *Secret History of the Mongols* makes no mention of Chinggis's funeral. Rashīd al-Dīn states that the Great Khan ordered that his death and funeral be kept secret, with care taken lest any public mourning, wailing, or any other signs of grief be seen until after the rebel leaders of the Tangut had emerged and were killed. Chinggis did not want news of his death to interfere with the final subjugation of Tangut territory and people. It was said that every living creature along the 1,600-kilometer procession route to the royal *ordu* was put to the sword. Marco Polo was aware of these stories, which he repeated in his own account of the death of royalty among the great Mongols.

All the Grand Kaans, and all the descendants of Chinghis their first Lord, are carried to a mountain that is called ALTAY to be interred. Wheresoever the Sovereign may die, he is carried to his burial in that mountain with his predecessors; no matter an the place of his death were 100 days' journey distant, thither must he be carried to his burial. Let me tell you a strange thing too. When they are carrying the body of any Emperor to be buried with the others, the convoy that goes with the body doth put to the sword all whom they fall in with on the road, saying: "Go and wait upon your Lord in the other world!" For they do in sooth believe that all such as they slay in this manner do go to serve their Lord in the other world. They do the same too with horses; for when the Emperor dies, they kill all his best horses, in order that he may have the use of them in the other world, as they believe. And I tell you as a certain truth, that when Mongou Kaan died, more than 20,000 who chanced to meet the body on its way, were slain in the manner I have told.[6]

Hülegü Khan, who died in 1265 in his kingdom of Persia, has never had his burial site disturbed as far as is known. Its exact location on Shāhī, now

Islāmī, Island in the Sea of Urumiya, Iranian Azerbaijan, has never been determined, so a veritable fortune in fabulous treasures and wealth, as well as the bones of six young virgins, awaits anyone who is able to find this elusive hoard. Hamd-Allah Mustawfī, writing in 1330, states:

People became doubled over in grief at the hero's death. Everyone placed themselves near, with their hair unbound. According to Mongol custom, men and women lamented, tearing their hair on his account. After the funeral preparations had been I made, a number of chosen princes placed the shah's body on a bier according to Mongol custom, and made the necessary ceremonies, and carried him to the Salt Sea, and there placed him secretly in his grave. In the Sea of Salmas, that shah found no royal throne; such is the justice of this world.[7]

Khwandamir, a Safavid bureaucrat and chronicler writing in the sixteenth century, embellished his account of Hülegü's death with more details, claiming that ministers "had an underground crypt dug for his funeral and sent several beautiful young girls bedecked with finery into the crypt so that the Ilkhan would not suffer from being alone."[8]

Worship was a simple outdoor activity for most Mongols. Churches and mosques were built, and Doquz Khātūn, wife of Tolui Khan and later wife of Tolui's son Hülegü, even constructed her own mobile church with bells. However, for their native religion there were no "houses" built. Instead, the Mongols often communed with their god by climbing a high mountain. They removed their hats and slung their belts over their shoulders as a sign of submission.

When Genghis Khan set out on his expedition to Cathay to do battle with the Altan Khan, as was his custom he went up alone on a hill, opened his belt and threw it over his neck, opened the ties of his tunic, dropped to his knees, and said, "O Ancient God, you know all things from long ago. You know that the Altan Khan initiated hostilities and began our enmity. Okin Barqaq and Hambaqai Qa'an were abducted by the Tatars and sent before the Altan Khan who killed them, my elders and ancestors, though they were innocent of any crime. [If you consider me right in what I think,] I ask for vengeance and retaliation for their blood. I want you to let men, fairies, and demons help and assist me." He prayed thus in all humility, and afterwards he arose and departed. Through his sincerity of intent, he gained victory over the Altan Khan, who was such a mighty and splendid emperor with vast lands and impregnable fortresses without number, and those realms came under his and his sons' control.[9]

Mountaintops and flowing water held spiritual significance. Taboos regarding water and washing created great problems in their contact with settled peoples, especially in the earlier decades. Flowing water was not allowed to be polluted on pain of death. Washing the body, clothes, dishes, or cooking utensils was forbidden. Ögödei Qa'an (ruled 1229–41) demonstrated the softening of these strictures in various well-known anecdotes reported during his reign. The Muslim historian

Tian Shan Mountains, Mountains of Heaven separating Xinjiang from central Asia. Courtesy of Xinjiang Qinshan Culture Publishing

Juwaynī (died 1282), who served as a minister under Hülegü Khan, the Mongol ruler of Iran (ruled 1256–65), recorded many stories in which Ögödei found ways of excusing those who had inadvertently transgressed the strict religious taboos of the Mongols. Finding a Muslim washing himself in a river, Ögödei's brother Chaghetai, a strict upholder of Mongol tradition, insisted that the man be punished. Ögödei arranged to have some gold placed in the river and instructed the unfortunate Muslim to claim that he had been in the water to retrieve the gold. In this way the transgressor escaped punishment.

DIVINATION

An important part in Mongol life and an essential duty of the shaman was divination. The shaman was the intermediary with the spirit world, and he could intercede with the spirits and foretell what they had planned and what the future held for the tribe. Dressed in white robes and riding a white horse, the shaman, with his insignia of staff and drum, was charged with various duties for the tribe, including exorcism, the recital of blessings, and prophecy. Prophecy was performed while in a self-induced trance or through the ritual burning and interpreting of sheep's shoulder blades. The cracks and splits that appeared in the bones after ritual burning had special significance that only the shaman could determine, though Möngke Qa'an (ruled 1251–59) was recorded as being able to read them by himself. William of Rubruck, very observant where matters of religion were concerned, was intrigued by the sight of servants carrying sheep's bones around the palace with a certain amount of reverence.

And as we were entering a servant came out carrying some sheep's shoulder-blades, burnt to coals, and I wondered greatly what he could do with them. When later on I enquired about it, I learnt that he does nothing in the world without first consulting these bones; he does not even allow a person to enter his dwelling without first consulting them. This kind of divination is done as follows when he wishes to do anything, he has brought him three of these bones not previously charred, and holding one, he thinks of the thing about which he wishes to consult it, whether he shall do it or not; and then he hands it to a servant to burn. And there are two little buildings beside the dwelling in which he lives, in which they burn these bones, and these bones are looked for diligently every day through-out the whole camp. When they have been charred black, they are brought back to him, and then he examines whether the bones have been split by the heat throughout their length. In that case the way is open for him to act. If, however, the bones have been cracked crosswise, or round bits have been started out of them, then he may not act. For this bone always splits in the fire, or there appear some cracks spreading over it. And if out of the three he finds one satisfactory, he acts.[10]

Bones were not the only means for divination, and according to the Armenian cleric Kirakos, all Mongol women had this gift bestowed upon them by heaven.

Their women are witches and divine everything. Without a command from the witches and sorcerers, they go on no journey; only if they permit it.[11]

CHRISTIANITY

With increasing contact with other religions, the Mongol tribes often converted or adapted the practices of other religions. Buddhism increased its influence as the Mongol Empire spread southward across China. Nestorian Christianity had converts among the Turco-Mongol tribes from at least the eleventh century. Such powerful Mongol tribes as the Kereit and Naiman were predominantly Christian. Other Mongol tribes such as the Merkits and Önggüt had many Christian followers. Hülegü Khan's major wife, Dokuz Khātūn was an active Christian, as was the Byzantine wife of his son, Abaqa (ruled 1265–82). The Mongols cynically exploited their Christian credentials when they sought European allies in the fight against the Muslim Mamluks of Egypt. William of Rubruck was not particularly impressed by the Mongols' displays of Christian piety, and he did not like the fact that the Nestorians had far more influence than other Christians at the royal court.

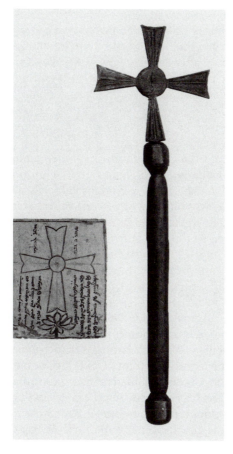

Christian relics from the Yuan dynasty,
Dengsheng Chinggis Khan Mausoleum.
Courtesy of Lan Tien Lang Publications

The Chan [Khan] had brought him our books, the Bible and the breviary, and made careful inquiry about the pictures, and what they meant. The Nestorians answered as they saw fit, for our interpreter had not come with us. The first time I had been before him, I had also the Bible in my bosom, and he had it handed him, and looked at it a great deal. Then he went away, but the lady remained there and distributed presents to all the Christians who were there. To the monk she gave one *iascot*, and to the archdeacon of the priests another. Before us she had placed a *nasic*, which is a piece of stuff as broad as a coverlid and about as long, and a buccaran; but as I would not accept them, they were sent to the interpreter, who took them for himself. The *nasic* he carried all the way to Cyprus, where he sold it for eighty bezants of Cyprus, though it had been greatly damaged on the journey. Then drink was brought, rice mead and

red wine, like wine of La Rochelle, and *cosmos*. Then the lady, holding a
full cup in her hand, knelt and asked a blessing, and the priests all sang
with a loud voice, and she drank it all. Likewise, I and my companion
had to sing when she wanted to drink another time. When they were all
nearly drunk, food was brought consisting of mutton, which was at once
devoured, and after that large fish which are called carp, but without salt
or bread; of these I ate. And so they passed the day till evening. And when
the lady was already tipsy, she got on her cart; the priests singing and
howling, and she went her way. The next Sunday, when we read: "*Nuptie
facte sunt in Chana,*" came the daughter of the Chan [Möngke Khan],
whose mother was a Christian, and she did likewise, though with not so
much ceremony; for she made no presents, but only gave the priests to
drink till they were drunk, and also parched millet to eat.[12]

THE MONGOLS AND THE ARMENIANS

Both William of Rubruck and Het'um, the king of Armenian Cilicia, had
firsthand knowledge of the relationship between Armenian clerics and the
Mongols. The Armenians of Cilicia became staunch allies of the Mongols in
their war against the Mamluks of Egypt, and they sometimes had intimate
contact with the Mongol court. William of Rubruck found Armenian priests
at every major stop on his travels during 1253–55. In Constantinople before
setting out into Mongol territory, he spoke with Armenian merchants and
clerics resident in the city. In Sarai on the River Volga, the effective capital
of the Golden Horde, he was a guest of Sartaq Khan, son of Batu Khan,
in whose court he encountered Armenian priests who knew Turkish and
Arabic and were employed as translators, a role he subsequently discovered that they carried out in Qaraqorum as well. In the Mongol capital the
Armenians were represented by a "swarthy and lank" Armenian cleric who
ran their small chapel. William of Rubruck dismissed him as an imposter
who had "lied, for he had taken no [religious] orders, and did not know
a single letter, but was a cloth weaver, as I found out in his own country,
which I went through on my way back." The papal envoy explained that

he had been a hermit in the country of Jerusalem, and that God had appeared
to him three times, enjoining on him to go to the Prince of the Tartars. But as he
neglected going, God threatened him the third time, striking him down to the
ground, and saying that he should die if he did not go; and that he should say
to Mongke-Khan that if he would become a Christian, all the world would come
under his rule, and that the great Pope would obey him.[13]

Rubruck was suspicious of the Armenians and uneasy at their obvious
closeness to the Mongols. Their numbers were large, as is indicated by

Nestorian Stele, Xi'an Museum of Steles. Courtesy of Lan Tien Lang Publications

Rubruck's reference to the Armenian Easter procession to the Great Khan's palace, which could only have taken place if there had been a sizable community in the capital. In his address to the pope, Rubruck expressed these fears, and in particular he was anxious that the pope's words and his own conversations might be erroneously reported to the Mongol leaders by the often Armenian translators.

I feared that as those who had interpreted your letters were Armenians from Greater Armenia—great haters of the Saracens—they had perhaps through hatred and for the discomfiture of the Saracens, gratuitously translated as had suited their fancy.[14]

Armenian petitioners were welcomed at the Great Khan's court, and their pleas were usually received sympathetically. While in Qaraqorum, William encountered an aristocratic petitioner to Möngke Khan who has been identified as the Armenian noble Smbat Orbelean.

A certain Armenian who had come with the monk had brought this said cross from Jerusalem, as he said, and it was of silver, weighing perhaps four marks, and had four gems in the angles and one in the center; and it did not have the image of the Savior, for the Armenians and Nestorians are ashamed to show the Christ fixed to the Cross. And they had presented it to Mongke-Khan, and Mongke asked him what he wanted. Then he said he was the son of an Armenian priest, whose church had been destroyed by the Saracens, and he asked his help to restore this church. Then [Mongke] asked him with how much it could be rebuilt, and he said two hundred *iascot*—that is two thousand marks. And he ordered that he should be given letters to him who receives the tribute in Persia and Greater Armenia, to pay him this sum of silver.[15]

The Flower of Histories of the East by the historian Hetoum verifies William of Rubruck's suspicions that indeed the Cilician Armenians had a strong and positive relationship with the Mongol Khans. Much of Hetoum's information is fanciful and some wishful thinking, but that Armenian Christians enjoyed considerable influence with different khans is undeniable. For the Mongols the Armenians were a useful if minor ally on the front line with the hostile forces of Mamluk Egypt. For the Armenians the Mongols were a lifeline and their only support against aggressive and threatening neighbors on all sides. They played up their contacts and friendship with their friends in the east as a matter of life and death. They used these contacts as a tactic of defense, and it was important for them that their enemies and their potential friends in Europe saw their alliance with the Mongols as rock solid and unbreakable. According to Hetoum, when King Het'um of Cilicia visited Möngke Khan in the early 1250s:

First he urged the Khan to convert to Christianity and to accept baptism together with his people; second, that eternal peace and friendship be established between Christians and Tatars; third, that it be possible to construct Christian churches in all of the Tatar countries and that the Armenians be freed from taxes and other burdens; fourth, that the Holy Land and the Holy Sepulcher be wrested from the Turks and given to the Christians; fifth, that the caliph in Baghdad, the head of the [Muslim] religion, be done away with.... When the Tatar Khan had consulted with his princes and grandees, he replied to the king of Armenia: "I accept your requests. I shall accept baptism and adopt the Christian religion and show concern that all my subjects do likewise."[16]

Hetoum wrote his *Flower of Histories of the East* in order to encourage his European audience to join an alliance with the Cilician Armenians and the Mongols against the Mamluks of Egypt. It was for this reason that he overplayed the Christian sympathies of the Tatar khans. There is no convincing evidence that Möngke Khan or any other Great Khan ever converted to Christianity or underwent baptism. However, Hetoum (circa 1245–1315), a noble and high official, hoped to convince his papal friends that the Mongols were good Christians.

Now after Mongke had accepted the requests of the Armenian king with charitable munificence, he had himself baptised by the chancellor of the Armenian kingdom, who was a bishop. With him [were baptized] his house and numerous other esteemed and grand men and women.[17]

The Mongols were good Christians, and the Cilician Armenians were exemplary defenders of the faith, if the words of Hetoum are to be taken literally. His king, Lewon III son of Het'um I (1269–89), is portrayed as defender of Christianity who on a visit to Abaqa's court

> beseeched him regarding freeing the Holy Land from the infidels. And Abaqa so promised, simultaneously advising the Armenian king to send emissaries to the Pope and to the orthodox kings [regarding this matter].[18]

The whole question of Christianity used as a link between the Mongols and Europe is explored in a new study by Professor Peter Jackson, *The Mongols and the West, 1221–1410*, and he examines how seriously both sides viewed the potential for an alliance. The tantalizing vision of what might have happened if those links had been forged remains an intriguing indulgence. By 1242 the Mongols had the military capacity, and fired by Tenggerism they had the will to continue their march of conquest into the heartlands of Europe. After 'Ain Jālūt in 1261 and the ignoble failure of the invasions of Japan in 1274 and 1281, the chastened Mongols were more open to compromise than in the past. But their cynical use of the Christian card with their willingness to clothe themselves in a Christian mantle alerted the suspicions of the papal court. Tenggerism did not exclude the superficial adoption of the rites and practices of other religions. Ghazan could proclaim his kingdom a Muslim state, but he would never subjugate the *yasa*. The diplomatic correspondence of the Il-Khans and other Mongol lords could adorn itself in the filigree of Christian niceties, but underneath the certainties of Tenggerism could not be diluted.

ISLAM

Islam increasingly gained ground among the Mongols as they moved westward. The Turks of central Asia had long had contact with Islam, but with the conquest of Persia and the forcible movement of the subject peoples eastward to man the bureaucracy of the empire, Islam began to take root. Berke Khan (1257–67) of the Golden Horde, which ruled Russia and the western steppe lands, was a Muslim. Many of the Mongols in Iran converted to Islam before the Mongol state itself, the Il-Khanate, became officially Muslim in 1295. The close cultural, trade, and political links between Iran and China in the thirteenth and fourteenth centuries ensured that Islam became entrenched throughout the empire.

The first Mongol khan in Iran to convert to Islam, Ahmad Tegüdar (1282–84), has often been overshadowed by the conversion of his nephew's son, Ghazan Khan (1295–1304). One reason has doubtless been the rather unorthodox strain of Islam that Ahmad adopted that scandalized the more conservative Persian members of the Il-Khanate court, an establishment that would have viewed some of Ahmad's Islamic practices with extreme disquiet and some of the Sufis who guided him in his religious

Phoenix Temple (thirteenth-century mosque), Hangzhou. Courtesy of Lan Tien Lang Publications

duties with extreme distaste. Il-Khan Ahmad surrounded himself with *qalandars,* members of an extreme antinomian strain of Sufism whose wandering adherents dotted the medieval landscape of greater Iran, central Asia, and Eurasia.

One influential figure, Hasan Mangolī, is mentioned in particular. Hasan Mangolī advocated a Sufi order that permitted and encouraged indulgence in hashish, and Sultan Ahmad was much taken by his company. Together they became involved in "blasphemy and corruption," and the sultan began to mix socially with *qalandars* and other such "unclean" persons that Hasan Mangolī collected around him. Mangolī attempted to use his position at court to further his own ends. He saw the revered sheikh and representative of the more respectable and socially acceptable form of Sufism, Sheikh Zāhid Gilānī and his son Jamāl al-Dīn ʿAlī, as impediments to his own advancement, which of course they were, and he set about poisoning the sultan's mind against the two respected holy men. However, events outside Mangolī's control overtook his nefarious schemes, and his patron, Sultan Ahmad, was deposed in a family coup by his nephew Arghun Khan. The new Il-Khan, Arghun Khan (1284–91) had his uncle, Ahmad Tegüdar, dispatched in the traditional Mongol fashion reserved for royalty. He was wrapped in felt and kicked to death. The felt or carpet was there to prevent any royal blood seeping into the earth, something the Mongols believed would bring calamity and disaster. Hasan Mangolī was also seized, though he was not dispatched in such a regal fashion. He was cast into a cauldron of oil and boiled alive.

QALANDARS

The *qalandars* were a very distinctive group seen on the medieval landscape of the Mongol Empire, and they became particularly prominent

Phoenix Temple, Hangzhou. Courtesy of Lan Tien Lang Publications

in the later thirteenth century in the Il-Khanate of Mongol Persia. They affected a characteristic coiffure, the so-called four blows *(chahār żarb)*, by shaving head, beard, moustache, and eyebrows, though such groups as the Haydarīs grew their moustaches excessively long. Their dress was sometimes completely absent, sometimes restricted to a simple loin-cloth, though often they dressed in more traditional Sufi garb, though the woolen or felt cloak was colored black or white rather than the usual Sufi blue. Others wore simple sacks. When they wore headgear it was invariably distinctive. Almost universally these *qalandars* went barefoot. Apart from their strange appearance *qalandars* could also be recognized as such by the paraphernalia they carried with them. The traditional black begging bowl and wooden club were ever present, but other equipment such as iron rings, collars, bracelets, belts, anklets, chains, hatchets, ankle-bones, leather pouches, and large wooden spoons distinguished these wandering *qalandars*. Most noticeable perhaps were the rings, which were sometimes pierced through the penis to enforce sexual abstinence. This deliberately provocative external appearance was further exaggerated by their eccentric and scandalous behavior, which itself was encouraged by their well-attested use of intoxicants and hallucinogenic drugs, cannabis in particular.[19]

The *qalandars* justified their outrageous behavior with clever, no doubt hashish-strengthened, logic, for they defiantly maintained their adherence to Islam and the teachings of the Prophet. They were, they would earnestly insist, engaged on the quest for God and enlightenment, and this of course entailed the suppression of self and selfishness. Too many, they claimed, were the Sufis who trod the path of self-denial and asceticism and yet who were ultimately defeated and seduced by the demon of self-aggrandizement. Too often these same ascetics took secret satisfaction and pleasure from the acclaim and admiration they elicited from their disciples and admirers and relished the fame that their hardship engendered. Their egos increased in proportion to the miseries they endured, and their public acclaim defeated the worldly self-denial they cultivated. The *qalandars* rejected such courting of public esteem and considered false this publicly paraded saintliness and piety. For them such public honor would undermine their attempts at self-abasement and true denial. It was therefore to avoid the pitfalls of public respect that they sought the opposite, namely public contempt and disgrace. They actively sought disapproval not only from the establishment but also from the public in general, and in this way they considered themselves freer to follow their spiritual path toward truth.

It was with this aim that the *qalandars* adopted their distinctive dress and practices, and it was with this as their justification that they took up with relish the consumption of, in particular, hashish, though it should be mentioned that alcohol, music, and various forms of less common sexual practices were also indulged in for the same pure reasons as mentioned above. Therefore, the *qalandars* were indulging in these excesses of sex, drugs, and trance-inducing music merely to throw people off their trail and to avoid the sin of vanity. They were not really hedonistic libertines but closet ascetics willing to endure public scorn and disgrace in the service of true humility.

The appearance of the *qalandars* was associated with the invaders from the east by the Arabs and by Muslims from the unconquered western reaches of the Islamic world. The Mongols and the Persians, who administered their kingdom, became the obvious targets of blame for the moral and material ills that beset the Islamic world in the second half of the thirteenth century, a decline exemplified by these wandering, hashish-partaking, foreign *qalandars*. Ibn Taymīyah (died 1328) was in no doubt that it was the Mongols who were responsible for introducing the evils of cannabis to the Islamic world. "It was with the Tatars that it [Hashish] originated among the people." "About the time of the appearance of the Tatars, hashish went forth, and with it, there went forth the sword of the Tatars."[20] His intention was to suggest not only that the Mongols introduced this vice to the people but that they did so with the intention of using it as a weapon to weaken resistance to their conquest. This belief was put forward by subsequent chroniclers, including al-Dhahabī and al-Zarkashī. Al-Zarkashī quoted an unnamed source when he claimed that the use of cannabis "was an evil restricted to Persia, until the Tatars gained control over its inhabitants. Then it moved on to Baghdad when the evil effect it had upon its people was already known." The thirteenth-century Spanish historian Ibn Saʿīd remarked

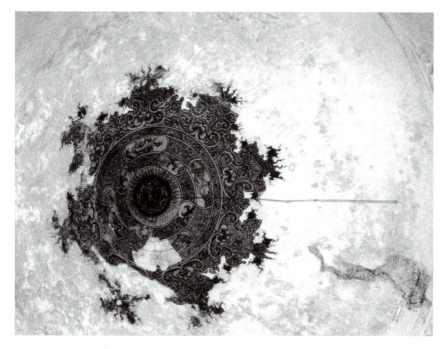

Ceiling inside prayer room of the Phoenix Temple. Courtesy of Lan Tien Lang Publications

disapprovingly on the use of hashish in Egypt, which he claimed was unknown in his native Islamic Spain. However, his remarks are significant when considered beside the verses, written in 1360, of Lisān al-Dīn ibn al-Khaṭīb, who drew attention to the appearance of widespread hashish use among both the low and upper classes of Granada in the fourteenth century.[21] Other than Sultan Ahmad, hashish use among the Mongols has not been recorded. They were heavy-drinking men and, as the poets of the time were fond of saying, the two drugs did not mix well.

> Their hashish covers the respectable person with ignominy
> So that you meet him like a killer acting with premeditation
> It produces upon his cheeks something like its own greenish colour....
> Our own wine covers the lowly person with respectability
> And dignity so that you find every master beneath him....
> It appears—and his secret appears and gladdens him.
> He resembles its colour with a rosy cheek.[22]

With the Turkish and Mongol population movements, there came westward a large influx of religious figures from Khorasan and central Asia, among whom were many dervishes loosely associated with the *qalandars* and their associated groups such as the Haydariyya.[23] These groups were

Inside prayer room of the Phoenix Temple. Courtesy of Lan
Tien Lang Publications

in no way so-called shamans in turbans, and any similarity between the
behavior and outward appearance of the Sufis and shamans was superficial. Shamanism was not generally practiced as a transcendental religion
and did not include such practices as *fanā* (annihilation in God) and
Gnosticism.[24] However, a distinction should be made between the many
wandering often antinomian dervishes, the larger establishment *Khanqāhs*,
and other more select centers where more ascetic, less flamboyant Sufis
might gather. Sultan Ahmad's Mangolī must surely represent one of the
first class of Sufi, the wandering antinomian dervishes, though it should
be remembered that this is a very unsatisfactory generalization because
the *qalandars* were hardly uniform in their practices, their social, religious,
or educational backgrounds, nor indeed in the depth of their spiritual
integrity.

An interesting anecdote is told about Hülegü that would suggest that the Mongols were not responsible for encouraging the westward spread of *qalandars* and that they were probably a purely Persian creation. Asked by Hülegü in about 1260 to explain a group of *qalandars* that the Il-Khan had encountered on the plain of Harrān, Tūsī answered that they were "the uncountered [surplus] of the world," leading Hülegü to immediately order the unfortunate dervishes' execution. Elaborating, presumably after the slaughter, Tūsī expounded to his master that mankind was divided into four categories: rulers, traders, craftsmen, and agriculturalists. Those who did not fall within these categories "were a burden [on the people]"[25] Though the details of this story are probably apocryphal, the message seems to be that Hülegü had not encountered such groups as the *qalandars* before.

MARCO POLO'S VIEWS ON RELIGION AND THE MONGOLS

If the Mongols were becoming involved with heterodox forms of Islam in the west, in the east they were able to maintain more traditional practices. Marco Polo, who served the Yüan dynasty for nearly three decades, provided various glimpses of the Mongols' spiritual life. In the following extract from his journal he summarizes their beliefs at the end of the thirteenth century.

CONCERNING THE RELIGION OF THE CATHAYANS, THEIR VIEWS AS TO THE SOUL, AND THEIR CUSTOMS[26]

As we have said before, these people are Idolaters, and as regards their gods, each has a tablet fixed high up on the wall of his chamber, on which is inscribed a name which represents the Most High and Heavenly God; and before this they pay daily worship, offering incense from a thurible, raising their hands aloft, and gnashing their teeth three times, praying Him to grant them health of mind and body; but of Him they ask nought else. And below on the ground there is a figure which they call *Natigai*, which is the god of things terrestrial. To him they give a wife and children, and they worship him in the same manner, with incense, and gnashing of teeth, and lifting up of hands; and of him they ask seasonable weather, and the fruits of the earth, children, and so forth.

Their view of the immortality of the soul is after this fashion. They believe that as soon as a man dies, his soul enters into another body, going from a good to a better, or from a bad to a worse, according as he hath conducted himself well or ill. That is to say, a poor man, if he have passed through life good and sober, shall be born again of a gentlewoman, and shall be a gentleman; and on a second occasion shall be born of a princess and shall be a prince, and so on, always rising, till he be absorbed into the Deity. But if he have borne himself ill, he who was the son of a gentleman shall be reborn as the son of a boor, and from a boor shall become a dog, always going down lower and lower.

The people have an ornate style of speech; they salute each other with a cheerful countenance, and with great politeness; they behave like gentlemen, and eat with great propriety. They show great respect to their parents; and should there be any son who offends his parents, or fails to minister to their necessities, there is a public office which has no other charge but that of punishing unnatural children, who are proved to have acted with ingratitude towards their parents.

Criminals of sundry kinds who have been imprisoned, are released at a time fixed by the Great Kaan (which occurs every three years), but on leaving prison they are branded on one cheek that they may be recognized.

The Great Kaan hath prohibited all gambling and sharping, things more prevalent there than in any other part of the world. In doing this, he said: "I have conquered you by force of arms, and all that you have is mine; if, therefore, you gamble away your property, it is in fact my property that you are gambling away." Not that he took anything from them however.

I must not omit to tell you of the orderly way in which the Kaan's Barons and others conduct themselves in coming to his presence. In the first place, within a half mile of the place where he is, out of reverence for his exalted majesty, everybody preserves a mien of the greatest meekness and quiet, so that no noise of shrill voices or loud talk shall be heard. And every one of the chiefs and nobles carries always with him a handsome little vessel to spit in whilst he remain in the Hall of Audience—for no one dares spit on the floor of the hall,—and when he hath spitten he covers it up and puts it aside. So also they all have certain handsome buskins of white leather, which they carry with them, and, when summoned by the sovereign, on arriving at the entrance to the hall, they put on these white buskins, and give their others in charge to the servants, in order that they may not foul the fine carpets of silk and gold and divers colours.

RELIGIOUS DEVELOPMENT AND TENGGERISM

With a tradition of shamanism, the Mongols were very open to the more sophisticated religious systems that they encountered as they spread their power bases outward. Often they adapted rather than adopted the beliefs that they encountered, but as their own culture drew away from its nomadic roots so, too, did their religious practices lose their anchorage in the steppe and the mountaintop. They needed a religion to sustain them as world imperialists. They needed a religion to underpin their globalization of trade and culture, and they needed a religion that could accommodate the various creeds that their expanding empire encompassed. The scholar Sh. Bira identified the emergence of Tenggerism, or Heavenism, as the Mongols assumed the mantle of world emperors. Shamanism envisages Tenggeri as a kind of supreme masculine being with dominion over all natural and social phenomena on earth. The feminine element is represented by Itügen, the Earth itself. Hence the expressions *etsege Tenggeri* (Father Tenggeri) and *eke gajar* (Mother Earth). Basic to their beliefs was the divine origin of the Qa'anship, which in the *Secret History of the Mongols* is expressed in the claim that Chinggis Khan ultimately originated from a divine blue wolf. However, in addition to this blue wolf, his ancestral mother, Alan-q'ao, divinely conceived three of her sons, the youngest of whom is considered the progenitor of Chinggis Khan's Golden clan *(Altan urug).*

Every night a shining yellow man slipped into the tent through the light of the smoke hole and the gap at the top of the door. He caressed my belly and his light seemed to sink into me....My sons are the children of heaven born to be lords of the land.[27]

This same story was told by the Armenian Kirakos, who heard it from a leading *noyan.*

They say that their king is a relative of God. God took heaven as his portion and gave earth to the Khan, for they say that Chingiz-Khan, the [grand] father of the [present] Khan was not born from the seed of man but that a light came from the unseen, entered through a skylight in the home, and announced to his mother: "Conceive and you will bear a son who will be ruler of the world." And they say that [Chinggis Khan] was born from that.[28]

The idea of immaculate conception is hardly original, and this concept is not alone in reflecting the influence of other ideas, myths, and beliefs that would have been stirring in the Mongol collective psyche as they swept across the globe in an unprecedented relentless tide. The conviction that their conquests and victories must have been ordained and sanctioned from above would have been unavoidable, and the Mongols were not alone in seeing the hand of God at work on his divine intent. As their *ordus* became ever larger and steadily more cosmopolitan, the emerging generation of Mongol princes were steeped in the learning, wisdom, and mythology of their Chinese, Persian, Turkish, Armenian, Tibetan, and Arab peers. The simple steppe lore of Tenggeri was interpreted and reinterpreted in the light of the more sophisticated and developed ideologies of those they were assimilating within the new and expanding world empire. As the young Mongols attempted to come to terms with the reality of their new world they tried to understand their position in the universe according to their God, Tenggeri, whose omnipotence was self-evident. Even if individual khans adopted the trappings of the local religion, such as the Il-Khan Ghazan's conversion to Islam in 1295, it was rare that the supremacy of the *yasa* was ever denied. Ghazan made Islam the state religion, but he also made it plain that he believed that he and his Golden clan had been divinely appointed and entrusted with a divine mission to rule over wherever Blue Heaven [*Köke Tenggeri*] covered, for all eternity [*Möngke Tenggeri*]. Writing to Pope Boniface VIII in 1302 about a joint assault on the Muslim Mamluks of Egypt, Ghazan twice urged prayer to Tenggeri for help.

At the moment we are doing exactly what we should be doing. You have to mobilise your troops and send them to the sultans of different peoples. Do not be late for the date we agreed! Praying to Tenggeri and understanding the significance of the great deed, let us complete it! Herewith we send to you as envoys Sedadm, Sananadm and Samsadin. Pray to Tenggeri, and have your troops prepared![29]

The Mongols' developing view of their status can be tracked through their official documents and from their correspondence with foreign states and rulers. The titles they awarded themselves reflected their actual and their perceived power. "By the power of eternal heaven, by the protection of the khan's charisma" is the standard opening of official documents and declarations. It expresses the dual nature of the godhead with Tenggeri in heaven and the khan on Earth. The khan embodies Tenggeri's power on Earth and enjoys his favor and protection. When the khan speaks, it "is the word of the son of God, which is addressed to you." In a letter sent to Pope Innocent IV with the spy Carpini, dated November 1246, the Great Khan Güyük (1246–48) explained the raids on European states and the massacres of the pope's Christian subjects.

The eternal God has slain and annihilated these lands and peoples because they have neither adhered to Chinggis Khan, nor to the Khagan, both of whom have been sent to make known God's command, nor to the command of God... all the lands have been made subject to me. Who could do this contrary to the command of God? If you do not observe God's command and if you ignore my command, I shall know you as my enemy.... If you do otherwise, God knows what I know.[30]

Möngke Khan echoed the same sentiments eight years later when he sent an ultimatum to Louis IX, king of France. Möngke appeared to view the Christian church as a rival ideology to this new divine force that Tenggerism was coming to represent. The Mongols justified their worldwide conquests as being divinely inspired and guided. The proof was their success.

It is the decree of eternal God, which we have made known to you. When you have heard and believed it, if you wish to obey us, send your envoys to us. In this way, we shall know for sure whether you wish to be at peace or war with us. When by the power of eternal God the whole world from the rising of the sun to the going down thereof shall be at one in joy and peace, then it will be made clear what we are going to do. If, when you hear and understand the decree of eternal God, you are unwilling to pay attention and believe it, saying "Our country is far away, our mountains are mighty, our sea is vast," and in this confidence you bring an army against us, we know what we can do: He who made what was difficult easy and what was far away near, eternal God, He knows.[31]

The Mongols now saw themselves as God's chosen people and Chinggis as his messenger. They were spreading the gospel of the Great *Yasa,* and they saw their conquests as a jihad, or crusade, legitimized by Tenggeri. Those who opposed them, therefore, were defying not only the Mongol-led armies but also the forces of good and God and the divine right of the Chinggisid Mongols to rule. In fact they were more successful in establishing themselves in this role in name rather than in practice, and for generations to come a claimed linkage to the Chinggisid Golden clan legitimized rulers as diverse as the Moguls of India and Turkoman dynasties of western Iran.

The Mongols did not see themselves as a state competing with, conquering, or challenging other states but more as a world empire enforcing its dominion on its resistant vassals. Other states were, first and foremost, expected to recognize the dominance and superiority of their Mongol overlords. For ideologies such as Christianity and Islam, this presented immediate deep-rooted problems. Some states, including Georgia, came to terms with the new world order painlessly, and coins struck in 1252 illustrate their acceptance of this reality. The inscription struck in Persian, reads, "By the Might of Heaven/By the Good Fortune of the Emperor of the World, Mungu Qa'an."

When Chinggis struck out from the steppe in 1206 as a nomad emperor his aims were conquest for the sake of plunder and power. When he thundered westward in pursuit of the ill-fated Khwārazmshāh, he did so in the spirit of revenge and destruction. But by the time his grandsons were negotiating submission and viewing new horizons of conquest, the philosophy of the conquerors had changed, and the transformation was positive and welcomed by those at the receiving end. The Mongols had become evangelical, and their message was one of spiritual, cultural, mercantile, and economic globalization.

NOTES

1. Rashīd al-Dīn, *Jāmi' al-Tavārīkh,* eds., Mohammad Roushan and Mustafah Mūsavī (Tehran: Nashr albaraz, 1994), 516.

2. J. A. Boyle, *The Mongol World Empire 1206–1370* (London: Variorum Reprints, 1977), 158.

3. Ala-ad-Din 'Ata-Malik Juvaini, *The History of the World Conqueror,* trans. John Andrew Boyle, intro. David Morgan (Manchester, U.K.: Manchester University Press, 1997), 39.

4. W. W. Rockhill, *The Journey of William of Rubruck to the Eastern Parts of the World, 1253–55, as Narrated by Himself, with Two Accounts of the Earlier Journey of*

John of Pian de Carpine, trans. from the Latin and ed., with an introductory notice, by William Woodville Rockhill (London: Hakluyt Society, 1900).

5. Ganjaks'i Kirakos, *Kirakos Ganjaks'i's History of the Armenians,* trans. Robert Bedrosian, *Sources for the Armenian Tradition,* 1986, available at: http://rbedrosian. com/kg1.htm.

6. Marco Polo and Rustichello of Pisa, *The Project Gutenberg EBook of the Travels of Marco Polo,* available at: http://www.gutenberg.net.

7. Hamd-Allah Mustawfi, *Nuzhat al-Qulub,* trans. G. Le Strange (Leiden, Netherlands: Brill & Luzac, 1919), 211.

8. Khwandamir, *Habib's-Siyar: The Reign of the Mongol and the Turk Genghis Khan, Amir Temur,* trans. W.M. Thackston, vol. 3 (Cambridge, Mass.: Department of Near Eastern Languages and Civilizations, Harvard University, 1994), 58.

9. Rashīd al-Dīn, *Jāmi' al-Tavārīkh,* 587.

10. Rockhill, *The Journey of William of Rubruck.*

11. Kirakos, *Kirakos Ganjaks'i's History of the Armenians.*

12. Rockhill, *The Journey of William of Rubruck.*

13. Ibid.

14. Ibid.

15. Ibid.

16. Hetoum, *Flower of Histories of the East.*

17. Ibid.

18. Ibid.

19. Ahmet Karamustafa, *God's Unruly Friends* (Salt Lake City: University of Utah Press, 1994), 21.

20. Franz Rosenthal, *The Herb: Hashish versus Mediaeval Muslim Society* (Leiden: E.J. Brill 1971), 48–51.

21. Moḥ ammad al-ᶜAbbādī, ed., Lisān al-Dīn ibn al-Khaṭ īb, *Nufāḍ at al-jirāb* (Cairo, 1968), 20, 183; Rosenthal, *The Herb,* 55.

22. Rosenthal, *The Herb,* 165.

23. For a contemporary picture of a Haydari Qalandar, see Pūr-i Bahā', "Kar-nameh Awqaf," 11–13, 17. See also Ahmet Karamustafa, *God's Unruly Friends* (Salt Lake City: University of Utah Press, 1994), 52–53, 57–58, 67–70.

24. Reuven Amitai-Preiss, "Sufis and Shamans," *JESHO* (1999): 38–39.

25. Ibn al-Fuwat, Kamāl al-Dīn Abū al-Fazl, *al-Hawādith al-Jāmī'a wa'l-Tajārib al-nāfi'a fi'l-mī'a al-sābī'a* (Baghdad: Carmel Press, 1932), 343.

26. Marco Polo and Rustichello of Pisa, *The Project Gutenberg EBook of the Travels of Marco Polo.*

27. Urgunge Onon, trans., *The History and Life of Chinggis Khan (The Secret History of the Mongols)* (Leiden, Netherlands: Brill, 1990), 3.

28. Kirakos, *Kirakos Ganjaks'i's History of the Armenians.*

29. A. Mostaert and F.W. Cleaves, "Trois documents Mongols des Archives Secretes Vaticanes," *Harvard Journal of Asiatic Studies* 52 (1952).

30. Christopher Dawson, ed., *The Mongol Mission,* trans. by a nun of Stanbrook Abbey (London: Sheed & Ward, 1955), 85–86.

31. Ibid., 203–4.

10

LAW AND MONGOL RULE

THE *YASA*

The term *yasa* is a Mongol word meaning "law, order, decree, judgment."
As a verb it implied the death sentence as in "some were delivered to the
yasa," usually meaning that an official execution had been carried out. It
was once generally accepted that Chinggis Khan had laid down a basic
legal code called the Great *Yasa* during the Great *Quriltai* of 1206 and written copies of his decrees were kept by the Mongol princes in their treasuries
for future consultation. This code, the so-called Great *Yasa,* was to be binding throughout the lands where Mongol rule prevailed, though strangely
the actual texts of the code were to remain taboo in the same way the text
of the *Altan Debter* (an official Mongol chronicle accessible only to Mongol
nobles) was treated. This restriction on access to the text explains the fact
that no copies of the Great *Yasa* have ever actually been recorded. Though
in reality it never existed in any formal physical sense, in later years many
assumed that these collected Mongol edicts known as the Great *Yasa* had
been compiled by Chinggis Khan.

The Great *Yasa* became a body of laws governing the social and legal
behavior of the Mongol tribes and the peoples of those lands that came
under their control. Initially it was based on Mongol traditions, customary law, and precedent, but it was never rigid, and it was always open to
very flexible and liberal interpretation and quite able to adapt, adopt, and
absorb other legal systems. Speaking of the *yasas*, the Muslim Juwaynī

(died 1282), historian and governor of Baghdad under the Mongol Il-Khans, was able to declare, "There are many of these ordinances that are in conformity with the *Shari'at* [Islamic law]."[1] The Great *Yasa* must therefore be viewed as an evolving body of customs and decrees that began long before Chinggis Khan's *quriltai* of 1206. His son Chaghatai was known to adhere strictly to the unwritten Mongol customary law, and many of his strictures and rulings would have been incorporated into the evolving body of law. Many of the rulings that appear to be part of this Great *Yasa* are based on quotations and *biligs* (maxims) of Chinggis Khan that are known to have been recorded. Another source of the laws that made up the Great *Yasa* is the Tatar Shigi-Qutuqu, Chinggis Khan's adopted brother, who was entrusted with judicial authority during the 1206 *quriltai*. He established the Mongol practice of recording in writing the various decisions he arrived at as head *yarghuchi* (judge). His decisions were recorded in the Uyghur script in a blue book *(kökö debter)* and were considered binding, thus creating an ad hoc body of case histories. However, this in itself did not represent the Great *Yasa* of Chinggis Khan, and it must be assumed that such a document never existed, even though in the years to come the existence of just such a document became a widespread belief.

IMPOSITION OF LAW

With or without the existence of a written Great *Yasa*, the Mongols, especially under Chinggis Khan, had a strict set of rules and laws to which they adhered, and their discipline was everywhere remarked on and admired. An intelligence report prepared by Franciscan friars led by Friar Giovanni DiPlano Carpini, who visited Mongolia in the 1240s, commented as follows:

Among themselves, however, they are peaceable, fornication and adultery are very rare, and their women excel those of other nations in chastity, except that they often use shameless words when jesting. Theft is unusual among them, and therefore their dwellings and all their property are not put under lock and key. If horses or oxen or other animal stock are found straying, they are either allowed to go free or are led back to their own masters.... Rebellion is rarely raised among them, and it is no wonder if such is their way, for, as I have said above, transgressors are punished without mercy.[2]

Even the Muslim historian Jūzjānī (died 1260) does not hold back.

Chinggis Khan moreover in [the administration of] justice was such, that, throughout his whole camp, it was impossible for any person to take up a fallen whip from the ground except he were the owner of it; and, throughout his whole army, no one could give indication of [the existence of] lying and theft.[3]

Nor does Jūzjānī refrain from treating Chinggis Khan's son and successor, Ögödei Qa'an, who was generally credited with having shown compassion and great sympathy for his Muslim subjects, with respect and positive treatment.

Religious tolerance became enshrined in the *yasa,* though some would say that the Mongols were just playing safe by safeguarding religious leaders of all faiths. Priests and religious institutions were all exempted from taxation. Water was treated with great respect, and it was strictly forbidden to wash or urinate in running water, streams and rivers being considered as living entities. Execution was the reward for spying, treason, desertion, theft, adultery and persistent bankruptcy in the case of merchants. Execution could take on various horrific forms and one particularly gruesome example has been recorded by Rashīd al-Dīn (died 1318), a prime minister of Iran during the Mongol Il-Khanid period. A rash Kurdish warlord had attempted to double-cross Hülegü Khan. He was apprehended and received this fate.

He [Hülegü] ordered that he [Malik Salih] be covered with sheep fat, trussed with felt and rope, and left in the summer sun. After a week, the fat got maggoty, and they started devouring the poor man. He died of that torture within a month. He had a three-year-old son who was sent to Mosul, where he was cut in two on the banks of the Tigris and hung as an example on two sides of the city until his remains rotted away to nothing.[4]

Reflecting the Mongols' respect for and superstitious fear of aristocracy, they were fearful of shedding the blood of the highborn upon the earth. They therefore reserved a special form of execution for kings and the particularly mighty. Such nobles, in recognition of their status, were wrapped in carpets and kicked to death.

Often portrayed as barbarians, the Mongols are not often credited with the discipline and law-abiding nature of their society. Though anarchy often followed in their wake, once established, serious measures were invariably enacted to ensure that the rule of law governed every aspect of life and all members of their society. Even in the north, far from the imperial cities that would emerge as the Il-Khanid and Yüan dynasties became established, the rule of law prevailed, as even the censorious eye of William of Rubruck conceded.

As to their justice you must know that when two men fight together no one dares interfere, even a father dare not aid a son; but he who has the worse of it may appeal to the court of the lord, and if anyone touches him after the appeal, he is put to death. But action must be taken at once without any delay, and the injured one must lead him (who has offended) as a captive. They inflict capital punishment on no one unless he be taken in the act or confesses. When one is accused by a number of persons, they torture him so that he confesses. They punish homicide with capital punishment, and also co-habiting with a woman not one's own. By not one's own, mean not his wife or bondwoman, for with one's slaves one may do as one pleases. They also punish with death grand larceny, but as for petty thefts, such as that of a sheep, so long as one has not repeatedly been taken in the act, they beat him cruelly, and if they administer an hundred blows they must use an hundred sticks: I speak of the case of those beaten under order of authority. In like manner false envoys, that is to say persons who pass themselves off as ambassadors but who are not, are put to death. Likewise sorcerers, of whom I shall however tell you more, for such they consider to be witche.

When anyone dies, they lament with loud wailing, then they are free, for they pay no taxes for the year. And if anyone is present at the death of an adult, he may not enter the dwelling even of Mangu Chan for the year. If it be a child who dies, he may not enter it for a month. Beside the tomb of the dead they always leave a tent if he be one of the nobles, that is of the family of Chingis, who was their first father and lord. Of him who is dead the burying place is not known. And always around these places where they bury their nobles there is a camp with men watching the tombs. I did not understand that they bury treasure with their dead. The Comans raise a great tumulus over the dead, and set up a statue to him, its face to the east, and holding a cup in its hand at the height of the navel. They make also pyramids to the rich, that is to say, little pointed structures, and in some places I saw great tiled covered towers, and in others stone houses, though there were no stones thereabout. Over a person recently dead I saw hung on long poles the skins of xvi horses, four facing each quarter of the world; and they had placed also cosmos for him to drink, and meat for him to eat, and for all that they said of him that he had been baptized. Farther east I saw other tombs in shape like great yards covered with big flat stones, some round, some square, and four high vertical stones at the corners facing the four quarters of the world. When anyone sickens he lies on his couch, and places a sign over his dwelling that there is a sick person therein, and that no one shall enter. So no one visits a sick person, save him who serves him. And when anyone from the great ordu is ill, they place guards all round the ordu, who permit no one to pass those bounds. For they fear lest an evil spirit or some wind should come with those who enter. They call, however, their priests, who are these same soothsayers.[5]

MONGOL LAW IN CHINA

In both China and Iran a complex legal system evolved and developed incorporating the existing body of laws already in practice. This was especially true in China, which had a centuries-old tradition of legal codes and a complex legal system. Paul Heng-chao Ch'en has written an excellent assessment of this subject in his book *Chinese Legal Tradition under the Mongols: The Code of 1291 as Reconstructed* and explains how those traditional codes and practices were adapted and incorporated into Mongol jurisprudence. In this slim tome he includes a reconstruction and translation into English of one of the key codes, the *Chih-yüan hsin-ko,* compiled in 1291.

After centuries of war the Liao, the Chin, and the Song were united under the Yüan dynasty, and Chinese legal institutions had to be adapted to reflect this fact as well as the reality of new nomadic rulers. Traditional historians, when recounting Chinese legal history, often jump straight from the Song to the Ming dynasties, omitting the Yüan period as a kind of black hole best ignored. However, this is an unjustified omission, and the evidence supports the view that the Yüan rulers adopted a new and substantial legal system that retained elements of Chinese legal tradition while incorporating laws to reflect the new realities. In 1291 a new legal code was promulgated, *Chih-yüan New Code,* and this code became the foundation for the later compilations of the *Ta Yuan t'ung-chih (Comprehensive Institutions of the Great Yüan),* and the *Yuan tien-chang (Institutions of the Yüan Dynasty).*

The *yasa* had been the principle source of legal rulings in the first years of Mongol domination but as this haphazard source of customary law increasingly proved deficient to meet the needs of Chinese society, the need for a unified Yüan code became obvious. The T'ang code had been standard in many parts of China since its drafting under the T'ang dynasty in 653. The articles of the T'ang code were grouped under 12 sections and covered most legal instances. The *T'ai-ho lü (T'ai-ho Statutes)* of the Chin dynasty, essentially a copy of the T'ang code, was used extensively, but when Qubilai Khan officially proclaimed the establishment of the Yüan dynasty in 1271 to formalize and legitimize Mongol rule in China, the *T'ai-ho* was officially annulled. The name *Yüan* was taken from the ancient book of Chinese divinity, the *I Ching (Book of Changes),* and suggested the "primal force of the Creative" or the "origin of the Universe," but its significance was its Chinese rather than Mongolian roots.

YÜAN LEGAL CODES

Yüan officials were reluctant to simply adopt the staid and rigid dictates of the T'ang code and favored codes of a more casuistic nature and less unified theme. Laws based on precedent were preferred, and collections of cases and the courts' rulings and decisions were compiled, and these in addition to various legal codes were employed in drawing up a national legal practice. The result was a compromise between the traditional Chinese reliance on codification and the flexibility of legal authority derived from precedent law. Though the *yasa* became effectively null and void, many of its laws, customs, and practices entered the new legal system through adoption into the codes or by their occurrence as precedents.

It was in this way that Qubilai Khan and his advisers were able to combine harmoniously Chinese legal tradition, Mongol customary law, and the new social and political realities that accompanied the establishment of the Yüan dynasty. From 1271 until 1320, changes in the legal system were initiated either to restore or create those Chinese institutions that would be necessary for the administration to function. From 1320 until the demise of the Yüan government, Mongol traditions were fully integrated within the Chinese institutions, and new codes were established. Not all were happy, and the words of one Confucian scholar were not an uncommon criticism.

All that is recorded [in the *Yuan tien-chang*] is, however, in the style of bureaucratic documents and, among them, seven- to eight-tenths are also mixed with colloquial language, common sayings, and vulgar expressions distorting the important essence. Its form is furthermore tangled and is loose without trace or order.[6]

This criticism of a Yüan legal code was a veiled reference to translations from Mongolian and the influence of Mongol and foreign overlords and administrators contained within the document. An eminent scholar from the Ch'ing era, Yao Nai (1731–1815) was more forthright in his criticism and prejudice, contemptuously condemning the *Yuan tien-chang* for its minute, rustic, and confusing use of expressions. Despite these shortcomings the Yüan leaders persevered in their work of codification. In 1324 copies of these new compilations were distributed to officials, and in 1328 Qa'an Toq Temür (ruled 1328–32) ordered the compilation of the *Ching-shih ta-tien (Great Institutions of Statecraft)*. The Yüan ruler considered himself a man of letters and had a great respect and love of Chinese arts and culture. It was Toq Temür who in 1329 established the Academy of the Kui-chang Pavilion to accommodate not only his scholars but his splendid collections of books, paintings, calligraphy, and curios.

The *Ching-shih ta-tien* documentary compilation was completed in 1331 and involved close collaboration between Mongol and Chinese officials in expediting numerous documents covering an array of institutions. This survey followed the style of Chinese collections from the T'ang and Sung dynasties and demonstrated a further growing acceptance of Chinese culture by the Mongol ruling elite. The section on judicial institutions, the *Hsien-tien*, comprised 22 subsections of all then-current regulations and an appendix containing all outdated legal material. Subsections included "Administrative Regulations," "Imperial Guards and Prohibitions," "Terms and General Principals," "Ordinances of Sacrifices," "Regulations of Study," "Family and Marriage," "Theft and Violence," "Food and Goods," "Complaints and Suits," "Homicides and Injuries," "Amnesties," "Grand Abominations," "Conflict and Battery," "Empty Prisons," "Evilness and Misdeeds," "Leniency of Punishments," and so on.

Various Chinese officials petitioned the Qa'an to pursue updates and modifications to these legal codes, arguing that the needs of a changing society demanded it. However, the relentless predominance of Chinese influence in these compilations suggests the bureaucrats had ulterior motives. The Qa'an Toq Temür was content to encourage this cultural trend with the Academy of the Hsüan-wen-ko (formerly Kui-chang) Pavilion expanding its literary activities. In 1334 he issued an edict ordering Mongols and central Asians resident in China to observe mourning of their parents. In 1343 he ordered the compilation of the "Three Histories," completed in 1345, which traced the histories of the Liao, Chin, and Sung dynasties with the implication of the continuity the Yüan represented. It was stressed that the study of these histories was necessary for scholars and officials to properly understand the present and to perform better in government.

The final major legal code of the Yüan dynasty was officially promulgated in 1346. This was the *Chih-cheng t'iao-ko*. which contained 150 decrees, 1,700 articles, and 1,050 precedents. Challenges to this code continued, but there is evidence that it continued to be used and consulted right up to the end. This follows the pattern established from the onset of Mongol domination of both Chinese and Mongol officials namely challenging, modifying, revising, and adding to the codes and legal compilations produced during the Yüan era. Chinese scholars continued to be apprehensive of their Mongol masters, often believing them incapable of the refined and sophisticated thought necessary to appreciate Chinese culture and Chinese legal systems. This was a demonstrably false impression of the Mongol elite as the cultural achievements of the Yüan government and of the brotherly state to the west, the Il-Khanate, clearly illustrate. In the field of Confucian studies and other intellectual pursuits, later, widely respected Chinese scholars have accepted that the record of the Yüan dynasty compares favorably with the records of other eras.

The Mongol rulers initially showed interest in Chinese legal codes and practices in respect to their new Chinese subjects, but as their knowledge of these codes grew and their acquaintance with Chinese culture developed, so too did their involvement in the Chinese institutions until those very institutions, suitably modified by exposure to Mongol sensitivities, became an integral part of the Yüan government. As the Mongols became increasingly familiar with Chinese ways, their initial mistrust decreased and their antagonism dissipated. After 1320 it was clear that Mongolian customs were becoming accommodated and integrated with the increasingly dominant Chinese institutions.

THE PENAL CODE

The penal code also underwent modification and change under the Yüan decades, and some of these changes became entrenched in the systems of later Chinese dynasties. For a people who have almost become synonymous with bloodshed and barbarity, it comes as a surprise to examine their record for legally sanctioned capital punishment under the Yüan government. The number of offences, recorded at 135, as listed in the *Yuan-shih* that carried the death penalty was less than the 293, 963, and 1,397 recorded under the T'ang (618–907), Sung (960–1260), and Ming (1368–1644) dynasties' codes, respectively. The number of executions carried out between 1260 and 1307 was 2,743, which, considering the huge population of China even then, is not a large figure. This figure was probably higher than the reality because many of these death sentences were commuted to life imprisonment at the last moment, but the record of an execution remained. In fact the Yüan rulers had a reputation for leniency, a fact that has often been overlooked by both Chinese and foreign historians unwilling to dispel the myth of the barbarian interlopers and the picture of the uncouth marauding hooligans trampling Chinese culture and sophistication underfoot.

The Yüan century saw a great expansion of Chinese urban society and accompanying commercial activity. With this expansion went the legal developments detailed previously, and to accommodate these new legal codes and institutions the penal system was reviewed and adapted. The rationale underpinning the penal system remained revenge, intimidation, prohibition, and rehabilitation. The traditional five penalties, the *Wu-hsing*, remained, but significant changes to form and content were implemented. Some of these changes died with the dynasty, but some outlived the Mongols and were adopted by the Ming and even the Ch'ing. In addition to the *Wu-hsing*, some supplementary financial and physical penalties were awarded on top of those five traditional punishments. These supplementary penalties reflect influence of the Mongol Great *Yasa*, and some of these characteristically Mongol punishments survived into the Ming and Ch'ing dynasties.

PUNISHMENTS

The standard form of the *Wu-hsing*, or five punishments, which goes back at least to the Sui dynasty (589–618 C.E.) code of 581–83, consisted of the following modes of punishment in descending degrees of severity: death by strangulation or decapitation; life exile with distances specified at 3,000 *li* (approximately 3 *li* = 1 mile), 2,500 *li*, and 2,000 *li*; imprisonment, with five periods between one and three years; beating with strokes of the heavy stick, awarded in units of 10 between 60 to 100; and beating with a light stick, in units of 10 between 10 to 50 blows.

The Yüan legislators introduced their own unique modification of the death penalty. Strangulation was generally replaced with *ling-ch'ih*, or slow slicing, which proved so popular that it was retained by both the Ming and the Ch'ing rulers. *Ling-ch'ih* was considered the severest form of punishment and was meted out for crimes such as treason. Cuts were applied to face, hands (2), feet (2), breast, stomach, and head, and these

8 cuts could be increased to 24, 36, or 120. The intention of the punishment was to prolong the death process to maximize suffering and pain. Strangulation was considered an easy option because the head was not separated from the body, and, according to Chinese belief, passage to the next world was not hindered. The Mongols abolished strangulation because they did not hold these beliefs and could not see its value as an alternative form of capital execution.

The leniency of the Yüan penal system was established from the outset by the strict edicts of Qubilai Qa'an, who ordered that any case resulting in the death sentence must be thoroughly reviewed before the sentence could be carried out. As early as 1260 it is recorded that he would personally review cases involving the death sentence and would commonly commute these to life sentences. The *Yuan-shih* records that in 1287, 190 people under sentence of death were reprieved at the last moment by Qubilai Qa'an, who exclaimed, "Prisoners are not a mere flock of sheep. How can they suddenly be executed? It is proper that they instead be enslaved and assigned to pan gold with a sieve." The Mongols did not invent the amnesty, but the granting of amnesties was common under Yüan rule, especially for Buddhist and Lamaist monks. The frequency of these amnesties provoked criticism from leading Chinese officials, with one senior official, Chang Yang-hao even suggesting that penalties should be more severe and amnesties greatly reduced.[7]

Once the death sentence was decided upon, however, leniency disappeared. For those for whom slicing was too lenient, other treatment was meted out. Political offenders might be pickled or chopped up into small pieces. Royalty whose blood could not be allowed to seep into the earth were wrapped in carpets and kicked to death, as the 'Abbasid caliph of Baghdad discovered in 1258.

Because the Mongols were a nomadic people, the idea of exile did not strike them as punishment in itself, and for this reason they added to the basic system in which prisoners were sent stipulated distances from their homes. Under the Yüan government, southern Chinese were exiled to Liao-yang and other northern districts, and northerners were exiled to Hunan and Hubei in the south. Koreans and Jurchen prisoners were also sent to exile stations in Hunan and Hubei. At the exile stations prisoners served at the postal relay posts or were set to work on the land. Banishment to a new land was not considered punishment, and therefore pain or slave labor was added to the sentence. In addition to the exile stations established to process exiles, the Yüan also introduced compulsory military service *(ch'u-chün)* and a measure *(ch'ien-hsi)* to deal with social undesirables that involved simply removing them from their village to some distant part of the empire.

Prison service was not considered enough unless accompanied by corporal punishment. A one-year sentence also included 67 blows from a heavy stick; 18 months, 77 blows; 2 years, 87 blows; and so on to the three-year maximum, which came with 107 blows with a heavy stick. Prison was not a cell but a mine or some such similar establishment. Here the prisoners were fettered and assigned heavy work for the day, a record of which would be kept.

The final forms of the *Wu-hsing*, or five punishments, were simple beatings with either a light stick or a heavy rod. Blows of 7, 17, 27, 37, 47, and 57 for the light stick and 67, 77, 87, 97, 107 for the heavy stick follow the Mongol tradition of using odd numbers, as has been noted by the Persian official and historian Waṣṣāf of Shiraz (died circa 1328). Marco Polo reports that these blows were often so severe that death resulted from the beatings.[8] The use of units of seven did not exist before 1260, and one of the earliest examples of the use of seven was the issuance of a decree in 1264 against walking in the capital after a certain time at night. The mandatory sentence for breaking this prohibition was 27 blows from a light stick. In fact a law also stipulated that the diameter of the light stick used for the chastisement be 0.27 Chinese inches at one end and 0.17 at the other.

WU-HSING SUPPLEMENTS

The supplementary financial and physical punishments imposed on top of the *Wu-hsing* were seen as a form of redemption. People who could not face physical punishment, such as children under 15 years, old people more than 70, cripples or severely injured people, or the very sick, were given the option to recompense the victim financially. Two types of formal compensation became common under the Yüan, namely *shao-mai-yin* (funeral expenses) and nourishment expenses, which meant, essentially, medical expenses. These practices were of Mongol origin and were designed to meet the demands of justice and avoid calls for revenge. The Great *Yasa* stated that in order to avoid capital punishment for murder, the culprit could pay, in the case of a Muslim victim, 40 *balish* (gold coins) or, in the case of a Chinese, one donkey. The *shao-mai-yin*, or payment of funeral expenses of the victim, became an important element in Chinese law, and it has often been forgotten that the origins of this practice are Mongolian customary law. The *Yuan-shih* stated unequivocally the nature of this law.

Any person who murders shall be executed. [The authorities] shall also exact from the person's relatives fifty *liang* of the *shao-mai-yin* for the [victim's family]. In cases of no silver, ten *ting* [ingots] of Chung-t'ung notes shall be exacted instead. If the person be pardoned by amnesty, [the sum] shall be doubled.[9]

The *shao-mai-yin* was generally fixed at 50 *tael* (between 1 and 2.5 ounces) of silver, and if the relatives were unable to pay they would be expected to perform manual services in lieu of payment. It has even been recorded that a family member was forced to work as a slave to pay off the *shao-mai-yin*.

The *Yuan-shih* also explained the practice of nourishment expenses, which covered the costs of medicine and medical care.

Any person who injures with an instrument another person and makes [the victim] crippled or seriously sick shall be punished 77 blows by beating with a heavy stick. [The authorities] shall also obtain [from the wrongdoer] ten *ting* of Chung-t'ung notes to give the injured person as "nourishment expenses."[10]

This penalty compares favorably with both the T'ang code, which specified that the offender receive three years' jail, and the Ming code, which demanded 100 blows from a heavy stick as well as the three years' imprisonment. Other examples reinforce the impression of the relative leniency of the Yüan penal system. As punishment for beating a sister-in-law to death, the Yüan code imposed a sentence of *shao-mai-yin* plus 107 heavy blows. In contrast the T'ang, Ming, and Ch'ing codes decreed strangulation as the appropriate penalty. The Yüan system, in other words, found a balance between the traditional Chinese practice of state-imposed punishment and the Mongolian custom of accepting redemption.

Another area in which Mongol law left its mark on Chinese laws and institutions was in provisions covering the crimes committed by slaves and servants.

In the case of a male or female slave or servant who has stolen a person's ox or horse and has been convicted and punished, [the slave or the servant] shall be given to the owner [of the stolen item]. If the master wishes to make redemption, let him do so.[11]

The option therefore existed for the master to surrender the slave or pay compensation. This option could be stretched to cover wives as well, and Mongol Oirat regulations stated that in the case of a wife murdering another's wife, the penalty fell on the husband, and he was given the choice of paying a heavy fine to the relatives of the victim or cutting off the ears of his homicidal wife and giving her away in marriage to the victim's family.[12]

Slaves were considered part of the family unit and, therefore, were regarded as legal relatives. As such they were viewed as being partners in a special relationship, and, therefore, the penalties imposed on them were comparatively lenient. From a traditional Chinese perspective, theft among relatives should be treated less seriously than ordinary theft because family members all had a moral obligation to support and aid each other financially. For the family unit, harmony and solidarity had to be maintained.

Bureaucrats and officials were usually granted the option of redemption, forfeiture of salary, demotion, or dismissal from the civil service for all but the most serious crimes. One development of these redemption options was the emergence of the nine-fold fine. This fine, calculated at nine times the value of the stolen item, was a feature of the Great *Yasa* of Chinggis Khan and was readily adopted for formal Chinese legal practice. The *Yuan-shih* states, "Any person who steals a camel, horse, ox, ass, or mule shall, for each one [stolen], compensate with nine." In the decrees of the *yasa* the law is equally clear. "The man in whose possession a stolen horse is found must return it to the owner and add nine horses of the same kind." This stipulation goes on to state that should the culprit be unable to pay in horses, his own children must be handed over instead, and "if he has no children, he himself shall then be slaughtered like a sheep."[13] Marco Polo also noted the nine-fold practice for the theft of cattle and sheep, the most serious of crimes for nomadic people. For other forms of theft, the two-fold fine was often considered sufficient.

In addition to these supplementary financial penalties, Yüan legal practice also developed some supplementary physical punishments. These penalties comprised forms of retaliatory punishment, which in essence amounted to the biblical practice of "an eye for an eye, a tooth for a tooth," according to the legal principle of talion. Though found in ancient Chinese practice by the time the T'ang codes were compiled, Chinese legal practices had moved far beyond such primitive concepts. One form of talion that was retained by the T'ang and passed into Yüan practice was the punishment for false accusation, which saw the false accuser suffer the penalty that might have been meted out to the object of his slander. "Any person who falsely accuses shall himself atone for the crime and suffer retribution."[14] The Yüan saw talion practiced in other cases, such as when religious figures were the object of attack. "He who beats a Lama monk shall have his hand[s] cut off; he who curses [a lama] shall have his tongue cut out."[15] The observant Marco Polo commented on this practice of retaliatory amputation. "If a man strikes with steel or with a sword, whether he hits or not, or threatens one, he loses his hand. He who wounds must receive a like wound from the wounded."[16]

Another supplementary penalty awarded either in addition to or instead of the five punishments was *tz'u-tzu*, which involved tattooing with a stylus or branding, and became institutionalized under the Yüan law makers. Tattoos branding the criminal were placed on the arms or neck instead of the forehead, as had previously been done under the Sung. In addition, the person so branded was also expected to act as a *ching-chi-jen*, a police informer, to alert the police to other social undesirables. This auxiliary police force of *ching-chi-jen*, or informers, became an integral part of the law-enforcement system, with various rewards allowed to enhance and extend the system. A *ching-chi-jen* could have his sentence reduced for diligence and supplying information that led to an arrest. Conversely, if a *ching-chi-jen* reoffended, he could be forced to serve as a *ching-chi-jen* for life. Three measures were enacted to ensure effective functioning of the *ching-chi-jen* institution. First, after the original sentence had been served, the criminal was sent back to his hometown to work as a *ching-chi-jen* and report and uncover local crime and criminals. Second, the name and offence of the *ching-chi-jen* was written in red paint on the wall outside his place of residence in order to subject him to local discrimination and surveillance, though this would seem self-defeating because it would surely hamper the criminal's undercover work as a *ching-chi-jen.* Third, the *ching-chi-jen* had to report regularly to the local authorities and account for his activities during this time. This twice-monthly visit had to be accompanied by reports from his neighbors and village headman attesting to his continued good behavior. Infringements of any conditions on his liberty, failure to report at the appointed time, or any additional criminal activity would result in not only punitive measures being taken against the culprit but also against the villagers charged with monitoring his behavior.

An edict specifying in detail the methods for tattooing was issued in 1302 on January 25 under the "General Precedents Concerning Robber and Thief."

Any thief shall be tattooed for the first offense by placing characters on the left arm. (This refers to the person who has already obtained goods by stealing.) For the second offense, he shall be tattooed on the right arm; and for the third offense, the neck. A robber shall be tattooed for the first offense on the neck. [Both of them] shall also serve as *ching-chi-jen.* The authorities shall examine and inspect [them] in accordance with the old methods [i.e., methods prescribed in the decree of 1264]. If a Mongol shall commit [such a crime] or a woman shall commit [it], the offender is not to be dealt with pursuant to the regulations concerning branding by tattooing.[17]

IMPLEMENTATION

The major challenge for the Yüan administrators, after having compiled their codes and established their complex system of laws and punishments, was the enforcement and execution of those laws over such a vast swathe of land and such a diverse patchwork of ethnic groups and communities, each with their own religious, social, and economic customs and traditions. The development of legal professionalism in formal trials and arbitration as well as informal settlements and legal understandings stands as testament to Yüan success and pride. The volumes of legal judgments, interpretations, rulings, cases, and other judicial material ensured that the law was open and accessible to all who could read and who might be interested in the administration of justice.

The basic hierarchy of legal administration was headed by the Secretarial Council, the *Chung-shu-sheng,* of the central government under which 10 *Hsing Chung-shu-sheng* or *Hsing-sheng* acted as provincial governments. The *Hsing-sheng* were split into four administrative divisions: *lu, fu, chou,* and *hsien.* Two further divisions, the army and the Bureau of Pacification, came under military control. The *hsien* became the basic judicial unit that could refer cases to the other divisions, and the *hsien* in turn was ranked upper, medium, or lower. By way of example, the following were officials of the upper *hsien:* magistrates *(hsien-yin)*, assistant magistrate *(hsien-ch'eng)*, record-keeper *(chu-pu)*, police commissioner *(hsien-wei)*, and regional overseer *(daru'chi)*. The police commissioner was entrusted with law enforcement and would patrol the area under his control with the authority to arrest suspects. To assist him in his duties he was assigned a team of archers *(kung-shou)* who acted as the police force. These archers were responsible for apprehending thieves and robbers, and failure to do so would result in their own punishment. Failure to arrest a thief or robber within a month was punished with 7 or 17 blows from a light stick, respectively; for two months 17 or 27 blows, respectively; for three months 27 or 37, respectively. However, the archer would receive an award for capturing the criminal before the deadline. The archers often relied on the *ching-chi-jen* for local intelligence. Once apprehended, the accused was handed over to the *hsien-yin*, the magistrate, for trial and sentencing.

Once the suspect entered the judicial system, he was confronted with a complicated and well-ordered organization. A complicated hierarchy of courts and a regulated setup of jails was headed by a commissioner of jails, the *ssu-yü*. The Yüan jailing system differed from other dynasties' systems because the Yüan jails were viewed more as holding jails utilized while the accused was going through the system. Because the emphasis of punishment was on forced labor rather than the deprivation of freedom, the cells were employed during those periods when the accused was awaiting or undergoing trial.

The prison commissioner *(ssu-yü)*, was responsible for four main areas: ensuring that the jails were clean and maintained; providing regular food and clothing for inmates; personally checking sick detainees; and reporting to the higher authorities any complaints, accusations, and problems concerning the prisoners. To prevent inmates from escaping, many prisoners were fettered. More serious offenders were forced to wear the cumbersome *cangue,* a kind of highly restrictive and heavy wooden collar. The weight of the *cangue* varied according to the crime. Murderers were obliged to wear wooden handcuffs. Chains and fetters of different weights and lengths were also employed. Torture was permitted but regulated and only allowed if other evidence existed pointing to the guilt of the accused. Torture had to be authorized and was theoretically restricted to beating. However, despite its prohibition, other more imaginative and cruel forms of torture existed. It was clearly stated that torture was not to be used unless clear evidence of guilt existed. Torture was deemed necessary because of the importance put on confessions.

In general, the judicial system of courts and jails was extremely well staffed by a complicated hierarchy of officials with a built-in system of checks and balances to counter irregularities and abuse of the system. The system ensured the accused legal rights and a system of appeal and redress for any perceived injustices. Verdicts and decisions often had to be signed by the accused, and a system of fingerprints was used to guard against forgery. Ink was smeared on the tip of the index finger and the back of the second and third joints and an impression made underneath the accused's name. This impression of three spots was apparently impossible to forge, and each person's impression was unique. This signature was necessary, and if it were not obtained the case had to be reviewed.

Until 1271 the judicial structure of the Yüan government was divided into three branches. These were the *Fa-ssu* (Bureau of Law), the *Hsing-pu* (Board of Punishments), and the *Tu-sheng* (the capital city's Secretarial Council). The *Fa-ssu* was dissolved in 1271, leaving the *Hsing-pu* and the *Tu-sheng* powerful institutions throughout the period of Yüan government. The *Hsing-pu* in particular became an important body, and even though final modifications were the preserve of the *Tu-sheng*, its decisions were rarely questioned.

The functions and structure of the judicial institutions were considered so well defined and transparent that no one could claim ignorance or confusion of the procedures in order to excuse bypassing the chain of command. Those who did were subject to punishment; however, those who found fault with the procedures or operation of justice were encouraged to air their grievances and seek recompense. The clear delegation of authority at all levels limited the potential for abuse or manipulation of the system. For cases of particular injustice it was possible to seek the intervention of the emperor himself. For this eventuality a drum was set up outside the imperial palace, and citizens were allowed to beat this drum in order to attract the attention of the emperor to their plight. The Yüan system of justice awarded more effective protection for its citizens against abuse of power, corruption, and the system itself than did earlier and later judicial systems under other dynasties.

ETHNIC DIFFERENCES AND LAW

With the vast expanses of land under Yüan government authority, the question of how to apply the law justly to the different ethnic groups became a potentially explosive situation. The Chinese had always harbored an innate sense of superiority to their various neighbors and believed that their Confucian ideals of culture and morality were suitable for all. Such attitudes were no longer sustainable, and the Chinese advisors to the Mongol rulers early realized that the judicial system would have to reflect the new reality. Four ethnic groups were recognized: Mongols, central Asians, northern Chinese, and southern Chinese; but where possible one court was convened to deal with a particular case with appropriate representation from the ethnic group of the defendant. The Yüan judiciary developed a system of joint representation in which the special interests of the different parties could be considered. A further development of these special courts convened to deal with ethnic conflicts of interest was the appearance of courts to deal with people who had special status, such as soldiers or members of certain professions or professional institutions.

IRAN

While the Yüan government was busy establishing the rule of law in China, in the west the Il-Khanate government of Iran was also trying to establish a stable legal framework in which to operate. However, in the Islamic lands the sharia law remained inviolable, and Mongol law and custom coexisted and adapted itself to Islamic practice. Juwaynī, historian and governor of Baghdad under Hülegü, famously claimed that the *yasa* and sharia law were often compatible.[18] This might have been an attempt at desperate self-delusion on Juwaynī's part more than a considered assessment of the two judicial systems. However, his statement does express a desire and willingness to reconcile Islamic teaching with the infidel rule. After the fall of Baghdad in 1258, Hülegü sought a *fatwa* (Islamic ruling) from Baghdad's *'ulamā* to legitimize his rule. The *fatwa* would resolve the question, "Who is preferable, an infidel ruler who is righteous, or a Muslim ruler who is unjust?" Ibn Ṭāwūs, a leading Shi'ite cleric from the holy city of Nejaf, found in his favor, declaring that a just infidel ruler was preferable to an unjust Muslim ruler.[19]

Prior to Hülegü's arrival circa 1255, the military government of Bayju Noyan had been essentially separate from the Iranian population, and the distinction between *'urfī* (customary law) and sharia jurisdiction was clear. With the establishment of the Il-Khanate and Mongol government, the distinction became increasingly blurred. The judicial system in Iran at this time was not as complex nor so bureaucratic as the system existing in China, nor were its workings committed to paper in such painstaking detail as has been found in the Yüan documents. However, the rule of law was enforced, and all were subject to its dictates.

Yarghu   The court of interrogation known as the *yarghu* was a fixed feature in the main cities but was also a mobile body, and *yarghuchi*, as its officers were known, traveled around the kingdom summoning those it wished to question. An *amīr yarghu* presided over the court and was helped by *umarā-yi yarghu* (emirs of the *yarghu* court) and the *yarghuchis* (lesser officials). The *yarghu* courts were present from the earliest appearance of the Mongols in Iran, and many examples exist of the *yarghu* being employed by the early military governors of this western province. However, details of procedure and the rules and regulations governing this institution are difficult to find in the sources. What was initially an extension of military rule developed into a respected and effective instrument of justice utilized by Mongol and non-Mongol alike with enough examples of its rulings against the Mongol governing class in favor of the subject people to demonstrate its impartiality. Whereas in the early decades its decisions were based on Chinggis Khan's *yasa*, in later years the sharia and local laws were increasingly used to arrive at final judgments.

In the decades before the establishment of the Il-Khanate in 1258, most cases that came before the *yarghu* courts concerned state affairs, Mongol officials and disputes between Mongols, and torture and beatings were commonly employed to elicit the all important confessions. The remarkable Arghun Aqa, a leading Mongol administrator in Iran, survived many *yarghu* hearings and lived to die a peaceful, natural death in 1273. Not so fortunate were other officials such as Körgüz, a rags-to-riches Uyghur governor who, after being shunted through a series of *yarghu* tribunals, insulted the wrong person and was killed. Juwaynī, who recounted the story of Körgüz, stated that at this time in pre-Hülegü Iran four points should be noted as regards the *yarghu*. First, procedures for the *yarghu* were not set down or formalized, and it was concerned not only with passing judgments but also with effecting reconciliation. Second, the various Mongol principalities exercised a degree of autonomy in the administration of justice. Third, those found guilty by the *yarghu* court might well be handed over to a third party for punishment. Finally, it should be noted that the long arm of the *yarghu* court could stretch across the empire, as Arghun Aqa found. He was summoned back to Qaraqorum and elsewhere from Iran on a couple of occasions, as were other administrators of the western province.

The earliest recorded case of a *yarghu* convened by Hülegü occurred on the march to Baghdad and concerned an official's failure to secure the submission of the fortress of Irbil in northern Iraq. The court found the official, the Kurd Tāj al-Dīn bin Salāyā Irbīlī, guilty, but his fate was not specified. In the reign of Ghazan, even though the government was now officially Muslim and therefore subject to Islamic law, the *yarghu* courts continued their work, and even top officials sought redress from their decisions. One case involved the chief accountant, or *mustawfi*, of Fars province suing the Sheikh al-Islam, who was also an immensely rich businessman, of embezzlement. Al-Tibī, the venerated sheikh, demanded that Ghazan himself conduct the *yarghu* hearing, and on November 8, 1296, the court sat to consider its verdict. The ruling went against al-Tibī, and he was summarily executed the following day.[20]

Why this case is noteworthy is that it demonstrates the confidence that the leading 'ulamā retained in this system of law and the fact that they recognized its validity and were prepared to use it in their personal disputes. Generally speaking, the *yarghu* proceedings were protracted and complex, but in cases in which the head of state was involved, matters were dealt with summarily. The historian and government accountant (*mustawfī*) Waṣṣāf, writing from Shiraz over the first three decades of the fourteenth century, recounted another case heard before the Il-Khanid Sultan Öljeitü (ruled 1304–16) in which Tāl al-Dīn Gūr Surkhī accused the grand vizier, Rashīd al-Dīn, of embezzlement. The case went against the plaintiff, and Rashīd al-Dīn's name was cleared. Tāl al-Dīn was executed, and some of his fellow plaintiffs were bastinadoed. Again, however, what is significant about this case is that the plaintiff obviously had enough faith in the system to risk his life bringing serious charges against one of the most powerful figures in the state. In this case also both plaintiff and defendant were Persians, not Mongols, though Waṣṣāf cast doubt on whether Tāl al-Dīn was Muslim, despite the honorific *al-Dīn*.

More light is cast on the nature of the *yarghu* courts during the later Il-Khanid period by the accountant and historian Mohammad ibn Hindūshāh Nakhchivānī in his report on the internal affairs and workings of the Il-Khanid government, *Dastūr al-Kātib*, completed circa 1366. Nakhchivānī stated that the Chinggisid innovators of the *yarghu* system had been scrupulous in ensuring that its decrees be based on truth (*rāstī*), and that justice and equity (*'adel va enṣāf*) would reach the utmost degree (*modārij, marātib*).[21] The Mongols created their own sharia, according to Hindūshāh Nakhchivānī, based on the *yasa* of Chinggis Khan and on the precedent of former *yarghu* decrees and *yarghuchis*. One clear influence from the early years of the *yasa* and the emerging *yarghu* courts was the idea of reconciliation. Judgments were passed, and a *yarghu-nāmeh* was issued to the party deemed by the court to be in the right. There matters stood unless the other party caused further trouble, in which case the aggrieved party was able to appeal to the court again to force the other party to pay the penalty specified in the *yarghu-nāmeh*.

Qāḍīs
Though the sharia courts had lost all preeminence, there was no attempt to abolish them, and tax concessions were granted to the leaders of the religious communities. Because there were not enough qualified officials to administer the emerging new legal system, the old courts and their cadre could still be employed. *Qāḍīs* (Islamic judges) were still appointed by the central government, and the chief *qāḍī*, the *qāḍī al-quḍāt*, remained an important figure with considerable influence. During the reign of the Il-Khan Geikhatu (ruled 1991–95) the post was held by the brother of the prime minister. The appointment of a joint leadership of two leading clerics was not uncommon, and there is evidence that the position was farmed out to the highest bidder. Rashīd al-Dīn claimed that the position of *qāḍī al-quḍāt* was secured through bribery and flattery during the tenure of Geikhatu's *ṣāḥib dīwān*, Sadr al-Dīn Khālidī, though the idea of corruption among the leading clergy was hardly a new idea. The *'ulamā* had long been viewed with considerable skepticism by various contemporary observers and commentators, and this view continued under the Il-Khanate. The noted Sufi and acclaimed poet and thinker Dayā, Najm al-Dīn Rāzī, complained of the moral decline among the *'ulamā* of his day.

With Ghazan's conversion to Islam in 1295 and the adoption of Islam as the state religion, the legal world was neither traumatized nor radicalized, and other than cosmetic changes little was different. A *yarligh* (edict) issued by Ghazan stated that a provincial *qādī* must be accorded the privileges and exemptions laid down in the great *yarligh* of Chinggis Khan. The *yasa* of Chinggis Khan, elusive though its reality might be, remained paramount. The question of the nature of Ghazan's conversion and how profound it was has long been a controversial question and a subject of debate. From the legal point of view its impact was cosmetic and *qādīs* remained state appointed and subject to state control.

The regulations that regulated the practices of the *qādīs* under Ghazan were strict and designed to prevent corruption and financial abuse or exploitation. Rashīd al-Dīn predictably painted a very unflattering picture of the behavior of *qādīs* before the implementation of his reforms. His reforms forbade them from accepting payments from plaintiffs or for writing legal documents. Scribes received payment for drawing up legal documents according to a strict scale. Their powers were curbed by a strangely ambiguous piece of legislation. Ghazan issued a *yarligh* stating that all provincial rulers, such as *maliks, basqaqs,* and governors, must refer all matters pertaining to sharia affairs to the local *qādīs*. However, it is also made clear that these same government appointees, the *basqaqs, maliks,* and governors, must summon the *qādīs* to their courts and obtain a written undertaking that the *qādī* would abide by the terms of all *yarlighs* issued by Ghazan.

TITLE DEEDS

One *yarligh* issued by Ghazan through his chief minister, Rashīd al-Dīn, concerned land title deeds and stipulated that cases that had not been preferred for 30 years were to be proclaimed null and void and the deeds physically destroyed. In order to prevent the circulation of false or invalid documents, all sharia courts were to have *ṭās-iᶜ adl* (bowls of justice) installed. Documents to be annulled were soaked in these bowls of water, and the ink was washed away permanently. New documents were then drawn up. Officials and ledgers were ordered installed in all courts, though provincial courts had to coordinate their work with the court officials in the capital cities where records could be checked and a master ledger maintained. Rashīd al-Dīn wrote in detail about these reforms, about the problems of implementation, and recorded a wealth of anecdotal records. He notes that *qādīs* were forbidden to hear cases while supporters of the plaintiff were present in court. Punishments *(taᶜzir)* laid down for contravening these new regulations could be bizarre. One penalty involved the guilty party having his beard shaved off and being paraded around the town on a donkey.

A *dīwān-i-maẓālim,* a court of grievances against government officials, was held two days a month in the Friday mosque and was presided over by the *shaḥna, malik, bitikchi, qāḍī,* or *'ulamā.* Cases involving a Mongol and a Muslim, government officials, or that were generally considered difficult to resolve were heard by the *maẓālim* court. In practice, according to the *Dastūr al-Kātib* of Hindūshāh, the *maẓālim* court was usually headed by an *amir ulus,* a military governor of a province.

A famous case in which the *yasa* was cited as justification of expropriation of land and the sharia invoked to resist these claims involved the powerful Mongol Emir Chopan. During Öljeitü's reign (1304–16) Emir Chopan laid claim to all the property belonging to a lady, Nāz Khātūn, on the grounds that her father had been captured during the siege of Baghdad in 1258 and had been declared war booty along with all his considerable landholdings. Chopan, claiming ownership of this war booty, attempted to eject many landowners from their estates because the titles to their lands fell under the title ownership of Nāz Khātūn. Under sharia law this would not be allowed. Öljeitü's minister Tāj al-Dīn ᶜAlī Shāh resolved the matter by granting Chopan ownership of a province in Anatolia in return for his renunciation of any rights to the lands of Nāz Khātūn.

A document referred to in the *Dastūr al-Kātib* allowed for the establishment of a new court that would reconcile the ambiguities and conflicts between the *yarghu* courts and the sharia courts. The office of arbitrator of the empire was created to decide cases according to custom, sharia, and justice *(ma'dalat).* All cases involving disputes between a governor and the peasants or ordinary citizens were heard by a court convened by this arbitrator of the empire. His salary was paid by the central government, and the plaintiff was also expected to contribute something if possible. It is not certain whether this court ever actually sat, but the fact that the need for such an institution was felt is indicative of the problems with the existing situation.

Village *qāḍīs* had very restricted powers, and they were primarily concerned with marriage documentation and the issuance of bonds connected with inheritance, *ḥujjathā-ye-furūd.* They were also responsible for ensuring that the *khuṭba* be read out in the right name and the right order. They were not authorized to issue title deeds or decisions without specific permission, and any such legal work that might be undertaken had to be carefully written down and submitted to a higher authority. Reliable clerks were appointed for such bookkeeping, and a daily record, a *rūz-nāmeh,* had to be kept up-to-date at all times, especially in matters pertaining to property.

Through the offices of Rashīd al-Dīn, Ghazan issued draft copies of various legal documents with the idea of creating a uniform legal system throughout his lands. Drafts of these documents are still extant because copies were included in Rashīd al-Dīn's *Compendium of Chronicles.* Very few actual legal documents have survived from the Il-Khanid years, however, which might suggest that many of Ghazan's reforms and legal edicts remained purely theoretical and were never implemented.

During the Il-Khanid period, therefore, both the sharia and the *yarghu* courts existed and functioned and often complemented each other. Whereas the sharia remained unchanged but generally subservient to the *yarghu*, the *yarghu* courts were in a state of permanent development and change and adapted themselves to the changing social mores and conditions. The legal institutions in Iran under the Il-Khans never reached the sophistication and elaborate complexity of the Yüan judiciary, but this may partly be because, with the widespread recognition and use of sharia rulings and precedents, there was no need for new codes.

NOTES

1. Ala-ad-Din 'Ata-Malik Juvaini, *The History of the World Conqueror,* trans. John Andrew Boyle, intro. David Morgan (Manchester, U.K.: Manchester University Press, 1997), 25.

2. R. A. Skelton, T. E. Marston, and George D. Painter, *The Vinland Map and the Tartar Relation* (New Haven, Conn.: Yale University Press, 1995), 97–98.

3. Maulana Juzjani, Minhaj-ud-Din Abu 'Umar-i-Usman, *Tabakat-i-Nasiri: A General History of the Muhammadan Dynasties of Asia; from 810–1260 A.D. And The Irruption of the Infidel Mughals into Islam,* trans. H. G. Raverty (reprint, Calcutta: Asiatic Society, 1995), 1078–79.

4. Rashid al-Din, *Rashiduddin Fazlullah Jami 'u' t-Tawarikh: Compendium of Chronicles,* trans. W. M. Thackston (Cambridge, Mass.: Sources of Oriental Languages & Literature 45, Central Asian Sources, Harvard University, 1998), 510–11.

5. W. W. Rockhill, ed. and trans., *The Journey of William of Rubruck to the Eastern Parts of the World, 1253–55, as Narrated by Himself, with Two Accounts of the Earlier Journey of John of Pian de Carpine* (London: Hakluyt Society, 1900), Internet version.

6. *Ssu-k'u ch'üan-shu tsung-mu t'i-yao,* 83:2b cited in Paul Heng-chao Ch'en, *Chinese Legal Tradition under the Mongols: The Code of 1291 as Reconstructed* (Princeton, N.J.: Princeton University Press, 1979), 32.

7. Ch'en, *Chinese Legal Tradition,* 46.

8. Marco Polo, *The Travels of Marco Polo,* trans. Teresa Waugh (London: Sidgewick and Jackson, 1994), 131.

9. Ch'en, *Chinese Legal Tradition,* 53.

10. Ibid., 54.

11. Ibid., 55.

12. Ibid., 56.

13. Ibid., 58.

14. Ibid., 62.

15. Ibid.

16. Marco Polo and Rustichello of Pisa, *The Project Gutenberg EBook of the Travels of Marco Polo,* available at: http://www.gutenberg.net.

17. Ch'en, *Chinese Legal Tradition,* 67.

18. Ala-ad-Din 'Ata-Malik Juvaini, *The History of the World Conqueror,* trans. John Andrew Boyle, intro. David Morgan (Manchester, U.K.: Manchester University Press, 1997), 25.

19. Ibn al-Tiqtaqa, cited by Etan Kohlberg, *A Mediaeval Muslim Scholar at Work: Ibn Tawwus and his Library* (Leiden: Brill, 1992), 10; A.K.S. Lambton, *Continuity and Change in Medieval Persia: Aspects of Administrative, Economic, Social History in 11th–14th Century Persia* (London: Taurus, 1988), 249, n. 119.

20. Lambton, *Continuity and Change,* 335; Wassaf, 268.

21. Nakhchavānī, *Dastūr al-Kātib,* 30.

11

WOMEN AND THE MONGOLS

TRADITIONAL ROLES

Women's role in Turco-Mongol society was ambiguous. On the one hand they often held considerable power both within the family and the community, but on the other hand they would appear to have sometimes been treated as just another commodity for barter or exchange. Men acquired wives as they might horses or cattle, and the richer and more powerful the man the more wives he would have. For the average Mongol herdsman, however, one wife was all he could afford, and the small nuclear family was the norm. Even among the rich and powerful there would be a chief wife whose sons would continue the bloodline, and her status was assured and greatly respected. The other wives would be subservient to her, though often the different wives, especially among the elite, would have their own *ordus* and retinues. Only the sons of Chinggis's chief wife, Börte, were considered for succession. On the death of the husband the lesser wives would be inherited by the sons, and another husband would be sought for the chief wife. Hülegü Khan (died 1265), ruler of Mongol Iran, inherited his chief and favorite wife, Dokuz Khātūn, from his father, Tolui, youngest son of Chinggis Khan. However, it was not unknown for a wife to remain unattached after the death of her husband, as the example of the many powerful Mongol women demonstrates.

It is also often forgotten that though women were sometimes treated as chattel, men were not necessarily treated any better. Life could be very hard on women, but generally men fared no better, and there was often equality in hardship.

FAMILY MAKEUP

The average Mongol family would not consist of more than two generations of adults, and the norm would be the two parents and their unmarried children. Common to many Eurasian families, the youngest son would continue to live with the family after his marriage because it was the youngest son who would inherit the homestead.

For the most part the women of the Mongol empire led a hard life, sharing most of the hardships but few of the pleasures with their men folk. Mongol women had the right to own property and to divorce, but full equality was far from a reality. In fact Mongol society was obviously a society in which some women were more equal than others, as a mission of Franciscan friars observed on a journey to the Mongol Empire in 1245–47.

[The Mongols] have as many wives as they can afford, and generally buy them, so that except for women of noble birth they are mere chattels. They marry anyone they please, except their mother, daughter, and sister from the same mother. When their father dies, they marry their step-mother, and a younger brother or cousin marries his brother's widow. The wives do all the work, and make shoes, leather garments, and so on, while the men make nothing but arrows, and practice shooting with bows. They compel even boys three or four years old to the same exercise, and even some of the women, especially the maidens, practice archery and ride as a rule like men. If people are taken in adultery and fornication, man and woman alike are slain.[1]

The friars were no apologists for the Mongols, and other reports suggest that women generally enjoyed more equitable treatment within the tribe. After Chinggis Khan's first wife, Börte, was kidnapped, Chinggis spared no effort to get her back, and once safely within his *ordu* (camp), she resumed her position of chief wife, and her unborn child, Chinggis's firstborn, Jochi, was later awarded the respect due to the firstborn son of the Great Khan despite his questionable parentage.

WOMEN'S WORK

Though women participated in all aspects of Mongol life, there were tasks in particular that were assigned exclusively to them. They were generally expected to drive the large wagons, so essential for these nomadic tribes, on which the family placed all their tents, dwellings, and household goods. William of Rubruck, the cleric who traveled among the Mongols between 1253 and 1255, claimed that one woman would drive as many as 30 connected wagons. One noble's dwelling could demand 200 wagons, and one noble with many wives could possess many dwellings. Because the terrain was relatively flat many wagons could be lashed together in sequence. The woman driver would sit on the front ox- or camel-driven wagon, and the rest would follow. If the terrain became difficult, the animals with their individual wagons could quite easily be separated and led one at a time. Women would also load and unload the wagons themselves.

When camp was struck, it was the woman's duty to saddle the horses and apportion the packs and loads to the camels and horses. When a suitable site for a camp was decided, it was the women who were expected to erect the tents and dwellings. The dwellings were pitched with the doorway facing south, the master's couch at the far end of the tent or yurt, and his wife's on the east side to her husband's left. The wife would place her own doll-like felt effigy on the wall over her head. By the entrance to the dwelling on the woman's side was placed another effigy. This effigy used a cow's udder and was considered protection for the woman, the cow milker. On the man's side of the door there was placed a mare's udder because this represented men's responsibilities for making koumiss (fermented mare's milk). Each wife would have her own residence, called *curia*, which might include a smaller dwelling, placed behind, for her maids. The chief wife would pitch her *curia* at the westernmost end, and the others would then position their own dwellings accordingly, "a space of one stone's throw between [them],"[2] until the last wife would have her own tent or yurt at the eastern end of the camp. William of Rubruck is not alone when he stated that these family units resembled small cities when they were finally assembled, though he adds that an absence of men was noticeable within their confines.

It is the duty of the women to drive the carts, get the dwellings on and off them, milk the cows, make butter and gruit, and to dress and sew skins, which they do with a thread made of tendons. They divide the tendons into fine shreds, and then twist them into one long thread. They also sew the boots, the socks and the clothing. They never wash clothes, for they say that God would be angered thereat, and that it would thunder if they hung them up to dry. They will even beat those they find washing them. Thunder they fear extraordinarily; and when it thunders they will turn out of their dwellings all strangers, wrap themselves in black felt, and thus hide themselves till it has passed away. Furthermore, they never wash their bowls, but when the meat is cooked they rinse out the dish in which they are about to put it with some of the boiling broth from the kettle, which they pour back into it. They also make the felt and cover the house.

The men make bows and arrows, manufacture stirrups and bits, make saddles, do the carpentering on (the framework of) their dwellings and the carts; they take care of the horses, milk the mares, churn the cosmos or mare's milk, make the skins in which it is put; they also look after the camels and load them. Both sexes look after the sheep and goats, sometimes the men, other times the women, milking them.

They dress skins with a thick mixture of sour ewe's milk and salt. When they want to wash their hands or head, they fill their mouths with water, which they let trickle on to their hands, and in this way they also wet their hair and wash their head.

> As to their marriages, you must know that no one among them has a wife unless he buys her; so it sometimes happens that girls are well past marriageable age before they marry, for their parents always keep them until they sell them. They observe the first and second degrees of consanguinity, but no degree of affinity ; thus (one person) will have at the same time or successively two sisters. Among them no widow marries, for the following reason : they believe that all who serve them in this life shall serve them in the next, so as regards a widow they believe that she will always return to her first husband after death. Hence this shameful custom prevails among them, that sometimes a son takes to wife all his father's wives, except his own mother; for the ordu of the father and mother always belongs to the youngest son, so it is he who must provide for all his father's wives who come to him with the paternal household, and if he wishes it he uses them as wives, for he esteems not himself injured if they return to his father after death. When then anyone has made a bargain with another to take his daughter, the father of the girl gives a feast, and the girl flees to her relatives and hides there. Then the father says: "Here, my daughter is yours: take her wheresoever you find her." Then he searches for her with his friends till he finds her, and he must take her by force and carry her off with a semblance of violence to his house.

Milking the cows, though not the koumiss-yielding mares, was considered women's work as well as making butter and curds. Both men and women tended the sheep and goats and both would on occasion milk these animals. Skin curing and leather preparation was a task left to the women as was shoemaking and the stitching and manufacture of all leather garments. Women also made other clothes such as socks and jerkins.

STATUS

Women generally enjoyed a high status in Mongol society and were involved in most aspects of life, including battle, along with their men folk. This is apparent when even a cursory look at the genealogical tables of the Mongol Great Khans reveals extended periods when women effectively ruled over the whole empire. Between 1241 and 1246 the Great Khan Ögödei's widow, Töregene, ruled as regent, and between 1248 and 1251 the Great Khan Güyük's widow, Oghul Ghaymish, became regent until Möngke was installed as the new Great Khan. After Chinggis Khan's youngest son, Tolui, died (1231–32), his formidable wife Sorghaghtani Beki resisted attempts to remarry her to Ögödei's son Güyük. Instead she ruled her late husband's domains herself, and eventually she was able to successfully promote her own sons as heirs to the Mongol throne. In

Mongol women's traditional dress, Hohhut Museum.
Courtesy of Xinjiang Qinshan Culture Publishing

Turkistan (central Asia) the Chaghataid homelands were long ruled by the widow of Chinggis's second son, Chaghatai.

The high status women enjoyed in Mongol society found reflection in the lands under their control, and both the Iranian provinces of Shiraz and Kirman experienced extended periods of rule by powerful women. Qutlugh Terkān Khātūn (ruled 1257–83) of Kirman maintained close personal, political, and cultural links with her Mongol overlords in the Iranian Mongol capital of Maragheh during her two decades of rule over this southern Persian province. The period she resided over as queen is considered a golden age in Kirman's history. Her namesake in the neighboring province of Shiraz, though not as illustrious nor so well regarded nor indeed so long-serving, was a powerful female monarch and reflected the Mongol influence on the society of the time.

The women whose biographies are examined later in this chapter are of course not typical, but their names, details of their lives, and their achievements would have been known and discussed by women in more mundane circumstances. These women would have inspired, and if they were not role models they were dream models for more ordinary women. Though the women examined led extraordinary lives, their lives illustrate attitudes to women and the potential allowed to women in an essentially patriarchal society. There are many aspects of Mongol society that contrasted with the sedentary societies on its borders. One of these is the role and status of women. In both China and Persia women faced far more oppression and lack of basic freedom than their sisters on the steppe. Women on the steppe endured a hard and at times harsh existence, but they shared this hardship with their men, and they faced their problems together on an equal footing. This was not the case in the urbanized societies outside the Eurasian steppe, and when the Mongol hordes swept southward and westward this contrast between the status of the women in the two societies came to the fore. This medieval clash of civilizations was not as dramatic as might have been expected, however. Prior to the irruption of the Mongols, cultural exchange and integration had already been taking place. In city-states such as existed in Kirman, the ruling family were Persianized Turks only one generation from the steppe. Turanian women had already settled into an Iranian court. Within two generations a Turkish queen had exchanged the saddle for a throne and the golden age of Kirman was presided over by a woman.

The women whose lives are now to be presented are Mongol and Turco-Mongol women who achieved greatness and gave hope, pride, and encouragement to the women who toiled over the pots, babies, and horses back in the *ordu*. Though a woman could not formally become Great Khan, women effectively achieved the highest office not infrequently at the local, regional, and highest imperial level.

These periods when women acted as regents, ruling the vast Mongol Empire, have often been dismissed merely as interludes in the main march of male-dominated Mongol history, but a closer examination of their reigns and the role these women played along with the influence they wielded suggests otherwise. Both Temüjin's mother and first wife were strong-willed, independent-minded women.

HÖ'ELÜN

Hö'elün entered the Borjigin clan and became Yesügei's wife in true Mongol fashion. During a falconry trip with his two brothers, Yesügei returned with more than the usual hunting trophies. He kidnapped and returned home to his yurt with a young woman from the Ongirrat tribe, part of the larger Merkit confederacy. Though she was already married to a Merkit man, Chiledu, whom she dearly loved, Yesügei made Hö'elün his

Mongol Khatun on the shores of Lake Sayram, north
of Yingin in the Heavenly Mountains, Tian Shan.
Courtesy of Xinjiang Qinshan Culture Publishing

wife, and she eventually bore him four sons. She was a fortunate choice
because when the family was still young, Temüjin's father died, believed
poisoned by his archrivals and enemies the Tatars. Following traditional
Mongol custom, Temüjin himself had been named after a slain Tatar chief
whom his father had killed in battle. The Tatars exacted their revenge and
Hö'elün soon found herself abandoned by family from both sides with five
small children to rear. "The deep waters have dried up, the sparkling stone
has shattered." Temüjin was too young to lead the clan, and for reasons
yet to be explained the Borjigin tribe in which Yesügei had been a leading
chieftain deprived the stricken family of most of their possessions and cast
them out on the steppe in the area around the source of the Onon River.
In addition to this, eight of their nine horses were stolen by thieves just as
they were about to begin their sorry exile. The children became proficient

in hunting and fishing from necessity. One of Temüjin's first prizes was the retrieval of those rustled horses, which with a lifelong friend, Bogorju, he hunted down and reclaimed.

It was Hö'elün's tenacity and perseverance that held the family together through those hard and, for Temüjin, formative years. His mother had a profound influence on her son, and her admirable qualities and character had long been recognized by friend and foe alike. The *Secret History of the Mongols* depicts her grubbing for fruit and roots in the forests that flanked the Burkhan Khaldun range, a sharpened juniper stick to hand, or fishing along the banks of the Onon, her skirts hoisted around her waist, but all the while with her aristocrat's hat planted firmly and proudly on her head. During those lean years Temüjin would have tasted poverty and smelled destitution.

> With wild onions and garlic
> The sons of the noble mother were nourished
> Until they became rulers.
> The sons of the patient noble mother
> Were reared on elm-seeds,
> And became wise men and law-givers.
> *The Secret History of the Mongols, translated by Urgunge Onon*

BÖRTE FÜJIN

There is no evidence of any romantic love between Chinggis and his chief wife, Börte, though he afforded her the greatest respect and listened to her advice throughout their lives. It was believed that she possessed special skills in magic and witchcraft, an art the Mongols believed resided within women in general. It was her lively face and flashing eyes that had first attracted the attention of Temüjin's father, and he decided that she would be a suitable partner for his young son even though she was a year older than Temüjin. Börte was a member of the Boskur, a subtribe of the leading Onggirat clan who pastured east of Lake Buir. The condition for the marriage was that Temüjin should live with his in-laws, a widespread practice among the nomadic tribes at that time. Because the boy was only eight at the time of his betrothal, however, this condition was for a future date. Unfortunately it was after concluding the marriage negotiations that Yesügei made that fateful trip home during which he encountered the Tatars who secretly and fatally poisoned his drink.

The marriage was consummated some seven years later when Temüjin was 15. Börte brought a black sable cloak as her dowry, which she presented to her mother-in-law, Hö'elün. When news spread over the steppe that Temüjin had brought home a new bride, however, the Merkits decided that the time was ripe to exact revenge for the abduction many years before of Temüjin's mother, Hö'elün. When 300 Merkit horsemen attacked his camp, Temüjin made provision for most of his family to escape, but because they were short of horses he decided that his new bride, Börte, was expendable, and he abandoned her hidden beneath a cart. This incident has never been conclusively explained and would appear to paint Temüjin in an extremely negative light as very selfish or coldly calculating. If at this early stage he already felt the heavy hand of history on his shoulders, as has been suggested, then saving himself had to take precedence over everything else. He more probably calculated that if a confrontation had been forced and a battle had been entered into then all would have perished. If Börte had shared a horse, she would have handicapped one of their party and ensured that they were pursued by the Merkit raiders. However, by leaving her behind, he and his followers, including Hö'elün, were able to escape, and Börte served as a decoy and distraction and the Merkits were unlikely to kill her. He would get his own revenge and rescue his wife at a later date.

The outcome of this story was to have long and deep repercussions that were to reverberate down through the rest of the turbulent history of the Mongol Empire. Börte was eventually rescued and restored to her former position of honor as Temüjin's chief wife. However, not long after she was snatched back from the Merkits, circa 1184, she gave birth to Temüjin's firstborn son, Jochi, and questions about his parentage have persisted from that time hence. Rashīd al-Dīn, as court historian of the House of Tolui, staunch allies of the House of Jochi, made up some implausible story about the abduction to silence any doubts that might be cast on Jochi's origins and to preserve Börte's honor. The *Secret History of the Mongols* recorded matter of factly that Börte was given as a wife to Chilger-bökö, younger brother of the deceased Chiledu from whom Hö'elün had been taken. That there were doubts about Jochi's paternity is indisputable even though the sources are either silent or circumspect about the matter, and because of this the rulers of the House of Jochi remained kingmakers rather than kings themselves, and the throne of the Great Khan was forever beyond their powerful reach. Chinggis Khan never alluded to these doubts concerning his firstborn, and there is no evidence that he was treated any differently from Chinggis's other sons as would accord with Mongol custom. However, some have read significance into Jochi's name, which means "visitor" or "guest" in Mongolian, a point others have explained by the fact that the family were at the time all guests at the *ordu* of Jamuka, Temüjin's *anda* (blood brother).

Chinggis Khan defended his wife's honor and reputation until the end, as is evinced in the *Secret History*'s account of the fierce fight between Jochi and his brother Chaghatai over the succession. When Chaghatai voiced doubts over Jochi's paternity, screaming out at one stage, "How could we let ourselves be governed by a Merkit foundling?," their father implored his sons to consider their mother, reminding them that she had been forced to go with the Merkits, and warning them that they would "harden the heart of butter" of their "wise mother" and "sour her heart of milk." He admonished them and emphasized that they had been born of the same "hot womb" and again warned them that if their "mother who had borne [them] from her heart has cause to be ashamed her love will cool," and should they "try to soothe her it will not work."[3] Börte died between 1219 and 1224 on the beautiful Avarga steppe in the vicinity of the Kherlen River.

TÖREGENE KHĀTŪN

According to Rashīd al-Dīn, Töregene, Ögödei's widow, was "no great beauty but of a very masterful nature," whereas Juwaynī, no great fan of the lady, described her as a "shrewd and capable" woman who had acquired power through "finesse and cunning." Both men, Muslim and Persian, reluctantly acknowledged her authority and status. Bar Hebraeus (died 1286), the Christian cleric, scholar, and historian, described her as "exceedingly wise and discreet." As early as 1240 her authorization as Yeke Khātūn (Great Lady), along with the seal of Ögödei, appears on an edict ordering the printing of Taoist texts, reflecting her interest in religion and education as well as her ability and determination to exercise power.

This determination to achieve her own ends regardless of the views of others was made brutally clear through her maneuvers to have her quarrelsome and arrogant son Güyük proclaimed Great Khan. This was against the wishes of her dead husband, Ögödei, and of the many who feared and hated Güyük. Immediately following Ögödei's death, Rashīd al-Dīn reported that Töregene Khātūn,

making full use of all the arts of diplomacy, seized possession of the kingdom without consulting *aqa* and *ini* [family] and wooed the hearts of kinsfolk and emirs with all manner of gifts and presents until they all inclined toward her and came under her control.[4]

Her immediate aim was to install Güyük instead of her husband's choice, his grandson Shiremün. Even though there was a general consensus that Shiremün was too young to take up the reins of office, Güyük was unpopular, and the requisite numbers of nobles and princes from the Golden family for a quorum at the *quriltai* summoned by Töregene failed to materialize. Thwarted but undaunted, Töregene as unopposed regent began to accrue authority and power. She was not Ögödei's senior wife, but none opposed her assumption of the throne because she was the mother of the eldest son. Once installed she lost no time in securing her position and replaced senior ministers and administrators with "a crowd of fools" whose loyalty she could depend upon. "Make haste, for time is a trenchant sword" as Juwaynī commented. Those who had slighted her during her husband's reign now paid the price for their indiscretion. Rashīd al-Dīn claims that "she resolved, now that she was absolute ruler, to wreak vengeance upon each of those persons."

To help her in her new position Töregene appointed a woman whose end was as gruesome as her reputation. Fatima Khatun had established herself as a procuress in the bazaar at Qaraqorum where she excelled "in the arts of shrewdness and cunning" so much so that "the wily Delilah could have been her pupil."[5] The prudish implication seems to be that Fatimah supplied the rich and idle with concubines, doxies, and rent boys. She doubtless soon became privy to much scandal and court gossip, all of which would have made her very valuable to one seeking to extend her power and influence at the top. She insinuated herself into the royal circles of the capital and eventually into Töregene's *ordu* where she quickly made herself indispensable. She became "the sharer of intimate confidences and the depository of hidden secrets" and also exercised political muscle being "free to issue commands and prohibitions," whereas older "ministers were debarred from executing business." As a result she aroused the intense hatred of those surrounding Töregene.

One of Fatimah Khātūn's first targets was the legendary Mahmūd Yalavach whom Ögödei had appointed *sāhib dīwān* (first minister), a man of immense power and prestige. She replaced Yalavach with a man of dubious ability and reputation, 'Abd al-Rahmān, and ordered his arrest. However, Yalavach had been informed of events and was prepared when the envoys arrived with instructions to bind him. He welcomed the envoys with great civility, honor, and hospitality, generously plying them with food and particularly drink. When they were thoroughly relaxed and beginning to enjoy themselves, the eminent Yalavach slipped away and sought refuge at the court of Köten, another son of Töregene. He found there another refugee, Chinqai, also a chief minister of Ögödei, who had earned the ire of Töregene and her nefarious confidant Fatimah. Köten defied his mother and refused to surrender his guests. His terse reply relayed to his mother:

The kite that takes refuge in a thicket from the talons of the falcon is safe from its fury. These too have sought sanctuary with us and touched the skirt of our authority. To send them back is forbidden by the code of magnanimity and humanity and is remote from the practice of generosity and liberality.[6]

As news of this crackdown spread, others also took flight, including Mahmūd Yalavach's son, the emir Mas^cud Beg, governor of Turkistan and Transoxiana, who fled to the court of Batu Khan of the Golden Horde. Others, like the Ögödei-appointed Uighur governor of Khorasan, Körgüz, a Muslim converted from Buddhism from the Christian town of Besh Baligh (modern-day Urumqi, capital of Xinjiang Province, western China), were not so fortunate. After his arrest Körgüz underwent a traditional Mongol execution and had his mouth filled with stones, which resulted in a particularly unpleasant and prolonged death.

Eventually Töregene Khātūn's will prevailed, and by a mixture of threats, charm, bribery, cajoling, intimidation, pleading, and dogged persistence she achieved a quorum at a *quriltai*, and all there from the Golden family agreed that Güyük of the House of Ögödei should assume the leadership of the empire. However, in reality Töregene continued to rule as she had before, and Güyük "took no part in affairs of state." Her writ continued until her death, and at least one observer has cast doubt on her having had a natural demise. Minhāj al-Dīn Jūzjānī, a historian writing outside the Mongol sphere of influence in Sind, hinted that others might have hastened her departure from this world. "They sent Turakīnah Khātūn to join Uktāe [Ögödei] and raised his son to the throne of sovereignty; but God knows the truth." Jūzjānī expressed more explicitly than Juwaynī and Rashīd al-Dīn the Persian hostility to an occurrence common in the realms of Turko-Mongol dominance, of women wielding power. "[During her rule] she displayed woman's ways, such as proceed from deficiency of intellect and excess of sensuality."[7]

When Töregene died a few months after Güyük's inauguration, her son came into his own, and the first person he and many of those around him cast the eye of revenge upon was the hated intimate, Fatimah Khatun. Prince Köten, who had offered protection to those fleeing the wrath of Fatimah, had previously intimated that the woman's malignant magic was the cause of his various physical ailments, so when he suddenly died, suspicion conveniently fell on Fatimah Khatun. Without her royal protection and surrounded by adversaries whose loathing and hatred had been honed by long and silent humiliation, Fatimah soon found herself before Güyük charged with witchcraft and sorcery, by which means she had brought about the sickness and death of Prince Köten. Her trial was public and ugly. Stripped naked, she was beaten and tortured until "she confessed to the calumny of a slanderous talebearer and avowed her falseness."[8] Her ending was particularly gruesome as Bar Hebraeus details in his chronography. "They sewed up the openings in her body, the upper and the lower, and they placed her in a cloth and cast her into the water and she was drowned. And they also killed all her kinsfolk who had gathered together about her."[9]

OGHUL GHAYMISH KHĀTŪN

Güyük's widow, Oghul Ghaymish Khātūn (ruled 1248–51), assumed the "throne of the world" upon her husband's death with the blessing of the Mongol kingmaker, Batu Khan, and the other princes of the royal household scattered over the vast empire. They endorsed her rule until such time as a *quriltai* could be summoned and a new Qa'an appointed. According to Juwaynī, loyal to his rival house of Tolui and no admirer of "uppity women," Oghul Ghaymish and her young sons busied themselves with intrigue and palace conniving, scheming away their future.

Juwaynī quoted a tenth-century Samanid poet to describe the situation under the last Ögödeid ruler.

> Two things with which the ascetic can do nothing are the counsel of women and the command of young men; As for women their inclination is towards passion, and as for young men, they run with loose bridle.[10]

It had already been quietly decided before the *quriltai* had been summoned that Güyük's successor should be Möngke Khan from the House of Tolui rather than a son of Güyük from the House of Ögödei. Batu and the formidable Sorghaghtani Beki, widow of Tolui Khan, sent messages to Oghul Ghaymish pleading with her to attend the *quriltai* and to abide by its decisions. Predictably, she did not, and the usual labels began to attach themselves to her. The papal envoy, William of Rubruck, claimed that Möngke Qa'an told him personally that Oghul Ghaymish was "the worst of witches, and that with her sorcery she had destroyed her entire family," charges that can also be found in the Chinese historical chronology the *Yuan Shih*, whereas Juwaynī referred to her spending most of the time "closeted with her *qan* [shaman] carrying out their fantasies and absurdities."[11] She refused to recognize Möngke Khan (ruled 1251–59) and was brought, her hands stitched in rawhide, to Möngke's mother's, Beki's, *ordu* to face trial. Though stripped naked before the court, she remained defiant and continued to claim the throne on behalf of the House of Ögödei, and for this she was wrapped in felt and cast to her death in a river.

SORGHAGHTANI BEKI

The role of Beki, that is Sorghaghtani Beki (died 1252), wife of Tolui and mother of Möngke, Qubilai, Hülegü, and Arigh Böqa, is noteworthy in the case of Oghul Ghaymish. The unfortunate regent met her cruel end in the *ordu* and under the ambitious eyes of Khātūn Sorghaghtani Beki. Sorghaghtani Beki was determined to see her sons and her family assume the reins of imperial power, and her ruthless determination would countenance no opposition or hindrance.

Sorghaghtani Beki was born into the Kereit tribe, the youngest daughter of Ja-Gambu, who was brother of the Kereit ruler Toghril Ong-Khan, whose support for Chinggis had been so crucial in the early years of the Great Khan's career. After the final defeat of the Kereit, Chinggis awarded his youngest son, Tolui, Sorghaghtani in marriage, and so began her formidable career, a career that earned her universal praise and admiration. In the words of a contemporary poet, "And if all women were like unto her, then would women be superior to men."[12] Her sister was married to Jochi, which led to a lifetime alliance between the two houses.

With her husband, Tolui, constantly away campaigning, more than any of the other sons of Chinggis Khan, Sorghaghtani Beki devoted her time to her own sons, instilling in them her own passion for learning and an appreciation for the values of sedentary society.

Thanks to her ability, when her sons were left by their father, some of them still children, she went to great pains in their education, teaching them various accomplishments and good manners and never allowing the slightest sign of strife to appear amongst them. She caused their wives also to have love in their hearts for one another, and by her prudence and counsel [she] cherished and protected her sons, their children and grandchildren, and the great emirs and troops that had been left by Chingiz-Khan and Tolui Khan and were now attached to them. And perceiving her to be extremely intelligent and able, they never swerved a hair's breadth from her command.[13]

Rashīd al-Dīn's portrayal of Tolui as "a great winner of battles" who conquered more countries than any other prince might well be the ultimate accolade for a Mongol man, but it does not suggest the perfect husband or father. His sons grew up under the very strong influence of their mother, especially after Tolui's premature death in 1231, brought about in true traditional Mongol fashion by excessive drinking.

After Tolui's untimely death, the Qa'an, Tolui's brother Ögödei, tried to arrange a marriage for the widow with his son Güyük, a union of aunt with nephew. By this politically inspired marriage, he hoped to preempt a power struggle following his death between the royal houses of the Ögödeids and the Toluids, a rivalry that was to ultimately rend the Mongols apart. Sorghaghtani Beki diplomatically declined the gracious offer, pleading that her responsibilities to the upbringing of her four sons outweighed her natural desire to be wed with the eligible Güyük.

Her sense of diplomacy and political sensitivity was a trait she encouraged in her sons. Though she was a Nestorian Christian, she patronized both Buddhists and Taoists in order to win favor with her Chinese subjects. She gave alms to poor Muslims, supported local Islamic leaders, and contributed to the funding of mosques and madrassas, including the Khaniyya of Bokhara. She donated 1,000 gold *balish* for the construction of a *khāngāh* in the region of Bokhara at the tomb of the renowned Sufi Sayf al-Dīn Bākharzī. In the same year, 1250–51, she had the surrounding villages bought and made into *auqāf* (plural *waqf*), a religious endowment the charitable status of which brought various advantages to the villagers. Her toleration of other faiths while at the same time quietly promoting her own Christian beliefs endeared her to contemporary writers and commentators throughout Eurasia and impressed her sons enough for them to emulate her example. Bar Hebraeus, a leading Nestorian cleric, said of her that "she was a Christian, sincere and true like [queen] Helena."[14]

Sorghaghtani Beki earned her honored place in the history books because of her work promoting her sons and ensuring the ascendancy of the House of Tolui. She was instrumental in the "coup" of 1251 that saw her eldest son Möngke firmly ensconced on the throne. It was her intelligence of Güyük's perfidy relayed to Batu that put the kingmaker and lord of the Golden Horde firmly in her debt. Güyük had been an admirer and had even entrusted Sorghaghtani with the distribution of gifts in his name, and she and her agents had no problem gleaning intelligence from the Ögödeid camp. In addition, with the support that she had enjoyed from the Qa'an, Ögödei, and "in the care and supervision of her sons and in the management of their affairs and those of the army and the ulus, [Sorghaghtani] laid the foundations of such control as no turban-weaver was or could be capable of."[15]

Though we are largely dependant on pro-Toluid sources for the history of this time, there can be little doubt that it was the widespread admiration, trust, and support that Sorghaghtani Beki enjoyed that fueled backing for Möngke during the vicious and bloody power struggle that followed Güyük's death. Batu had called a *quriltai* in 1250 near Lake Issykul in the Tian Shan (Mountains of Heaven), and Möngke was elected Qa'an. However, this was boycotted by the Ögödeids on the grounds that not only was it not held in Qaraqorum but it was held outside Mongolia proper and therefore could not be deemed legitimate. It was Sorghaghtani Beki who devised an ingenious solution. Though she lacked access to Qaraqorum, as widow of Chinggis Khan's youngest son, Tolui, she controlled the heartlands of the empire where the founder of the empire had been born, elected ruler, and was reputedly buried. No one could refuse to attend a *quriltai* in such a sacred place or question the legitimacy of its location. A second election was duly held on July 1, 1251, and the 43-year-old Möngke was proclaimed Qa'an. The day represented the climax of Sorghaghtani Beki's life. Her sons and family were now destined to rule over the empire. Unlike the sons of Chinggis, who had been prone to drink and excess, her sons had had a stricter upbringing and were trained and ready for the positions of power that awaited them.

Rashīd al-Dīn unequivocally recognized Sorghaghtani Beki's role in his account of Möngke's succession.

After the death of Guyuk Khan most men were of one mind as to the entrusting of the Khanate to her eldest son, Möngke Qa'an. And so she continued to conciliate every side until the time when God Almighty, through the mediation of her experience, laid the bride of kingship in the bosom of Möngke Qa'an. And though she was a follower and devotee of the religion of Jesus she made great efforts to declare the rites of the law of Mustafa and would bestow alms and presents upon imams and shaikhs. And the proof of this statement is that she gave 1,000 silver *balish* that a *madrasa* might be built in Bukhara, of which the shaikh al-Islam Saif al-Dīn of Bākharz *(may God sanctify his noble spirit!)* was to be administrator and superintendent; and she commanded that villages should be bought, an endowment made, and teachers and students accommodated [in the madrassa]. And always she would send alms to all parts and dispense goods to the poor and needy of the Muslims. And she continued to tread this path until *Dhu'l-Hijja* of the year 649 [February–March 1252], when she passed away. And God knows best and is most able to decide.[16]

In China her legacy spread indirectly though her influence on her son Qubilai. Qubilai was born on September 23, 1215, the year his grandfather, Chinggis, seized what was to become the Yüan capital, Beijing [then

Zhongdu]. Sorghaghtani ensured that as well as the traditional Mongol skills of riding, hunting, archery, and combat, her son was literate and educated, and to this end she recruited an Uyghur named Tolochu to teach him Mongolian literary skills. Surprisingly, though a Chinese speaker, Qubilai never mastered Chinese writing. Sorghaghtani had persuaded the Qa'an Ögödei to grant her an appanage after her husband's, Tolui's, death, and in 1236 she received lands in Chen-ting, today part of northern China's Hebei province. In the same year Qubilai also received lands, the appanage of Hsing-chou, which supported 10,000 households. His appanage was close by the lands of his mother. His attitude was initially laissez-faire, and he ignored the abuses by his administrators, who imposed crippling taxes and demanded excessive labor services from the peasants and farmers in the manner of any other absentee landlord. The result was a dramatic exodus of farmers from his lands.

Qubilai's mother, Sorghaghtani, had recognized that this often brutal suppression and exploitation of the peasants condoned by many of the new landowning Mongols was self-defeating, shortsighted, and usually disastrous for the economy of the region. In her own appanage she encouraged the native agrarian economy with no attempt at imposing the pastoral practices more suited to Mongol nomads. Her wisdom was reflected in increased tax returns, and the lesson was not lost on her son Qubilai, who as soon as he realized the extent of the migration from his lands began taking a direct interest in the administration of his appanage. He had many of the Mongol officials immediately replaced with Chinese officials and dismissed his retainers, replacing them with regular administrators who made up what he named the *an-ch'a shih*, or Pacification Commission, a predominantly Chinese body. Their first task was to draw up a system of regular taxation and the abolition of extraordinary levies with the aim of enticing the farmers back to their lands, and by the early 1240s this policy could be seen to be working.

Sorghaghtani Beki left a more concrete form of immediate legacy in the shape of the Parisian goldsmith Guillame Boucher and his exotic, idiosyncratic works. On one of Batu's early campaigns in Europe, Prince Böchek, a paternal half brother of Möngke, captured the French goldsmith, possibly in Belgrade, and presented him to his father's chief wife, who resided with her youngest son, Arigh Böqa. It was Boucher who designed and had manufactured the elaborate silver drinking fountain that so amazed visitors to the Mongol capital, including the papal envoy William of Rubruck.[17] On Sorghaghtani's death, Arigh Böqa inherited not only his mother's estate but also the renowned craftsman.

In the small, leafy market town of Maragheh, once capital of the Il-Khanid state, hidden in a warren of buff, windowless backstreets in the playground of a small girls' school can be found an ancient tomb tower still in reasonable condition. It is known as the Tomb to the Mother of Hülegü Khan. In fact, this obscure monument with its clear Saljuqid design features could have been constructed as early as 1186 C.E., as the tomb tower beside it, long before Sorghaghtani Beki's birth. However, its dedication to this illustrious woman is indicative of her enduring reputation and regard.

DOQUZ KHĀTŪN

Doquz Khātūn (died June 16, 1265) was the last wife of Tolui Khan, who upon her husband's death, according to Mongol tradition, passed to his son. Hülegü inherited Doquz Khātūn from his father but made her his chief wife though not mother to his heirs. Despite having other wives who were mothers to his heirs, her status as chief wife was never in question, and she earned great praise and honor in her own right as well as for being partner to the founder of the Il-Khanid dynasty of greater Iran.

Doquz Khātūn was the granddaughter of Wang (Ong) Khan, leader of the Nestorian Christian Kereit tribe whose pastures were based near present-day Ulaanbaatar. After Wang Khan's defeat by Temüjin in 1203 she was given to the latter's youngest son, Tolui. The marriage was apparently not consummated, and when Tolui died in 1233 she passed into the care of his son Hülegü, who married her during his expedition to Persia in 1256–58. He had considerable respect for her judgment, and she was able to intercede for the Christians after the Mongol sack of Baghdad in 1258; she was also instrumental in securing the election of Mar Denha as Nestorian catholicos in 1265. The Great Khan Möngke, in his parting address to his brother, had strongly advised Hülegü to heed the words and advice of Doquz Khātūn during his campaign in the west to establish stability and imperial rule over Iran, Rum, and Syria. A mural found in a church in eastern Turkey originally thought to depict Helen and Constantine is now thought more likely to represent Hülegü and the lady so beloved of the local Christians, Doquz Khātūn, complete with saintly halo.[18] A church with *naqus* (clappers) was erected in her own *ordu,* and she encouraged the building of churches throughout the realm. *Naqus* were used instead of bells in Eastern Orthodox practice to summon the faithful to prayer. She survived Hülegü by only four months; there is no evidence to support the thirteenth-century Armenian historian Stephannos Orbelian's claim that she was poisoned by the *sāhib dīwān,* Juwaynī.[19]

Although Doquz Khātūn produced no children, Hülegü had offspring from several concubines in her entourage, and her influence continued to be felt; she helped to ensure the succession for his son Abaqa (ruled 1265–82). Indicative of her influence and the esteem in which she was held is the frequency of references to Doquz Khātūn that occur in sources. Bar Hebraeus claims "she raised on high the horn of the Christians in all the earth" and lamented the departure of "the believing Queen."[20] Two Mamluk historians, certainly no apologists for the Mongols, recounted the story of a young Ayyubid prince forced to present his father's submission to the feared King of the World, Hülegü Khan. Also present at the audience was Doquz Khātūn who immediately attempted to put the eight-year-old ambassador at ease. She was so taken with the young boy that she inquired through an interpreter if the young prince would like to stay with her and be adopted:

"I do not have a child, and this King is an old man, and no child will come from him." AL-ᶜAzīz ᶜUthmān was silent and [then] said, "I want my mother and father." Dokuz Khātūn turned to Hülegü and spoke with him two words.[21]

The Armenian cleric and scholar Vardan Arewelc'i, who became the queen's confidant and spiritual mentor, spoke of the grief of the Christians when three months after destiny "broke the staff of the powerful, valiant, and victorious Hulawu," the pious queen also died, leaving "the Christian nations heart-broken with manifold distress and grief."[22]

The Armenian monk Grigor of Akanc, though writing around 1260–70, based some of his history on hearsay, and some of this same hearsay can be found in the royal Armenian historian Het'um. Both writers repeated the fulsome praise of Hülegü's wife and recount her tireless work for the Christians, but they went farther and make quite unfounded claims that Doquz Khātūn encouraged ill-treatment and harassment of her Muslim subjects. Grigor claimed that pigs were taken from the Armenians as annual tribute, and that from these, 2,000 pigs were sent to every Arab city. These pigs were delivered with strict orders that the Muslim Arabs were to feed them fodder every morning, almonds and dates every evening, and that every Saturday these same pigs were to be washed ready for slaughter and eating. Every Muslim man was to eat the flesh of these swine, with orders given that any who refused were to be decapitated. Hetoum's claims were not so dramatic. He claimed that Doquz ordered the rebuilding of all churches that had suffered damage at Muslim hands and the destruction of "all the temples of the Saracens." He further claimed that such was the oppression felt by the Muslims that they were fearful of going outside. Though there is no evidence of any of this (in fact Muslims fared well under the early Il-Khans) these reports were used by both Christians and Muslims in subsequent centuries to promote their own propaganda and their own interpretation of events at this time. Kirakos reported that Doquz tried to dissuade her husband from lavishing money and attention on magicians and soothsayers, but there are no other serious suggestions or evidence that, despite promoting her own faith, Doquz showed any animosity to other religions.

KÄLMISH AQA

Kälmish Aqa was a granddaughter of Tolui through his third son, Qutuqtu, born to his wife Linqum Khātūn. She was married to and outlived Salji'udai Gürägän (died 1301), who served in the Golden Horde, and as such she served as a bridge between warring factions of the Golden family. Toqta Noyan, ruler of the Golden Horde (ruled 1291–1312) held her in high esteem, and she had the highest regard for Ghazan Khan (ruled 1295–1305) of Iran, with whom she kept in contact informing him of events in the neighboring state. Her late husband's memory secured her position in the court of the Golden Horde, and her Toluid blood ensured her close ties with the Il-Khanate khans. She provided a much-needed line of communication between the two rival houses. When Qubilai Khan's son Nomoghan was seized by his cousins and taken prisoner to the court of Möngke Temür (ruled 1267–80), ruler of the Golden Horde, it was Kälmish who secured his release and ensured that he was returned with honor to his father in China. Though she was a relatively minor figure and is rarely mentioned in the history books, Kälmish's role in these affairs of state reflects the importance given to women and the influence they wielded even though it was often behind the scenes.

QUTLUGH TERKĀN KHĀTŪN OF KIRMAN

Terkān Khātūn, though a minor figure in the grand history of the Mongol Empire, is significant for the light she throws on the Mongols' relationship to their subjects and as reflective of the status of women under their rule. Women had always played a leading role in Mongol society, and women from steppe societies in general enjoyed a higher status than their cousins from the plateau lands to the south. Marriage alliances were usually political, and remarriage was not uncommon. Terkān Khātūn effectively ruled the southern Iranian province of Kirman for 26 years, from 1257 until 1283, and her reign is generally considered the golden age of the rule of the Qutlugh-Khanids, rulers of the southern Iranian province of Kirman for 85 years (1222–1307). Two generations from the steppes of central Asia, this Turkic dynasty, especially under Terkān, bridged the divide between the Mongol overlords and their Persian subjects.

Terkān Khātūn's rise to fame is an epic story in itself. She was born into a noble Khitai (central Asians of Turco-Mongol descent) family in Transoxiana (modern-day Uzbekistan and Turkmenistan), but during the violent political upheavals of the early thirteenth century, she was taken captive and sold into slavery. She had a succession of wealthy masters who all fell in love with her beauty and intelligence until finally she ended up with the Qutlugh Khan, Baraq Hājib (died 1235), the powerful ruler of Kirman. When he died, following steppe tradition, not only his crown but also his wife went to his son Qutb al-Dīn. It was early recognized that his wife, Terkān Khātūn, held considerable influence over her husband, Qutb al-Dīn, and when he ascended the throne of Kirman in 1251 she was seen as the real power behind the throne.

Terkān Khātūn realized official power in 1257 upon the death of her husband when she was proclaimed Qutlugh (an honorific meaning "fortunate one") Terkān and regent for her young son Hajjāj Sultan. To cement her position and spread her influence she sought political marriages both for her son, Hajjāj, and her favorite daughter, Pādeshāh Khātūn. Hajjāj

married the daughter of a leading member of the Mongol elite and governor of Khorasan, Arghun Aqa, and Padeshāh married the future Il-Khan
himself, Abaqa Khan, son of Hülegü Khan. Terkān Khātūn ignored the
fact that her Muslim daughter was forbidden by Islamic law to marry a
non-Muslim, the Buddhist Abaqa. Qutlugh Terkān Khātūn maintained
close links with the Il-Khanid court in Azerbaijan and enjoyed the Mongol
court's favor and support.

Terkān Khātūn of Kirman was famed for her justice, the stability she
brought to the province, and her charitable works. Many stories are told
of her wise resolutions to the disputes that her subjects took before her. An
old man appeared before her to complain that his wealth and jewels had
gone missing from his house. When she learned that he had a young wife,
she ordered that some of her own special perfume be presented to the old
man as a gift for his young wife. She then ordered her night watchmen
to search the city and arrest anyone smelling of that distinctive perfume.
A young man was duly discovered and soon confessed to a liaison with
the wife. Threatened with punishment, he returned the old man's wealth,
the young wife was divorced and cast out with her lover, and the reputation of the Queen soared. Stories such as these and of her acts of charity
abounded and she was well regarded by all her subjects. As one contemporary chronicler, Munshī, expressed it:

She was a queen whose character was righteous, whose mystery was pure, whose
outer garments were modesty, whose insignia was chastity, . . . whose days were
resolute. She was the jeweled knot and springtime of the kings of the Qarā Khitā'ī
of Kirman.[23]

PĀDESHĀH KHĀTŪN

Pādeshāh Khātūn was Qutlugh Terkān's favorite daughter, and during
her upbringing she enjoyed all the comforts of Kirman's courtly life. This
life was far from the rough life of the steppe, even though for the Mongol aristocracy of the second half of the thirteenth century, life in their
ordus had long since ceased to be incommodious or unpalatable. Palace
life had not eradicated a pining for her roots on the steppe, and she clearly
expressed her strong sentiments in verse, poetry being an unusual occupation with which she has since become associated.

> Although I am the child of a mighty Sultān
> And the fruit of the garden that is the heart of the Turks,
> I laugh at fate and prosperity,
> But I cry at this endless exile.[24]

She had been promised in marriage to the new Il-Khan Abaqa (ruled
1265–82), but it was not until 1271–72 that her mother overcame her

misgivings about her beloved child becoming a minor wife in a Mongol harem and the marriage was able to take place. Significantly, it was these fears rather than the fact that her Muslim daughter would be marrying an unbeliever, a union strictly forbidden in Islam, than caused her disquiet. When a high-ranking ambassador, Qarghai Ilchi,[25] arrived in Kirman from Abaqa's *ordu*, Qutlugh Terkān realized that there was no alternative but to obey the marriage request. However, she was most concerned as to how her "delicate and sensitive," "proud and well-bred," "precious," "illustrious," "exalted," "beloved" but "hot-tempered" "dainty coquette"[26] would be able to deal with the rigors of harem life where she would have to adapt to the dictates of Mongol customs and rules. The princess Pādeshāh would invariably have to join Abaqa Khan's close relatives and older more senior wives, to whom she would be expected to defer. One of her duties would include presenting them with a vessel of wine and filling their drinking goblets. Her mother was fearful that due to her hot temper and great sensitivity she might not behave suitably submissive, and she wondered how such a "fragile girl" would manage to carry that demeaning and heavy wine flagon. However, Qutlugh Terkān's fears were allayed when her "divine guardian angels brought forth words of comfort" and reminded her of when she had been in a similar situation in her own troubled past and had faced a comparable dilemma and stressed that eventually the circumstances had developed to the later benefit of both mother and daughter.[27] In fact, these qualms proved to be unfounded because the death of Abaqa's mother, Yisunjin Khātūn, almost coincided with Princess Pādeshāh's arrival at his court.[28] After this venerated lady "had been transferred from her throne in the House of Frailty to the great sepulchre of eternity," as the Persian chronicler described her sickness and death, the problem of how to dispose of her considerable personal *ordu*, comprising estates, provinces, servants, domestics, her throne, and crown, still remained.[29] The problem was solved when Abaqa met his new wife and recognized in her character intelligence, royalty, and leadership and in her actions capability and suitability. A royal charter was therefore issued in Pādeshāh's name, and she was confirmed in office and the king's mother's crown was placed on her head. Day by day and hour by hour she gained acceptance from the other wives and the emirs and the religious grandees who eventually acknowledged her qualities.[30] The court administrator and historian Wassāf felt that it was the special love that Abaqa felt for Pādeshāh that caused him to promote her above all his other women, and that it was the couple's inseparability that partially accounted for her mother, Terkān Khātūn's 30-odd year reign over Kirman.[31]

Other than an intriguing history, Pādeshāh Khātūn has also left behind a small body of verse. The following are examples of translations from the Persian of this verse:

> An apple that from your hand secretly reaches me,
> From that, the scent of eternal life reaches me.

From your hand and palm a goblet reaches me
At that, like a pomegranate, my heart smiles from joy.[32]

That day in the infinite past that they formed him,
They created him to soothe the souls of the love-sick,
Candy laid claim to his sugar-like lips,
In Egypt they put three skews in his mouth.[33]

Who has ever seen writing in musk on a ruby?
When has perfume ever done injustice to wine?
O my soul, the trace of a black mole on your lip,
Is darkness and the water of life together.[34]

Today, until my hand rests on your shoulder,
How much grief must spring from your fountain of pleasure?
In your ear I see seeds of pearl
That surely my tears must water?[35]

QUTULUN KHĀTŪN

Qutulun was the daughter of the Ögödeid rebel Qaidu (1236–1303), who came to represent and champion traditional Mongol values and virtues. Qaidu, a cousin of Qubilai, espoused the morality and traditions of the steppe over the sown (the settled, urban people) and rebelled against what he saw as the corrupted regimes of his cousins in Iran and China. His daughter, Qutulun, became a symbol of Turco-Mongol womanhood and crystallized some of those values he fought for and he perceived as now dying in the lands that the Mongols had conquered.

Qutulun was her father's pride and joy. She campaigned with him and was considered on her own merits a warrior of the first rank. Even if some of the stories told about her are apocryphal, they enhanced her status as the ideal representation of Mongol womanhood. Regardless of their strict historical accuracy, the portrayal of Qutulun is important because it provides a portrait of the aspirations of many Mongol men and maybe even women who considered themselves Turco-Mongols.

It was said that Qutulun had vowed not to wed any man who could not first defeat her in physical combat. The woman who Marco Polo described as "very beautiful but also so strong and brave that in all her father's realm there was no man who could outdo her in feats of strength" had no shortage of suitors. Though her parents wanted her to marry, she was insistent that the successful suitor must first prove himself superior in contests of physical strength and endurance as well as military skills. The many shamed princes had to pay for their "courtship" with their horses and arms. Any suitor's challenge was accepted on condition that 100 horses and the challenger's pride were staked on the outcome. Her stable is said to have contained 10,000 steeds. A woman who felt at home in the saddle and enjoyed time spent as a warrior, preferring the open spaces to the camp, was a Mongol ideal that was exemplified in Qaidu's daughter. Qutulun sought a partner who excelled in the martial arts and who was proficient in the saddle rather than a scholar refined in intellectual combat who was proficient in the court. She represented the world of the nomad and pastoral traditions, and her values contrasted sharply with the sedentary, agricultural, and urban society of the new generations of Mongols more at home with their centralized governments and hordes of bureaucrats.

One version of Rashīd al-Dīn's histories claimed that rumor mongering forced Qutulun into a marriage against her will. Qaidu, of whom she had said, "I will become your wife. I want no other husband," was forced to marry her off to a Mongol named Abtaqul of the Qorolas clan, whom she chose herself. After her father's death she had two sons with Abtaqul, and the family lived contentedly two weeks' journey east of Samarqand on the slopes of the Shinqorliq mountain between the rivers Ili and Chu in what is today Kazakhstan.

OF THE DAUGHTER OF KING KAIDU, HOW STRONG AND VALIANT SHE WAS[36]

You must know, then, that King Kaidu had a daughter named, in the Tartar language, Aigiarm, which means shining moon. This damsel was so strong, that there was no young man in the whole kingdom who could overcome her, but she vanquished them all. Her father the king wished to marry her; but she declined, saying, that she would never take a husband till she met with some gentleman who should conquer her by force, upon which the king, her father, gave her a written promise that she might marry at her own will. She now caused it to be proclaimed in different parts of the world, that if any young man would come and try his strength with her, and should over-come her by force, she would accept him for her husband.

This proclamation was no sooner made, than many came from all parts to try their fortune. The trial was made with great solemnity. The king took his place in the principal hall of the palace, with a large company of men and women; then came the king's daughter, in a dress of cendal, very richly adorned, into the middle of the hall; and next came the young man, also in a dress of cendal. The agreement was, that if the young man overcame her so as to throw her by force to the ground, he was to have her for wife; but if, on the contrary, he should be overcome by the king's daughter, he was to forfeit to her a hundred horses. In this manner the damsel gained more than ten thousand horses, for she could meet with no one able to conquer her, which was no wonder, for she was so well-made in all her limbs, and so tall and strongly built, that she might almost be taken for a giantess. At last, about the year 1280, there came the son of a rich king, who was very beautiful and young; he was accompanied with a very fine retinue, and brought with him a thousand beautiful horses.

Immediately on his arrival, he announced that he was come to try his strength with the lady. King Kaidu received him very gladly, for he was very desirous to have this youth for his son-in-law, knowing him to be the son of the king of Pamar; on which account, Kaidu privately told his daughter that he wished her on this occasion to let herself be vanquished. But she said she would not do so for anything in the world. Thereupon the king and queen took their places in the hall, with a great attendance of both sexes, and the king's daughter presented herself as usual, and also the king's son, who was remarkable no less for his beauty than for his great strength. Now when they were brought into the hall, it was, on account of the superior rank of the claimant, agreed as the conditions of the trial, that if the young prince were conquered, he should forfeit the thousand horses he had brought with him as his stake. This agreement having been made, the wrestling began, and all who were there including the king and queen, wished heartily that the prince must be the victor, that he might be the husband of the princess. But, contrary to their hopes, after much pulling and tugging the king's daughter gained the victory, and the young prince thrown on the pavement of the Palace, and lost his thousand horses. There was not one person in the whole hall who did not lament his defeat. After this the king took his daughter with him into many battles, and not a cavalier of the host displayed so much valour; and at last the damsel rushed into the midst of the enemy, and seizing upon a horseman carried him off to her own people.

The stories that have endured, idolizing Qutulun the daughter of Qaidu Khan (died 1301), a great-grandson of Chinggis Khan and an upholder of traditional Mongol values and virtues, suggest an aspirational ideal for Mongol women and an idealized wife or daughter or even sister for Mongol men. Qaidu fought a losing battle to retain traditional, pastoral Mongol values, and his daughter shared this passion.

BAGHDĀD KHĀTŪN

Baghdād Khātūn was the daughter of the immensely powerful emir Chopan Suldus, who in 1307 was appointed senior emir to Ghazan Khan (ruler of the southwestern lands of the Mongol empire) and became effective ruler of the Il-Khanate when the 11-year-old Abū Saʿīd ascended the throne in 1316. Chopan was married to Sati Beg, Abū Saʿīd's sister, so his children and his daughter Baghdād Khātūn in particular were brought up almost as royalty. The fate and intrigues of this influential Mongol woman are of interest because they stand in such contrast to her contemporary Qutulun Khātūn of the house of Ögödei. Baghdād Khātūn excelled at the more common womanly guiles of seduction, charm, and stealing men's hearts, which worked on Mongol men as much as on any other men. She also suffered such jealousy that she was suspected of poisoning her eventual husband, the last Il-Khanid sultan, Abū Saʿīd (died 1335).

By all accounts the 20-year-old sultan, Abū Saʿīd, formed an uncontrollable, all-consuming passion for the daughter of Chopan, his chief emir. "The ruler of the world, in a corner of his palace, thought only of his beloved."[37] Unfortunately, the daughter, Baghdad Khātūn, was already married to Shaykh Hasan-i-Buzorg (Big Hasan), a powerful notable of the Mongol Jalayrid tribe. According to a *yasa* of Chinggis Khan, the sovereign has the right to demand the hand of any woman, married or not, for whom he might feel an attraction. Abū Saʿīd cited this *yasa* when he revealed his turbulent emotional state to the lady's father, who reacted with cold though controlled anger. His sultan ominously said nothing and remained impassive.[38]

All reports tell of the young sultan's obsession with this "moon-faced beauty." Abū Saʿīd was "at his wits end and could neither sleep nor settle himself."[39] It is said that when "his vision fell on Baghdād [Khātūn] a river flowed from his eyes like the Tigris. Love brought black misery and agony to the Sultan and on the battlefield of love [*maidān-i-ʿeshq*] his heart was soon smitten and the kingdom of [his] heart conquered."[40] "When under the gaze of her narcissus eyes, the heart was abandoned to intoxication—whether king or beggar, all were lost."[41] Even though the sultan heeded reports of Chopanid intrigue and conspiracy and ended up having both her brother, Khwaja Damashq, and father, Chopan, executed, to comply with Islamic practice, he still insisted on her divorce from Shaykh Hasan the Great and their subsequent marriage. Initially the fortunes of Iran reflected the happiness of the love-smitten couple, and the house of the Chopanians continued to serve its sovereign though now in a different capacity.[42] "The road to the royal court, magnificence, pomp, the highest rank, was once again open to the Chopanians."[43] The passion did not last long, and Abū Saʿīd later married Baghdād Khātūn's niece, Delshād Khātūn. It was anger and jealousy for this younger woman, as well as a desire to avenge her father and brother, that led Baghdād to conspire with Sultan Özbek of the Golden Horde to murder by poison the last Il-Khanid sultan. Baghdād Khātūn did not outlive her husband long, and in 1336 she was murdered in her bath on the orders of Arpa Khan, a Mongol aspirant to the Iranian throne.

TSA CHÜ OPERA SINGING GIRLS[44]

To conclude this section on women, a tradition that started at the time of Qubilai Khan and proved a most popular form of entertainment should be included since it illustrates one way in which girls from humble backgrounds could find fame and fortune or at least an escape from the drudgery of the urban sprawls that were becoming a feature of the Yüan years. The *Tsa Chü* opera has also been called drama since two-thirds of the performance involves prose dialogue with only the star performer singing his or her part. This form of stage show appeared and was popularized in Besh Baliq in the 1260s. The show was divided into four acts, with only one key being used for all songs included in each act. In addition, there was a prelude called "the wedge," which consisted of one or two short songs that were performed at the beginning of the show.

The star performer of these *Tsa Chü* operas was treated as a celebrity, and the audience often attended in order to see one particular singer. In one performance, the star of the *Tsa Chü* opera would be expected to sing forty or fifty arias almost without pause (the performance broken only by the interludes of prose dialogue by the chorus), a quite extraordinary feat. Though male singers were also assigned the star role, women were more common and were also sometimes expected to take on male roles.

During the Yüan period, troupes of performers were often composed of family units with the only outsiders being sons-in-law or daughters-in-law. If the star roles in *Tsa Chü* operas were usually female, men would play women in other forms of entertainment, burlesque in particular, where men would play such roles as the old procuress that appears in many plays of the time. There was a law at that time stipulating that marriage between actors and those outside the profession was illegal. In 1278, a law enforcing this decree only applied to actors belonging to the Imperial Music Academy, and the object of the law was to prevent trained and therefore valuable actors from being taken away either as spouses or concubines to positions in the provinces. In 1311, a stricter edict was passed by the Great Khan himself. "Henceforth *yüeh-jēn* [public entertainers] are only to marry *yüeh-jēn*. If any of those on close attendance upon me, or any official, or anyone else takes a *yüeh-jēn* as his wife, it will be accounted a crime."[45] A certain Mongol official, Hsin Ha-erh-ti, was executed for breaching this new law.

Much of the information that is known about the performers in *Tsa Chü* opera comes from a manuscript known as the *Green Bower Collection* (*Ch'ing Lou Chi*), which records details of the careers of one hundred singing girls involved in this kind of entertainment between the period circa 1270–1374. Many of the women whose careers are detailed in the *Green Bower Collection* and who did not marry fellow actors became concubines of well-to-do theatre proprietors. Though not a legal wife, the position of concubine was a recognized and acceptable social position, and for a girl from very humble origins it was a desirable position in which to find herself. With a repertoire of songs, dances, and stories, they formed the link between high culture and popular culture, a service traditional to concubines throughout history. The fact that the author of the *Green Bower Collection* considers this function of concubinage noteworthy suggests that most of the girls were illiterate. They were not all possessed of good looks, and examples of hunchbacks and girls with other physical defects are recorded. What all the girls had in common were exceptionally beautiful singing voices. It was their golden voices that were prized by their patrons, whose positions ranged from high local officials to Mongol generals and chief ministers, and who were mainly Mongols and Uyghur Turks, though instances of simply well-to-do lovers of song holding minor government posts or of private means are noted. Since the abolition of the discriminatory examination system and its replacement in 1313 by more straightforward, modern exams, a new, popular, vernacular culture was supplanting the old, and this favored the *Tsa Chü* opera singers.

The *Green Bower Collection* was compiled by Hsia Po-ho in 1364. He came from a prominent family of Sungkiang and had inherited a great fortune, which a fortune teller warned him he would very shortly lose to a great calamity that would beset him. With the aim of being penniless by the time this calamity struck, he began spending lavishly and entertaining on a grand scale, during the course of which he encountered many of the *Tsa Chü* opera girls, many of whom he showered with his largesse. Calamity did strike, and he was forced to flee his native town with only his books and memories for comfort. It was then that he started writing out the details of the many girls he had encountered in his previous life.

One girl was Chang "Harmonious Cloud" who was good at reciting both *Shih* and *Tz'u* poetry. She was witty in conversation and was the best singer among her contemporaries. She had a fine reputation in Da-du (Beijing), and her portrait had been painted by the leading painters of the day. Countless famous people had composed poems in her honor, and two local notables gave drinking parties held in her name. A story is recounted concerning the chief minister of state, who it is said waylaid two known friends of Harmonious Cloud in the street. Knowing that they were on their way to her house, he asked if he could accompany them. When they assented, the chief minister immediately gave orders for his servants to follow him after fetching wine and provisions, including gold goblets and silver platters of the finest foods, and delicacies to take to the lady's home. Harmonious Cloud was honored to receive such an illustrious guest and sang for him. He was in turn so impressed that when it was time to leave and his servants began to pack up the gold and silver items that they had brought with them, the minister stopped their packing and insisted that the items should remain in Harmonious Cloud's house just in case he should visit her again.

Another singer mentioned is Ts'ao E-hsiu, who was also renowned in the capital. Hsia Po-ho states that she was extremely intelligent and unrivaled in her looks and art. A certain Po-chi gave a small party in her honor at which a number of high-ranking officials were invited, and a story was told that demonstrated her quick wit and confident manner.

Kao "Natural Elegance" was singularly distinguished-looking and refined and carried a "woodland air" about her. She was particularly famous for her portrayal of "boudoir-repining," that is, upper-class women mourning their absent lovers. However, she also played court scenes and "flowered" female roles. She married a famous actor and, on his death, married the head clerk Chiao T'ai-su, after whose death she once again became an actress. "This loss of one who ranked as a leading beauty in good society was deeply regretted; but she continued to conduct herself with the most scrupulous propriety."[46]

Wang Golden Belt was unrivaled in beauty and in her singing. She was taken as a concubine by a leading provincial official with whom she had a child. However, she came to the notice of the great Boyan Noyan, Qubilai Khan's greatest general, and he wished to enroll her in the capital's Imperial Music Academy. Her lover was desperate for her to stay with him and in despair appealed to General Boyan's wife. His appeal was successful, and Golden Belt remained with him.

Wei Tao-tao was famed for her rendition of the Partridge Dance. She performed it as a solo act, and so great was her performance that she had no successor. The Partridge Dance was a Chin Tatar dance with flute and drum accompaniment.

Mi-Li-ha was a Muslim girl who played leading female roles in dramas. Her clear and pure voice was particularly noteworthy, and she was most famous for her portrayal of "flowered" women, that is, women heavily made-up with paint and cosmetics.

In all, the lives and careers of a hundred girls are told in the *Green Bower Collection* as well as stories of famous musicians and performers of the Yüan years. Arthur Waly's translation of extracts and research into the collection's writer and the background to the *Tsa Chü* opera are a very welcome addition to our understanding of the Mongol years ruling China and the role women played.

NOTES

1. R. A. Skelton, T. E. Marston, and George D. Painter, *The Vinland Map and the Tartar Relation* (New Haven, Conn.: Yale University Press, 1995), 94, para. 49.

2. William of Rubruck, *The Mission of William of Rubruck,* trans. and ed. Peter Jackson with David Morgan (London: Hakluyt Society, 1990), 74.

3. Urgunge Onon, trans., *The History and Life of Chinggis Khan (The Secret History of the Mongols)* (Leiden, Netherlands: Brill, 1990), 141–42.

4. Rashid al-Din, *The Successors of Genghis Khan,* trans. John Andrew Boyle (New York: Columbia University Press, 1971), 176.

5. Ala-ad-Din 'Ata-Malik Juvaini, *The History of the World Conqueror,* trans. John Andrew Boyle, intro. David Morgan, vols. 1 and 2 (Manchester, U.K.: Manchester University Press, 1997), 245.

6. Ibid., 242.

7. Maulana Juzjani, Minhaj-ud-Din Abu 'Umar-i-Usman, *Tabakat-i-Nasiri: A General History of the Muhammadan Dynasties of Asia; from 810–1260 A.D. And The Irruption of the Infidel Mughals into Islam,* trans. H. G. Raverty (Reprint, Calcutta: Asiatic Society), 1144.

8. Ala-ad-Din 'Ata-Malik Juvaini, *The History of the World Conqueror,* 246.

9. Gregorius Bar Hebraeus, *The Chronography of Gregory Abu'l-Faraj Bar Hebraeus' Political History of the World, Part I*, trans. Ernest A. Wallis-Budge (Piscataway, N.J.: Gorgias Press, 2003), 412.

10. Maulana Juzjani, Minhaj-ud-Din Abu 'Umar-i-Usman, *Tabakat-i-Nasiri*, 265.

11. Ala-ad-Din 'Ata-Malik Juvaini, *The History of the World Conqueror*, 265.

12. Ibid., 552.

13. Rashid al-Din, *The Successors of Genghis Khan*, 168.

14. Gregorius Bar Hebraeus, *The Chronography of Gregory*, 398.

15. Rashid al-Din, *The Successors of Genghis Khan*, 199.

16. Ibid., 200.

17. William of Rubruck, *The Mission of William of Rubruck*, 224; see also internet version, http://www.locksley.com/locksley/rubruck.htm or http://depts.washington.edu/uwch/silkroad/texts/rubruck.html.

18. J.M. Fiey, "Iconographie Syriaque Hulagu, Doquz Khatun ... six Ambons," *Le Museon* (1975), 59–64.

19. Stephannos Orbelian, *Histoire de la Siounie*, trans. M. Brosset (St Petersburg, Russia: Académie imperiale des sciences, 1864), 234–35.

20. Gregorius Bar Hebraeus, *The Chronography of Gregory*, 419.

21. Reuven Amitai-Preiss, "Hülegü and the Ayyubid Lord of Transjordan," *Archivum Eurasiae Medii Aevi* 9 (1995–97): 14.

22. Vardan, "The Historical Compilation of Vardan Arewelc'i," trans. R.W. Thomson, *Dumbarton Oaks Papers* 43 (1989): 222.

23. Naṣīr al-Dīn Munshī, *Simṭ, al-'ulā* (Tehran: Inteshārāt Esatir 1983 / 1362), 37.

24. Munshī, *Simṭ, al-'ulā*, 70; Anon, *Tārīkh-i Shāhī*, ed. Ibrāhīm Bāstānī (Tehran: Inteshārāt Baniād Farhang, Iran 1976), 61; Moḥammad Shabānkāra'ī, *Majma'-'Ansāb*, (Tehran: Inteshārāt Amīr Kabīr, 1984), 201.

25. Possibly Emīr Qarakhai, mentioned in Munshī's *Sim't al-ᶜula*, 47.

26. Anon, *Tārīkh-i Shāhī*, 139.

27. Ibid.

28. Ibid., 140; Rashīd al-Dīn, *Jāmi' al-Tavārīkh*, Mohammad Roushan and Muṣtafah Mūsavī (Tehran: Nashr albaraz, 1994), 1055.

29. Anon, *Tārīkh-i Shāhī*, 140.

30. Ibid.

31. Āyātī, 177–78; Waṣṣāf 291; Hamdu'llah Mustawfī-i-Qazwīnī, *Tarīkh-i-Guzīda: The Select History*, trans. Edward G. Browne, (London: Luzac, 1913), 531; Khwandamir, *Habib's-Siyar: The Reign of the Mongol and the Turk Genghis Khan, Amir Temur*, trans. W.M. Thackston, vol. 3 (Cambridge, Mass.: Department of Near Eastern Languages and Civilizations, Harvard University, 1994), 268; Khwandamir, *Habib's-Siyar*, 155.

32. Munshī, 70; *Tārīkh-i Shāhī*, 61; Shabānkāra'ī, 202.

33. Munshī, 70; *Tārīkh-i Shāh*, 60; Shabānkāra'ī, 201.

34. Khwandamir, *Habib's-Siyar*, 271; Ibid., 156.

35. Anon, *Tārīkh-i Shāhī*, 61.

36. Marco Polo, *The Travels of Marco Polo*, trans. Teresa Waugh (London: Sidgewick and Jackson, 1994), ch. 49, 417–19.

37. Khwandamir, *Habib's-Siyar*, 119.

38. Shabānkāra'ī, 295; Mustawfī, *Ẓafarnāmeh*, 1463, Ward's tr., 649.

39. Al-Razzaq Samarqandī, 92.

40. Mustawfī, *Zafarnāmeh*, 1462, tr. 648.

41. Al-Razzaq Samarqandī, 92.

42. Hamdallah Qazvīnī Mustawfī, *Ẓafarnāmeh of Mustawfī*, trans. L. J. Ward (PhD thesis, University of Manchester, 1983), 666.

43. Ibid., 117.

44. For more detail on this subject, see Arthur Waley, "The Green Bower Collection," in *The Secret History of the Mongols, and Other Pieces* (Thirsk, Yorkshire: House of Stratus, 2002), 67–106.

45. Waley, 90.

46. Ibid., 96.

12

FOLKTALES FROM MONGOLIA

Folktales say much about a people and much about the history of that people. In a society with a strong oral tradition rather than a literary tradition, the folktales are all the more important. Mongol society had a strong tradition of folk stories that served the function of entertainment, the communication of wisdom, the preservation of history, and the transmission of tradition and customs.

THE GREEDY DOG

Once upon a time, a long, long time ago, there was a greedy dog living in the Altai Mountains.

One day while the greedy dog was walking along he found a nice bone on the ground near a bridge. He stopped to pick up the bone and looked across the river to the other side. He thought it looked nicer on the other side of the river and decided to go on across the bridge. As the greedy dog was walking across the bridge with the bone in his mouth he looked down into the water. There in the water he saw his own reflection and thought it was another dog with a bone. The greedy dog thought to himself, "I am going to take that bone away from the other dog as it is bigger than the bone I have." So the greedy dog jumped off the bridge into the water; he splashed around for a while but never found the other dog and lost his own bone at the same time.

THE COLT AND THE MARE

It is said that there was a spotted mare from Choht who had a colt named Morning Star. After she led him around for three nights, they would go to water; after three more nights, they would go to graze. Once, while on the way to water, they came to a bird's egg.

At this, it is said that a goose came and pleaded, "Don't step on my egg or you'll kill it!" kowtowing to the mare. The mare responded, "Don't talk to me about killing your egg, my throat is parched with thirst and I can hardly walk." The mare swerved on purpose and kicked the egg, killing it. Then they went off in the direction of water.

The goose was enraged. "On your way back I am going to kill your Morning Star!"

When this mare and her colt came back by, the goose flew at the colt; when pecking from the south the mare would move the colt to the north, when pecking from the north she would move him to the south, when pecking from the west she would move him to the east, when pecking from the east she would move him to the west. Not letting the goose get near the colt, it is said, the mare led him off and away from there.

The small colt noticed his mother's ears were not shifting back and forth as usual, rather now they were sagging. His mother must be thirsty, he thought. The colt noticed again how his mother's gait was not the usual sound of clip-clop, rather now it was more of a dragging sound. His mother must be tired, he thought.

The colt wondered why his mother's fur was disheveled and dirty. He thought it was from the trek through the brush on Shabakt Peak where the mud and dirt got caked to her fur. The colt also wondered what the red spots were that were on his mother's body. He thought it was from the trek over Hont Peak where the sulfur and sand got caked to her fur. The colt also wondered what the blue spots were on his mother's body. He thought they must be from the trek over Bingt Peak where the rocks and pebbles stuck to her fur.

At this and after they crossed the peak, the mare stopped with tears streaming from her eyes. She said, "My son, your dear mother is going to die soon." Tears began to well up in the colt's eyes as he moved away from his beloved mother.

"Where will I go, what will I do? I don't know anything from above or below, I can't remain alone. Without your sweet milk what will I eat? Please try and bear it my dear mother," said the little colt, tears filling his beautiful, big, bright eyes as he began crying.

It is said that the mare wished her son well. "My son, death is a predetermined part of life. Behind the Baraad Peak you will find a herd of horses a thousand strong. In that herd is your older sister, but you can't get along together. Behind the Argalt Peak is a herd of horses ten thousand strong. In that herd is your older brother, but you can't get along together.

From there if you go in that direction is a herd of horses one hundred thousand strong, in that herd is your old mother. It is there where you can live together with her. Grass and greens will be milk for you. There will be many friends and nieces and nephews for you there. Be good to your master; when you are saddled, be a prized horse. If you go to far places you will not get thin, if you go to near places you will not get tired. You will become the best of the riding horses, a friend to the children of man. In the herd you won't be at the head or the tail. You will eat the tender shoots of grass and be like a son of gold to any father."

After she finished saying these things the mare died.

Poor little Morning Star colt looked at his dead mother as the tears that filled his eyes streamed down his face. He began turning around and around and said in remorse, "My mother has already said these things."

The Mongolian horse-headed fiddle. Courtesy of Xinjiang Qinshan Culture Publishing

Morning Star went to the herd where he found his older sister. She kicked him when he was behind and bit him when he was in front, not letting him get near her. He then went to the herd where he found his older brother, but he would not let him get near either. Finally, he went to the herd where he found his old mother. When she saw him she said, "A portion of my flesh and bones has come!" When asked where his mother was, he responded, "My mother has already died."

At this she said, "If this is so then you stay at my right and left sides and don't wander. My teats are already dry, but if you try hard you may get milk." He stayed at her right and left sides and didn't wander. After trying and trying, he was able to get milk from her teats.

Morning Star grew up to become the head of this herd and many others, the fastest and best of all the horses.

HUNTER-BOY

They say that, in this remote beauty spot, there is a game-wealthy Hunter-Boy. His winter camp is in the Altai Mountains, and his summer camp in the back tablelands. When he rides his chestnut colored pony eastward he hunts buck and doe, after heading westward there is always an antelope tied to his saddle, if traveling south he tracks deer, if galloping to the north he kills fox and wolf. After hunting he always comes back with something strapped to his saddle. He is never selfish with his catch; whenever around his neighbors he shares the meat. Hunter-Boy is a grown man, able to reach the saddle ties and put his foot into the stirrups. Therefore, over these years, the neighboring families there have never gone without.

One day, when Hunter-Boy was on his way to go hunting, a hawk came flying over and swooped down to catch a thin, white snake curled up in the tall grass near the river shore. As the hawk flew back by, the small snake called out, "Hunter-Boy, help! Help!" Hunter-Boy, feeling sorry for the snake, thought to himself, "Poor thing, the little creature has run into trouble and is pleading me, how can I refuse to help!" He pulled out an arrow and shot the hawk, and the thin, white snake fell to the ground. "Hunter-Boy, your grace must be repaid!" said the little snake as it disappeared into the tall grass.

That evening, after strapping a roebuck to his saddle, Hunter-Boy headed back along the river shore. On the way he happened upon a multitude of snakes lying crisscross along the path. "Are you having a gathering today?" asked Hunter-Boy out of curiosity. Then, just ahead, the thin, white snake came out, saying to everyone, "This is Hunter-Boy, the one who graciously saved my life." All of the snakes circled around Hunter-Boy in a loud commotion. "Our master has invited you to visit him." Then the small, white snake said, "I am the Dragon Master's youngest daughter.

Yesterday you saved my life, and my father wishes to show his appreciation by inviting you to visit his palace." "How can I ever get to the Dragon Master's palace?" asked Hunter-Boy. "Close your eyes, and I will lead you there," replied the thin, white snake.

While walking along, the thin, white snake whispered into Hunter-Boy's ear, "My father is going to offer you precious objects of silver and gold, but don't accept them. Instead, ask for the small, round precious stone that my father always keeps in his mouth. Once you place it in your mouth you will be able to understand the languages of all four-legged and winged creatures. However, I will warn you about one thing. After you have put the precious stone into your mouth, and can understand the language of the flying creatures and know what they are saying, whatever you do, you cannot tell what you have heard to any human being. If you do, your body will immediately turn to stone. Please, don't ever forget this." Hunter-Boy, understanding what she had said, nodded his head. After walking a ways further, he opened his eyes only to find that they had already arrived at the Dragon Master's palace.

The Dragon Master, wanting to express great thanks to Hunter-Boy, opened the doors to his one hundred and eight treasure houses, saying, "Hunter-Boy, you may choose anything from among these treasures of mine." Hunter-Boy walked up to the door of the treasure house to peer inside. Gold and silver glittered in his eyes, and the pearls were piled high like mountains. Treasures to revive the dead, to bring sight to the blind, to bring sound to deaf ears and speech to the speechless. There was enough for a lifetime of grains, for garments that the sun and wind could not penetrate; the universe would never lack from these treasures.

Hunter-Boy bowed to the Dragon Master and said, "Dragon Master, I live as a hunter, a guardian of the remote spaces, I have need of the small, round stone that you keep in your mouth. Please bestow that upon me."

The Dragon Master looked to the right and laughed, looked to the left and cried, took the precious stone from his mouth and gave it to Hunter-Boy. From that time on Hunter-Boy, able to understand the languages of the four-legged and winged creatures, became an even more successful hunter.

One day, as Hunter-Boy went up the mountain to go hunting, he overheard the mountain birds in discussion, "Tomorrow, they say that Sir Tiger, our mountain creature king, will be celebrating his birthday. They also say that he is going to eat the flesh of those two children who always come up the mountain to fetch firewood.... The two of them don't know that they will die tomorrow."

Hunter-Boy was very surprised to hear this and wanted to tell those two children; however, he remembered that if he were to tell them, his own body would turn to stone. But then, if he didn't tell them, when the two poor children go to gather firewood and are eaten by the tiger . . . The fear tore at him all night. Suddenly, at the break of dawn, an idea came to him.

He took his bow and arrows and headed up the mountain. He arrived at a cliff and sat down to wait. Shortly after, the two children came up the mountain gathering firewood and were paying no attention to what was going on around them. All of a sudden, the fierce tiger jumped out roaring, "MEAT! MEAT!" They say, just as the tiger hurled himself toward the two children, Hunter-Boy, with a single arrow, shot the tiger through the neck, killing him instantly. The two children bowed down in front of Hunter-Boy, their lifesaver, thanking him. All of the mountain animals who, time and time again, had been humiliated and taunted by the tiger also came to show their appreciation at his deed.

As the days and nights passed, Hunter-Boy became more and more skilled at hunting on horseback, and at the same time continued to answer to the needs of the neighboring families. One summer day, it is said, Hunter-Boy went to a far-off mountain behind his home to go hunting. The Emperor and Empress of the bird kingdom were leading their subjects on a long journey to a faraway place. All of the four-legged animals were growling and quarreling; they say even the bunnies and gophers were grouping together, fleeing in excitement. At this, Hunter-Boy, in a state of wonderment, got down from his horse and sat in the shadow of the trees to listen to the birds in conversation.

"Tomorrow this mountain is going to burst and create a large flood. All creatures must take their belongings, not leaving anything behind in the village, and head out," they exclaimed.

At that instant, Hunter-Boy jumped up and took off toward home. As soon as he reached the village he began, "Quickly, we all have to move away from here! Tomorrow the mountain behind us is going to burst, and there is going to be a dangerous flood...." As he spoke, it is said, not even one person believed his words. He moved away and thought to himself, "I am an orphan, and these people have cared for me since my birth. They have taught me the difference between right and wrong. How can I just leave them with this threat of death?" He spoke up, "Hurry, get away from here! Hurry! There is really a flood coming!" Hearing this, the people badgered him, asking over and over, "How do you know about this flood? Who told you?" They say not even one person was prepared to flee.

At this, very worried and excited, he thought to himself, "How can I be afraid of turning to stone and let all of these people and animals die." Then Hunter-Boy began by telling them about saving the thin, white snake and the Dragon Master summoning him to visit his palace to show his gratitude, about the precious stone that the Dragon Master kept in his mouth, and how he begged the Dragon Master to give him the stone. How, once he placed the stone in his own mouth, he could understand the languages of all creatures, therefore killed the tiger and saved the two children gathering firewood. He explained how today he overheard the mountain animals talking. He told them that the Dragon Master's youngest daughter strictly told him not to tell any of this to any other humans, otherwise his body would change into stone. As he was speaking, his body slowly began to harden, and just as he stood he turned to stone. Everyone around blinked as they watched in disbelief, then their eyes grew larger and larger. Only after witnessing this did the people believe what Hunter-Boy had said. All of the sudden, as everyone began frantically running to and fro to get away, there was a loud noise, "Ka boom!" The mountain behind them had really burst, and they could hear the sound of the rushing water crashing down toward them.

The people gazed at the stone figure of Hunter-Boy from afar as it stood firm in its place, not even the water caused it to budge. At a safe distance, everyone sobbed and cried, saying, "Hunter-Boy turned to stone for us!" From this time on, the people who were saved from the flood continue to pass the memory of Hunter-Boy on from generation to generation.

There in the Altai Mountains, standing upright next to the source of a natural spring, is a blue rock formation, and they call this spring Hunter-Boy's Spring.

THE THREE SISTERS[1]

Long ago there were three sisters who lived together with their mother in a one-room log cabin. The older sister's name was Big Turnip, the second sister's name was Carrot, and the third, or youngest, sister's name was Radish.

One day the three sisters' mother went out to see their grandmother. About halfway down the mountain road the mother ran into a Mangai. Now a Mangai is a frightfully ugly and extremely stupid mountain monster. The Mangai asked the mother some questions, like where are you going? How many children do you have? What are their names? Then after asking the questions the Mangai ate the mother.

After eating the mother the Mangai put on her clothes and went back to their home in the evening. He went up to the door and knocked, "Big Turnip, open the door." Big Turnip heard the voice and knew it wasn't their mother and refused to open the door. "Carrot, open the door." Carrot heard the voice and knew, too, that it wasn't their mother and refused to open the door. "Radish, Open the door." Little Radish heard the voice. "Momma's home!" she hollered and went running to the door and had it open before the other two girls could stop her.

The Mangai walked into the house, bong bong bong, and went in to lay down on the bed. "Big Turnip, come sleep with me." "No," said Big Turnip. "you're not my mother!" "Carrot, come sleep with me." "No," said Carrot, "you're not my mother!"

"I'll come sleep with you," called out little Radish as she jumped in bed with the Mangai.

In the middle of the night the two older sisters heard some crunching. Big turnip asked, "Momma, what are you eating?"

"I'm eating a fat radish I got from the neighbors," said the Mangai.

Then Carrot asked, "Momma, what are you eating now?"

"I'm eating a thin radish I got in the garden," said the Mangai.

"Let us have some too," the girls responded. He broke off a thumb and threw it to Big Turnip and threw a pinkie to Carrot. At this they knew that the Mangai had eaten their baby sister. They whispered to each other, "We have to get away."

The two girls stood up, and the Mangai asked, "Where are you going?"

"We are going to the outhouse," they said.

Now a Mangai is a very mean monster but also extremely stupid. He let them go.

As the girls ran out of the house, they grabbed their mother's small, wooden comb box. The two girls ran and ran as fast as they could. But after a while, the Mangai knew that they had tricked him, and he went after them.

The girls could hear him coming, bong bong bong, and even saw his shadow behind them in the light of dawn. Big Turnip stopped and opened up their mother's wooden box, took a comb out, "The comb used by my mother, become a large forest," she said and she threw it over her head toward the Mangai. The comb became a big forest and separated the girls from the monster, but he just used his big arms to sweep the trees aside and kept on chasing the girls.

Bong bong bong, the Mangai was catching up with the girls again. Big Turnip stopped and took a fine-tooth comb out of the box. "The fine-tooth comb used by my mother, become a dense forest," she said and threw the fine-tooth comb over her head. The comb became a dense forest that stopped the Mangai. But the monster swung his strong arms and used his sharp teeth to cut a way through the dense forest.

Bong bong bong, the Mangai was catching up with the girls again. Big Turnip stopped and took a small mirror out of the box. "The mirror used by my mother, become a large lake," she said and threw the mirror over her head. The mirror became a large lake, and the Mangai was stopped on the other side.

The two girls looked back over the lake at the monster, and he hollered out, "Big Turnip, Big Turnip, how did you get across to the other side?"

The Mangai is a big but dumb monster!

Big Turnip answered, "We cut open our gut and pulled out our intestines, tied a rock to it and threw it across the lake to make a bridge." "Can I get over that way?" asked the Mangai. "Yes," said Big Turnip, "hurry on across!"

The nails on a Mangai are razor sharp. He slashed open his gut and pulled out his intestines, then tied a rock to it and threw it to the other side of the lake. Just at that time a gull was flying past and saw the intestine in the lake. He dove down and bit off a piece, cutting the intestine in two. At that, the Mangai sank to the bottom of the lake and drowned.

The two girls, safe and sound, returned to their home and lived in peace. The moral of the story is that a mother's love can protect and help her children even when she is far away from them.

A STORY OF TWO FRIENDS

Once upon a time, in a small village there lived two very special personalities, one was named Beseech-No-One and the other was named Help-No-One. The two of them would never ask for help or help the other, a sort of "you live your life and I live mine" kind of attitude.

One summer day Beseech-No-One had no firewood at his home and took off, pulling his cart to the nearby mountains to chop wood. Just as he was on the way back home, one of the wooden wheels on his cart ran over a large rock and broke, making it impossible to continue. "If I don't get the wood home, we will have nothing to burn," he thought to himself, "but my cart. . . . " After thinking about the situation for quite some time, he finally had no other choice but to go to Help-No-One's house and borrow a cart. Beseech-No-One went through the door to the house and with a smile on his face said, "Hey Help-No-One, good ole buddy, we don't have any firewood at home, and I thought maybe I could borrow your cart to make one quick run. What do you think?"

Help-No-One, just to make things difficult, responded, "The cart . . . that's not a problem, but the canvas cover and the rope are all up on the roof, and there's no way to get them down. We don't have a ladder either, so I don't know how I can help you out."

After hearing this, Beseech-No-One knew that Help-No-One was not willing to let him use the cart and turned angrily to leave.

Interestingly enough, just a few days had passed when Help-No-One's well completely dried up. He took a look at his garden, and everything was beginning to wilt. At this, Help-No-One started to get real concerned. After thinking about the situation for quite some time, he finally had no other choice but to go to Beseech-No-One's house and ask to use his well so he could water his garden. Help-No-One went through the door to the house, and with a smile on his face said, "Hey Beseech-No-One, good ole buddy, my well has gone dry and my garden is wilting, so I thought maybe I could use your well to water my garden. What do you think?"

Beseech-No-One, out of spite said, "The well . . . it has a lot of water, but . . . the key to the well cover is hanging in the cellar, and neither of us has a ladder, so I don't know how I can help you out."

Help-No-One didn't get the water he needed and just left.

The moral of this little story is that if people don't help each other, humanity will not persist. Besides, there is no such person as Beseech-No-One. People cannot separate themselves from others and survive.[2]

THE REASON WHY THE FIR, CEDAR, AND RED BILBERRY BECAME EVERGREENS

Once upon a time, there was a kindly swallow who had discovered the spring of eternal life. He sipped a few drops and held them in his beak and then went out searching for a worthy human being. He flew high and low, hoping to find someone to whom he could grant eternal life and everlasting youth. However, a mean-spirited bumblebee, who knew the secret that the swallow was carrying in his bill, stung the bird in flight. The swallow uttered a groan from the pain, and the precious liquid spilled from its bill. The drops of magical liquid fell down from the sky and splashed onto the outspread leaves and branches of the fir, cedar, and red bilberry, and as a result the leaves of these three trees became forever green.

The swallow, realizing that it would not be able to grant a human being the gift of eternal life and youth, chased the bumblebee, and in its grief and anger he pulled out the bumblebee's tongue. From that day forth, the bumblebee has been unable to sing beautifully but instead is able only to utter an ugly droning noise.

THE SWALLOW AND THE WASP

Many, many years ago, the Garida Khan, who ruled over the world of feathered creatures and birds, summoned a wasp and a swallow before him in order to discover which creature possessed the tastiest and most delicious meat in the world. When they arrived, the Garida Khan immediately dispatched them on a mission around the world and told them that whoever discovered the answer first should report back to him immediately and inform him which creature had the sweetest meat. The swallow and the wasp flew away at the command of Garida Khan. On that day the weather was very fine, the sun shone brightly, and it was very warm and hot, so the swallow forgot the king's order and spent his day swooping in the blue sky, singing beautifully, bathing in the sun, and enjoying himself at ease.

However, the evil and vicious wasp spent the whole day stinging all the animals that crossed his path, and he also tasted all their hot blood as he stung them. When the sun began to set, the two creatures returned to the agreed meeting place and together they began their journey back to the Garida Khan. The swallow asked the wasp if he had managed to find out which animals' meat was the sweetest. The wasp answered that the creature with the sweetest meat was the human being. Men had the tastiest meat, and therefore their king, the Garida Khan, must always be fed human meat.

The swallow was most distressed when he heard the wasp's words, and he grieved for the fate of mankind and wondered what he could do to save all the kind human beings that he knew.

Then he asked himself, "How shall I save those poor human beings from disaster?" And he asked the wasp, "How could you taste the hot blood of living man?" The wasp answered, "Oh, that is very easy. I pierced him with my sting and tasted with my tongues," said the wasp.

Then the swallow asked, "Where is your great tongue?" And when the wasp opened its mouth and showed its tongue, saying, "This is my tongue . . . ," the swallow pecked it out. It is from that time that the wasp has not been able to sing beautifully and only makes a buzzing, droning sound.

When they arrived at the King of the Feathered Creatures and Birds court, the wasp began to complain loudly and flew around the king, buzzing with all his might, but because he had lost his tongue, nobody could make out what he was saying and what his problem was.

The king demanded to know what the wasp was saying and what kind of noise he was making and angrily complained that he could understand nothing of what the wasp was saying. In the end, he asked the swallow to explain the outcome of their quest and to tell him what creature on the Earth had the tastiest and most delicious meat. The swallow replied that it was the snake that had the sweetest and tastiest meat in the world.

The King of the Feathered World believed the swallow's words, and from that day forth he began to catch and eat snakes. Today only the hawk remains of the descendants of the Garida Khan, and this bird loves to hunt and eat snakes, just like the king.

THE GUESSING BOYS

Many moons ago, there were three orphan boys who between them possessed only one cow with a calf. The orphans were completely dependant on the cow for their sustenance. They each used to suck three of the cow's nipples, and the calf used to suck the fourth. One day, their cow went out to pasture and did not return. They waited for a day, but the cow did not return. They waited for a second day, but the cow did not return. A third day passed, and the calf died of starvation. The boys searched for their cow, but they could find no trace. Eventually they came to their *noyan*.[3] The *noyan* was cooking a shoulder of beef, and he offered to share it with them. When they began to eat it, the eldest brother said, "This is our meat." Then the second brother said, "This is a shoulder of beef." Finally, the youngest brother said, "If it is our meat and a shoulder of beef, this then is our cow's shoulder."

Then the *noyan* demanded to know how they knew it was their cow's shoulder. The brothers immediately answered, "We know, because we guessed." To which the *noyan* responded, "Are you good at guessing?"

They answered, "We can guess what we can guess." And the *noyan* retorted, "You will go outside, and we will see how good you are at guessing." And after they had gone outside, he hid some things under three china cups and turned them upside down. Then he called to the boys and told them, "Now come in!"

When they came in, the *noyan* said, "Guess what is in the first cup?" The eldest boy answered, "There is something the shape of a ball." The second boy said, "Something pure yellow." Then the youngest boy guessed, "If there is something the shape of a ball and it is colored pure yellow then it has to be a sparrow's egg." When the *noyan* turned up the cup, there was a sparrow's egg underneath.

Next the *noyan* asked what was in the middle cup. The eldest boy answered, "There is something pure red in the cup." The second brother added, "There is something very tasty in the cup." Then the youngest brother said triumphantly, "If there is something pure red and something very tasty, it must be a red plum." And the *noyan* turned up the cup to reveal a red plum.

Then the *noyan* asked, "What is there in the last cup?" The eldest boy said, "There is something round in that cup." The second boy answered, "There is something that has a square hole in the middle." Then again the youngest boy guessed, reckoning that if there were something round that had a square hole in its middle then it must surely be a brass coin.[4] Thus, all three boys had guessed all three things in the three cups. The *noyan* ordered a sheep to be killed and cooked in honor of the boys, and he commanded that his mares be milked and a *ger* be erected as a sign of respect for the three boys, and a big feast was held.

The *noyan* secretly instructed his servant to listen to what the three boys were discussing after they had been left alone and to report back his findings immediately. When the servant went and listened to the boys, they were discussing the various parts of the meal. They commented that the *airaq*[5] was the best that they had ever tasted but that it contained human blood. The meat that had been served, the boys observed, had been of excellent quality but that it had been dog's meat. Lastly they revealed that the *noyan* was one of the best men, most caring of hosts, and finest of *noyans* but that he was not in fact a Mongol but was in reality of Chinese descent.

The *noyan* was furious and immediately summoned the shepherd from whom he had purchased the sheep for that night's feast and demanded why he had sold him dog instead of sheep. The shepherd pleaded innocence and insisted that the sheep had been of the finest quality. However, he added that particular sheep they had eaten that night had been reared within the shepherd's family circle, and because the sheep's mother had died, the sheep as a lamb had been suckled at a dog's nipple.

Next the *noyan* went to his horse breeder and demanded to know if he had given him human blood in place of his order for the finest *airag*. The horseman then explained that when he had been out catching a horse with a lasso, the lasso pole ripped his hand and blood had seeped out and it had dripped into the water. It was the same water that his mares had been drinking from, and this would explain how blood had contaminated the mare's milk from which the *airag* was made.

Lastly when the *noyan* returned home that night, he confronted his mother and asked her, "What man's son am I?" Then with a sigh, his mother answered, "Your true father was a Chinese." Hearing this, the *noyan* was disappointed, but he called the three orphan boys to his *ger* and he apologized for having stolen and eaten the boys' cow. Then the *noyan* renounced his position and appointed the eldest boy as *noyan* and his two brothers as his officials, and he lived happily ever after.

HOW IT CAME ABOUT THAT THE CAMEL TUMBLES INTO THE ASHES

The Mongol 12-year calendar was assigned its animal names long ago by the Buddha. He had no problem assigning the first 11 animals, but he could not decide the animal who should represent the first year of the cycle. Both the camel and the mouse had submitted their names, and the Buddha was reluctant to chose between them for fear of upsetting one of the two. Therefore, at the Buddha's prompting, it was decided that they should resolve the issue between themselves. The animal who would represent the first year of the calendar cycle, they decided, would be the one who saw the first light of the morning sun.

Whereas the camel faced the east to await the sunrise, the mouse, climbing up onto the camel's hump, fixed his eyes steadily toward the west on a mountain top. So it was that when the time came for the appearance of the first rays of the sun and the beam fell upon the top of the western mountain, the mouse cried out that he had seen the light first and was therefore the winner. The camel became furious at losing the bet and attempted to kill the mouse by trampling him underfoot. Fearing for his life, the mouse scurried away and hid himself under a pile of ashes.

It is for this reason that whenever a camel sees a pile of ashes, he stamps his feet or lies down in order to completely flatten his detested enemy, the mouse who came to represent the first year of the calendar cycle. However, even though the camel was left out of the 12-year animal cycle, in fact it was discovered that he was present in each of the 12 years. The camel possesses characteristics of each of the 12 animals in individual body parts so that the camel in this way also became present in the cycle.

These body parts that the camel possesses are as follows:

1. The ears of a mouse.
2. The stomach of a cow.
3. The paws of a tiger.
4. The nose of a hare.
5. The body of a dragon.
6. The eyes of a snake.

7. The mane of a horse (the long hair under his neck).

8. The wool of a sheep.

9. The hump of an ape.

10. The head crest of a chicken.

11. The legs of a dog.

12. The tail of a pig.

ARSLANTAI MERGEN KHAN

Many years ago there lived a khan called Arslantai Mergen. This khan's kingdom held the belief that correct practice insisted that all horses be herded together and grouped on low ground. Among his many fine horses there were some special steeds, among them a wild chestnut horse. One day, when the khan came out to check on his horses, he found to his astonishment that they were not together in a herd on the low ground. He could not understand this because he personally checked the horses every night. His guess was that three wolves must have eaten some of his horses. So without further ado, he prepared to hunt those three wolves and bring back their heads as trophies. He chose, as his special mount for this special hunting trip, his chestnut horse, which was born of a chestnut mare.

News of the khan's expedition soon reached the ears of the three wolves, and they began to discuss strategy.

"Arslantai Mergen Khan intends to kill us by hunting us on his chestnut horse, the foal of a chestnut mare. Since it is also the foal of a young mare, we shall have to try to escape, first up to the top of a mountain, and then we should change direction quickly and run away down the mountainside, so that he can not catch up with us." The other wolves quickly agreed with him.

Next day, Arslantai Mergen Khan found the scent of the wolves and quickly gave chase after them. The wolves, as they had agreed, fled first up to the top of a mountain, and then they turned swiftly down the mountainside, and Arslantai Mergen Khan could not catch up with them.

Arslantai Mergen Khan decided to continue the hunt for the three wolves using instead his foal of a chestnut mare with a blaze of white down its nose, so he went back home to prepare for the hunt.

The wolves learned of this and said to themselves, "Arslantai Mergen Khan is getting ready to pursue us on the foal of a chestnut mare with a blaze of white down its nose. However, this foal is the foal of an old mare, so we can make good our escape by turning swiftly down the mountainside and then turning quickly up to the top of the mountain each time he tries to reach us. Then he will never be able to catch up with us, and we will escape his clutches forever." The other two wolves agreed that this plan would allow them to escape from the khan.

The next day, once again Arslantai Mergen Khan galloped after the wolves, riding on his blazed chestnut horse, which was the offspring of a blazed chestnut mare, but he was unable to catch up with the wolves because, just as they had agreed, after running away down the mountain-side they abruptly turned and sped back up to the top of the mountain.

Again Arslantai Mergen Khan went home to devise a better strategy to ensnare these scheming predatory wolves. This time, he decided to hunt them with his lean and bony wild chestnut horse. Again, the three cocky wolves heard of the khan's plans, and they laughed derisively at the thought of being chased by this old, skinny horse. They sneered at Arslantai Mergen Khan's audacity in coming after them on such a "steed." That night the wolf said to its companions, "Let's feast on that bony chestnut horse from among the herd of Arslantai Mergen Khan!" The other two wolves replied, "It would be bad for our digestion if we ate such a lean and skinny horse. Let us choose a filly mare with more flesh," but they could not agree among themselves which horse they would honor that night with their hungry teeth.

Finally, the chief wolf said to the others, "Listen, we can decide this matter later. Let us first agree where to meet. Now listen to me. First, we will meet on the shady back-top of the Altai Khangai mountain! Second, we will meet on the backside of that wild and chestnut horse! And third," the wolf continued, laughing and sneering with contempt, "we will meet on the shoulders of the Arslantai Mergen Khan!"

The next morning Arslantai Mergen Khan pursued the three wolves on his wild chestnut horse. It was not long before he caught up with them and swiftly killed all three of them. He had caught and killed them all on the back-top of the Altai mountain. Having killed the wolves, he put their skins on the back of his lean and wild chestnut horse and then returned home. At home, Arslantai Mergen Khan fashioned a jacket for himself from the wolf-skins. From that day forth, both the khan and his steed wore their coats made from the skins of the three wolves.

So it came to pass that those three wolves had in fact spoken the truth and had correctly foreseen the future. For they truly met each other on the three occasions they had mentioned, namely, on the back of the Altai mountain, on the rump of the poor wild chestnut horse, and around the shoulders of Arslantai Mergen Khan!

NOTES

1. "The Three Sisters" is a story from the Daur minority. The storyteller was Audeng, and told in 1996 at Hohhot, Inner Mongolia.

2. The stories quoted previously have been translated by Todd Cornell for CultureEvolution (http://www.ezlink.com/~culturev/CulturMythology.htm). Permission was sought but no reply received. However the stories appear on other sites without restrictions: http://www.gwinnett.k12.ga.us/PinckneyvilleMS/Media/B_MG_E_G/MediafestivalHOME.htm and http://drlee.org/mongolia/mythology.html#center.

3. A *noyan* is a lord, noble, general.

4. Thirteenth-century Mongolian coins were round with a square central hole.

5. *Airaq* is the finest distilled kumiss.

APPENDIX A

Years According to the Animal Cycle: 1168–1371

RAT	1168	1180	1192	1204	1216	1228	1240	1252
OX	1169	1181	1193	1205	1217	1229	1241	1253
TIGER	1170	1182	1194	1206	1218	1230	1242	1254
HARE	1171	1183	1195	1207	1219	1231	1243	1255
DRAGON	1172	1184	1196	1208	1220	1232	1244	1256
SNAKE	1173	1185	1197	1209	1221	1231	1245	1257
HORSE	1174	1186	1198	1210	1222	1234	1246	1258
SHEEP	1175	1187	1199	1211	1223	1235	1247	1259
MONKEY	1176	1188	1200	1212	1224	1236	1248	1260
HEN	1177	1189	1201	1213	1225	1237	1249	1261
DOG	1178	1190	1202	1214	1226	1238	1250	1262
PIG	1179	1191	1203	1215	1227	1239	1251	1263

RAT	1264	1276	1288	1300	1312	1324	1336	1348	1360
OX	1265	1271	1289	1301	1313	1325	1337	1349	1361
TIGER	1266	1278	1290	1302	1314	1326	1338	1350	1362
HARE	1267	1279	1291	1303	1315	1327	1339	1351	1363
DRAGON	1268	1280	1292	1304	1316	1328	1340	1352	1364
SNAKE	1269	1281	1293	1305	1317	1329	1341	1353	1365
HORSE	1270	1282	1294	1306	1318	1330	1342	1354	1366
SHEEP	1271	1283	1295	1307	1319	1331	1343	1255	1367
MONKEY	1272	1284	1296	1308	1320	1332	1344	1356	1368
HEN	1273	1285	1297	1309	1321	1333	1345	1357	1369
DOG	1274	1286	1298	1310	1322	1334	1346	1358	1370
PIG	1275	1287	1299	1311	1323	1235	1247	1259	1371

APPENDIX: PERSONAGES

Abish Khātūn	r.1263–82	Ruled Shiraz; married Möngke Temür son of Hülegü
Abū Saʿīd	r.1316–35	Last Il-Khan of Iran; son of Ghazan
Ahmad Tegudar, Sultan	r.1282–84	Son of Hülegü; third Il-Khan of Iran
Alans		Persian speaking semi-nomadic people from the north Caucasus, ancestors of Ossetians
Arghun Aqa	d.1273	Mongol administrator of Iran; governor of Khorasan
Arghun Khan	r.1284–91	Il-Khan of Iran, son of Abaqa, grandson of Hülegü
Arigh Böqa	d.1266	Youngest son of Möngke Khan; rival of Qubilai Khan
Ascelin, Lombard	1247–48	Dominican envoy who encounted Baiju
Baidu	d.1295	Il-Khan for six chaotic months, killed by Ghazan
Baiju/ Baichu	1228–1259	Military commander of western Asia for Batu
Bar Hebraeus	1226–86	Christian historian from Syria/Anatolia
Batu Khan	d.1255	Founder & ruler of Golden Horde
Baybars, Sultan	d.1277	Mamluk Sultan of Egypt; with Qutuz victor of 'Ayn Jālūt [1260]
Berke Khan	r.1256–66	Brother of Batu, ruler of Golden Horde

(*Continued*)

Bolad Aqa	c.1240–1313	Mongol administrator, envoy; ambassador to Iran from China. Married former concubine of Abaqa
Börte		First wife of Temüjin, mother of Batu etc.
Bujir	1206–1260	Mongol Successor administrator to Mahmūd Yalavač
Carpini, Giovanni de Plano	1245–47	Papal emissary to the Mongols
Ch'ang-Ch'un	1148–1227	Spiritual advisor to Chinggis Khan
Chin		Jurchen dynasty ruling northern China defeated by Chinggis c.1215
Cumans/Pecheneg/Qipchaq		Turkic people from western Eurasian steppes
Dokuz Khātūn	d.1265	Wife of Tolui Khan, then primary wife of Hülegü Khan
Ghazan Khan	r.1295–1304	Proclaimed Mongol Iran, Muslim.
Gog and Magog		Biblical enemies of God; in Ezekiel Gog is the ruler of the land of Magog, while in Revelations Gog and Magog are nations that are under Satan's rule. Mongols thought to be their emissaries.
Grigor of Akanc'	d. circa 1275	Armenian cleric and Historian
Güyük Khan	r.1246–49	3rd Great Khan, son of Ögödei
Het'um, King	1224–68	King of Armenian Cilicia, Lesser Armenia, staunch ally of the Mongols
Ho'elün		Chinggis's mother
Hsi-hsia aka Tangut		Originally Tibetan semi-nomadic trading tribe. Victims of Chinggis's last campaign.
Hu Szu-hui	Presented book, 1330	Author of *Yin-shan cheng-yao* [*Proper and Essential Things for the Emperor's Food and Drink*]
Ibn Batutta	1304–69	Traveller from Tangiers, journeys 1325–54
Jebe Noyan	d.1224	One of four 'Hounds of War'. 1221–4 epic reconnaissance trip.
Juwaynī, ᶜAṭa Malik	d.1282	Historian, Ilkhanid governor of Baghdad
Juwaynī, Shams al-Dīn	d.1280	Grand Vizier under Hülegü and Abaqa Khan
Jūzjānī, Minhāj al-Dīn	d.1260	Anti-Mongol historian from Delhi Sultanate
Kart, Shams al-Dīn	d.1278	Founder of Kart dynasty of Herat; 1245–1389

(Continued)

Kereits		Turco-Mongol tribe among whom were many Nestorian Christians.
Ket-Buqa	d.1260	Mongol general, Nestorian, killed by Mamluks after defeat at 'Ayn Jālūt.
Khwārazmshāh, Jalāl al-Dīn Mingbirdi	d.1231 [?]	Killed murdered for his clothes by Kurdish bandits who did not realise who he was.
Khwārazmshāh, Sultan Mohammad	d.1221	Hunted by the Noyens Jebe and Subodei, he died of pleurisy on the island of Abeskum
Kirakos	1200–72	Armenian historian and cleric
Mahmūd Yalavač	d.1254	Merchant and top administrator for Mongols
Mamluks	1250–1517	Rulers of Egypt and Syria
Marco Polo	1254–1324	VenetianTraveller and official of the Yuan dynasty under Qubilai.
Mar Yaballaha	1245–1317	Nestorian monk who travelled from China to Europe, later Patriarch of Nestorian Church in Tabriz [1281–1317]
Mas'ud Beg	d.1289	Son of Mahmūd Yalavač. Top administrator
Merkits		Turco-Mongol tribe
Möngke Khan	r.1251–1258	4th Great Khan, son of Tolui
Möngke Temür	1256–82	Son of Hülegü; ruled Shiraz with Abish Khātūn
Musta'şim, Caliph	r.1242–58	Caliph in Baghdad until executed by Hülegü.
Mustawfī Qazvīnī, Hamdallah	1282–1344	historian, geographer, government tax official, and notable
Naiman		Turco-Mongol tribe
Nestorians		Eastern Christians, who follow the teachings of Nestorius, archbishop of Constantinople.
Noghai Khan	d.1300	Rival of Toqta fror Golden Horde; founded Noghai Khanate in Dubrudja
Oderic of Pordenone, Friar	1286–1331	Cleric, traveller in Far East 1316–1330
Oghul-Qaimish Khātūn	r.1248–51	Ruled empire as Güyük's widow
Ögödei Khan, Qaqan	r.1227–41	Successor to father Chinggis Khan
Ong Khan/ Toghril	d.1203	Ruler of Kereyit tribe, early ally, *anda* of Yisugei
Orda	d.1206	Batu Khan's elder brother, khan of White Horde

(Continued)

Pādeshāh Khātūn	r.1292–95	Queen of Kirman, wife of Abaqa Khan.
Paris, Matthew	1200?–1259	English chronicler and monk.
Qaidu Khan	1236–1303	Mongol traditionalist, ruled Turkistan for Ögödeids until his death.
Qara-Khitai		Descendants of semi-nomadic Turko-Mongol Khitans from northern China who settled in Turkistan from 1120 until advent of the Mongols
Qipchaq/ Kipchak/ Cumans/ Pecheneg		Turkic people from western Eurasian steppes
Qubilai Khan	r.1260–1294	
Qutulun bint Qaidu	After 1303	Daughter of Qaidu Khan, famous for her military prowess.
Qutuz, Sultan	d.1260	Mamluk Sultan of Egypt; victor of ʿAyn Jālūt
Rabban Sauma	1225–94	Chinese Nestorian who travelled to Europe
Rashīd al-Dīn	d.1318	Historian, Ilkhanid prime minister
Rūmī, Jalāl al-Dīn	1207–1273	Sufi poet from Turkistan who settled in Anatolia [Rum].
Shiremün	d.1258	Grandson of Ögödei, executed by Qubilai
Sorghaghtani Beki	d.1252	Chief wife of Tolui, mother of Möngke Khan
Subodai Bahadur Noyan	1176–1248	One of four 'Hounds of War'. 1221–4 epic reconnaissance trip.
Süldüs		Turco-Mongol tribe, sheltered Temüjin from Tayichi'ut
Sung/Song		Chinese dynasty ruling southern China until final defeat by Qubilai in 1279. Capital in Hangzhou.
Suqunjaq Noyan	d.1290	General from the Süldüs tribe, governor of Shiraz in 1280s
Tangut aka Hsi-hsia		Originally Tibetan semi-nomadic trading tribe. Victims of Chinggis's last campaign.
Tatars		Turco-Mongol tribe, killers of Temüjin's father.
Tayichi'ut		Turco-Mongol tribe, early enemy of Temüjin
Teb Tenggeri	d.c.1206	Chief shaman, killed after challenging Chinggis.
Tegudar Ahmad, Sultan	r.1282–84	Son of Hülegü; third Il-Khan of Iran
Temüjin	1167–1227	Became Chinggis Khan in 1206

(Continued)

Temür Öljeitü	r.1294–1307	Yuan Great Khan, grandson of Qubilai
Tenggeri		Heaven, Mongols' sky God
Terkan Khātūn of Kerman,	r.1257–1283	Queen of Kirman, titled 'Qutlugh'
Terkan Khātūn of Shiraz	d.1283	Would-be ruler of Shiraz, murdered by her husband
Töde Möngke	r.1280–87	Ruler of Golden Horde when Turkish officially replaced Mongolian.
Toghrul aka Ong-Khan or Wang-Khan	d.1203	Leader of Kereits and Temüjin's powerful protector
Tolui Khan	d.1232	Youngest son of Chinggis and Börte
Toqta Khan	r.1291–1312	Khan of the Golden Horde
Töregene Khātūn	d.1246	Wife of Ögödei; regent 1241–46
Ṭūsī, Naṣīr al-Dīn	1201–74	Philosopher, scientist, advisor to Hülegü
Uyghurs		Turkic people today living in Xinjiang Province of western China. Early allies of Mongols active in administration.
Vanakan	d.1251	Armenian cleric and historian
Waṣṣāf	d. (circa) 1330	Historian, administrator in Shiraz, history covers 1257–1328
William of Rubruck	d.1266?	Papal emissary to Mongols 1253–55
Yesügei	d.1174	Father of Chinggis Khan, poisoned by Tatars.

GLOSSARY

ᶜ**Abbāsids** A dynasty of Islamic sultans ruling from Iraq and Baghdad, 750–1258 (1517, in Cairo).

Abu, Abū "Father of ...," often used as main form of address. Compare bin, ibn (son of ...).

Alamūt Headquarters of Nizārī Ismāᶜīlīs, north of Qazvin. This castle was destroyed by Hülegü in 1256.

ᶜ**Alids** Followers of the Imam 'Alī; Shi'ites.

anda "Brother-by-oath," sealed with blood. A strong pact made between Mongol friends vowing loyalty and support.

appanage Land or other provision granted by a king for the support of a member of the royal family.

aqa Elder brother with the connotation of senior prince. *Aqa* and *ini*, all the family including elder and younger brothers or, by implication, princes.

aqa Title for noble (e.g., Arghun Aqa).

arbans Ten men.

atabeg Local ruler. Originally this term denoted the personal tutor and guardian of a royal prince.

autarkic Economic self-sufficiency.

Ayyubids Kurdish sultans who ruled in Syria and Iraq and who dominated the Islamic world between 1169 and 1260. Saladin (Salāḥ al-Dīn, d. 1193) is the most famous of the Ayyubids for his seizure of Jerusalem and his final defeat of the Fatimids as well as his justice and wisdom.

Bahadur Hero, brave warrior; often given as a title.

baksi Lama, Buddhist priest, sage.

basqaq Overseer appointed by the Great Khan, or Il-Khan, to oversee the provincial administrations. *Basqaq* (Turkish), also *darugha, darughachi* (Mongol), *shaḥna* (Arabo-Persian).

bāṭin Esoteric interpretation of Islam.

B.C.E. Before the common era; a religiously neutral alternative to B.C., now growing in usage, especially in academic publications.

beg Tribal leader, prince (Turkish), lord.

bilig Saying, maxim; especially, *biligs* of Chinggis Khan.

bin, ibn, b "Son of . . .," often written *b.*

bint, bt "Daughter of . . .," often written *bt.* (e.g., Abish Khātūn bint Terkān Khātūn).

bocca/boghta Large headdress worn by Mongol ladies.

böge Shaman.

bökä'ül Court taster, officer in charge of army provisions.

bulqaq Disturbance, chaos, confusion.

C.E. Common era; a religiously neutral alternative to A.D., now growing in usage, especially in academic publications.

cangue Wooden implement of punishment and restraint that traps the hands and head in a vice.

catholicos Head of the Nestorian Church.

ch'ao Chinese paper money used also in Il-Khanate in 1290s.

ching-chi-jen Branded police informer.

Chinggisid Related to the House of Chinggis Khan and his descendants.

Chung-shu-sheng—Secretarial council under the Yüan dynasty.

dānishmand—Learned scholar, though often used to mean Muslim cleric.

Dar al-Ḥarb "Abode of war." All territory not under Islamic law.

Dar al-Islam "Abode of Islam." All lands under Islamic law.

darugha, darughachi See *basqaq*.

Dīwān, Dargāh The royal court (Persian).

elchi, ilchi Envoy, ambassador, representative.

emir, amir Noble, lord, or prince. A title of Arabic and Persian origin.

emir/amir al-umarā Commander in chief.

farr Persian term meaning "majesty," "nobility."

farsang, parsang, farsakh 6.42 kilometers.

fatwa Islamic legal ruling.

fida'i Islamic warrior, holy warrior, ghazi.

ger Yurt; tent made with cloth and a wooden frame as support.

ghazi Fida'i, holy Islamic warrior, fighter who has declared war on infidels.

ghulām Slave. See Mamluk.

Ghurids Afghan dynasty ruling central and eastern Afghanistan, Ghur, from 1011 to 1215.

Gog and Magog Devils who at the end of time will wage war on the Christian church but who will finally be destroyed by the forces of God (Revelation 20:8–10); a prince and the land from which he comes to attack Israel (Ezekiel 38).

Golden Horde The Mongol *ulus* founded by Batu, based in Russia, Ukraine, Eastern Europe.

Great Saljuqs Turkish dynasty ruling in Persia.

gurkhan Title, leader of a clan or tribe.

harban Ten men.

haran Commoners.

hsien Basic judicial unit.

hsien-yin Magistrate.

Hsing Chung-shu-sheng Regional secretarial council under the Yüan dynasty.

il, el Turco-Mongol for "friendly," "at peace," "submissive," as opposed to **bulgha,** "at war," "rebellious."

īlchi Messenger, representative.

Il-Khanate, Il-Khan The Mongol kingdom in western Asia comprising Iran, Afghanistan, Iraq, eastern Turkey, and the southern Caucasus. The kings were called Il-Khans. Founded by Hülegü circa 1258.

ini Younger brother or prince. **Aqa** and *ini*, all the family including elder and younger brothers or, by implication, princes.

inju Mongol crown lands.

iqṭā Assignment of land or its revenue.

Iran/Persia These terms are often used interchangeably. The Persian Empire, centered traditionally in Fars/Pars province with its capital in the vicinity of modern Shiraz, has in its history encompassed Afghanistan, central Asia, Anatolia, Mesopotamia, and modern Iran. Iran, or more correctly *Iranzamin*, usually referred to the lands of the Iranian plateau and Afghanistan, that is, those lands south of the Oxus River facing Turan, the land of the Turk.

Ismāᶜīlī Sevener Shi'ites, Fatimids of North Africa, Assassins of Iran and Syria. Also known as 7ers.

Itügen Earth; the earth goddess.

jagun One hundred men.

jihād, jihadist Jihad means "holy war" and is understood to be either the great jihad, in which evil is confronted within the believer's heart, or the lesser jihad, war against those who would oppress Muslims or occupy their lands. Jihadists are those who believe in perpetual holy war against the infidel. It is a term adapted by followers of militant Islam, such as Osama bin Laden.

Jochids Supporters and descendants of Jochi, eldest son of Chinggis Khan, and Batu, who founded the Golden Horde.

Jurchen Seminomadic tribe that founded the Chin (gold) dynasty of northern China.

keshig Imperial guard.

Kereits Turco-Mongol tribe, many of whom were Nestorian Christians of Turkic origin.

Khan, the Great Khan, Qa'an Lord, noble, also a title (e.g., Chinggis Khan). The Great Khan, or Qa'an, was the ruling khan, or emperor, of the Mongol Empire.

khānaqāh, khāngāh Hospices, retreats, or monasteries for Sufis, sometimes open to the public.

khātūn Lady; title given to a woman of noble birth.

khilᶜat Robe of Honor.

Khorasan Province of northeastern Greater Iran.

khuṭba The Friday sermon given by the head Imam of the mosque. It was very important because blessings were traditionally invoked for the current ruler, thus any changes in regime or dynasty would be announced in the Friday *khuṭba.*

koumiss, kumiss, *qumis, airag.* Alcoholic drink fermented from mare's milk, very popular with the Mongols.

kung-shou Archers, that is, Yüan police officers.

malik Local king or ruler.

Mamluk (*ghulām***)** A slave soldier. Mamluks were often captured as children during battles or raids on central Asian, Caucasian, Anatolian, and African territory and brought up in military camps as Muslims and soldiers. The Mamluks were the ruling elite of Egypt from 1250 to 1517. Their armies defeated the Mongols in 1261 at 'Ain Jālūt.

mangonel War engine used to throw stones and rocks; giant catapult.

Manichaeans Mani was born in 216 c.e. St. Augustine was a follower before his conversion. From his home in southeastern Iran, Mani traveled extensively and gained many followers. He considered the quest for truth the essence of all religion and saw the universe as a cosmic battlefield between good and evil. He recognized the role of all the great religious figures.

maphrian Armenian patriarch, elder of the Church.

Merkits Powerful Mongol tribe, and early enemies of Temüjin; lived south of Lake Baikal. Hunters and fishermen.

minbar Pulpit for the reading of the Friday *khuṭba,* or sermon.

minghan One thousand men.

Moguls Descendants of Timurlane, who claimed Mongol heritage. They ruled India until the advent of the British.

mustawfī Revenue accountant.

naccara Mongol war drums.

Naimans Turco-Mongol tribe of steppe nomads, mainly Buddhist but also Nestorian Christians.

nasij Gold and silk brocade and embroidery.

nerge The elaborate hunt of the Mongols that served also as military training.

Nestorian Christianity Eastern Christian church with followers in China, central Asia, and among the Mongols. Followers believed that Christ was two distinct persons, divine and human, implying a denial that the Virgin Mary was the mother of God.

noker, nöker, nökhöd (pl.) Ally, close friend; later it came to imply follower. Used in Mongolian, Turkish, and Persian, hence the variety of spellings.

noyan Mongol general or noble.

nur/nuur Lake (Turco-Mongol).

oghul Turkish for "son," applied as a title to Mongol princes of the blood.

Oirats Forest Turco-Mongol tribe of hunters and fishermen; shamanists.

ongghot Images of family ancestors retained within the tent home for worship.

ordu Mongol camp.

ortaq Merchant in partnership with a prince or high official and operating with the latter's money.

pādeshāh Persian king.

paiza Chinese *p'ai tzū*, a kind of laissez-passer, Marco Polo's "tablet of authority"; facilitated travel and ensured favorable treatment.

parsang/farsang 6.42 kilometers, a league less 3 miles.

paykān Relay runners.

Pervāna Mongol appointed governor of Sultanate of Rum.

Prester John A legend that grew among the crusader states of an eastern Christian king who would come from the east and defeat the Muslim sultanates on the way to rescue the besieged crusader states of Palestine.

Qa'an The Great Khan; often used alone with reference to Ögödei.

qādī Islamic judge.

qalandar Wandering dervish.

qanat Underground canal system still operating in Iran and Afghanistan.

Qipchaqs (Kipchaks), Cumans, Polovtsy A loosely organized Turkic tribal confederation that by the mid-eleventh century occupied a vast, sprawling territory in the Eurasian steppe, stretching from north of the Aral Sea westward to the region north of the Black Sea.

qïshlaqs Winter camps.

qubchur Mongol all-purpose tax, poll-tax.

qumis, **koumiss** Alcoholic drink fermented from mare's milk, very popular with the Mongols.

quriltai A Mongol assembly of khans, princes, and nobles.

Rasadkhana The observatory at Maragheh, northwestern Iran, built by Hülegü for Ṭūsī.

Rum Anatolia, modern-day Turkey.

ṣāḥib dīwān Chief minister, prime minister, grand vizier.

Saladin (Salāḥ al-Dīn) Born Ayyūb (1137–93); retook Jerusalem from the crusader armies in 1187 c.e.

Saljuqs Turkish dynasties ruling in Rum, Iran, and central Asia, from 1055.

Samanids Persian dynasty ruling eastern Persia, 819–1005.

Saracen Term commonly used in Christian sources to mean Muslim.

shaḥna Overseer; also *basqaq* (Turkish), *darugha* (Mongol), *shaḥna* (Arabo-Persian).

shaman Steppe holy man and divinator; *böge.*

shao mai yin Funeral expenses.

Shi'ism, Shi'a, Shi'ite A major branch of Islam that recognizes 12 holy Imams descending from ᶜAlī and the Prophet's daughter Fatima. Also called 12ers.

Sinicize To manifest the influence and infiltration of Chinese culture.

ssu-yü Police commissioner.

steppe and sown, or settled A term used to contrast nomads from the steppe lands with their settled, urbanized, or agriculturalist neighbors.

Sufi, Sufism Sufism is the mystical branch of Islam that blossomed under the Il-Khans in particular.

Sunnism, Sunni, Sunnite The branch of Islam practiced by the majority of the world's Muslims.

supratribal polity An amalgamation or federation of tribes working toward a common objective.

talio, talion The system or legal principle of making the punishment correspond to the crime (Latin); retaliation.

al-tamgha A vermillion seal of authentication attached to documents by the Mongols.

tamma **system** An army of contingents allotted from the total available Mongol manpower whose aim was to maintain and extend Mongol rule in conquered territory.

tangsuq Novelty, rarity, precious object (Turco-Mongolian).

tanistry System of succession whereby the leadership goes to the most powerful.

Taoism, Daoism Teachings based on Dao De Jing and Zhuang Zi (circa 300 b.c.e.), celebrating the merits of inaction and mysticism and contemplation.

taqiyya Dissimulation, or the option to deny their religion and true beliefs should they feel themselves in danger.

Tatar, Tartar Strictly speaking the Tatars are one of the Mongol tribes. However, Tatar, meaning Mongol, has been commonly used in European and western Asian sources since the founding of Chinggis Khan's empire.

Ta-tu Beijing; "Great Capital" in Chinese, Khanbaliq (City of the Khan) in Turkish, and Daidu/Dadu for the Mongols.

Tenggeri Heaven; the universal sky god.

Tenggerism or Heavenism Development of the Mongols' basic religious beliefs.

tigishmishi Ceremony of presenting gifts to the ruler.

tulughma Military tactic of encirclement and frontal, shielded attack.

Toluid Supporters and descendants of Tului, youngest son of Chinggis Khan.

tümen Ten thousand.

Turan Traditionally the lands of Turkistan north of the Oxus River (Amū Darya) facing Iran, the lands of Persia south of this once mighty river.

Turkistan The lands of central Asia including Xinjiang Province in western China, most of whose people speak Turkic languages.

tz'u-tzu Tattooing with a stylus; branding.

Uighur/Uygur A Turkic tribe from the area of Turkistan today known as Xinjiang in the far west of China. Mainly Muslim, the Uighur were early allies of the Mongols and held important administrative positions throughout the empire. The Uighur script was used to write Mongolian.

culamā' (**sing.** *cālim*) Religious classes, Islamic scholars.

ultimogeniture/primogeniture Rights of the last born/first born.

ulus Allotment of people and tribes granted to Mongol princes.

'urfī Customary law.

waqf Islamic endowment.

wazir, vizier Government minister, top adviser.

wu hsing Five traditional forms of Chinese punishment: strangulation or decapitation, life exile, imprisonment, beating with a heavy stick, beating with a light stick.

yam The Mongol postal system, comprising relay stations equipped with food, accommodation, and horses.

yarghu, yarghuchi Mongol court of interrogation and its officials.

yarligh Mongol edict, legal ruling.

yasa Traditional Mongol laws.

yaylaqs Summer camps.

yurt. *Ger;* tent made with material, often felt, with a wooden frame support.

Primary Sources and those Available in Translation

Altangerei, Damdinsurengyn, trans., Choi Luvsanjav and Robert Travers, eds. 1988. *How Did the Great Bear Originate? Folktales from Mongolia.* Ulaanbaatar, Mongolia: State Publishing House.

Anonymous. 1976. *Tārīkh-i Shāhī,* ed. Ibrāhīm Bāstānī. Tehran: Inteshārāt Banīād Farhang, Iran.

Āyātī, 'Abdul Moḥammad, ed. 1993. *Taḥrīr-e Tārīkh-i Waṣṣāf.* Tehran: Ministry of Culture and Education. This is an abridged and edited version of Waṣṣāf's virtually unreadable history. Even Iranians find Waṣṣāf extremely difficult to read. This excellent book makes Waṣṣāf accessible to those with a reasonable level of Persian.

Bar Hebraeus, Gregorius. 2003. *The Chronography of Gregory Abu'l-Faraj Bar Hebraeus' Political History of the World, Part I,* trans. Ernest A. Wallis-Budge. Piscataway, N.J.: Gorgias Press.

———. 1932. *The Chronography of Gregory Abu'l-Faraj Bar Hebraeus' Political History of the World, Part I,* trans. Ernest A. Wallis-Budge. London: Oxford University Press.

This Christian bishop had access to Naṣīr al-Dīn Ṭūsī's remarkable library in Maragheh and was witness to many of the events that took place in eastern Turkey, Syria, and Iranian Azerbaijan. In many ways his history is a relatively impartial account of his times.

———. [1897] 1976. *The Laughable Stories,* trans. E. A. Wallis-Budge. 1897. Reprint, New York: AMS Press. Bar Hebraeus collected stories, anecdotes, and maxims from all over the Mongol empire and beyond. Having access to the libraries and the international scholars who flocked to the Mongol capital, he was in a unique position to amass this intriguing collection of tales. They give a vivid picture of the medieval world.

Bar Hebraeus, Gregory. 1993. *Ethicon,* trans. Herman Teule. Vol. 2. Louvain, Belgium: E. Peeters. This book reveals another, spiritual side to Bar Hebraeus.

Bedrosian, Robert. (n.d.). *Sources for the Armenian Tradition.* Available at: http://rbedrosian.com/kg1.htm. Robert Bedrosian studied medieval Armenian history at university in the 1970s and was awarded a doctorate for his study of the lords of Armenia and their relationship with invaders from the east, namely the Turks and the Mongols. Since gaining his doctorate, Bedrosian has veered sharply away from history and entered more lucrative waters. However, in recent years, much to the enduring gratitude of medieval scholars of the Middle East and the Mongols in particular, he has resumed his interest in history and has made available in hard copy and on the Internet his translations of medieval Armenian texts. These include Kirakos's history, Grigor of Akanc's *History of the Nation of Archers,* Het'um's *Flowers of History,* Sabeos's history, T'ovma Metsobets'i's *History of Tamerlane and His Successors, The Chronicle of Smbat Sparapet, The Georgian Chronicle,* and other early texts covering the period before the Mongol invasion. Though he does not claim his translations attain the highest standard of scholarship, they are very readable and immensely valuable contributions to our field of academic research. For many years these Armenian texts have been virtually inaccessible to most scholars interested in the Mongol period because few had mastered Armenian, let alone medieval Armenian, and the only translations available were long out of print and available in very few libraries. Robert Bedrosian fully deserves the gratitude that so many scholars have expressed for making freely available the fruit of so many years of hard work and research on the Internet for anyone to easily browse and enjoy at no cost.

Bretschneider, E. [1910] 1967. *Mediaeval Researches from Eastern Asiatic Sources.* Vol. 2. Reprint, London: Routledge & Kegan Paul. This provides the English reader access to many valuable primary sources from China and East Asia that would otherwise be completely unavailable. It includes extracts from the Yuan Shih.

Brosset, Marie, trans. 1969. *Histoire de la Georgie* [The Georgian Chronicle], St. Petersburg: Académie des Sciences 1849–58. This is a French translation of another important Caucasian text, and it contains firsthand descriptions of the events and relations between the Mongols and the Georgians and Armenians.

Buell, Paul D., and Eugene N. Anderson. 2000. *A Soup for the Qan.* London: Kegan Paul. This is an absorbing, fascinating, and practical guide to the culinary practices and delights of Mongol cuisine during the Yüan period. As well as translating the medieval text of the Uyghur cook Hu Szu-hui, Buell and Anderson have provided a scholarly analysis of the text and provided a wealth of background material about the Mongols and their empire. This is a book not to be missed.

Carpini, Giovanni DiPlano. 1996. *The Story of the Mongols Whom We Call the Tartars: Historia Mongalorum,* trans. Erik Hildinger. Boston: Branden. This is a new translation of the journey of the thirteenth-century mission to the Mongols undertaken by the papal envoy, though some would say spy, Friar Giovanni DiPlano Carpini. It provides a vivid, firsthand account of the Mongols in Russia and of the court of the Great Khan Güyük. The longer quotations in this book are taken from an earlier edition translated and annotated by W. W. Rockhill. *The Journey of William of Rubruck to the Eastern Parts of the World, 1235–55, as narrated by himself, with two accounts of the earlier journey of John of Pian de Carpine* (London: Hakluyt Society, 1900).

Cleaves, Francis Woodman, trans. 1956. "The Biography of Bayan of the Barin in the Yuan Shih." *Harvard Journal of Asiatic Studies* 19 (3/4): 185–303.

Clavijo, Ruy Gonzalez de Clavijo. 1928. *Clavijo. Embassy to Tamerlane 1403–1406,* trans Guy Le Strange. New York and London: Harper. Available on the Internet http://depts.washington.edu/uwch/silkroad/texts/clavijo/cltxt1.html. This is a fascinating and vivid description by a European envoy of the lands of the Middle East and the Far East after the Mongols had fallen from power. However, it is revealing in that it reports people's attitudes to the Mongols with the hindsight of history.

Dawson, Christopher, ed. 1955. *The Mongol Mission,* trans. by a nun of Stanbrook Abbey. London: Sheed & Ward. This collection contains an older translation of the journey of the thirteenth-century mission to the Mongols undertaken by the papal envoy, though some would say spy, Friar Giovanni DiPlano Carpini. It provides a vivid, firsthand account of the Mongols in Russia and of the court of the Great Khan Güyük. Also included are William of Rubruck's account and other narratives and letters of the Franciscan missionaries in Mongolia and China in the thirteenth and fourteenth centuries.

Daya, Najm al-Din Razi. 1982. *The Path of God's Bondsmen from Origin to Return,* trans. Hamid Algar. Delmar, N.Y.: Caravan Books. Daya was an Iranian Sufi poet who witnessed the initial occupation of Iran and eastern Anatolia by the Mongols and the anarchy that prevailed until the advent of Hülegü Khan in 1254.

de Somogyi, Joseph. 1933–35. "A Qasida on the Destruction of Baghdad." *Bulletin of the School of Oriental and African Studies* 2: 41–48 This poem is a thirteenth-century description of the destruction of Baghdad by someone not very sympathetic to the Mongol cause.

Fakhru'd-Din Iraqi. 1939. *The Song of Lovers: 'Ushshaq-nama,* trans. Arthur Arberry. Islamic Research Association, no. 8. Oxford: Oxford University Press. Iraqi was a Sufi poet of the Il-Khanid period and a friend of the Juwaynīs and other powerful figures of the time.

Gold, Milton, trans. 1976. *Malik al-Shu'ara' Bihar: The Tarikh-e Sistan.* Persian Heritage Series. Tehran, Iran: Istituto Italiano Per Il Medio Ed Estremo Oriente and The Royal Institute of Translation and Publication of Iran. This history of Sistan (S. E. Iran) is an example of a local history composed by contemporaries. It includes the Mongol period.

Grigor of Akanc'. 1954. *History of the Nation of Archers,* trans. R. Blake and R. Frye. Cambridge: Harvard University Press. The Armenian cleric Grigor gives a vivid and fascinating picture of the Mongols (the Archers), much of it from firsthand knowledge. His history extends to the rule of Abaqa Khan (1265–82).

Ḥamdallāh Mustawfī Qazvīnī. 1919. *Nuzhat al-Qulub,* trans. G. Le Strange. Leiden, Netherlands: Brill & Luzac. (see also under Mustawfī) Mustawfī, a government financial administrator, lived toward the end of the Il-Khanid period. This geographical account of Iran, Afghanistan, and northeastern Turkey is rich in detail and economic, social, and commercial data.

———. 2000. *Nuzhat al-Qulūb,* eds. M. Dabīrsyāghī and Nashr Hadis. Qazvin: al-Hādī Publishers. This is a new edition with an up-to-date introduction in Persian. It does not contain the chapters dealing with the countries outside of Iran and the Arab world.

———. 1913. *Tarikh-i-Guzida: The Select History,* trans. Edward G. Browne. London: Luzac. Printed for the trustees of the E.J.W. Gibb Memorial. This translation is an abridged, summarized version of the original text.

Hetoum. 1988. *A Lytell Cronycle,* ed. Glenn Burger, trans. R. Bedrosian. Toronto: University of Toronto Press. Available at: *History of the Tartars (The Flower of Histories of the East),* http://rbedrosian.com/hetumint.htm. Another Armenian text, here translated into medieval English. Hetoum was very much pro-Mongol, and his account gives a different view of the Mongol conquests.

Hu Szu-hui. 2000. *Yin-shan cheng-yao* [Proper and essential things for the emperor's food and drink] trans. Paul D. Buell and Eugene N. Anderson. A "Soup for the Qan" See under Buell.

Ibn 'Abd al-Zahir, al-Qadi Muhi al-Din, ed. 1956. *Baybars I of Egypt: al-Rawd al-Zahir fi Sirat al-Malik al-Zahir,* trans. Syedah Fatima Sadeque. Dacca, East Pakistan: Paramount Press. This biography of the Mamluk leader, who was the only serious challenge to the Mongols in the thirteenth century, gives a unique view of the Mongols from Egypt.

Ibn Battuta. 1983. *Travels in Asia and Africa 1325–1354,* London: Routledge & Kegan Paul.

———. 1999. *The Travels of Ibn Battuta* A.D. *1325–1354,* trans. H.A.R. Gibb. Vols. 1–3. New Delhi: Munsharim. Born in Tangier in 1304, Ibn Battuta traveled from North Africa to the Middle East, where he performed the hajj, and on to Turkey, Iran, and through central Asia to China. He is estimated to have covered some 75,000 miles between 1324 and 1354 and left the world a remarkable account of his adventures in the medieval world.

Ibn al-Fuwaṭī, Kamāl al-Dīn Abū al-Fazl. 1932. *al-Hawādith al-Jāmī'a wa'l-Tajārib al-nāfi'a fī'l-mī'a al-sābī'a.* Baghdad: Carmel Press.

Ibn Isfandiyar. 1905. *Ibn Isfandiyar's History of Tabaristan,* trans. Edward G. Browne. Leiden, Netherlands: E.J.W. Gibb Memorial Trust, E.J. Brill. Another local history that includes events in the Caspian regions of Iran during the Mongol years.

Iraqi, Fakhruddin. 1982. *Fakhruddin 'Iraqi Divine Flashes,* trans. William Chittick and Peter Lamborn. London: SPCK, Holy Trinity Church. This is a translation of the well-know Persian Sufi poet Iraqi, who wrote in Mongol Iran and enjoyed the patronage of top officials.

Juvaini (Juwaynī), Ala-ad-Din 'Ata-Malik. 1997. *The History of the World Conqueror,* trans. John Andrew Boyle, intro. David Morgan. Vols. 1 and 2. Manchester, U.K.: Manchester University Press. The historian and later governor of Baghdad, 'Ata Malik Juwaynī (Juvaini) served at the Mongol court from childhood. He witnessed many of the events firsthand and traveled extensively throughout the empire. He served Hülegü in a personal capacity until he was appointed governor of Baghdad circa 1260. His history is a major source for information about the Mongols. Juwaynī concludes his history after the destruction of the Ismāʿīlīs at Alamut but before the fall of Baghdad.

———. 1912, 1916, 1937, *Tārīkh-i Jahān Gushā*, ed. Moḥammad Qazvīnī. Vols. 1, 2, and 3. London: E.J. Brill. This early edition printed in London contains a lengthy and extremely useful introduction in English by E.G. Browne, including a paraphrased translation of Juwaynī's autobiography of the troubles which beset him towards the end of his life.

Juzjani, Maulana, Minhaj-ud-Din Abu 'Umar-i-Usman. [1881] 1995. *Tabakat-i-Nasiri: A General History of the Muhammadan Dynasties of Asia; from 810–1260* A.D. *And The Irruption of the Infidel Mughals into Islam,* trans. H.G. Raverty. Reprint, Calcutta: Asiatic Society. Writing at approximately the same time as his fellow Persian, Juwaynī, the histories of Jūzjānī are particularly interesting because they were written from outside the sphere of Mongol domination and are, therefore, virulently anti-Mongol in character. For this reason they provide a contrast and counterweight to Juwaynī. However, what is interesting is that both historians agree on most of the major facts and chronology of events even though there was no chance of collusion between the two. Jūzjānī's history covers all the Muslim dynasties of the Indian subcontinent from 864 C.E. and the Mongol invasions to 1260 C.E.

Khusraw, Nasīr-i. 2001. *Book of Travels,* trans. Wheeler M. Thackston. Costa Mesa: Mazda Publications. Though this book was written before the age of the Mongols, I am including it because it gives a vivid picture of the Medieval Islamic world into which the Mongols irrupted. In fact Nasir-i-Khusraw lived at the time of the first great irruption of Turks, the Saljuqs, into the Islamic world, and historians frequently compare and contrast the coming of the Saljuq Turks and the Mongols nearly two hundred years later. However, the world that Nasir-i-Khusraw describes would not have been so different from the world which the Mongols would have encountered.

Khwandamir. 1994. *Habib's-Siyar: The Reign of the Mongol and the Turk Genghis Khan, Amir Temur,* trans. W.M. Thackston. Vol. 3. Cambridge, Mass.: Department of Near Eastern Languages and Civilizations, Harvard University. This sixteenth-century history provides a comprehensive account of the Mongol period and draws on many local sources, now lost.

Kirakos Ganjaks'i. 1986. *Kirakos Ganjaks'i's History of the Armenians,* trans. Robert Bedrosian. *Sources for the Armenian Tradition.* Available at: http://rbedrosian. com/kg1.htm. The Armenian cleric Kirakos lived in the thirteenth century and witnessed the coming of the Mongols and life under the Il-Khans. He was imprisoned and then employed by the Mongols, and his histories reflect his ambivalent attitude.

Lewis, Bernard, ed. and trans. 1974. *Islam.* Vol. 1, *Politics and War.* London: Macmillan.

———. ed. and trans. 1987. *Islam.* Vol. 2, *Religion and Society.* New York: Oxford University Press. Two excellent books of various medieval primary sources in English translation.

Meyvaert, Paul, ed. 1980. "An Unknown Letter of Hülegü, Il-Khan of Persia, to King Louis IX of France (10 April 1262)." *Viator* 11: 245–59. This is an early example of the style of letter written to persuade the Europeans to join forces with the Mongols to defeat the Muslim Egyptians.

Michell, R., and Nevill Forbes. 1914. *The Chronicle of Novgorod 1016–1471.* Camden Third Series, vol. 25. London: Offices of the Society. These early Russian texts contain harrowing accounts of the first appearances of the Mongols in Europe. It is these early accounts that gave rise to much alarm in the rest of Europe.

Mostaert, A., and F. W. Cleaves. 1952. "Trois documents Mongols des Archives Secretes Vaticanes." *Harvard Journal of Asiatic Studies* 52: 419–506–Important primary source material.

Munshī, Naṣīr al-Dīn. 1983. *Simt al-'ulā.* Tehran: Inteshārāt Esatir.

Mustawfī, Ḥamdallah Qazvīnī. 1983. *Zafarnāmeh of Mustawfi,* trans. L. J. Ward, PhD thesis, University of Manchester. (See also under H amdallāh). Facsimile copy, 1999. Tehran: Iran University Press. Written at the end of the Ilkhanid era, this little-known history was written by a courtier at the heart of the Mongol government of Iran. Mustawfi's other works are far better known but this work equals them in historical importance. (See under Ḥamdallāh).

———. 1983. *Tārīkh-i Guzīdeh.* Tehran: Entashārāt Amīr Kabīr.

———. 1999. *Zafarnāmeh.* Tehran: Publication of the University of Iran.

Nakhchavānī, Moḥammad bin Hindūshāh. 1964. *Dastūr al-Kāteb fī ta'yin al-marātib,* ed. 'Abdul Karīm 'Alīzādeh. 3 vols. Moscow: Asia Institute.

Oderic, Friar Oderic of Pordenone. 2002. *The Travels of Friar Oderic of Pordenone,* trans. Sir Henry Yule. Grand Falls, Michigan: William E. Eerdmans Publishing Company. This is a reprint of the original Yule translation published in *Cathay and the Way Thither,* detailed below.

Onon, Urgunge, trans. 1990. *The History and Life of Chinggis Khan (The Secret History of the Mongols).* Leiden, Netherlands: Brill. This is an insider's account of the rise of Chinggis Khan and the rule of his son and successor, Ögödei, the Qa'an. It is the only Mongolian primary source still extant.

Orbelian, Stephannos. 1864. *Histoire de la Siounie,* trans. M. Brosset. St Petersburg, Russia: Académie imperiale des sciences. The Orbelian family were Armenian nobles who established close relations with the Mongols and were loyal servants of the Il-Khans. This French translation from the Armenian gives valuable insight into the relationship between the rulers and the ruled during the Mongol period in western Asia.

Polo, Marco. 1985. *The Travels of Marco Polo,* trans. Teresa Waugh. London: Sidgewick and Jackson. A modern translation but a beautifully and lavishly illustrated edition. Many editions of the travels of Marco Polo are available in varying degrees of erudition including the Everyman Edition, 1983. In addition, the travels are available online in extracts and in their entirety. Marco Polo remains one of the most important sources for the Mongols and the Yüan dynasty. Quotations in the text are taken from the freely accessible online Complete Yule-Cordier Edition of Marco Polo's travels by Marco Polo and Rustichello of Pisa, *The Project Gutenberg EBook of the Travels of Marco Polo,* vols. 1 and 2, available at: http://www.gutenberg.net.

Pūr-i-Bahā' (Tāj al-Dīn Nasā'ī). 1960 (1339). "Kārnāmeh-ye Awqāf." *Farhang-e Īrān Zamīn.* Vol.8. Tehran.

——. 1956. "Mongol Ode" and "Pūr-i-Bahā' and his Poems." In V. Minorsky. *Iranica: Twenty Articles*. Tehran: Publications of Tehran University, 1960. Pūr-i-Bahā' was a satirical poet during the time that the Juwaynī family was at the height of its power in thirteenth-century Iran. The fact that Pūr-i-Bahā' felt free to write such biting satire against the government of the time is indicative of the freedom of expression which prevailed in Ilkhanid Iran. His most famous poem, the *Mongol Ode*, demonstrates just how many Mongolian and Turkish idioms, phrases, and words were in current usage in the Persian of the thirteenth century. Other translations of his poetry appear in E. G. Browne's *Literary History of Persia*.

Rashīd al-Dīn. 1968. *Histoire des Mongols de la Perse,* trans. Étienne Quatremere. Amsterdam: Oriental Press. This is a French translation, extremely well annotated, of Rashīd al-Dīn's history of Hülegü, taken from the Compendium of Chronicles. It provides details of Hülegü's wives and sons and of his establishment of the Il-Khanate, up until his death in 1265.

——. 1971. *The Successors of Genghis Khan,* trans. John Andrew Boyle. New York: Columbia University Press. Another scholarly translation from Rashīd al-Dīn's *Compendium of Chronicles,* this section covers the rule of the Great Khans until Temür Qa'an (d. 1307).

——. 1998/9. *Rashiduddin Fazlullah Jami 'u' t-Tawarikh: Compendium of Chronicles,* trans. W.M. Thackston. 3 vols. Cambridge, Mass.: Sources of Oriental Languages & Literature 45, Central Asian Sources, Harvard University. Thackston's translation of the great statesman and historian Rashīd al-Dīn's epic *Compendium of Chronicles* is an admirable achievement. This work is considered the world's first universal history. Rashīd al-Dīn was able to draw on a great variety of sources both Eastern and Western, and he had the full cooperation of the Mongol courts in his endeavors. This is by far the most important translated text for the study of the Mongols.

——. 1994. *Jāmi' al-Tavārīkh,* eds. Mohammad Roushan and Muṣtafah Mūsavī. Tehran: Nashr albaraz. This is the latest four-volume edition of this important work. It contains two volumes of indexes, glossaries, notes, and black and white illustrations.

——. 1972. *Tanksūq-nāmeh yā ṭibb ahl-i-Khitā,* ed. Mujtabā Minuvī. University of Tehran. Facsimile edition with some wonderful illustrations.

al-Razzāq Samarqandī, 'Abdul. 1993. *Maṭla' al-Sa'dayn,* ed. M. Shafī'. 2 vols. Tehran: Institute for Humanities and Cultural Studies.

Redhouse, James. 1976. *Legends of the Sufis: Selections from Menaqibu' l'Arifin,* trans. and preface by Idries Shah, Shams al-Din Ahmad, el-Eflaki. London: Theosophical Publishing House. Aflaki was a follower of the Sufi order founded by Rūmī. These stories, both mythical and factual, provide valuable information about the life and teaching of the great Sufi poet Jalāl al-Dīn Rūmī.

Reynold Nicholson, trans. *Selected Poems from the Dīvān-i-Shams-i-Tabrīz.* Richmond, U.K.: Curzon. This is a literal translation with accompanying Persian text. For lovers of Rūmī this is an indispensable volume. See also under Shams-i-Tabrīzī.

Riley-Smith, J.S.C., U. Lyons, and M.C. Lyons. 1971. *Ayyubids, Mamlukes, and Crusaders: Selections from Tarikh al-Duwal wa'l-Muluk.* Cambridge, U.K.: Heffer. These are selected translations from the Arabic and provide a view of the events in western Asia and of the Mongols from an Egyptian, Mamluk perspective.

Rumi, Jalal al-Din. 1993. *The Discourses of Rumi,* trans. A. J. Arberry. London: Curzon
    Press. This is a translation of Rūmī's speeches and public addresses, including
    his views on his Mongol masters. A new translation by Wheeler Thackston,
    Signs of the Unseen (London: Shambhala, 1999), is also available.

Reynold Nicholson, trans. 1926. *The Mathnawī.* London: Gibb Memorial Trust. This
    is Rūmī's greatest work and various translations are available. It is a literal
    translation and more suited to the Persian speaker. Arberry's *Tales from the
    Mathnavi* (London: Curzon, 1993) would be more suited to the nonspecial-
    ist reader.

Sa'di Shirazi. 1975. *Morals Pointed and Tales Adorned: The Bustan of Sa'di,* trans.
    G. M. Wickens. Leiden, Netherlands: Brill. Sa'di wrote for the Salghurid
    rulers of Shiraz. The Salghurids were for the main part faithful servants
    of their Mongol masters. Sa'di's words of wisdom and advice reflect the
    society and customs of his time but also have a timeless relevance quite
    applicable to modern times.

Shabānkāra'ī, Moḥammad. 1984. *Majma' al'ansāb.* Tehran: Inteshārāt Amīr Kabīr.
    This Persian history was written in the fifteenth century and covers the rul-
    ers of Iran from the Saffarids to the end of the Ilkhanid period. The writer
    was a poet as well as a historian. He was Kurdish and therefore he presents
    the history of the times from a local perspective.

Shams-i-Tabrīzī. 2004. *Me and Rumi: an Autobiography of Shams-i-Tabrīzī,* trans
    William C. Chittick. Louisville, Kentucky: Fons Vitae. This is an extremely
    welcome translation of an extremely important though little-known docu-
    ment. Shams-i-Tabrīzī was the wandering dervish that made such an impact
    on the Sufi poet, Jalāl al-Dīn Rūmī. It was rumored that Rūmī's family had
    Shams-i-Tabrīzī murdered so fearful were they of his influence on and hold
    over Jalāl al-Dīn, who had changed from a sober, rather austere and serious
    cleric to a wild, ecstatic poet who held evenings of dance and music in place
    of prayer and Quranic readings.

Shirley, Janet, trans. 1999. *Crusader Syria in the 13th Century: The Rothelin Continua-
    tion with Part of the Eracles or Acre Text.* Aldershot, U.K.: Ashgate. These are
    crusader chronicles, but they cover the period of Mongol engagement.

Simon de Saint Quentin. 1965. *Histoire des Tartars,* ed. Jean Richard. Paris: Libraire
    orientaliste.

Smpad. 1959. "The Armenian Chronicles of Constable Smpad, or The Royal Histo-
    rian," trans. S. Der Nersessian. *Dumbarton Oaks Papers* 13: 141–68. Constable
    Smpad (1208–76) was a high-ranking official at the Armenian court of Cili-
    cia and brother of King Het'um. The Armenians of Cilicia made a pact with
    the Mongols in the 1240s and became allies. Smpad had firsthand knowl-
    edge of the Mongols, the court in Mongolia, and the Il-Khans.

Skelton, R. A., T. E. Marston, and George D. Painter. 1995. *The Vinland Map and the
    Tartar Relation.* New Haven, Conn.: Yale University Press. This account of
    the Franciscans' journey to the Mongol court was written by a member of
    Carpini's party. It contains additional details and facts not found in Carpi-
    ni's version of the journey.

Tusi, Nasir al-Din. 1950. *Tasawwurat or Rawdatu't-Taslim,* trans. W. Ivanow. Leiden,
    Netherlands: Ismaili Society, Brill. Another example of Tusi's philosophical
    and religious works.

———. 1963. "The Longer Introduction to the Zij al-Ilkhānī of Naṣir-al-Dīn Ṭūsī," trans. and intro. John Andrew Boyle. *Journal of Semitic Studies* 8. This is a technical piece of work written for Hülegü by Tusi.

———. 1964. "Nasir al-Dīn on Finance," trans. M. Minovi and V. Minorsky. *Iranica* 775: 64–85.

———. 1964. *The Nasirean Ethics,* trans. G. M. Wickens. London: George Allen and Unwin. This is Tusi's most famous work. It is in the tradition of *Mirror for Princes* and gives moral and political advice to rulers.

———. 1971. "The Death of the Last 'Abbasid Caliph: A Contemporary Muslim Account," trans. John Andrew Boyle. *Journal of Semitic Studies* 6.

Boyle, J. A., 1977. *The Mongol World Empire 1206–1370.* London: Variorum Reprints. Tusi wrote this account of the destruction of Baghdad, an event in which he played a leading role, and amended it to Juwaynī's *History of the World Conqueror.* In the Persian editions of Juwaynī's history, Tusi's amendment is usually included.

———. 1998. *Contemplation and Action: The Spiritual Autobiography of a Muslim Scholar,* trans. S. J. Badakhchani. London: Tauris and The Institute of Isma'ili Studies. This is the spiritual autobiography of Tusi, who became a close adviser to Hülegü. It was for Tusi that Hülegü built the observatory and library, the Rasadkhāneh, in Maragheh, northwestern Iran, in about 1260.

Vardan. 1989. "The Historical Compilation of Vardan Arewelc'i," trans. R. W. Thomson. *Dumbarton Oaks Papers* 43: 125–226. The Armenian cleric wrote this general history, which continues to the reign of Abaqa Khan (d. 1282). Vardan was particularly close to Hülegü's wife, Dokuz Khātūn.

Wallis-Budge, E. A., trans. 1928. *The Monks of Kublai Khan, Emperor of China.* London: Religious Tract Society. This is the account of the embassy of the Nestorian (eastern Christian) patriarch, Yaballaha III, and his vicar, Bar Sauma, from Qubilai Khan to the courts of Europe at the end of the thirteenth century. This is now available online.

Waṣṣāf, Shihab al-Dīn 'Abdallah Sharaf Shīrāzī. 1959. *Tārīkh-i Waṣṣāf.* Tehran: Ketābkhāneh Ibn Sina.

Wiley, Arthur, trans. 1991. *The Travels of an Alchemist.* Taipei, Taiwan: SMC Publishing. This account of Chinggis Khan's spiritual advisor, who accompanied the Great Khan in his final years, has recently been republished. It is an account of the travels of Ch'ang Ch'un, summoned to central Asia by the Great Khan, whom he then accompanied southward across Afghanistan into Sind and then back again to central Asia. The story is recounted by the holy man's disciple, Li Chih Ch'ang, and provides important insights into the personality of Chinggis Khan.

William of Rubruck. 1990. *The Mission of Friar William of Rubruck,* trans. and ed. Peter Jackson with David Morgan. London: Hakluyt Society. This account of the journey of the Franciscan missionary, William of Rubruck, to the court of Möngke Khan is an invaluable source of information and descriptions of the Mongols and the lands under their domination. Quotations used in the present text are taken from W. W. Rockhill, ed. and trans., *The Journey of William of Rubruck to the Eastern Parts of the World, 1253–55, as Narrated by Himself, with Two Accounts of the Earlier Journey of John of Pian de Carpine* (London: Hakluyt Society, 1900), available at: http://www.locksley.

com/locksley/rubruck.htm or http://depts.washington.edu/uwch/silkroad/texts/rubruck.html.

Yule, Henry. [1914] 1967. *Cathay and the Way Thither.* 3 vols. Reprint, Millwood, N.Y.: Kraus Reprint. This three-volume set is a wonderful collection of early source material, much of it unavailable elsewhere. In particular, it contains the travels of friar Oderic of Pordenone, who traveled extensively in the Far East between 1316 and 1330, and his observations of life under the Yüan administration form a useful comparison with Marco Polo's reports. Also found in this collection are letters and reports of other missionary friars and medieval travelers to the Orient, such as Pegolotti (1330–40) and Marignolli (1338–53), and a letter to the pope in Avignon from the Great Khan.

Yūnīnī, al-. 1998. *Early Mamluk Syrian Historiography: al-Yūnīnī's Dhayl Mir' āt al-zamān,* trans. and ed. Li Guo. Leiden, Netherlands: Brill. Li Guo provides a scholarly translation and a detailed introduction to an important Mamluk text written in Arabic covering the period 1256 to 1311. This period deals with Egypt and Syria under the rule of Ayyubid princes, the crusaders, the Bahri Mamluks, and the Mongols. Al-Yūnīnī was born into a family of scholars and was a wide traveler in this volatile region and a close observer of events. This is an important source on Mongol history written in Arabic rather than Persian. The Persian sources tend to dominate Mongol history and were often written from within the regime. Al-Yūnīnī wrote from outside the Mongol Empire, from lands under the control of the Mamluks, enemies of the Mongols.

SECONDARY SOURCES: ANNOTATED BIBLIOGRAPHY

Adams, Robert. 1965. *Land behind Baghdad.* Chicago: University of Chicago Press. This is a description of Baghdad and its hinterland during the decades before the Mongol invasion that demonstrates that the decline in this city's fortunes had begun long before the arrival of Hülegü.

Allsen, Thomas. 1987. *Mongol Imperialism: The Policies of the Grand Qan Mongke 1251–1259.* Los Angeles: University of California Press. This is an important analysis of the split in the Mongol ruling family and the development of the Tuluids under Möngke.

———. 1989. "Mongolian Princes and Their Merchant Partners 1200–1260." *Asia Major* 2: 82–126 Princeton, N.J.: Princeton University Press. Allsen investigates the relationship between merchants and their royal financial backers and demonstrates the close links between the Mongols and international commerce.

———. 1997. *Commodity and Exchange in the Mongol Empire: A Cultural History of Islamic Textiles.* Cambridge: Cambridge University Press. This important study shows the crucial role that precious fabrics, and gold cloth in particular, played in the expansion and development of the Mongol Empire.

———. 2001. *Culture and Conquest in Mongol Eurasia.* Cambridge: Cambridge University Press. Allsen's study of Iran and China focuses on the roles of the Mongol Yüan official Bolad Aqa and the Persian Il-Khanid minister Rashīd al-Dīn. He demonstrates just how involved the Mongols became in the transfer of culture between the different parts of their empire and shows that their role was very much proactive and directional at all levels of the administration and government. Allsen is able to draw on his knowledge of both western Asian and eastern Asian languages to investigate much primary source material never before so intimately compared. A review of this book in the *Bulletin of the School of Oriental & African Studies* states, "Any new publication by Thomas T. Allsen is justly followed by ripples of excitement. . . . A new book excites those ripples to tidal proportions" (George Lane, "Culture and Conquest in Mongol Eurasia," *Bulletin of the School of Oriental & African Studies* 65 [2002]: 411–12).

Amitai, Reuven, and Michal Biran, eds. 2005. *Mongols, Turks, and Others: Eurasian Nomads and the Sedentary World*. Leiden, Netherlands: Brill. This is an excellent collection of articles from many of the big names in the world of Mongol studies, including Morgan, Jackson, Endicott, Khazanov, Manz, and others.

Amitai-Preiss, Reuven. 1995. *Mongols and Mamluks: The Mamluk-Ilkhanid War 1260–1281*. Cambridge: Cambridge University Press. Amitai-Preiss gives a detailed breakdown of the wars between the Mamluks of Egypt, who stopped the Mongols' conquest of the whole Islamic world, and the Il-Khanids, or Mongols, of Iran.

———. "The Conversion of Tegüder Ilkhan to Islam." 2001. *Jerusalem Studies in Arabic and Islam* 25: 15–43. Tegüdar was the first of the Iranian Mongols to convert to Islam, although the rest of his court did not follow his example. This is a very interesting and informative study of Tegüdar's short reign.

———. 1995–97. "Hülegü and the Ayyubid Lord of Transjordan." *Archivum Eurasiae Medii Aevi* 9.

———. 1999. "Sufis and Shamans." *Journal of Economic and Social History of the Orient* 17 (1): 27–47.

Ball, Warwick. 1976. "Two Aspects of Iranian Buddhism." *Bulletin of the Asian Institute of Pahlavi University* 1–4.

———. 1979. "The Imamzadeh Ma'sum at Vardjovi: A Rock-cut Il-Khanid Complex Near Maragheh." *Archaeologische Mitteilungen aus Iran* 12.

Barthold, V. V., trans., and T. Minorsky. 1968. *Turkestan down to the Mongol Invasion*. London: Luzac. This study is a classic and explores in depth the historical development of the Turkish steppe people and Central Asia. Its central subject is the land of Turkestan before and after the Mongol invasions.

Bedrosian, Robert. 1979. *The Turco-Mongol Invasions and the Lords of Armenia in the 13th–14th Centuries*. Long Branch, N.J.: Sources of the Armenian Tradition. Available at: http://rbedrosian.com/hsrces.html. Robert Bedrosian has made his doctoral dissertation available on the Internet as well as in hard copy and provides the most welcome translation of the medieval Armenian sources. His dissertation contains many translations of sources unavailable elsewhere.

Biran, Michal. 2005. *The Empire of the Qara Khitai in Eurasian History*. Cambridge: Cambridge University Press. This extremely important book is the definitive account of the precursors of the Mongols, the Qara Khitai. It has sometimes been said that the coming of the Qara Khitai from Northern China to Central Asia circa 1125–30 was the first Mongol invasion. It differed from the invasion of the Chinggisids in that it was relatively peaceful and that the Qara Khitai established strong and peaceful relations with the Muslims of the region. With the publication of this scholarly study, the Qara Khitai should enter the consciousness of the more general reading public.

———. 2000. *A Fight between the Mongols: The Battle of Herat (1270).* Jerusalem: Institute of Advanced Studies, Hebrew University of Jerusalem. This short paper is an excellent model for students interested in probing deeper into the details of Mongol history.

———. 1997. *Qaidu and the Rise of the Independent Mongol State in Central Asia.* Richmond, U.K.: Curzon Press. A useful and readable portrait of a little-known figure and an analysis of an under-studied area of Mongol history, Michal Biran's book would be welcomed by students wanting new, relatively untouched territory to further their studies.

Boase, T.S.R., ed. 1978. *The Cilician Kingdom of Armenia.* Edinburgh: Scottish Academic Press. The Armenians of Cilicia were early and willing allies of the approaching Mongols. The Armenians are a good example of a small kingdom that opted to cooperate rather than oppose the invaders, and they even tried to recruit their fellow Christians in Europe and in Palestine to join them.

Bosworth, C. E. 1996. *The New Islamic Dynasties.* Edinburgh: Edinburgh University Press. This reference book is a must for any student interested in Islamic political history.

Bowman, John, and J. A. Thompson. 1966. "The Monastry-church of Bar Hebraeus at Maragheh in West Azerbaijan." *Abr-Nahrain* 5. Department of Semitic Studies, University of Melbourne.

Boyle, J. A. 1968. *The Cambridge History of Iran.* Vol. 5. Cambridge: Cambridge University Press. This work contains the standard studies of the Mongol period in Western Asia.

———. 1977. *The Mongol World Empire 1206–1370.* Aldershot, U.K.: Variorum Reprints. This book collects various papers of the late John Boyle from Manchester University and covers all aspects of Mongol society and politics. Boyle is most famous for his linguistic expertise and his translations from various Asian languages.

Browne, Edward G. 1915. *A Literary History of Persia.* Vol. 2, *From Firdawsi to Saʿdī.* London: Unwin.

———. 1920. *A Literary History of Persia.* Vol. 3, *Persian Literature under Tartar Domination 1265–1502.* Cambridge: Cambridge University Press. Both of these volumes by Browne, two from a four-volume work, provide a wonderful introduction to the Mongol period. Though no Mongol apologist, Browne gives an entirely different perspective on the Mongol period in his translations from the Persian. At one stage, Persian was almost the lingua franca of the Mongol Empire, and Iranians held important positions in administration, commerce, and cultural life throughout the empire. Browne has put together an excellent collection of translations and extracts from a wide variety of sources. These books have recently been reprinted.

Bruijn, J.T.P. de. 1997. *Persian Sufi Poetry: An Introduction to the Mystical Use of Classical Poems.* Richmond, U.K.: Curzon Press. The Mongol period saw an upsurge in the popularity of Sufism in western Asia, central Asia, and beyond. For those interested in this aspect of Mongol rule, this book is a valuable introduction.

Burman, Edward. 1987. *The Assassins: Holy Killers of Islam.* London: Crucible. Another contribution to the study of this medieval sect.

Cahen, Claude. 1968. *Pre-Ottoman Turkey,* trans. J. Jones-Williams. London: Sidgwick & Jackson.

———. 2001. *The Formation of Turkey,* trans. and ed. P. M. Holt. London: Longman. These two books by Cahen provide a vivid picture of Anatolia (Turkey) before the coming of the Ottomans. The second book concentrates more on the Mongol period.

Chambers, James. 1979. *The Devil's Horsemen.* London: Book Club Associates. This classic is a very readable study of the Mongol invasion of Eastern Europe and Russia. It paints a vivid picture of the early Mongol invaders and gives a balanced account of their impact on Russia and its neighbors. This is an excellent introduction to the history of the Mongols.

Chaudhuri, K. N. 1985. *Trade and Civilisation in the Indian Ocean: An Economic History from the Rise of Islam to 1750.* Cambridge: Cambridge University Press. Trade in the Indian Ocean is often seen as peripheral to the study of the Mongols. This study proves otherwise and puts the events of the thirteenth century into context.

Ch'en, Paul Heng-chao. 1979. *Chinese Legal Tradition under the Mongols: The Code of 1291 as Reconstructed.* Princeton, N.J.: Princeton University Press. A detailed study of Mongol law as practiced under the Yüan administration.

Ch'en Yüan. 1966. *Western and Central Asians in China under the Mongols,* trans. and annotated by Ch'ien Hsing-hai. Monumenta Serica Monograph, no. 15. Los Angeles: University of California Press. The Yüan dynasty attracted visitors from Europe and western Asia to its fabulous courts. This is a book written from a Chinese perspective.

Cleaves, Francis Woodman. 1954. "A Medical Practice of the Mongols in the Thirteenth Century." *Harvard Journal of Asiatic Studies* 17 (¾ December): 428–44

Cramer, Marc. 2003. *Imperial Mongolian Cooking: Recipes from the kingdoms of Genghis Khan.* New York: Hippocrene Books. This little book contains a wide range of dishes from the four main *ulus* of the Mongol Empire. The recipes have been adapted to modern times so the ingredients should all be easily accessible.

Dabashi, Hamid. 1996. "The Philosopher/Vizier: Khwāja Naṣīr al-Dīn Ṭūsī and the Ismāʿīlīs." In *Mediaeval Ismāʿīlī History and Thought,* ed. F. Daftary, 231–246 Cambridge: Cambridge University Press. This is an interesting and thought-provoking study of Tusi.

Daftary, Farhad. 1966. *Mediaeval Ismāʿīlī History and Thought.* Cambridge: Cambridge University Press.

———. 1990. *The Ismāʿīlīs: Their History and Doctrines.* Cambridge: Cambridge University Press. Daftary has written the definitive study of this Muslim sect.

———. 1994. *The Assassin Legends: The Myths of the Ismāʿīlīs.* London: Taurus. Daftary's study clears up many of the misconceptions and myths about the medieval Ismāʿīlīs. He explains why they became known as the Assassins.

DeWeese, Devin. 1994. *Islamization and Native Religion in the Golden Horde.* University Park: Pennsylvania State University Press. This book is interesting for its study of the process of Islamization and its research into the nature of religion in the Golden Horde.

Eboo Jamal, Nadia. 2002. *Surviving the Mongols.* London: Institute of Ismaili Studies, I. B. Tauris. This is an interesting account of the survival of the Ismaili community in Mongol-ruled Iran. Though it is rather clichéd and dated in its portrayal of the Mongols, the book contains some valuable insights into life in Mongol Iran and how the secretive Ismaili community managed to survive and prosper against considerable odds.

Endicott-West, Elizabeth. 1986. "Imperial Governance in Yüan Times." *Harvard Journal of Asiatic Studies* 46 (2): 523–49. For serious students of the Mongols in China, Endicott-West is indispensable.

Fischel, Walter J. 1937. *Jews in the Economic and Political Life of Mediaeval Islam.* London: Royal Asiatic Society Press. The Jews were far more active and influential in western Asia during the medieval period than they are given credit for.

Fletcher, Joseph. 1986. "The Mongols: Ecological and Social Perspectives." *Harvard Journal of Asiatic Studies* 46 (1): 11–50. This paper has now become an oft-quoted classic. Lucidly and simply explained, it puts the Mongols in historical, political, and even anthropological context. This is a must for all students of the Mongols.

Foltz, Richard. 1999. "Ecumenical mischief under the Mongols." *Central Asiatic Journal* 43: 42–69.

Fiey, J. M. 1975. *Chrétiens Syriaques sous les Mongols.* Louvain: Secrétariat du Corpus SCO

——. 1975, "Iconographie Syriaque Hulagu, Doquz Khatun ... six Ambons," *Le Museon* 88.

Franke, Herbert. 1978. *From Tribal Chieftain to Universal Emperor and God: The Legitimation of the Yüan Dynasty.* Munich: Verlag der Bayerischen Akademie der Wissenschaften. Herbert Frank has written widely on the Mongols and is a recognized expert. In this book he discusses the question of legitimacy.

Galstyan, A.G. 1975. "The Conquest of Armenia by the Mongol Armies," trans. R. Bedrosian. *The Armenian Review* 27: 4–108.

——. 1976. "The First Armeno-Mongol Negotiations." *The Armenian Review* 29: 1–113. These studies examine the relationship of both the Caucasian and Cilician Armenians with the Mongols.

Gibb, H.A.R., J.H. Kramer, J. Schacht, and F. Levi-Provençal, eds. 1960. *The Encyclopaedia of Islam.* New ed. Leiden, Netherlands: Luzac and Brill. This is a comprehensive and useful reference work.

Gibbons, Edward. 1910. *Decline and Fall of the Roman Empire.* London: Everyman's Library. 6 vols.

Golden, Peter B. 1992. *An Introduction to the History of the Turkic Peoples.* Wiesbaden, Germany: Otto Harrassowitz.

——. 2003. *Nomads and Their Neighbours in the Russian Steppe.* Aldershot, U.K.: Variorum Reprints, Ashgate. Peter Golden's book is an excellent starting point for students embarking on the study of the Turkic and steppe peoples of central Asia. The Variorum collection includes some key papers on the people from the steppe.

Grousset, Rene. 1991. *The Empire of the Steppes,* trans. Naomi Walford. New Brunswick, N.J.: Rutgers University Press. This book has become a modern classic and puts the Mongol years into the perspective of steppe empires.

Gumilev, L.N. 1987. *Searches for an Imaginary Kingdom: The Legend of the Kingdom of Prester John.* Cambridge: Cambridge University Press. An unusual work but full of valuable research and insights.

Halperin, Charles J. 1983. "Russia in the Mongol Empire in Comparative Perspective." *Harvard Journal of Asiatic Studies* 46 (2): 239–61. This article examines the Mongol conquests from a Russian point of view.

———. 1986. *The Tatar Yoke.* Columbus, Ohio: Slavica. Halperin examines the reasons behind the reluctance of Russian writers to deal with the Mongol domination of Russia.

———. 2000. "The Kipchak Connection: The Ilkhans, the Mamluks and Ayn Jalut." Bulletin of the School of Oriental & African Studies 63 (pt. 2): 229–245. This is a survey of events to the south in Iran and Syria from the view of the Golden Horde.

de Hartog, Leo. 1989. *Genghis Khan: Conqueror of the World.* London: Taurus.

———. 1996. *Russia and the Mongol Yoke: The History of the Russian Principalities and the Golden Horde, 1221–1502.* London: British Academic Press, Taurus. De Hartog has written two very readable accounts, though the second study takes the traditional Russian view of the Mongol years. His book on Chinggis Khan is thoroughly researched, very readable, and clearly presented.

Hawting, G. R. 2005. *Muslims, Mongols, and Crusades.* London: RoutledgeCurzon. This is a useful collection of articles published by SOAS [School of Oriental and African Studies], part of the University of London, which is concerned with the Mongols. The collection includes such articles as Joseph de Somogyi's 1933 translation and analysis of an Arabic poem written as a reaction to the destruction of Baghdad.

Heissig, W. 2000. *The Religions of Mongolia.* 3rd ed., trans. Geoffrey Samuel. London: Kegan Paul. This book provides an excellent general background of religion and the medieval Mongols.

Heywood, Colin. 1999. "Filling the Black Hole?: the Emergence of the Bithynian Atamanates 1298–1304." *Yeni Turkiye Dergisi,* 1–10. Colin Heywood outlines his ideas concerning the origins of the Ottomans. He explains how the collapse of the Noghai Khanate in the eastern Balkans coincided with the appearance of an ambitious and militant tribe in western Anatolia. Various large movements of people and tents are mentioned in various sources and nowhere is it adequately explained what became of the *ulus* Noghai. Heywood has discovered no unequivocal evidence that binds these various events together, but his theories are convincing.

Howorth, Henry H. 1965. *History of the Mongols from the 9th to the 19th Century.* 4 vols. New York: Burt Francis. This four-volume work is an immense achievement, incorporating all of the then-known primary sources: Armenian, Georgian, Persian, Arabic, Mongolian, Chinese, Chaghetaid, Turkic, and so forth. Unfortunately, Howorth is not widely acknowledged because his research is based on translations rather than on primary sources and because he does not offer the detailed or accurate citations in his text with copious footnotes demanded by modern scholarship. However, he presents in English translation large extracts from most of the contemporary histories, and his work can be utilized as a guide to the primary sources. For researchers his monumental work is of limited value. Most academics find his volumes extremely useful as background material, but when citations are needed he cannot be utilized, and the sources themselves or accepted translations must be sought. For undergraduates and the general reader,

Howorth is an excellent introduction to history based directly on primary source material.

Humphreys, R. Stephen. 1977. *From Saladin to the Mongols.* Albany: State University of New York Press. This is the Mongols as seen from an Arab perspective.

Ipsiroglu, M. S. 1967. *Painting and Culture of the Mongols,* trans. E. D. Philips. London: Thames and Hudson. This book contains a large collection of little-known artworks from the Mongol era that often depict the daily life of ordinary Mongols.

Irwin, Robert. 1986. *The Middle East in the Middle Ages: The Early Mamluk Sultanate 1250–1382.* Carbondale: Southern Illinois Press.

——. 1989. *The Age of Calamity* A.D. *1300–1400.* Amsterdam: Time-Life Books. Robert Irwin's study of the Mamluks presents the Arab world at the time of the Mongols. His chapter on Timurlane in the Time-Life book is included with other pieces concerned with the Mongol conquests.

Jackson, Peter. 1978. "The Dissolution of the Mongol Empire." *Central Asiatic Journal* 32: 186–243.

——. 2000. "The State of Research: The Mongol Empire, 1986–1999." *Journal of Mediaeval History* 26 (2): 189–210.

——. 2005. *The Mongols and the West, 1221–1410.* London: Longman. Peter Jackson's study of the breakup of the Mongol Empire is already a classic and the basis of most other studies and research on this subject. His work cannot be ignored. Jackson's latest book retains his distinctive eye for detail and exhaustive investigation and will become an indispensable volume in any library of the Mongols.

Jay, Jennifer W. 1991. *A Change in Dynasties: Loyalism in Thirteenth-Century China.* Bellingham: Western Washington. Jennifer Jay studies the Sung Chinese loyalists and their attempts to resist cooperating with the Mongol Yüan dynasty.

Karamustafa, Ahmet. 1994. *God's Unruly Friends.* Salt Lake City: University of Utah Press. A detailed and scholarly study of the wandering dervishes, *qalandars,* and other eccentrics who populated medieval Persia.

Khazanov, Anatoly M. 1994. *Nomads and the Outside World.* Madison: University of Wisconsin Press. This is a collection of essays and papers concerned with Mongol society and its interaction with its sedentary neighbors. The collection includes work by Peter Golden, Reuven Amitai-Preiss, and Thomas Allsen.

Kohlberg, Etan. 1992. *A Mediaeval Muslim Scholar at Work: Ibn Tawwus and his Library.* Leiden, Netherlands: Brill.

Komaroff, Linda, and Stefano Carboni, eds. 2002. *The Legacy of Genghis Khan: Courtly Art and Culture in Western Asia 1256–1353.* New York: Metropolitan Museum of Art. This long-overdue contribution to the field of Mongol studies is a lavishly illustrated book, rich in writing as well as pictures, that makes the case for a serious reassessment of the Mongol epoch. It would be difficult to view the Mongols as barbarian invaders after viewing the wealth and diversity of their cultural contributions and their patronage of the artistic life of their subject peoples.

Koprulu, Mehmed Fuad. 1992. *The Seljuks of Anatolia. Their History and Culture According to Local Muslim Sources,* trans. Gary Leiser. Salt Lake City: University of Utah Press.

———. 1993. *Islam in Anatolia after the Turkish Invasion (Prolegomena).* Salt Lake City: University of Utah Press. Both of Koprulu's books include valuable information on Mongol influence in Anatolia.

Krader, Lawrence. 1966. *Peoples of Central Asia.* Bloomington: Indiana University Press. A wide study of the cultural diversity of central Asia.

Kramarovsky, Mark G. 1991. "The Culture of the Golden Horde and the Problem of the 'Mongol Legacy'." In *Rulers from the Steppe: State Formation on the Eurasian Periphery,* ed. G. Seamans and Daniel Marks. Los Angeles: Ethnographics Press. An interesting study of the Mongol successor state, the Golden Horde.

Lambton, A.K.S. 1988. *Continuity and Change in Medieval Persia: Aspects of Administrative, Economic, Social History in 11th–14th Century Persia.* London: Taurus. The legendary Ann Lambton is an acknowledged authority on medieval Persia, and she was one of the first to look at the Mongol period in depth. Another classic study.

Lane, George. 1999. "An Account of Bar Hebraeus Abu al-Faraj and His Relations with the Mongols of Persia." *Hugoye Journal of Syriac Studies* 2 (2): http://syrcom.cua.edu/Hugoye/Vol2No2/HV2N2GLane.html.

———. 2000. "Arghun Aqa: Mongol Bureaucrat?" *Iranian Studies* 32 (4): 459–482.

———. 2003. *Early Mongol Rule in Thirteenth Century Iran.* London: RoutledgeCurzon.

———. 2004. *Genghis Khan and Mongol Rule.* Westport, Conn.: Greenwood Press. George Lane's earlier works are primarily concerned with the Mongols in Iran and how this whole period was one of cultural, spiritual, and economic renewal rather than of confrontation, stagnation, and oppression, as it has been previously characterized. The picture is of Mongol rulers rather than Mongol conquerors. His interest in China and other parts of the Mongol Empire is reflected in his more recent work, however.

Le Strange, Guy. 1966. *The Lands of the Eastern Caliphate.* London: Frank Cass. This is a geographical survey of medieval Persia, much of it based on primary sourcebooks.

Lewis, Bernard. 1968. *The Assassins: A Radical Sect in Islam.* New York: Oxford University Press. Lewis has produced a small, concise, and very readable account of this widely misunderstood Muslim sect. Essential reading for students of the Mongols in western Asia.

———. 1987. *The Jews of Islam.* Princeton, N.J.: Princeton University Press. This is a study of a neglected area and includes information on the Jews and the Mongols.

———. 1993. *Islam in History: Ideas, Peoples, and Events in the Middle East.* Chicago: Open Court Publishing. Included in this collection is Lewis' memorable paper on the Mongols in which he dares to suggest that Western scholarship has been perhaps more unkind and unfair to their memory than they deserve. Subsequent scholarly studies have often agreed with him.

Lewis, Franklin. 2000. *Rumi: Past and Present, East and West.* Oxford, U.K.: Oneworld. This is the definitive book on the Sufi poet Rumi and a comprehensive study that also allows insight into the medieval Mongol-dominated world of western Asia and beyond. This very readable book provides a view of this period of history from an angle different from the usual political analysis but is equally valid. The book also contains a very practical and comprehensive bibliographical survey.

Lewisohn, Leonard. 1995. *Beyond Faith and Infidelity*. Sufi Series. London: Curzon Press. A detailed study of the Sufis and poets of western Asia under Mongol domination.

Lockhart, L. 1968. "The Relations between Edward I and Edward II of England and the Mongol Il-Khans of Persia." *Iran: Journal of the British Institute of Persian Studies* 28: 22–31. This paper deals with the Mongols' approaches to the Europeans and the English monarchs, Edward I and II in particular.

Man, John. 2004. *Genghis Khan: Life, Death, and Resurrection*. London: Bantam Books. An apologist for Chinggis Khan who provides a vivid picture of the land in which the Great Khan grew up. The author writes his book around his quest for the final burial place of Chinggis Khan, which remains a mystery at the close of the book.

Marshall, Robert. 1993. *Storm from the East*. London: BBC Books. This book accompanied a television series, with David Morgan as the academic advisor. The result is a beautifully illustrated, clearly presented, simply explained account of the Mongols' rise and rule. Unfortunately out of print, this book is well worth the effort of a search.

Martinez, A.P. 1987–91. "Changes in Chancellery Languages and Language Changes in General in the Middle East, with Particular Reference to Iran in the Arab and Mongol Periods." *Archivum Eurasiae Medii Aevi* 7: xx–xx. This is a thought-provoking paper that researches language change during the Mongol period, which suggests that the Mongols were far more integrated into the societies that they conquered than had been previously thought.

Mazzaoui, Michel M. 1972. *The Origins of the Safawids*. Wiesbaden, West Germany: Franz Steiner Verlag. The Safavids, who came to power in Iran in 1500, trace their roots and the founding of their so-called family to the Il-Khanid period when their eponymous founder Safī al-Dīn was close to the Mongol royal family. This book casts new light on the relationships between the Mongols and their subjects.

Melville, Charles. 1990. "Pādeshāh-i Islam: The Conversion of Sultan Ghazan Khan." *Pembroke Papers* 1: 159–77.

———. 1990. "The Itineraries of Sultan Oljeitu: 1304–16." *Iran: Journal of the British Institute of Persian Studies* 28: 55–70.

———. 1996. "'Sometimes by the Sword, Sometimes by the Dagger': The role of the Ismāʿīlīs in Mamluk-Mongol relations in the 8th/14th Century." In *Mediaeval Ismāʿīlīs History and Thought*, ed. Farhad Daftery, 247–264. Cambridge: Cambridge University Press. Charles Melville is an authority on the Mongols and the later Il-Khans in particular. His work is extremely important, and his paper on the conversion to Islam of Ghazan Khan is particularly interesting.

Mills, Margaret A. 1991. *Rhetoric and Politics in Afghan Traditional Storytelling*. Philadelphia: University of Pennsylvania Press. Among the various interviews, storytelling sessions, and other oral transmissions are references to the Mongols, suggesting that the memory of the Chinggisid era is still very much alive in Afghanistan.

Minorsky, Vladamir. 1964. *Iranica Twenty Articles*. Vol. 775. Tehran: Publications of the University of Tehran.

———. 1978. *The Turks, Iran and the Caucasus in the Middle Ages*. London: Variorum Reprints.

——. 1982. *Medieval Iran and Its Neighbours.* London: Variorum Reprints. Vladamir Minorsky, onetime Russian ambassador to Ottoman Turkey and later scholar and lecturer at London University's School of Oriental and African Studies, has written widely and knowledgeably about Iran, central Asia, and the Mongols, and his work is still highly regarded today.

Morgan, D.O., ed. 1982. *Medieval Historical Writing in the Christian Worlds.* London: School of Oriental and African Studies.

——. 1986. *The Mongols.* Oxford, U.K.: Blackwell.

——. 1988. *Medieval Persia, 1040–1797.* London: Longman.

——. 1997. "Rashīd al-Dīn and Gazan Khan." *Bibliothèque Iranienne* 45.

——. 1996. "Mongol or Persian: The Government of Il-Khan Iran." *Harvard Middle Eastern and Islamic Review* 3: 1–2, 62–76. David Morgan is considered one of the foremost authorities on the Mongols, and his book *The Mongols* has been translated into many languages and has been reprinted many times. All his work is well worth reading, and *The Mongols* should be the constant companion of any student of the Mongols. His deceptively readable style should not obscure the solid academic content. His *Medieval Persia, 1040–1797* contains a particularly useful and comprehensive bibliographical survey of primary and secondary source material relevant to the period.

Morgan, D., and R. Amitai, eds. 1999. *The Mongol Empire and Its Legacy.* Leiden, Netherlands: Brill. An important collection of papers by many of the leading experts on the Mongols.

Nebenzahl, Kenneth. 2004. *Mapping the Silk Road and Beyond.* London: Phaidon. A valuable collection of medieval maps, covering the Silk Road east and west. Each map is accompanied by an insightful text.

Nicolle, D., and V. Shpakovsky. 2001. *Kalka River 1223: Genghiz Khan's Mongols Invade Russia.* Oxford: Osprey Publishing. This is a beautifully illustrated, detailed account of the historic Mongol campaign which opened up Europe to the storm from the East. It is well served by clear maps and diagrams.

Patton, Douglas. 1991. *Badr al-Dīn Lulu Atabeg of Mosul 1211–1259.* Seattle: University of Washington Press. An interesting study of a Kurdish warlord who ruled during the Mongol period and who allied himself with Hülegü.

Petech, Luciano. 1990. *Central Tibet and the Mongols: The Yüan-Sa-skya Period of Tibetan History.* Rome: Serie Orientale Roma.

Rachewiltz, Igor de, Hok-Lam Chan, Hsiao Ch-i-Ch-ing, and Peter W. Geier, eds. 1993. *In the Service of the Khan: Eminent Personalities of the Early Mongol-Yüan Period 1200–1300.* Wiesbaden, Germany: Harrassowitz Verlag. An excellent study of officials from the Yüan dynasty, many of whom have not been dealt with elsewhere.

Ratchnevsky, Paul. 1993. *Genghis Khan: His Life and Legacy.* Oxford, U.K.: Blackwell. For the serious student of the Mongols, Ratchnevsky's book is indispensable. He is meticulous in his attention to detail and in his scrutiny of the sources, especially where differences occur.

Rosenthal, Franz. 1971. *The Herb: Hashish versus Mediaeval Muslim Society.* Leiden: E.J. Brill.

Rossabi, Morris. 1988. *Khubilai Khan.* Berkeley: University of California Press. This is an excellent and indispensable study of the founder of the Yüan dynasty of China.

———. 1992. *Voyager from Xanadu.* New York: Kodansha International. This is the story of two Christian clerics, the embassy from China on behalf of the Yüan dynasty, through Iran to the courts of Europe.

Roxburgh, David J. 2005. *The Turks.* London: Royal Academy of Arts. This catalog was published to accompany the exhibition of the same name held in London, and the book is worthy of what was a major and justly celebrated show. Of great interest to those concerned with Mongol matters is the artist Siyah Ghulam, or Black Pen, whose work is covered extensively in the catalog just as it was in the exhibition. Peter Golden, Filiz Cagman, and others contributed articles.

Runciman, Steven. 1965. *A History of the Crusades, 1, 2, 3.* London: Penguin. The Mongol impact on western Asia and on the crusader states is examined in Runciman's classic study.

Smith, John Mason. 1984. "ʿAyn Jalut: Mamluk Success or Mongol Failure?" *Harvard Journal of Asiatic Studies* 44 (2): 307–45. A detailed study of this famous battle that became a turning point in Mongol history. It was the first major and decisive military confrontation that the Mongols lost, and it halted their westward advance in Asia. Its significance is still debated today.

Smith, Paul J. 1998. "Fear of Gynarchy in an Age of Chaos: Kong Qi's Reflections on Life in South China under Mongol Rule." *Journal of Economic and Social History of the Orient* 41: 1–95. This study considers the impact of foreign rule on the indigenous culture and the dissolution of the existing world order into apparent chaos.

Spuler, Bertold. 1972. *History of the Mongols.* London: Routledge & Kegan Paul.

———. 1994. *History of the Muslim World: The Mongol Period.* Princeton, N.J.: Marcus Wiener. Bertold Spuler is considered among the foremost authorities on the Mongols, and his books are treasure troves of details and data. Unfortunately, his studies of the Golden Horde and the Il-Khanate are available only in German.

Thorau, Peter. 1992. *The Lion of Egypt: Sultan Baybars I and the Near East in the 13C,* trans. P. M. Holt. London: Longman. Baybars, the legendary leader of the Mamluks of Egypt, successfully kept the Mongols at bay and even challenged them in Anatolia. This is a thorough and informative study and essential reading for an understanding of Baybar's role in medieval western Asia.

Turnbull, S. R. 2003. *Genghis Khan and the Mongol Conquests, 1190-1400.* Oxford: Osprey Publishing.

Turnbull, S. R. 2003. *Mongol Warrior, 1200—1350.* Oxford: Osprey Publishing. This entire series is excellent, and the artwork is accurate and detailed. All three books by Turnbull are recommended.

Turnbull, S. R., and A. McBride. 2000. *The Mongols.* Men-at-Arms Series, no. 105. Oxford, U.K.: Osprey Military.

Vernadsky, George. 1953. *The Mongols and Russia.* New Haven, Conn.: Yale University Press. This is still one of the most thorough studies of the Mongol period in Russian history and contributes greatly to our understanding of the dynamics of the Golden Horde.

Voegelin, Eric. 1941. "The Mongol Orders of Submission to European Powers, 1245–1255." *Byzantion* 15: 378–413. It is interesting to contrast these early communiqués from the Mongols to the European courts with their later, more conciliatory correspondences.

Vryonis, Speros, Jr. 1971. *The Decline of Medieval Hellenism in Asia Minor and the Process of Islamization from 11th Century through 15th Century.* Los Angeles: University of California Press. This is a bold and searching book that traces the changes in Anatolia brought first by the Turkish invasions and then later by the Mongol invasions and the decline in Greek influence. This book can be usefully read alongside the works of Claude Cahen.

Weatherford, Jack. 2004. *Genghis Khan and the Making of the Modern World.* New York: Crown. Another apologist for Chinggis Khan, Weatherford writes an interesting book because he approaches his subject primarily not as a historian but as an anthropologist. A readable and challenging study of the Great Khan.

Wiencek, Henry, and Glen D. Lowry, with Amanda Heller. 1980. *Storm across Asia: Genghis Khan and the Mongols. The Mogul Expansion.* London: Cassell. A useful introduction to Chinggis Khan and his successors.

INDEX

About the Author

GEORGE LANE teaches in the Department of History, School of Oriental and African Studies, University of London. Dr. Lane's focus is on Islamic history, particularly in the Central Asia region. He has also worked on relations between Iran and China during the 13th and 14th centuries. He contributed to *The Greenwood Encyclopedia of Daily Life* (Greenwood, 2004), and is the author of *Genghis Khan and Mongol Rule* (Greenwood, 2004) and *Early Mongol Rule in 13th Century Iran* (2003).

The Greenwood Press "Daily Life Through History" Series